HISTORY OF N

HISTORY OF
Nebraska

JAMES C. OLSON & RONALD C. NAUGLE

Third Edition

University of Nebraska Press

Lincoln & London

Publication of this volume was assisted
by The Virginia Faulkner Fund, established in
memory of Virginia Faulkner, editor-in-chief
of the University of Nebraska Press.

∞ The paper in this book meets the minimum
requirements of American National Standard for
Information Sciences–Permanence of Paper for
Printed Library Materials, ANSI Z39.48-1984.

Typeset in Carter & Cone Galliard

Library of Congress
Cataloging-in-Publication Data
Olson, James C.
History of Nebraska / James C. Olson and Ronald
C. Naugle. – 3rd ed.
p. cm.
Includes bibliographical references, (p.) and index.
ISBN 0-8032-3559-3 (alkaline paper). –
ISBN 0-8032-8605-8 (paperback : alkaline paper)
1. Nebraska – History. I. Naugle, Ronald C.
(Ronald Clinton), 1942-   . II. Title.
F666.O48 1997 978.2–dc20
96-27320 CIP

CONTENTS

v

ILLUSTRATIONS

TABLES

PREFACE TO THE THIRD EDITION

It has indeed been a daunting task to undertake the revision of the *History of Nebraska*, first produced by James C. Olson in 1955. I hope that the vision that guided the first edition at a time when Nebraska had just celebrated its territorial centennial, as well as the second at the state's centennial twelve years later, is kept alive in this edition as Nebraska's 125th anniversary fades from memory. Jim's recognition of the need for a one-volume general survey of the history of Nebraska to serve both the college student and the general reader as a text and a reference has been affirmed enthusiastically by nearly three generations of readers; this edition strives to serve the needs of one more as the state's leaders grapple with challenges, both present and future.

Nebraska's history has attracted numerous scholars over the past thirty years, and, just as previous editions sought to synthesize the scholarship of their day, this edition also attempts to integrate and synthesize the scholarly contributions that illuminate the people, events, and issues important to an understanding of the state's present and past. It seeks also to celebrate the achievements of its entire citizenry with sensitivity to issues of gender, race, and ethnicity. Readers familiar with previous editions will find many of the same features with a modest reorganization and infusion of new material throughout the work. Readers will also find that the section, "Suggestions for Further Reading," so appreciated in previous editions, has been maintained and expanded. The scope and breadth of the narrative have been expanded and enhanced without sacrificing substance. Scholarly research is ongoing and much remains to be done to achieve a complete synthesis of Nebraska's past. Within the limitations of present research and my judgment, it is hoped that readers will find here an enlightening and valuable addition to their understanding and appreciation of the Nebraska spirit.

I owe a debt of gratitude to many colleagues and friends who assisted in the preparation of this edition. I count it a great honor and privilege to have become acquainted and to work with James Olson, and I appreciate his faith and trust that I could produce a new edition that remained true to his original vision. Jim and I met several times over the course of the project, and he made numerous helpful and insightful comments as the work progressed. I am particularly indebted to Jana Beddow, who assisted me in the initial stages of the project by tracking down the many books and articles relevant to the state's history that had been produced since the publication of the second edition, and to Kara Mickle and Kären Larson, who provided invaluable assistance in the later stages of updating the bibliography.

I am also grateful to the administration at Nebraska Wesleyan University, who granted me a sabbatical leave during the 1994–95 academic year for the purpose of researching the book, and to the Nebraska Humanities Council for granting me a Summer Scholar's Stipend in 1994 to help with expenses. I was ably assisted by the staffs of the Nebraska Library Commission and the Nebraska State Historical Society, who kept their humor as I searched their collections. I am particularly grateful to John Carter, curator of photographs at the Nebraska State Historical Society, who made many suggestions for photographs to be included in the book. I also appreciate the help provided in photograph selection by Jim Potter and Gail DeBose Potter of the Nebraska State Historical Society, Donald Rundquist of the Conservation and Survey Division of the University of Nebraska, and Pat Sloan of the *Lincoln Journal Star*. I deeply appreciate the assistance of Reid Hester, who did yeoman service tracking down citations and materials during the last stages of research. I am also indebted to my good friends Frederick Dahlstrand, professor of history at the University of Ohio–Mansfield, and Stanley Carlson, retired from the Nebraska Department of Education, who read the final manuscript and ably and graciously pointed me in the right direction.

I also deeply appreciate the scores of colleagues and friends who remained so during the course of this work, particularly my colleagues in the History Department at Nebraska Wesleyan University, Elaine Kruse, Patrick Hayden-Roy, Kim Risedorph, Marge Cathcart, and my secretary, Debra Davis, all of whom had faith that I would once again become human.

My greatest debt of gratitude is to my family. My wife, Gretchen, and teenage daughter, Meredith, both had faith that someday life would return to normal.

RONALD C. NAUGLE

HISTORY OF NEBRASKA

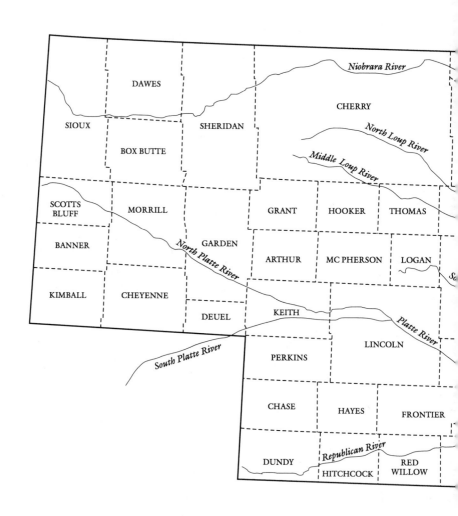

CHAPTER I

The Land

When Major Stephen H. Long of the Army Engineers returned from his epochal expedition to the Rocky Mountains in 1820, he confirmed what many white Americans had suspected all along, that most of the area between the Missouri River and the Rocky Mountains was a vast desert wasteland. "In regard to this extensive section of country," he wrote, "I do not hesitate in giving the opinion, that it is almost wholly unfit for cultivation, and of course uninhabitable by a people depending on agriculture for their subsistence." Dr. Edwin James, chronicler of the expedition, stated that he had "no fear of giving too unfavourable an account" of the region. The apparent lack of timber, navigable streams, and water in general made it "an unfit residence for any but a nomad population." He hoped it would remain forever "the unmolested haunt of the native hunter, the bison, and the jackall." The expedition's cartographer likewise dismissed the area's future potential by labeling it "The Great Desert."[1] The designation stuck and could be found on maps of the United States for the next fifty years.

A GREAT AMERICAN DESERT?

Meriwether Lewis and William Clark, who only skirted Nebraska as they followed the Missouri River northward in 1804–6, had also suspected that the area was useless. Lieutenant Zebulon M. Pike, who went out along the Republican River in 1806 and then down to Santa Fe, was the first to report officially on the conditions on the plains. He had written of "barren soil, parched and dryed up for eight months in the year," and had hazarded a guess that America's western plains would "become in time equally celebrated as the sandy desarts of Africa."[2]

Indeed, Thomas Jefferson, whose principal concern in 1803 was the acquisition of the area around the mouth of the Mississippi River, saw

I

no great promise for the vast trans-Mississippi region. He believed it had simply been thrown into the bargain by France to increase the purchase price.

By the end of the first quarter of the nineteenth century most Americans accepted the notion that the region between the Missouri and the Rockies was a vast, uninhabitable desert. It is little wonder that in the late 1820s and early 1830s the suggestion that the area west of the Missouri River be set aside as a permanent home for the Indians found ready acceptance. As the years wore on, others added their testimony to the cumulative condemnation of the plains. Historians, geographers, and journalists, now supplied with an abundance of apparently reliable source material, described in detail the Great American Desert.

Walter Prescott Webb, studying the plains in the early 1930s, expressed the nature and geographical boundary of the problem in his work, *The Great Plains*: "As one contrasts the civilization of the Great Plains with that of the eastern timberland, one sees what may be called an institutional fault (comparable to a geological fault) running from middle Texas to Illinois or Dakota, roughly following the ninety-eighth meridian. At this fault the ways of life and of living changed. Practically every institution that was carried across it was either broken and remade or else greatly altered." The reason, Webb suggested, was clear. "In the new region—level, timberless, and semi-arid—they were thrown by mother necessity into the clutch of new circumstances. . . . East of the Mississippi civilization stood on three legs—land, water, and timber; west of the Mississippi not one but two of these legs were withdrawn,—water and timber,—and civilization was left on one leg—land."[3]

A few people disagreed with the prevailing notion. As early as 1817, the English naturalist John Bradbury wrote that Americans were misled in their thinking about the plains because they were accustomed to "a profusion of timber." To say that whites could not inhabit a land barren of timber simply because Americans had not yet pushed settlement beyond the region of the great timber was, in Bradbury's eyes, sheer nonsense. He expressed a definite opinion that the region could be cultivated and, "in the process of time, it will not only be peopled and cultivated, but it will be one of the most beautiful countries in the world."[4] Bayard Taylor, who went through the country in 1866, also disagreed with the common

Satellite image of Nebraska showing the varied terrain and formations of the state. A National Oceanic and Atmospheric Administration Advanced Very High Resolution Radiometer Image of August 1993. Courtesy, Earth Resources Observation Systems (EROS) Data Center, U.S. Geological Survey, Sioux Falls SD; and Center for Advanced Land Management Information Technologies (CALMIT), Conservation and Survey Division, University of Nebraska–Lincoln.

view. Reflecting on his trip to Colorado via the Smoky-hill route, he was "fast inclining toward the notion that there is no American Desert on this [the eastern] side of the Rocky Mountains."[5]

By the time Taylor's book appeared in 1867, a great many people had acquired a vested interest in the land west of the Missouri. Nebraska had been admitted to the Union and was in the process of claiming its landed endowment; millions of acres had been or shortly would be withdrawn for the benefit of the Union Pacific and the Burlington Railroads; speculators were busy locating large tracts which they hoped to turn at a profit; settlement by homesteaders was well under way. These people were gambling that the desert concept was erroneous. Experience on the wet prairies east of the Missouri had demonstrated that trees were not essential to grow bountiful crops of corn, wheat, and oats. A brief experience west of the Missouri had shown that this area, too, would produce good crops.

The Missouri, then, was not the dividing line between farmland and desert. But where was such a line? Did it even exist or was it simply myth?

Even the most pessimistic of the early observers had admitted that some of the land just west of the Missouri was not bad. Some, impressed by the rolling hills and tall, waving grass, had even praised its beauty and fertility. Almost all agreed, however, that as one got out on the flat land—well before reaching Fort Kearny—the country began to deteriorate: the grass became short and parched, streams failed, and even the creek bottoms seemed unable to support anything more than low, sickly shrubs.

Agreement as to the exact location of any "line of civilization" would not be soon in coming. Indeed, a whole generation of Nebraskans stoutly denied that it existed at all. Major John Wesley Powell, chief of the Department of the Interior's Survey of the Rocky Mountain Region, stated in 1878 that nonirrigable farming was not possible west of the one hundredth meridian because the area had less than twenty inches of annual rainfall. Samuel Aughey, chairman of the Department of Natural Sciences at the University of Nebraska, denounced Powell's findings as bureaucratic nonsense. Others agreed. Powell, of course, was not talking about a desert; he was talking about a region in which irrigation would be necessary if farming were to be successful over the years. There was a vast difference.

Indeed, Powell was much more optimistic regarding the prospects of western Nebraska and Kansas than Ferdinand V. Hayden, chief of the United States Geological Survey, had been six years earlier. Hayden's report of 1872 had predicted that occupation of the area would be indefinitely postponed because of insufficient rainfall, a lack of building material, the scarcity of fuel, and an insufficient number of running streams to provide water for livestock.

Though Powell was much and unjustly abused by his own generation for his pessimism about the West, he was, if anything, too optimistic. There were many areas east of the one hundredth meridian where farming needed the aid of irrigation. In general, however, Powell's appraisal was correct. If his contemporaries had appreciated his vision, our history might have been vastly different.

A CLOSER LOOK

History has made inconsequential whether Webb's ninety-eighth meridian, which enters the state at Niobrara and leaves it at Superior, or

Powell's one hundredth, which runs down the main street of Cozad, more accurately defines the outer limits of agrarian advance. So too the voices of Zebulon Pike, Long, and a host of others pessimistic about the plains and its potential for sustaining future settlements of agrarian people would over time prove less than prophetic. Their views were shaped by the realities of their present. To a large extent, they saw in the plains an environment vastly different from that farther east and could not imagine agriculture as they knew it thriving in these conditions. Their vision was limited by a paradigm that defined three environmental conditions essential for the support of civilization: land, timber, and water.

Factors that were not apparent were equally important to an understanding of early assessments of the land. Clearly a considerable portion of Nebraska was treeless, and large areas were without running streams. Yet not all of the state lacked these "necessities." Nor was the area of the plains that would become Nebraska devoid of human habitation. Many observers failed to grasp that centuries before them, men and women had made the plains their home, adapting to its conditions in ingenious and resourceful ways. And finally, many could not see what would become apparent to those who finally put the shovel to the earth, a vast, rich diversity in the area's major resource: the land itself.

MINERAL RESOURCES

From the earliest days of white exploration and settlement there was occasional excitement in the expectation that the land would yield up riches from beneath the ground. Coal and salt deposits were believed to exist in the area, and entrepreneurs, encouraged by promoters and even governors, periodically attempted to launch commercial enterprises to reap the profits inherent in these and other natural resources.

Ultimately Nebraskans learned that their state, like much of the plains, possessed relatively few mineral resources. Coal and salt did exist but not in paying quantities. Likewise, there was neither iron nor precious metals. The minerals that did exist in commercially significant quantities were stone, sand, gravel, clay, oil, and gas. There was enough potash in certain sections of the Sand Hills to make government-financed production during World War I seem feasible, and for a time volcanic ash, known commercially as silica, was produced.

Stone deposits, including limestone, chalk rock, sandstone, granite, rock salt, and gypsum also exist in the state but at too great a depth to make their production commercially feasible. Large sand and gravel deposits in various parts of the state are useful for road building and the manufacture of concrete. Clay, which also occurs at various places, but principally around Hastings, Lincoln, and Nebraska City, has been used in the manufacture of brick, tile, and terra-cotta. Since World War II oil and gas wells have added to the prosperity of southwestern Nebraska. Yet nothing compared to the state's most important natural resource, which most came ultimately to recognize was not under the ground but under their feet, the land itself.

TOPOGRAPHY

On any generalized, small-scale map of the United States, Nebraska appears as part of the great prairie-plains flatland that constitutes the central portion of the country. Within this general classification, however, there is considerable diversity. There is a gradual rise in altitude, at the rate of about 9 to 10 feet per mile, from 825 feet in Richardson County in the southeastern corner of the state to 5,330 feet in Banner and Kimball Counties on the western border. There are considerable areas of flat land in the south-central portion of the state and on the high table around Alliance, but most of the state's surface has been roughened by glacial action and by wind and water erosion.

The entire state lies within the drainage area of the Missouri River, which forms its eastern border. The Platte, most important of the Missouri's tributaries, sprawls like a huge snake across the state, its broad valley providing easy access to the mountains. The Platte's principal tributaries are the Loup and the Elkhorn, which drain the Sand Hills. The swift Niobrara flows across the northern part of the state. The South Platte section is drained by the Republican and the Blue, tributaries of the Kansas River.

Topographically, Nebraska is divided into some nineteen regions, which embrace the following general topographic types: alluvial lowlands, loess, sand hills, high plains, and badlands. The alluvial lowlands lie along the rivers, principally the Missouri, the Platte, and the Republican, with the broad, fertile Platte Valley being the most important. The loess region occupies about 42,000 of the state's 77,237 square miles and includes rich farming areas in the eastern, central, and southern parts. There are both loess plains and loess hills. In the plains, generally south of the Platte and west of Saunders, Lancaster, and Gage Counties, the land flows in gentle waves toward the southeast; along the Missouri and between the Platte and the Sandhills the waves converge into moderate hills.

The Sand Hills, the state's most distinctive topographic feature, occupy some 18,000 square miles west and northwest of the loess region, with outliers extending to the southwest as far as Dundy County. The Sand Hills, for the most part, consist of sloping hills twenty-five to a hundred feet higher than the valleys between but sometimes stretching into gentle plains as well as rising into sharp pinnacles. They are dotted with rich valleys, lakes, and fertile tablelands. West and northwest of the Sand Hills stretch the high plains, some 12,000 square miles of level tablelands, broken occasionally by deep canyons. The general area includes two low groups of evergreen wooded mountains, the Wild Cat range in Scotts Bluff and Banner Counties and the Pine Ridge in Sheridan, Dawes, and Sioux Counties.

Conspicuous on the high plains are the rugged isolated buttes rising hundreds of feet above the surrounding tableland. The badlands, or Pierre Hill region, occupy about a thousand square miles, principally in Sioux County, with minor sections in Dawes and Sheridan Counties. Most valuable economically as rangeland, their weathered slopes and valleys, together with the Wild Cat range and the Pine Ridge, make northwestern Nebraska an area of rare scenic beauty.

SOILS

Nebraska is also blessed with a diversity of soils, which with the notable exception of the Sand Hills and a small area of the badlands on the northern edge of the panhandle, fall into five general groupings. Prairie soils, Chernozem soils, and Chestnut soils are among the most productive in the world. This is indeed fortunate for a state whose economy is almost entirely dependent on agriculture.

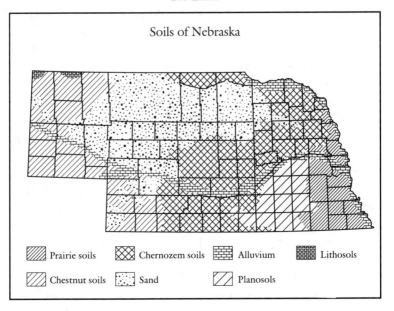

Soils of Nebraska

Prairie soils   Chernozem soils   Alluvium   Lithosols

Chestnut soils   Sand   Planosols

Prairie soils, found in southeastern Nebraska, are the soils of the great midwestern corn belt. They have developed in cool, moderately humid climates under the influence of a grass vegetation. In general the Prairie soils are unexcelled for corn and sorghum production, and oats, barley, soybeans, clover, and timothy hay are also evident. Certain varieties of Prairie soils, however, erode easily under cultivation, and twentieth-century farmers in southeastern Nebraska have become increasingly alert to the necessity for erosion control.

The dark brown to black Chernozem soils, which extend in a broad belt through the northern plains, are the richest of all. In most years, however, they do not get sufficient rainfall to make them as productive as the slightly less fertile Prairie soils to the east. In general, these soils are well suited for the production of corn, soybeans, oats, and barley. The existence of a particular variety of Chernozem soil in the northeastern corner of the state makes that area comparable to some of the best corn lands of Iowa.

Occupying the southwestern corner of the state and most of the panhandle west of the Sand Hills are the Chestnut soils, which cover a vast area of the northern plains from the Arkansas River to the Canadian border. The area is part of a high, smooth, treeless plain dissected at wide intervals by comparatively narrow valleys. In the twentieth century these soils have been found preeminently suited to winter wheat and produce good crops whenever moisture is adequate. In the panhandle, wheat, corn, and oats have been the principal crops. Rye, barley, and potatoes are also grown there. Relative acreage of each crop tends to fluctuate with price levels. The nonarable lands provide range for cattle, and wild hay is cut on the meadows and smooth upper lands. Again, lack of moisture is the principal problem.

The Sand Hills, as distinctive in soil composition as they are topographically, occupy a larger area in Nebraska than any other single soil type. The soil characteristic of this area is found only in Nebraska and in small parts of North Dakota, South Dakota, Colorado, and Texas. The Nebraska Sand Hills are primarily wind-blown sands released by disintegration of tertiary sandstones. They have accumulated considerable organic matter and with adequate moisture will support a relatively luxuriant grass cover. They are well adapted to livestock, providing range in summer and nutritious hay for winter use, but experience has shown that when broken with the plow they are apt to lose their grass cover with disastrous results.

Three additional soil types deserve mention. Relatively important in south-central Nebraska are a series of Planosols, which extend in a belt from two to four counties wide through Nebraska and Kansas between the Platte and the Arkansas Rivers. Commonly referred to as Claypan soils, they produce wheat, corn, oats, and alfalfa as principal crops, although they are better suited to small grain than to corn because in dry weather the water supply over the Claypan is inadequate. Alluvial soils, occurring along the river bottoms, principally the Platte, Republican, and Missouri, are much more important than their area would indicate. Those of the Platte Valley provide some of Nebraska's richest farmland. Missouri River bottoms are equally fertile but are subject to periodic flooding, which greatly reduces their dependability. The region known topographically as the badlands, or Pierre Hills, consists primarily of a series of the Lithosols, shallow, stony soils on rough, hilly terrain of little use except as rangeland.

The soil map of Nebraska thus exhibits wide variation, accounting in large measure for the highly diversified nature of the state's twentieth-century agriculture. Except for the Sand Hills, the dominant areas are extremely fertile and well suited to the production of cultivated crops. Just as the principal conditioning factor in the year-to-year productivity of the various soils is the amount of moisture available, the variation in rainfall has been an important factor in the development of the soils themselves.

THE CLIMATE

There is an old saying in Nebraska, and in other states as well: "If you don't like the weather, just wait a minute and it'll change." Like many other old sayings, this one contains just enough truth to keep it going. The climate in Nebraska, in common with that of the plains region generally, is subject to violent and seemingly unpredictable fluctuations. There can be extremes of heat and cold, violent thunderstorms, and hot, dry winds, blizzards, tornadoes, and hailstorms. The variation, particularly in rainfall, is long as well as short term; the west differs markedly from the east. Nebraska's climate is typical of the interior of large continents in the middle latitudes, exhibiting light rainfall, low humidity, hot summers, and severe winters.

Nebraska's climate is controlled primarily by the state's latitude, its altitude, its inland position, and its location to the east of the Rocky Mountains. Mean annual temperature ranges from about 53° Fahrenheit in the southeast to about 45° in the northwest; summer temperatures rise above 100° in most of the state, and winter readings reach as low as minus 45° in the northwest. The average length of the growing season varies from 164 days in the southeast to 122 in the northwest.

The most important climatic feature is rainfall. It determines the type of agriculture, the prosperity, and the very way of life of the state's citizens. The mean rainfall is 22.8 inches, varying from 27.8 inches in the eastern division to 22.3 in the central and 17.9 in the western division. In Iowa, by comparison, the mean annual rainfall is 30.9 inches, and in Illinois, 36.6 inches. Fortunately, 77 percent of Nebraska's yearly total falls in the six months from April to September and 45 percent in the three months of May, June, and July. There is a great deal of fluctuation from month to month and from year to year.

WATER RESOURCES

That early observers dismissed Nebraska's agricultural potential because of the apparent lack of adequate water is not surprising. Precipitation is uncertain and varies greatly across the state; and its major rivers—the Platte and its larger tributaries, the Elkhorn and the Loup, and the Niobrara across the northern part of the state, as well as the Republican and the Big and Little Blue in the southern and eastern part of the state—are all subject to great variation in flow, depending both on the season and year. Yet surface water in lakes, streams, and rivers proved a deceptive indication of the state's true water resources, for Nebraska is blessed with vast groundwater resources which help to replenish the rivers and lakes and provide water for irrigation.

The stored groundwater in Nebraska amounts to nearly 2 billion acre-feet. The amount as well as its accessibility, however, varies greatly across the state but is found in the greatest quantity in the Sand Hills, where the Ogallala Aquifer stores from 700 to 800 million acre-feet of water. Although groundwater serves many needs in both urban and rural areas across the state, its major importance is in irrigation. In fact, 92 percent of all the water consumed in Nebraska is used for irrigation, and groundwater provides nearly two-thirds of the 8.4 million acre-feet used annually for that purpose.

TREES AND PLANTS

To the early white settlers the most obvious characteristic of the landscape west of the Missouri was the absence of trees. Only about 3 percent of Nebraska was forested, and most of the trees that did exist were concentrated in the eastern part of the state and along streams. Characteristic trees found all over the state were the cottonwood, elm, ash, box elder, hackberry, various varieties of willow, and red cedar. Oak grew along the Missouri River, and the bur oak was found throughout the eastern half of the state. Western yellow pine was found in the valleys of the North

Platte and Niobrara Rivers and quaking aspen in the northwest corner of the state. Many other varieties existed in small quantities. Among the fruit trees were wild plum and chokecherry.

Nebraska, however, like other plains states, was primarily grass country. Professor Samuel Aughey, pioneer student of the state's natural resources, collected 149 species of grass native to the state and 150 species of sedges.[6] The grass varied according to the rainfall. In the more humid eastern portion of the state tall prairie grasses, particularly the bluestem, abounded; the less humid western section was covered with short grasses, particularly grama and buffalo. Indeed, buffalo grass originally covered much of the state, and there was a legend among the old settlers that its disappearance was caused by the destruction of the buffalo.

NEBRASKA TODAY: A LANDED HERITAGE

Nearly two centuries after the acquisition of the vast trans-Missouri plains, the fortunes of the people are tied to the land. Indeed, even as Nebraskans look toward the twenty-first century, life remains conditioned by the state's primarily agricultural economy and its outlook. Though the trend toward the cities, begun early in the twentieth century, has continued, in 1990 only two places, Omaha with a population of 335,795 and Lincoln with a population of 191,192, were classified as metropolitan areas. Only eleven places, outside of Omaha and Lincoln, have populations greater than 10,000. The population of Grand Island, the third city, was only 39,386 in 1990. Even in the cities, the point of view remains agricultural, hardly surprising considering that the state's most important industry is the processing of farm products.

Agriculture in Nebraska has been subject to violent fluctuations, caused by both human and natural causes; rarely has it enjoyed uninterrupted prosperity for as much as a decade. This, of course, has had a significant impact on the economy, as well as the politics, of the state and has further underscored the importance of the land as its major natural resource.

CHAPTER 2

The First People

Until very recently most archaeologists accepted with little question the theory that the first immigrants to the North American continent came from Asia across a frozen Bering Strait toward the end of the Pleistocene or Ice Age, about 12,000 years ago. Although the details of why and how they migrated continue as topics of debate, the general acceptance of the timing of their arrival has been based on well-documented evidence from archaeological sites, largely in New Mexico and the southern plains. This research places these early immigrants, generally referred to as Paleo-Indians, into three groups: the Clovis people, dating from 11,500 to 11,000 years ago; the Folsom people, who followed from 11,000 to 10,500 years ago; and the Late Paleo-Indians, who appear to have been here from about 10,500 to 8,000 years ago.

PRE-CLOVIS PEOPLES

Although there is little question about the presence of Paleo-Indian peoples, archaeologists debate whether they were the first to inhabit the Western Hemisphere. Evidence from excavations in southern Chile, southwestern Pennsylvania, and a recent site in Frontier County in Nebraska suggests that the first Americans may have arrived earlier than 12,000 years ago, as previously thought. Scientists working at the Chile and Pennsylvania sites have suggested that human beings may have been here as much as 40,000 years ago.

The Nebraska site is of particular interest because evidence found there suggests that people were hunting on the plains some 18,000 years ago, 10,000 years earlier than previously believed. In 1987, archaeologists discovered a mammoth in the eroded shoreline of Medicine Creek Reservoir in Frontier County. Archaeologists have been working at this site, known as the La Sena Mammoth site, since 1988. Radiocarbon dates prove that the La Sena mammoth died about 18,000 years ago. Of most interest, however, is the condition of the bones, which appear to have been scattered in a random manner. The fractures and bone flakes also suggest the use of flint tools manufactured by humans. Archaeologists working at the site have found other signs of human butchering. The excavations at La Sena will undoubtedly be followed with great interest by historians while archaeologists seek more conclusive evidence.

Although it is uncertain whether human beings made their home on the plains as early as 18,000 years ago as the La Sena evidence suggests or only 8,000 years ago as traditional theory holds, clearly the first inhabitants were followed by a succession of peoples whose varied cultures reflect human efforts to meet the challenges presented by the environment. The work of archaeologists provides a necessary and useful perspective on the prehistory and ethnohistory of the plains before the relatively brief period of white occupation.

PALEO-INDIAN CULTURES

Although no Clovis or Folsom sites have been excavated in Nebraska, weapons found in fields and streambeds provide considerable evidence that people associated with these cultures were present on the Nebraska plains. The Clovis and Folsom peoples appear to have been nomadic hunters of large game animals, now extinct—mammoths and mastodons, ground sloths that grew to as long as twenty feet, giant beavers the size of modern-day horses, giant saber-toothed cats with canines as long as seven to eight inches, and others. Paleo-Indians also appear to have been skillful stone workers. The Clovis culture, particularly, is identified by a fine fluted spear and well-made tools of both stone and bone for cutting and scraping.

Late Paleo-Indian sites have been excavated in western Nebraska, and perhaps in time a Nebraska site representing earlier cultures will be located since such sites have been excavated in southern South Dakota, eastern Colorado and Wyoming, and western Kansas.

What happened to the Paleo-Indian peoples is not certain. Some scientists have suggested that they overhunted the game, extinguishing their food supply; others posit that they may have been forced by drought and other difficulties to abandon the plains; they may have struggled for survival and, with reinforcements from Asia, became the ancestors of later American Indians. There is evidence of periodic—and perhaps, in certain areas, continuous—occupation of the plains during the long period between about 10,000 B.C. and approximately A.D.1000. There is also evidence that conditions on the plains were much less desirable during this period than they had been earlier: lakes, marshes, and streams were drying up; vegetation was not as lush; trees were becoming scarcer; and many animal forms had disappeared.

THE FORAGERS

By 8,000 B.C. mammoths, mastodons, giant bison, and many other large animals were extinct or nearly extinct. By the early Archaic period, beginning around 6500 B.C., nomadic hunters still roamed the plains, but life was changing in significant ways. Archaeologists refer to this era as the second major period of cultural change. Several archaeological sites around the state—on Lime and Medicine Creeks, tributaries of the Republican River; in western Nebraska at Signal Butte in Scotts Bluff County and Barn Butte in Garden County; and an important site in northeastern Nebraska at Logan Creek, south of Oakland in Burt County—have produced important information on the adaptation of these people to changing environmental conditions. The Signal Butte and Logan Creek sites are of particular interest because multiple layers of culture have been excavated there. Radiocarbon dating has been used to provide significant information to help in defining the orderly succession of cultures between the Clovis and Folsom peoples of more than 10,000 years ago and the pottery makers who occupied the plains from about A.D. 400 to 600.

The climate warmed during this period, and the plains were subjected to cycles of wet and dry that benefited the grasslands as well as other vegetation. Large herds of smaller bison could be found throughout the plains region, but hunters stalked a much greater variety of game. The bones of many species of birds and animals have been excavated at most of the archaic sites in the state, suggesting an indiscriminate pursuit of

One of many archaeological excavation sites in the state which are providing valuable information about Nebraska's first people. This photograph of a site near Gretna was taken by *Omaha World-Herald* photographer Jim Denney. Courtesy, Nebraska State Historical Society (NSHS), Jim Denney Collection, T7:11-8.

food. Many different spear points, much more finely crafted than those associated with the Clovis and Folsom traditions, have been found.

These people, known generally as foragers, were not solely dependent on game but enjoyed a diverse diet. Evidence suggests that they gathered and ground vegetation for food. They also used fire. Hearths as well as charcoal and burned stones have been excavated. A wide variety of stone and flint tools such as chipped flint scrapers and points, bone awls, and gouges, as well as bone beads, have been discovered. Late Archaic sites have produced an even greater array of tools, including chipped stone knives, drills, and awls for working bone, shell, and hides. Pottery first appeared among these people, who were less nomadic than the Paleo-Indians who preceded them. There is also evidence that as they became more sedentary, they began to practice burial ceremonies, which, along with pottery, were characteristic of the Eastern Woodland culture, whose influence clearly had reached the plains by the late Archaic period.

PLAINS-WOODLAND PEOPLE

The Plains-Woodland people, also known as pottery-making people, appear to have spread over much of the plains during the years A.D.1 to A.D.1000, and their remains have been found in virtually all parts of Nebraska. They lived primarily by hunting but may have practiced simple horticulture. They also appear to have been less nomadic than their predecessors on the plains.

The dwellings associated with the Plains-Woodland people were simple, semisubterranean houses, equipped with a central fireplace (a depression in the ground) and probably covered with skins or mats supported by light poles. The pottery they produced was generally large and coarse with large openings and presumably was used for food storage.

A particular expression of Plains-Woodland culture in south central Nebraska and northwestern Kansas, known as the Keith phase, indicated the use of large stone points, probably on spears and lances. Archaeologists have also found small, serrated points, suggesting that these people may have been the first to use bow and arrow weaponry in Nebraska.

VILLAGE FARMERS

The Plains-Woodland people appear to have been succeeded, at least in many areas of Kansas and Nebraska, by a more sedentary people who lived in relatively large, unfortified villages. In addition to hunting and fishing, these people practiced a fairly intensive corn and bean horticulture. They occupied the plains from about A.D.1000 to approximately A.D.1400 and may represent the westernmost extension of the eastern maize culture complex.

Archaeologists have discovered sites representing two major variants of this culture: the Nebraska, along the Missouri River between Omaha and Sioux City, and the Upper Republican, in the valleys of the Loup and Republican Rivers and generally throughout southern and central Nebraska. These village farmers raised maize and a variety of other crops but also gathered wild fruits and berries and fished in nearby streams. Hunting remained important, and the bow and arrow was now the principal weapon, but hunting had become a seasonal activity, after which the hunters returned to their home base. As a result of relative peace, agricultural advance, new influences, and perhaps new people from the south, their arts were relatively more advanced than those of their predecessors: they produced high-grade pottery and a wide variety of stone, bone, horn, and shell tools and ornaments.

The houses constructed by these people were grouped together to form small villages. They were much sturdier and more substantial than those of previous cultures. Floors were often a foot or more below the surface of the ground. Large posts were set along the perimeter of the square or rectangle and in the center and covered with a combination of thatch and mud. A hearth was located near the center, and beds were positioned along the outer walls. Pits were dug for food storage and to dispose of refuse.

No one knows for sure what happened to these people. They may have been forced to abandon the plains in the late fifteenth century. There is evidence of a prolonged drought and dust storms during the latter part of the fifteenth century—many of the village sites are buried under a heavy mantle of dust.

HISTORIC INDIAN PEOPLES

By the early seventeenth century the Plains-Woodland Indians appear to have been succeeded by a related culture. Archaeological sites on the Republican and Lower Loup Rivers date this culture, known as lower Loup or protohistoric Pawnee, from about 1600 to 1750, and evidence suggests that these people may have descended from the Upper Republican culture and may be ancestors of the historic Pawnee. They lived in earth lodges in villages, much as did the Upper Republican people, but were more dependent on horticulture. There is evidence of a more deliberate and systematic cultivation of crops, particularly maize, yet they continued to hunt and fish. Their tools of stone and bone are similar to Upper Republican ones, and the bow and arrow appears to have been their principal weapon. These sites also contain evidence that the occupants had domesticated dogs, using them to drag heavy items.

At about the same time that the early Pawnee people were flourishing in southern and central Nebraska, another distinct culture appeared in western Nebraska and particularly in the Sand Hills. Archaeological sites have produced evidence that this Dismal River culture existed from the late 1600s to the early 1700s. These people were more nomadic than the early Pawnee and Upper Republican people and were more dependent on hunting for their subsistence. Their standard of living appears to have been lower, and their houses were less substantial, probably small structures covered with skins rather than the earth lodges used by the early Pawnees. Their pottery was not as highly decorated, and their stone tools were considerably cruder. A few metal objects and glass beads suggest that they had some contact with whites, most likely Spanish explorers on excursions north from the southern plains and French explorers pushing west from the Mississippi into the Missouri River basin. Archaeologists believe that these people were Apaches who had drifted north and settled on the plains.

THE PAWNEES

Of the historic tribes, the Pawnees were the most closely associated with Nebraska. The name is of uncertain origin, and the origins of the tribe as well are clouded in obscurity. The name Pawnee may come from the word, *Pa-rik-i*, meaning a horn, a reference to the typical Pawnee method of dressing the scalplock in an erect manner. It has also been suggested that the name may derive from the seventeenth-century French *pani*, or Spanish *panani*, meaning the feathers of a bird, since the Pawnee were particularly attracted to feathers, frequently wearing them as ornaments. The modern French word *penne*, which means feather, may derive from the older *pani*.

According to one tradition, the Pawnees moved into the valleys of the Platte and Loup from the south and southwest; another tradition points to a southeastern origin. They probably were in Nebraska by 1541, when Francisco de Coronado explored the central plains, and certainly by 1673, when they appear on Father Jacques Marquette's map. Archaeological evidence suggests that they may have been here much earlier if the Upper Republican people of A.D.1200–1500 were in fact the ancestors of the historic Pawnee.

The First People

Throughout the eighteenth century, French explorers and traders came in contact with the Pawnees, and the detailed accounts of Lewis and Clark, Pike, Long, and other Americans in the early nineteenth century corroborate and amplify earlier information that showed the Pawnees occupying large villages in an area centering around the Platte, although they hunted over a much wider area.

Linguistically, the Pawnees were part of the Caddoan family. They were divided into four bands, each of which had earlier occupied one or more separate earth-lodge villages: the Chaui, or Grand; the Kitke hahki, or Republican; the Pitahauerat, or Tappage; and the Skidi, or Wolf. Tribal organization was based on the village. Each village had its name, its shrine containing sacred objects, and its priest, as well as its hereditary chiefs and leading men. The tribe was held together by ceremonies pertaining to a common cult in which each village had its place and by the tribal council, composed of the chiefs of the various villages.

The Pawnees were essentially a farming people and lived in permanent villages. The characteristic dwelling was the communal earth lodge, a circular structure consisting of a framework of four or more center posts with rafters covered with brush and dirt. The floor was excavated slightly below the ground level, and an opening in the center of the roof served as a smoke hole for the fireplace directly below. The entrance was covered and usually faced the east or southeast. Periodically, usually twice a year, the entire community abandoned the village and went off on a buffalo hunt. While hunting, they lived in the skin tipis associated with the nomadic tribes. In the village and on the hunt, the women did most of the work and generally endured a hard life. There were some compensations, however. The women owned the property, and the chieftainship descended through the existing chief's sister.

That the Pawnees lived by both agriculture and hunting accounts for the diverse elements in their culture. During part of the year they were sedentary farmers, living in permanent villages; during the remainder they were nomadic hunters, adopting dwellings and habits generally associated with the wandering tribes of the plains. At heart, however, they were farmers, particularly corn growers, and this preference is reflected in their religion. Each dwelling probably had its sacred buffalo skull, but corn was their mother, figuring in their rituals and in their mythology even more prominently than did the buffalo. The sacred bundles of the tribe contained two ears of corn, and their most important ceremonies, including the sacrifice of a maiden to the Morning Star by the Skidi, were directed primarily toward securing a bountiful crop of corn.

Pawnee cornfields were small, usually not more than an acre or so. The primitive tools—principally a hoe made from the scapula of a buffalo—were not suited to working heavy turf, and the women located their fields at the mouths of ravines or in similar spots where the soil was loose and fertile. Sometimes they were compelled to go several miles from the village to find a suitable plot of ground. The corn was planted in hills and was usually hoed twice a year. The ears were small, generally not more than four inches long, although in one instance ears from sixteen to eighteen inches in length were reported as being not uncommon. Corn was gathered while it was still green, boiled, cut from the cob, dried, and placed in leather bags to be stored in caches for future use. In addition to corn, the Pawnees cultivated beans, pumpkins, and squash. They also seem to have been fond of the wild potato, which grew plentifully in the sand of the Platte and Loup valleys.

The buffalo, object of at least two great hunts each year, was an important source of food. Its hide, hair, sinew, horns, and even hooves were also important to the Pawnees. The summer hunt began immediately after the corn had been hoed the second time, usually about the middle of June, and occupied the tribe until September, when they returned to harvest the corn and other crops. Near the end of October, after the corn had been stored, the tribe set out on the winter hunt, remaining away until April, when the people would return to plant corn. A favorite hunting ground lay between the Republican and Arkansas Rivers, necessitating a trip of from four hundred to nine hundred miles on each hunt. The meat was eaten fresh whenever possible, and the hunt, if successful, was a time of great feasting. What could not be eaten fresh was cut into strips and dried in the sun to preserve it for future use. In addition to buffalo, the Pawnees ate elk, deer, bear, beaver, otter, raccoon, badger, dogs, rabbits, and squirrels. Fish seem to have been of little importance to them.

Before their contact with white people, the Pawnees had developed expertise in the art of making pottery and tools from stone and bone. After they secured metal containers from the whites, they stopped making native pottery. Likewise, the arrow points, knives, scrapers, and other tools once chipped from hard native stone were abandoned in favor of substitutes furnished by white traders. At first, the stone arrow points were replaced by metal ones, and these in turn gave way to guns. The Pawnees did continue to do considerable woodworking, making mortars, bowls, whip handles, platters, and cradle boards, even after they had become heavily dependent on metal goods furnished by the traders.

The decline in traditional Pawnee culture appears to have begun when they acquired horses. This, too, was the result of white contact, even if indirect. By 1800 every village possessed many animals, and their use had become an integral part of Pawnee culture. Other evidence of Pawnee decline as a result of white contact is supplied by population figures. In 1838 the missionaries John Dunbar and Samuel Allis estimated that there were ten thousand Pawnees. Increasing white contact, particularly as a result of the heavy overland migration through the Pawnee country in the 1840s, introduced disease and dissipation and left the Pawnees in a weakened condition. In particular, they were less able to defend themselves against the almost continuous attacks by the Lakota. In 1849 they were reported to have lost one-fourth of their number from cholera, leaving a population of only about forty-five hundred. In 1856 their numbers had increased to 4,686; five years later they were reported at 3,416. In 1857 the Pawnees ceded all of their land in Nebraska to the federal government except for a small reservation on the Loup River, where they remained until their complete removal from Nebraska to Indian Territory in 1874.

SEDENTARY SIOUAN TRIBES

While the Pawnees dominated central Nebraska, the sedentary Siouan tribes were a major presence along the Missouri River. These included Omahas, Poncas, Otos, Iowas, and Missourias. The great Siouan linguistic family embraced many groups, tribes, and subtribes. The family also included the Lakota, as well as the sedentary tribes. The Omahas and Poncas belonged to the Dhegiha group, along with the Quapaws, Osages, and Kansas, who lived further south. The Iowas, Otos, Missourias, and

Winnebagoes made up the Chiwere group, which, though similar, spoke a dialect that could not readily be understood by the Dhegihas.

It is likely that the Siouan peoples lived east of the Allegheny Mountains at one time and pushed westward, either in search of food or in response to the pressure of enemies. The precise pattern of their migration and occupations is unclear, but they were well ensconced along the west bank of the Missouri when the first white people arrived in the region.

The Omahas probably moved up the Mississippi River from the mouth of the Ohio River, remaining for a while at the mouth of the Missouri River, then going north into Iowa and southern Minnesota, and finally turning to the southwest across the Missouri. They appear to have been in Nebraska from about 1650, settling on Bow Creek in the northeastern part of the state. in the early nineteenth century they occupied the bluffs along the Missouri River from the mouth of the Platte to Sioux City. They were seriously hit by smallpox in 1802 but made a rapid recovery: their population increased from 300 in 1802 to 600 in 1804; in 1829 it was estimated at 1,900, but by 1843 it had declined to 1,600.

During the chieftainship of Black Bird in the late eighteenth century, the Omahas were a strong, warlike tribe, striking fear into the hearts of their neighbors and occasional white traders who ventured into their country. During the early nineteenth century, however, pressure from the Lakotas and from whites steadily reduced their will and their ability to defend themselves. In 1854, under the leadership of Logan Fontenelle, a mixed-blood, they ceded all their land west of the Missouri River except 300,000 acres in northeastern Nebraska, which they retained as a reservation.

The Poncas and the Omahas were once part of the same tribe. The precise date of separation is uncertain; estimates range from the late fourteenth century to the late seventeenth century. Traditional accounts of their migration up the Missouri River are somewhat obscure, but there is evidence that they were in Nebraska at least by the beginning of the eighteenth century. Juan Baptiste Munier is said to have "discovered" the Poncas at the mouth of the Niobrara in 1789, but they appear on P. C. LeSeur's map of 1701. They suffered heavily from smallpox near the end of the eighteenth century and were estimated by Lewis and Clark in 1804 as having a population of only 200. They had increased to 600 in 1829 and

800 in 1842. In 1874, while the entire tribe was living on the Niobrara River, they numbered 733. Like the Omahas, the Poncas were under almost constant attack from the Lakotas. They were abruptly removed to Indian Territory in 1877—an experience that almost destroyed the tribe.

Though anthropologists find many differences between them, until the debasement of their cultures through contact with whites, the Omahas and Poncas appear to have followed a way of life similar to that of other semisedentary tribes on the eastern plains, depending on both agriculture and hunting for their subsistence. They lived in earth lodges and skin tipis; they farmed a little and went on periodic buffalo hunts; they made pottery, tools, and weapons from native materials.

The Otos, Iowas, and Missourias, along with the Winnebagoes, were once part of a single nation, the Chiwere group that lived near the Great Lakes. The Otos, Iowas, and Missourias separated from the Winnebagoes in the early 1600s and wandered to the southwest, taking up positions west of the Missouri River and south of the Platte River. The Otos and the Missourias settled farther north than the Iowas. The Otos eventually split off from the Missourias and established their own settlements even farther to the north. By the early 1700s they were settled along the Platte River near the present site of Ashland. During historic times, at least, these tribes were never very large or important, and when first observed by white travelers they seem to have been much less highly developed than the Pawnees or the Omahas and Poncas. They lived semisedentary lives, farming a little and hunting a little, but they appear never to have been able to achieve the degree of mastery over their environment accomplished by their neighbors. Lewis and Clark, for example, speak of Otos they saw near Council Bluffs as being almost naked, having no covering except a sort of breechcloth with a loose blanket or painted buffalo robe thrown over the shoulder. Their permanent villages consisted of large earth lodges, and while traveling they lived in tipis.

The Otos were found by Lewis and Clark on the south side of the Platte, about thirty miles from the mouth of the river. Earlier they had lived about twenty miles north of the Platte on the Missouri River. They, too, suffered from a siege of smallpox in the late eighteenth century, but unlike the Poncas, they never regained their former numbers. The Iowas were reported by Lewis and Clark as occupying a single village along the Platte of approximately eight hundred persons, including some two hundred warriors. The Missourias moved south of the Kansas River in the late eighteenth century but were driven out by the Sauk and Fox. When Lewis and Clark came along, they were living in small villages south of the Platte, but smallpox reduced their numbers so severely that the remainder were absorbed by the Otos. By the middle of the 1880s all three tribes were on reservations in Indian Territory.

THE WESTERN TRIBES

In addition to the Pawnees and the sedentary Siouan tribes who lived more or less permanently in Nebraska, various divisions of Teton Sioux, or Lakota, as well as Cheyennes, Arapahoes, Comanches, and possibly Kiowas, roamed over western Nebraska during the historic period. The seven divisions of the Lakota—Brule, Oglala, Miniconjou, Two Kettle, Sans Arc, Sihapasa or Blackfoot Sioux, and Hunkpapa—were particularly significant in resisting white occupation of western Nebraska and the northern plains.

The Lakotas were relative latecomers to the plains. Louis Hennepin placed them on the upper Mississippi as late as 1680. Suspension of French trade along the lower Mississippi by the 1690s and the increasing difficulty of defending themselves against encroaching tribes supplied with English weapons forced them to relinquish more and more of their woodland habitat until they were driven out completely by the Chippewas in 1736.[1]

P. C. LeSeur's map shows the Lakotas and Yanktons just east of the Missouri River in western Iowa by 1702, but the first record of their being west of the Missouri is probably that of French frontiersman Pierre Gaultier de Varennes, sieur de La Vérendrye, who referred to a band of "prairie Sioux" which he met in 1743 somewhere west of the Missouri River in what is now South Dakota. In 1842 John C. Frémont found the Lakotas between the north and south forks of the Platte River, near the Laramie plains. In the early years of the nineteenth century they were raiding and hunting through western and central Nebraska and even harassing the Pawnees and the sedentary Siouan peoples along the Missouri. By the 1870s they were well established on the northern and western plains, where, under the leadership of such men as Red Cloud and Crazy Horse, they provided significant resistance to white occupation.

THE HORSE TRANSFORMS INDIAN LIFE

By the time the first white people began to venture out on the plains in the early years of the nineteenth century, the region was occupied by a variety of Indian tribes, speaking diverse languages and following various ways of life. There were, to be sure, vast differences, but all shared one important element. Whether semisedentary or nomadic, the trans-Missouri Indian's culture centered around the horse. Without it, the extended wanderings, the methods of hunting, and even the hit-and-run style of warfare between tribes would have been impossible. For many tribes, wealth and stature came to be measured in terms of horses.

When first acquired from the Southwest in the early eighteenth century, the horse greatly modified life for the plains Indians. Traditional aspects of plains culture such as the tipi, the travois for transportation, the controlled buffalo hunt, and many ceremonies were reorganized around the horse. It allowed a greater emphasis on hunting and less on horticulture, and tribes such as the Cheyennes abandoned the permanent village for the nomadic camp. Others, like the Pawnees, retained their permanent villages but intensified their hunting activities.

CHAPTER 3

Spain and France on the Plains

Although white settlement of the trans–Missouri River country came about through the westward extension of the people of the United States, the earliest white explorers of the region were Europeans who came from the Southwest more than half a century before the English established their first tentative settlement at Jamestown. When Lewis and Clark ventured up the Missouri in 1804, the Spanish had known the plains for more than two and a half centuries. They had given the rivers as far north as the Platte melodious names such as Rio de Jesus and Rio de San Lorenzo and had designated the more important Indian tribes. The French, penetrating the region from the Northeast, were well established at St. Louis, knew intimately the Indians as far north as the Niobrara, and had entered the Mandan country in present North Dakota. Despite their presence over these long years, however, neither the Spanish nor French made much impression on the area.

Both the Spanish and French had been impelled onto the plains by the age-old search for gold and by the hope, associated with virtually all of the early explorations of North America, that one of the beckoning rivers might lead to the Western Sea. They found no gold, and the rivers seemed to lead nowhere. They had to content themselves with trade and the exploitation of the native peoples. The peoples were widely scattered, and the trade was difficult and not particularly profitable. Little wonder, then, that neither they nor the territory made much of an impression on one another.

The first white people on the plains were the Spanish soldiers under Francisco Vasquez Coronado, who marched north out of the valley of the Rio Grande in April 1541 to search for the Kingdom of Quivira, a rich land where even the poorest people ate from dishes made of gold. Many of Nebraska's earlier historians located Quivira within Nebraska. Modern scholarship suggests that it was several villages of Wichita Indians

27

in central Kansas, near present-day Lindsborg. The Nebraska connection or myth, however, is kept alive by the Knights of Ak-Sar-Ben, who each fall, in an elaborate social function, crown the king and queen of Quivira.

For the purposes of history, the exact location of Quivira is of minor importance. The significance of Coronado's search is that, for the first time, it exposed white people to the central plains. Those who came in search of gold were doomed to disappointment. Sadly, Coronado wrote the king of Spain: "What I am sure of is there is not any gold nor any other metal in all that country, and the other things of which they had told me are nothing but little villages, and in many of these they do not plant anything and do not have any houses except of skins and sticks, and they wander around with the cows."[1] The cows, of course, were buffalo, an animal that fascinated the Spanish. For the colonists there might have been some hope in his subsequent observation: "The country itself is the best I have ever seen for producing all the products of Spain, for besides the land itself being very fat and black and being very well watered by the rivulets and springs and rivers, I found prunes like those of Spain and nuts and very good sweet grapes and mulberries."[2]

It is interesting that Coronado recognized in the new land an agricultural potential that would escape the first American explorers. But the Spanish were not after farms. They wanted gold, and when they found none, Spanish interest in the plains waned, except for their desire to keep others, particularly the French, out of the area.

Throughout the remainder of the sixteenth century and well into the seventeenth, individuals and small groups of Spanish and French continued to probe the central plains, but it was not until the early 1700s that the rivalry between them proved critical for the northern plains. From the 1660s on the Spanish became increasingly suspicious that the French were trading with the Pawnees. In 1699 rumors of French presence on the plains were confirmed when a Navajo war party returning from a raid on the Pawnees brought French carbines, powder flasks, clothing, and other equipment. The Spanish stirred to check their rivals, and, late in 1718, the viceroy at Mexico City ordered countermoves against the French on both the Texas and New Mexico frontiers. In the fall of 1719, Governor Antonio Valverde of New Mexico led a fainthearted expedition

A detail from a hide painting of the August 13, 1720, massacre of Pedro de Villasur's Spanish army near present-day Columbus by Pawnee and Oto Indians. This painting in the collection of the Museum of New Mexico in Santa Fe is over seventeen feet long and believed to be the oldest recorded scene in what is now Nebraska. Courtesy, Museum of New Mexico, Segesser II, 149803.

against the Comanches and Utes, and the next year Lieutenant Colonel Pedro de Villasur was sent to reconnoiter enemy positions on the northern plains.

Accompanied by forty-five white soldiers, sixty Pueblo Indians, a priest, and an interpreter, Villasur set out from Santa Fe on June 16, 1720. Heading generally northeastward, the party crossed the Arkansas River and eventually came to the Platte River near the present site of Grand Island. He proceeded to cross the Platte and went to the Loup River to the north. Here they came upon villages of Pawnee Indians. Several efforts to open a parley were rebuffed, and in the ensuing attempts, a Pawnee Indian scout with the Villasur expedition was detained by the Indians. Frustrated by the loss of his scout, Villasur fell back to plan his next move. He camped for the night in a meadow of tall grass just south of the present site of Columbus. At daybreak on August 13, the Pawnees suddenly attacked. The tall grass proved advantageous to the Pawnees, who were able to surround the camp unnoticed. Villasur was killed before he could reach his weapons. Most of the Pueblos apparently had scented the danger in time to escape, but only thirteen of the Spaniards survived to make their bedraggled way back to Santa Fe.

When the news of the defeat reached Mexico City, the troubled viceroy ordered an investigation. The deceased Villasur was a convenient scapegoat. For entrusting the expedition to an obvious incompetent, Governor Valverde was required to pay 50 pesos for charity masses for the souls of the dead soldiers and 150 pesos to purchase ornaments for certain of the missions. Regardless of who was to blame, Spanish influence on the upper plains after 1720 was nonexistent, and at Santa Fe and Mexico City everyone was sure that the French were at the root of the difficulty.

Whether or not the Villasur massacre had been led by Frenchmen, as the survivors maintained, the French by 1720 were becoming well established in the trans-Missouri country. Louis Joliet and Father Jacques Marquette passed the mouth of the Missouri River in June 1673. Impressed by its turbulent waters tumbling into the Mississippi, Marquette reported that it might lead to California. Robert Cavelier, sieur de La Salle, followed in February 1682 and was able to gather from the Indians a fairly accurate description of the river and the peoples along it perhaps as far north as the Platte.

Spurred on by La Salle's dream of empire and the obvious missionary opportunities, the French made plans to extend their imperial embrace to the people of the Missouri. Missionaries in the Illinois country picked up a great deal of information about the Indians of the region, and many legendary accounts grew up concerning traders who were reputed to have ventured up the river.

The first significant exploration of the Missouri River was accomplished by Etienne Veniard de Bourgmont in 1714. Bourgmont, a *coureur de bois* of adventuresome spirit, deserted his post as commandant of Fort Detroit to marry an Indian woman and live among the tribes of the Missouri. (He first became aware of them when they showed up unexpectedly in 1712 to assist the French in a siege of Fort Detroit being levied by the Fox.) Bourgmont reported in considerable detail on his travels, noting in particular that the tributaries of the Missouri, as described to him by the Indians who had roamed the Southwest, might provide a route to the Spanish settlements. Bourgmont's reports also contain the first recorded use of the word *Nebraska*: "Higher up the river, one finds the Large river, called Nibraskier by the French and Indians."[3]

French officials, who were learning that it would be difficult to reach the Spaniards by way of the Red or the Arkansas Rivers, were impressed by Bourgmont's reports. The French in Louisiana, unlike the Spanish, were not content to let the trans–Missouri River country remain a no-man's-land and took steps to consolidate their position in the area. Villasur's defeat removed the threat of Spanish competition. All that was needed now was to cement the allegiance of the tribes and persuade them to live together in peace. To do this, the Company of the Indies commissioned Bourgmont, who was now in Paris, where he was honored with the Cross of St. Louis, commandant of the Missouri, with instructions to establish a fort on the Missouri River, make an alliance with the Padoucas, and then return to France with some Indian chiefs.

Bourgmont established Fort Orleans on the Missouri in 1723, probably on an island in the river near Brunswick, Missouri. He visited the Padoucas and various other tribes in the spring of 1724, holding long and apparently successful powwows, and later in the year returned to Paris with a delegation of Oto, Osage, and Missouria chiefs, among them the noted Chicago, and a young Indian woman. Had French officials

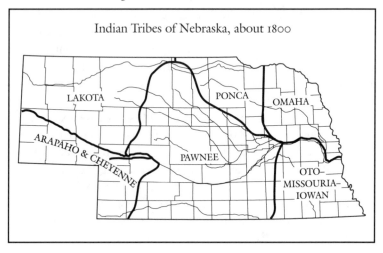

Indian Tribes of Nebraska, about 1800

LAKOTA

PONCA

OMAHA

ARAPAHO & CHEYENNE

PAWNEE

OTO-
MISSOURIA-
IOWAN

in America been as vigorous in carrying out their plans as they were in developing them, Bourgmont might well have laid the foundations for a successful imperial adventure in the Missouri Valley. The governor of Louisiana, Jean Baptiste le Moyne, sieur de Bienville, however, lost enthusiasm for adventures in upper Louisiana and failed to support the Fort Orleans project; two years after Bourgmont returned to France, the fort was abandoned. Bienville even reduced the number of Indian delegates Bourgmont was allowed to take with him to France. During the remainder of their period of dominion in North America, the French contented themselves with relatively insignificant trading expeditions among the Indians and somewhat more significant efforts to strike up a trade with the Spanish in New Mexico after 1739, when the way to Santa Fe was opened by Pierre and Paul Mallet.

Under the assumption that the Missouri would lead to New Mexico, the Mallet brothers ascended that river to the mouth of the Niobrara, where they concluded that they were traveling in the wrong direction. They retraced their steps by land, almost parallel to the Missouri, striking a river which they called the Platte (probably between South Bend and Fremont). They followed it to a point about twenty-five miles beyond the Loup River fork, where they turned southward. They probably crossed the Republican River between Superior and Red Cloud, continuing their southwestward course until they reached the Arkansas River. In due time they found an Indian who was able to guide them to the Spanish settlements.

The Spanish tried to prohibit the French from trading with their New Mexican settlements, but after the Mallet brothers had opened the way, numerous pack trains crossed the wilderness each year to the Spanish settlements, and during the 1740s and 1750s the contraband trade took on large proportions. Meanwhile, the French continued to trade with the Indians of the lower Missouri River, and from Canada French traders had opened traffic with the tribes of the upper river. By the late 1750s, however, the French were losing their hold on North America, and in the Treaty of Paris in 1763, all the land west of the Mississippi River became Spanish.

The Spanish were slow to exploit the upper Missouri. For the most part, they seem to have been content to trade with the tribes adjacent to St. Louis. Even as late as 1785 they appear to have had little definite knowledge of the river beyond the mouth of the Niobrara. Following the close of the American Revolution, however, the Spanish began to press their claim to the upper Missouri River. The Americans, who had succeeded the British as masters of the Illinois country, were aggressive and ambitious and were looked upon as a definite threat to Spanish influence over the Indians. More important, the British, who retained economic control of the upper Mississippi Valley after the Revolution, were pushing into Spanish territory from the north and east, taking over the trade with the Lakotas and competing seriously for that of the Pawnees, Omahas, and Iowas. Finally, traders in St. Louis were becoming so numerous that ruinous competition was developing in the trade with the nearby tribes.

In 1789, Juan Munier "discovered" the Poncas living near the mouth of the Niobrara and in return was given exclusive trading privileges with them. The next year, Jacques d'Eglise obtained a license to hunt on the Missouri and wandered as far north as the area of the Mandans. In 1793, d'Eglise and an apparent rogue named Garreau set off up the river with goods advanced by Bentura Collell and Joseph Robidoux. According to d'Eglise, this venture failed because of Garreau's deceit and the hostility of the Lakotas and the Arikaras. As reimbursement for his efforts, d'Eglise requested a monopoly on the trade with the Mandans similar to that which had been granted to Munier among the Poncas. Spanish officials in St. Louis, however, had already granted a monopoly on the trade of all the tribes above the Poncas.

The Company of Explorers of the Upper Missouri, organized in St. Louis on October 15, 1793, under the leadership of Jacques Clamorgan, was the first and only large-scale Spanish effort to extend their trade to the upper Missouri. Spanish officials were enthusiastic. In addition to giving the company the monopolistic privileges it demanded, Governor-General Francisco Louis Hector, Baron de Carondelet offered a prize of $2,000 (later raised to $3,000) to the first Spanish subject who should reach the Western Sea by way of the Missouri River. Though the company included, in addition to Clamorgan, such well-known and experienced traders as Bentura Collell, Joseph Robidoux, Gregoire Sarpy, and Antoine Roy, Jean Baptiste Truteau, a schoolmaster, was chosen to lead the first expedition.

Accompanied by eight men in a pirogue, Truteau left St. Louis for the Mandan villages on June 7, 1794. He spent a miserable winter near Fort Randall, trading a little with the Lakotas, the Omahas, and the Poncas. The next spring he headed north but got no further than the Arikaras. He appears to have got along well with the Arikaras and apparently was in contact with the Cheyennes, but he was back in St. Louis by the early part of 1796 with little to show for his efforts.

In April 1795, the company had dispatched a second expedition under the leadership of a man named Lecuyer. It was much better equipped than Truteau's, costing twice as much, but it never got beyond the Poncas. Lecuyer is reported to have taken two wives among the Poncas and wasted much of the company's goods. Near the end of August 1795, the company sent out a third expedition. This, the best equipped of all, was led by James Mackay, a Scot who had traded among the Mandans for the British and who had changed his allegiance to Spain. The party stopped for a few days at the Oto village near the mouth of the Platte. They built a cabin nearby for those who were left to trade with the Otos. Mackay himself spent the winter at the Omaha village in present Dakota County, building Fort Charles (about five miles southeast of the Omaha village) and forming an alliance with the celebrated chief Black Bird.[4] From Fort

Charles, Mackay sent his trusted lieutenant John Evans on a mission to the Arikaras. Stopped by the Sioux, Evans returned to Fort Charles, to be sent out again—this time to discover a passage across the continent to the Pacific.

Evans, of course, did not find a passage to the Pacific. Both he and Mackay were back in St. Louis in 1797, and though the company still hoped that it would find a route to the Western Sea, its activities after Evans's abortive effort were confined to developing trade with the tribes along the Platte and, as its resources permitted, extending its influence up the Missouri. The company underwent numerous reorganizations, but it remained under the domination of Jacques Clamorgan and for a time operated under the name of Clamorgan, Loisel and Company.

By the turn of the century the Spanish were trading as far north as the Mandans and knew the river as far as its confluence with the Yellowstone. Given time, they might have made their way to the Pacific. But Spanish days on the Missouri were numbered. The destiny of the valley was being determined not by the traders on the river but by the diplomats in Paris and Madrid.

CHAPTER 4

The Louisiana Purchase

In the secret Treaty of San Ildefonso, signed on October 1, 1800, the Spanish agreed to turn Louisiana back to France, thus paving the way, under Napoleon Bonaparte, for rebuilding the French empire in North America. Napoleon, however, ultimately concluded that this plan was impractical, and on April 11, 1803, Charles Maurice de Talleyrand-Périgord, the French foreign minister, asked Robert Livingston, resident U.S. minister in Paris, what he would give for all of Louisiana. Livingston, who had been trying unsuccessfully to buy New Orleans, seized the opportunity, and on April 30 he and James Monroe signed a treaty transferring Louisiana to the United States for 80 million francs—about $15 million, or four cents an acre.

There were those in and out of Congress who doubted both the wisdom and the constitutionality of adding this vast territory to the United States. It would more than double the nation's size. Many more, however, agreed with President Thomas Jefferson, who pushed it through, altering the destiny of his own as well as America's first people.

THE LEWIS AND CLARK EXPEDITION

The Louisiana Purchase enabled Jefferson to realize a long-standing ambition—the exploration of the Far West. As early as 1783 he had tried to interest George Rogers Clark in exploring the country from the Mississippi River to California; in 1786, while minister to France, he had persuaded John Ledyard to try to explore the country from west to east, an effort that failed when the Russians objected to Ledyard's transit across Siberia; and in 1792 he had been the leading spirit in the American Philosophical Society's ill-fated attempt to send André Michaux across the continent. The presidency brought new opportunities, and on January 18, 1803, Jefferson sent a secret message to Congress urging that efforts be made to establish trade with the Indians of the Missouri River and to extend the external commerce of the United States. Congress responded on February 23 by appropriating $2,500.

Jefferson chose Meriwether Lewis, age twenty-eight, son of an Albemarle County neighbor and his private secretary, to head the expedition. Jefferson instructed Lewis to ascend the Missouri River, cross the mountains, and descend by the most practicable river to the Pacific; to make geographic and scientific observations; to ascertain the routes of Canadian traders in their traffic with the Indians; to determine the feasibility of collecting furs at the source of the Missouri and transporting them downstream; and to cultivate friendship and trade with the native tribes.

Lewis selected as his companion and co-leader William Clark, a younger brother of the famed Revolutionary War hero George Rogers Clark. On Jefferson's authority, Lewis, a captain of infantry, also offered Clark a captaincy. When the commission came through, however, it was a second lieutenancy. Nevertheless, to their men and to history they were Captain Lewis and Captain Clark, and they shared the leadership of the expedition equally. Both were seasoned campaigners with vast frontier experience: Lewis had served in the army from the Whiskey Rebellion to his detachment as Jefferson's secretary; Clark, member of a famous military family, had served four years with Anthony Wayne in the Indian wars of the Northwest.

Lewis embarked at Pittsburgh on August 31, 1803. The trip down the Ohio was slow and tiresome, and it was October 26 before he left Louisville with Clark, the latter's black slave, York, and a group of young Kentucky hunters.[1] They reached the DuBois River, just across the Mississippi from St. Louis, in mid-December and there went into winter camp. The winter months were spent drilling the men and making preparations for the trip up the Missouri River. Lewis spent a great deal of time in St. Louis making arrangements and talking to traders who knew the river. On March 9, 1804, he was the chief official witness to the formal transfer of Upper Louisiana from Spain to France and from France to the United States.

On May 14 the Lewis and Clark party, known also now as the Corps of Discovery and numbering forty-five in all, broke camp at the DuBois River "in the presence of many of the Neighbouring inhabitents and

A black-and-white photograph of a painting by Karl Bodmer depicting the American Fur Company's steamboat, *Yellow-Stone*, when it ran onto a sandbar in the Missouri River on April 19, 1833. The decision of the American Fur Company to abandon keelboats and use steamboats was an important factor in the company's acquisition of a virtual monopoly of the fur trade of the Far West. Courtesy, Joslyn Art Museum, Omaha, gift of the Enron Art Foundation.

proceeded on under a jentle brease up the Missourie."[2] Clark, who kept the journal during much of the trip, was an acute observer and an ingenious speller. Their equipment consisted of a fifty-five-foot keelboat with twenty-two oars, an open pirogue with seven oars, and another with six. All three were equipped with sails, push poles, and tow lines—the latter items being much more frequently used than the first. The boats were loaded with arms, ammunition, extra clothing, scientific instruments, food, and presents for the Indians. Two horses were taken along for the use of the hunters.

On July 15, they made camp near the mouth of the Little Nemaha River, their first in Nebraska. Clark reported: "I saw Great quantities of Grapes, Plums, of 2 Kinds, wild Cherries of 2 Kinds, Hazelnuts, and Goosberries."[3] On July 21 they reached the Platte. The next day they went ten more miles up the river, where they decided to remain for a few days to explore the country and try to persuade chiefs of the neighboring tribes, particularly the Otos, to come in for a conference. After some difficulty—including the desertion of Liberté, a French hireling sent after the Otos, and Private Reed, who was later recaptured—on August 3 the explorers met with a group of Otos and Missourias at a point they called the Council Bluff (near the present town of Fort Calhoun) fifty miles up the river. Clark's account of this first parley west of the Missouri between representatives of the United States and the Indians shows that he and Lewis were skilled diplomats:

mad[e] up a Small preasent for those people in perpotion to their Consiqunce. also a package with a meadile to accompany a Speech for the Grand Chief (which we intend to send to him) after Brackfast we Collected those Indians under an orning of our Main Sail, in presence or our Party paraded & Delivered a long Speech to them expressive of our journey the wirkes of our Government, Some advice to them and Directions how They were to Conduct themselves, (made one) the princapal Chief for the nation (to whom) being absente we sent him the Speech flag *Meadel & Some Cloathes. after hering what they had to say Delivered (two of) a medal of Second Grade to one for the Ottos & one for the Missourie (part of the nation) present and 4 medals of a third Grade to the inferior Chief two for each tribe.*[4]

Yet for all the diplomacy, there was little meeting of minds. Lewis and Clark were staking claim to the new territory for the United States and identifying sites for trading and defense posts. As Clark noted about the site of this first meeting:

The Situation [wc: 25 Days from this to Santafee] of our last Camp Councill Bluff or Handssom Prarie, appears to be a verry proper place for a Tradeing establishment & fortification. The Soil of the Bluff well adapted for Brick, Great deel of timers abov in the two Points. many other advantages of a Small nature . . . one Days march from the Ottoe Town, one Day & a half from the great Pania village, 2 days from the Mahar Towns, two 1/4 Days from the Loups *Village, & Convenient to the Countrey thro: which Bands of the*

Soux hunt. perhaps no other Situation is as well Calculated for a Tradeing establishment. The air is pure and helthy So far as we can Judge.[5]

The expedition also sought to make peace among the several tribes and establish trade. These first contacts with the Otos and Missourias, however, revealed a fundamental difference between the aims and expectations of the Corps of Discovery and those of the Indians. The Indians wanted trade, to be sure, but it mattered little with what nation. And intertribal conflicts would not be solved by the intervention of these outsiders; promises made to Lewis and Clark would be binding only for the brief moment.

A few days after the meeting with the Otos and Missourias the party suffered its only fatality. That there was only one is perhaps one of the most remarkable aspects of the whole trip. On August 19, Sergeant Charles Floyd was "taken verry bad all at onc with a Beliose Chorlick." Recent scholarship suggests that Floyd was suffering from appendicitis. The next day he died, probably from peritonitis following the rupture of his appendix.[6] He was buried on top of a bluff one-half mile below the mouth of a small river. Both the bluff and the river were given his name.

The party was along the Nebraska shore until September 7, then proceeded into South Dakota. By late October they had put the Lakotas and the Arikaras behind them and were at the Mandan villages near present Bismarck, North Dakota. There they built winter quarters. On April 7, 1805, they set out again. After a season of almost unbearable hardship, they came in view of the Pacific on November 7. They had found a route to the Western Sea.

It was not a good route, and the explorers knew it. Hence, during a miserable winter at Fort Clatsop, which they built on Young's Bay, the leaders decided that on the return trip they would divide the party. They were sure that there were other routes through the tangled mountain wilderness, and they must try to find them. They parted at Travellers' Rest Creek on July 3, 1806. Lewis would go directly to the falls of the Missouri River and then explore the Marias River region; Clark would go to the head of navigation of the year before and then cross over to the Yellowstone River. When they came together a few days later, on August 12, below the mouth of the Yellowstone, their earlier optimism was gone: any route to the Pacific would involve a long and difficult land carry.

They were back in St. Louis on September 23, 1806. Others would find a better route to the Western Sea, but Meriwether Lewis and William Clark had pointed the way. The significance of their achievement can hardly be overestimated.

Along with President Jefferson, Americans in the West moved quickly to exploit the Louisiana Purchase. In 1805, General James Wilkinson, governor of Louisiana territory, sent twenty-six-year-old Lieutenant Zebulon M. Pike to find the headwaters of the Mississippi. No sooner had the young lieutenant returned to St. Louis—after having dealt successfully with the Indians of the region, even though he mistook Leech Lake for the source of the Mississippi River—than General Wilkinson sent him into the Southwest to explore the headwaters of the Arkansas and Red Rivers and conclude a treaty with the Comanches. His first duty, however, was to escort a group of Osages and Pawnees back to their homeland and arrange peace between the two tribes. When he left St. Louis on July 15, 1806, with his party of twenty-two, he had with him about fifty Indians. By September 25 he was at the Pawnee villages on the Republican River.[7]

The Kansas and Osage tribes were willing to smoke the pipe of peace, but the Pawnees were not so agreeable. They had recently been visited by a large party of Spaniards under Don Facundo Melgares, who had been sent out to turn back the Americans. Characterish, the Pawnee chief, had a commission from the governor of New Mexico; several of the chiefs had medals from Melgares; and the Spanish flag flew at the head chief's door. Despite his small force, however, Pike was able to persuade Characterish to haul down the Spanish flag and raise the Stars and Stripes in its stead. He then set out to the southwest, following the homeward trail of Melgares.

While Pike was penetrating the Southwest, St. Louis traders continued to move up the Missouri River. Indeed, on their outbound journey in 1804, Lewis and Clark met no less than eight parties of traders coming downstream before they reached the Platte River; on their homeward journey in 1806, they encountered eleven separate parties heading up the river.

Lewis and Clark returned to St. Louis with glowing reports of the profits that could be made in furs. Thereafter the trade increased rapidly, continuing as the most important activity in the trans–Missouri River region until about 1843, when the high tide of western migration set in. The traders and trappers roamed everywhere, involving themselves and their government with the Indians and even with foreign powers, drinking, gambling, womanizing, and carousing, making huge fortunes almost overnight and losing them even more rapidly. Through it all, however, they were exploring this vast, wild country, both plains and mountains, seeking the sources of its rivers and finding new roads to the West. The map of the West was indeed first drawn on a beaver skin.

THE FUR TRADE

The fur trade of the Far West had its headquarters at St. Louis, whose warehouses bulged alternately with trade goods and furs and whose port became the center of a commerce almost as widespread as that of New York. Nebraska's role was primarily that of providing a highway. To be sure, the Nebraska tribes—particularly in the early years—were the source of a fairly profitable trade, but once the traders had penetrated to the tribes dwelling in the rich beaver grounds of the upper Missouri River and the Rocky Mountains, the relative significance of the Nebraska trade steadily declined. The Missouri River, however, and later the Platte, were the highways to the rich grounds farther on, and the traffic to and from the Far West played an important role in Nebraska's preterritorial history. Trading posts flourished along the Missouri, particularly near the mouth of the Platte and in the Scotts Bluff region. Fort Atkinson provided protection for the early upriver trade and was the point from which the first Rocky Mountain expedition was launched.

The first of the large-scale operators to penetrate the upper Missouri after Lewis and Clark was Manuel Lisa, who left St. Louis in the spring of 1807 with a keelboat full of trade goods. At the mouth of the Platte he met John Colter, who had been with Lewis and Clark, and persuaded him to go back up the river. After encounters with various hostile tribes, especially the Lakotas and Assiniboines, he halted at the mouth of the Bighorn River in the heart of the Crow country. Here he built a post, variously known as Fort Lisa, Fort Manuel, and Manuel's Fort. His activities during the winter are somewhat obscure, but the next spring he was back in St. Louis, elated with his success and eager to expand the trade. To accomplish this, the St. Louis Missouri Fur Company was organized on March 7, 1809, as a copartnership. Lisa's partners in this venture included some of the best-known men in St. Louis—Pierre and Auguste Chouteau, William Clark, Andrew Henry, Sylvestre Labadie, Reuben Lewis, Pierre Menard, William Morrison, and Benjamin Wilkinson. Even so, the company's early efforts were not successful.

The first expedition left St. Louis in June 1809 with 172 men and nine barges loaded with goods worth $4,269, including whiskey valued at $165. By the time they reached Fort Osage, sickness and desertion had reduced the crew to 153 men, and though trade on the Big Horn River was fairly successful, they lost most of their goods and many men to the Blackfeet. After much difficulty and some dissension, the company was reorganized in 1812. Also in that year pressure from the British and Indians forced Lisa, who continued to be the company's principal agent in the field, to abandon the upper river. He retreated to a point near the Council Bluff and there built a new post (Fort Lisa), which soon became the most important fort on the Missouri River.

Fort Lisa controlled the trade of the Omahas, Pawnees, and Otos and after the war of 1812 served as a base for the revival of trade on the upper river. Manuel Lisa exercised dominion over the Nebraska country. Hot-tempered and erratic, he was one of the most forceful and controversial figures in the fur trade. Though hated by his competitors and some of his employees, he seems to have established good relations with the Indians. After the custom of most fur traders, he took an Indian wife, a beautiful Omaha woman, who bore him two children and helped solidify his position with the tribe. Lisa served as agent for the tribes on the Missouri River above the Kansas River and appears to have been instrumental in preventing the British from winning these tribes as allies. Through all this he was successful financially, and by 1818 business had revived to the extent that he was considering the possibility of reestablishing trade at the headwaters of the Missouri and even beyond the Rocky Mountains. He died in 1820, however, before he had had an opportunity to carry out his plans.

After Lisa's death, Joshua Pilcher took over the management of the company. He tried to carry out Lisa's plans for reestablishing trade on the upper Missouri but was no more successful than Lisa at first had been. He withdrew altogether from trade above the Omahas, retiring to the main establishment at Fort Lisa. The company continued to do business for several years and may have operated in the Rockies, but its activities were of little importance in comparison with the growing power of the Western Department of John Jacob Astor's American Fur Company.

Lisa himself had had a brush with this colossus, which would soon largely dominate the fur trade of the Far West. In 1811, on his last trip to the upper river, Lisa got involved in a desperate keelboat race and even more desperate maneuvering for the favor of the upriver tribes with Wilson Price Hunt, who was making his way to Astoria, the American Fur Company's projected post at the mouth of the Columbia River.[8] Though Astoria, like Lisa's upper Missouri enterprises, was a casualty of the War of 1812, failure there did not dull Astor's ambition to control the trade of the Far West. Following the war he moved seriously to achieve his monopolistic goal.

Meanwhile, the War Department, under the leadership of Secretary John C. Calhoun, was moving aggressively to exploit the advantage won in the war. A succession of treaties at Portages des Sioux in 1815 had provided a basis for peace with thirteen of the western tribes, including the Omahas, Poncas, Iowas, and Lakotas. To preserve the peace and counteract remaining British influence, Calhoun proposed to build a series of self-sustaining military posts at strategic points along the Mississippi and Missouri Rivers and their tributaries and to connect them with adequate roads. Fort Snelling was to be the principal post on the upper Mississippi River. On the Missouri River, posts were to be constructed at the Council Bluff, the Mandan villages, and possibly at the great bend and at some point above the Mandan villages, perhaps the mouth of the Yellowstone River.

The Missouri enterprise, commonly referred to as the Yellowstone Expedition, consisted of a military force under Colonel Henry M. Atkinson and a scientific party under Major Stephen H. Long of the Army Engineers. Atkinson had the Sixth Infantry and the United States Rifle Regiment, commanding a total of 1,126 men. Abandoning keelboats in favor of steamboats, previously untried on the Missouri River, Atkinson found himself in trouble from the beginning. Of the five steamboats provided by the contractor, a corrupt and inefficient operator, two never entered the river at all, a third was abandoned thirty miles below Franklin, Missouri, and the other two stopped below the mouth of the Kansas River. Atkinson's men were lucky to reach the Council Bluff before winter set in. Major Long was more fortunate. His steamboat, the *Western Engineer*, was much better suited to the Missouri River than were the others. It was of lighter draft and a stern-wheeler, probably the first ever built. The *Western Engineer* made it all the way to the Council Bluff, the first steamboat to ascend the Missouri River to that point.

Atkinson's troops spent a scurvy-ridden winter at Camp Missouri, in the bottoms below the Council Bluff; Long's fared little better at Engineer Cantonment, five miles down the river. With spring, news came that Congress, weary of the expense and dubious of the whole Northwest project, had clipped the War Department's wings. Long, who had spent the winter in Washington, returned to lead a small exploring party up the Platte River; Atkinson's troops were to go no farther. The Council Bluff was to be the outpost of the nation's Northwest defenses. Another small expedition led by Captain Matthew J. Magee of the Rifle Regiment was sent to open a route from the Council Bluff to Fort Anthony, later Fort Snelling.

Long's force, consisting of twenty men, left Engineer Cantonment on June 6, 1820. The most notable result of the expedition was the unfavorable impression it fostered regarding the country west of the Missouri River. At the Loup fork, the party came upon the Pawnee villages. Long estimated their population at something less than the 6,223 found by Pike in 1806. Around the villages were six to eight thousand horses, grazing on the plains during the day but confined in corrals at night. Picking up two French guides at the villages, Long followed the north side of the Platte River to the forks and then crossed over to the south side. The party reached the Rocky Mountains, and Dr. Edwin James, scientist for the expedition, scaled Pikes Peak, the first white man to do so. They continued south to the Arkansas River, and Long divided his party in an unsuccessful effort to find the headwaters of the Red River. Finally, in mid-September they were reunited at Fort Smith, having suffered much but accomplished little.

Meanwhile, the Sixth Infantry, thwarted in its plan to go farther up the Missouri River, was occupied in transforming Camp Missouri from a temporary cantonment into a permanent post, to be designated Fort Atkinson. The camp was moved to higher ground, and new barracks, covered with shingles and furnished with brick chimneys, were erected. Because of the experience with the scurvy epidemic, Colonel Atkinson suggested that the men be allowed to supplement their army-supplied rations by raising their own vegetables and livestock. Calhoun agreed. The experiment was a success. The soldiers raised good crops of corn, turnips, and potatoes and large herds of cattle and hogs. A sawmill was built and a brickyard established. Colonel Atkinson was promoted to the command of the western wing of the Western Department, and Colonel Henry Leavenworth arrived to take command of the Sixth Infantry. As Calhoun had written the chairman of the House Committee on Indian Affairs: "The position at Council Bluffs is a very important one. . . . It is believed to be the best position on the Missouri to cover our flourishing settlements in that quarter and ought, if it were wholly unconnected with other objects, to be established for that purpose alone."[9]

But there were "other objects." The fur trade, in decline since the war, was showing marked signs of revival. The *Missouri Intelligencer* on September 17, 1822, estimated that a thousand men were employed on the waters of the Missouri River. The American Fur Company had established its Western Department at St. Louis. The Columbia Fur Company had entered the field the year before. The Missouri Fur Company was carrying on Lisa's business. Others new in the business or with increased capital were Stone, Bostwick and Company, Bernard Pratte and Company, and Ashley and Henry. They all had designs on the dangerous upper Missouri River country. They would all need protection.

Trouble was not long in coming. Men from the Missouri Fur Company, floating downriver with a load of furs, were attacked by the Blackfeet on the Yellowstone River on May 31, 1823. The leaders of the party and five men were killed, and all their furs and equipment were lost. On June 2, General William H. Ashley, returning upriver from St. Louis (his partner, Andrew Henry, had wintered on the Yellowstone River), was attacked by the Arikaras near the mouth of the Grand River. He retreated down the river to a fortified point near the present town of Chamberlain, South Dakota, and sent calls for help to Colonel Leavenworth at Fort Atkinson and Major Henry on the Yellowstone River. Henry promptly came down the river with most of his party, and by early August Colonel Leavenworth had arrived with 220 regulars from Fort Atkinson. Also on hand were Joshua Pilcher with a party of men from the Missouri Fur Company and a sizable band of Lakotas. These forces were at cross purposes from the beginning. The Lakotas were interested only in plunder, and when they saw no prospect of that, left in disgust. The traders wanted the Arikaras exterminated, to get them out of the way and to serve as an example to other tribes. Colonel Leavenworth, however, wanted only to punish the offenders. As a result, the so-called Arikara War settled nothing. Leavenworth got a peace treaty with the Arikaras, but it was not satisfactory to the traders. Ashley and Henry decided to transfer their activities to other fields. In so doing, they opened the fur trade of the rich Rocky Mountain area and blazed the Platte Valley trail, soon to become the West's great emigrant road.

Robert Stuart had come down the Platte River in 1812–13 when returning from Astoria with word for John Jacob Astor about the plight of that post. The significance of the Platte Valley as a route was not fully appreciated, however, until the spring of 1824, when Thomas Fitzpatrick and James Clyman also followed it from the mountains to the Missouri River, reporting to Ashley, who had returned to St. Louis after the Arikara trouble, about the rich beaver grounds in the Green River country and the practical road to reach them.[10] Ashley, who had spent the summer unsuccessfully campaigning for governor of Missouri, immediately organized an expedition to the Rocky Mountains. He set out from Fort Atkinson with a party of twenty-five men, fifty pack horses, and a wagon on November 3, 1824. It was very late in the season to begin such a venture. He followed the Platte River to its forks and decided to continue up the South Fork. Mid-April 1825 found him at the Green River. Here he divided his men into four groups with instructions to trap the region and rendezvous on the Green River, near Henry's Fork, in July. Thus Ashley, in addition to pioneering a new route and opening a new trade region, also pioneered a new system for the fur trade that did not rely on fixed trading posts. The resulting summer rendezvous annually brought together traders, trappers, and Indians for a period of dealing, double-dealing, and carousing.

Meanwhile, Fort Atkinson continued to flourish. The agricultural experiment of 1820 was repeated annually on an ever-increasing scale; the post was improved and became the center of white activity on the Missouri River. It was not very effective, however, in fulfilling its original mission, the protection of the fur trade, and the War Department began to question the need for its continuance. General Atkinson and Major Benjamin O'Fallon had gone up the river in 1825 and concluded treaties with seventeen of the tribes. The success of this expedition made it appear that a post on the upper Missouri River was unnecessary. Perhaps there was little need for Fort Atkinson either. Inspector George Croghan, who visited Fort Atkinson in 1826, denounced it as the weakest fort with the worst trained garrison he had ever seen. To him, the key to its uselessness was that the soldiers had so much time for agriculture. With great irritation, he wrote:

Our military have lost character among the Indians. No officer seems to know his place in case of an alarm. . . . The men say there is no danger—well then as well argue that there should be no army and I would as soon argue there be none. The present system is destroying military spirit and making officers the base overseers of a troop of awkward ploughmen. Let the soldier be one. Let him no longer boast of his skill as a tiller of the soil, but as a soldier. . . . Look at Fort Atkinson and you will see barnyards that would not disgrace a Pennsylvania farmer, herds of cattle that would do credit to a Potomac grazier, yet where is the gain in this, either to the soldier or to the Government? Why all the corn and hay? To feed to cattle. Why the cattle? To eat the corn and hay.[11]

Shortly thereafter, in June 1827, Fort Atkinson was abandoned, and the Sixth Infantry was transferred to Jefferson Barracks, near St. Louis. Later in the year, a new post, Cantonment Leavenworth, was established farther south near the jumping-off place for the growing Santa Fe trade and for an ever-increasing number of expeditions to the Rocky Mountains. Fort Atkinson was too far north to protect this trade and too far south to protect the trade of the upper river. It was generally vilified as an unfortunate and expensive aftermath of the abortive Yellowstone

Expedition. Even so, the post at the Council Bluff played an important, if brief and neglected, role in frontier history. Nationally, it gave protection to the fur trade when the need was greatest, and it represented a significant extension of the military frontier line. Locally, it was the site of initial farming operations by whites in a state that in less than a century would become noted for its agriculture. The success of the agricultural experiment proved significant for the army as well. In spite of Inspector Croghan's dim view of the soldier-farmer, the army adopted an agricultural program and encouraged its implementation at its western posts through the remainder of the century.

Fort Atkinson had also served as the site for the Council Bluffs agency operated by John Dougherty for the Oto, Omaha, Missouria, Pawnee, Lakota, Arikara, and other northern tribes. When the fort was abandoned in 1827, Dougherty moved with the army to Fort Leavenworth, where he continued to operate the agency until the spring of 1832, when he decided to move north to a post which was owned by Lucien Fontenelle at Bellevue. Fontenelle, who had acquired the post shortly after Fort Atkinson was abandoned, sold it to Dougherty for $1,000 and rebuilt a short distance down the river. Peter Sarpy and the American Fur Company subsequently opened a post at Bellevue, which after 1840 became a well-known rendezvous for Indians, traders, and travelers.

THE MISSION FIELD

The fur trade had a profound effect on the Indians. The traders not only brought with them symbols of white progress such as implements and clothing but also weapons, alcohol, and vices. The result was an almost complete breakdown of the native way of life. Particularly disastrous to the Indian was the trader's "firewater" for which they had as little tolerance as they did to the diseases brought by whites. And trade whiskey was far worse than the liquors consumed by most whites. The trader's basic recipe called for one gallon of grain alcohol, three gallons of water, and a pound of chewing tobacco. To this might be added a variety of other ingredients such as red pepper, ginger, and black molasses, depending on their availability. It was, indeed, a concoction so vile that its deleterious effect was not limited to Indians.

The Indian Intercourse Act of 1834 prohibited the importation of liquor into the Indian country, and inspectors were stationed at Leavenworth, Bellevue, and other points to enforce the prohibition. Efforts at enforcement, however, were ineffectual. Liquor had become the one indispensable article in the fur trade, and the St. Louis traders argued that they needed it to meet competition from Hudson's Bay Company representatives, who had free use of it. Hence, in spite of the best efforts of federal authorities, or with their connivance, vast quantities of liquor were smuggled into the Indian country each year.

Striving hard to counteract the traders' influence among the Indians was a small band of missionaries. As early as November 1830, the Baptist Missionary Union had made preliminary arrangements with the government to establish a mission among Nebraska tribes. The following year Reverend Johnston Lykins started a mission among the Shawnees in present eastern Kansas but though he might have intended to reach tribes north along the Missouri River, his work never extended into Nebraska.

Baptist mission work in present Nebraska was begun by Moses P. Merrill, who was sent in 1833 to establish a mission among the Otos near Bellevue. Accompanied by his wife, Eliza, Cynthia Brown, and Ira D. Blanchard, the Reverend Mr. Merrill arrived at the Bellevue agency on November 8. Eliza Merrill opened a school on the seventh day after their arrival. In 1835, Moses Merrill was appointed a government teacher, thus making it possible for him to augment the meager support provided by the Missionary Union. Merrill was particularly active in providing literature in the Oto tongue—a spelling book, a reader, and a small collection of hymns. He worked diligently, but he was only partially successful. This he attributed to the evil influence of the traders. In 1839 he accompanied the Pawnees on their autumn hunt. He was ill when he returned and died in 1840.

Interest in missions to the Indians spread to other denominations as well. The Methodists sent Jason Lee to Oregon with the trapper caravan of 1834. Lee was the first missionary to be sent to Oregon country. That same year, John Dunbar and Samuel Allis were sent by the Presbyterians to work among the Pawnees, and in 1838 a Jesuit, Father Pierre Jean DeSmet, briefly visited the Potawatomis near present Council Bluffs, Iowa.

John Dunbar and Samuel Allis were perhaps the most adventurous of the early missionaries in Nebraska. They arrived at Bellevue in October, hoping to spend the winter with the Pawnees. When the Pawnees came in for their annuities later in the month and learned of the desires of the two men, they welcomed them with open arms. There was only one difficulty. Two Pawnee bands each wanted a missionary. Dunbar and Allis had assumed that they would spend the winter together, but, laying their apprehensions aside, they decided to separate, Dunbar going with the Grand Pawnees and Allis with the Loups. Both men were treated with the utmost consideration by their hosts, who, in turn, felt that the missionaries had brought them good fortune. The buffalo were lower down the Platte in 1834–35 than they had been for twenty years. The Pawnees told Dunbar that it was because he had come to live with them: "They say the buffalo have been gone a long time, but now a man has come to live with them who loves Te-rah-wah, and he has sent back the buffalo."[12] Allis was to spend one and Dunbar two more years with the tribes.

In 1835, just a year after sending Dunbar and Allis, the Presbyterians sent out Samuel Parker and Marcus Whitman. Whitman went only as far as the Green River, however, and returned to the United States. He started out again the following year, this time with his bride, Narcissa, and the Reverend and Mrs. Henry H. Spalding. Accompanying the party was another young woman, Emeline Palmer, who was betrothed to Samuel Allis. After Samuel and Emeline were married in April 1836, the Whitmans and the Spaldings set out for Oregon country. Narcissa Whitman and Eliza Spalding thus became the first white women to traverse the overland trail.

Missionary work was becoming a family venture. Like the Merrills, Samuel Allis and his wife, Emeline, established themselves in the vicinity of Bellevue, from which they would continue their missionary work among the Pawnees. In November 1840, Emeline gave birth to a daughter, Martha, and later to two sons. Along with Dunbar, they established a mission to the Tappage, Republican, and Grand Pawnee on present Council Creek, then called Plum Creek, not far from the present town of Fullerton, in the spring of 1841. Dunbar thought this was good corn country, and he believed wheat could be easily cultivated as well. By the autumn of 1842, the Tappages, together with many Grands and Republicans, had a village of forty-one lodges near the mission. The Plum Creek mission failed to prosper, however. Dunbar and Allis became estranged, and much of their time seems to have been occupied in fruitless controversy over both temporal and spiritual matters. Moreover, the Lakotas were a constant threat and in 1846 forced an abandonment of the mission and a return to Bellevue.

That same year the Presbyterians established a mission for the Omahas at Bellevue under the charge of Edward McKinney and his wife. They opened a school in 1847, and despite much opposition and many difficulties, the mission prospered. The Reverend William Hamilton took charge in 1853, continuing with the Omahas, except for the decade 1857–67, until 1870, when the tribe was assigned to the Society of Friends. Father Hamilton, as he was called, was much beloved by both Indians and whites and was to play an important role in early territorial history.

It is difficult to assess the work of the missionaries. They had the welfare of the Indians at heart and worked to promote it, particularly against the influence of the traders, which, all the missionaries agreed, was particularly baneful. Moreover, whereas the trader was merely indifferent to the Indian's culture, the missionary saw in it something that must be changed. Both contributed to its ultimate dissolution.

Although explorers and traders were seemingly uninterested in establishing permanent settlements and domesticating the wilderness, the missionaries and their families were. It is interesting that the oldest quilt in the collection of the State Historical Society is a dower quilt made by Martha Allis, which she began in the 1850s. Long before the major period of settlement, the women, as well as men, who sought to spread the Gospel were changing the domestic face of the frontier. It is also significant that in the Oregon country the missionaries were able to win ground where the traders had failed. They may not have been successful in converting all with whom they came in contact, but their efforts were a major force in calling the country's attention to Oregon and inducing a migration that in less than a generation would completely transform the face of the West.

CHAPTER 5

The Great Platte River Road

The broad, flat valley of the Platte River with its easy ascent to the foothills of the Rockies provided westward-moving Americans with one of the world's great natural highways. The Platte Valley provided an incomparable roadbed for wagons. Robert Stuart, who led a group overland from the Pacific Fur Company outpost, Astoria, on the Columbia River, to St. Louis, had reported its potential as a wagon route in 1813. Stuart's route, which crossed the continental divide near South Pass in southern Wyoming and followed the Sweetwater and Platte Rivers to the Missouri River, later became the eastern end of the Oregon trail.

The first wagons to leave their tracks on what was to become the Oregon Trail were those taken west by Jedediah Smith, David Jackson, and William Sublette in 1830. Successors to William Ashley's Rocky Mountain Fur Company, the firm of Smith, Jackson, and Sublette set out from St. Louis with ten wagons, each drawn by five mules, and two Dearborns, four-wheeled carriages with curtained sides, each drawn by one mule. Leaving the Santa Fe Trail about forty miles west of Independence, Missouri, they angled to the northwest across the Kansas and the Blue Rivers to the Platte River, arriving ultimately at the head of Wind River. Here they stopped to gather furs, but as they observed, "the wagons could easily have crossed the Rocky mountains, it being what is called the Southern Pass."[1]

In 1832 Benjamin L. E. Bonneville took wagons through South Pass and as far west as the Green River. In 1836 Dr. Marcus Whitman and his party tried to take a two-wheeled cart all the way to Oregon but were forced to abandon it at Fort Boise. Finally, in 1838, Reverend W. H. Gray and party managed to get a two-wheeled cart all the way.

THE OREGON TRAIL

Beginning in 1814, when the Lewis and Clark journals were published, through the next two decades, individuals and groups periodically attempted to heighten the nation's interest in Oregon country. "Oregon country" referred to a vast geographical area, generally encompassing the land west of the continental divide as well as a portion of southwestern Canada. In it lay the future states of Washington, Oregon, and Idaho and portions of Montana and Wyoming.

It was not until the 1830s that "Oregon Fever" began to catch on. Ironically it was the missionaries who unintentionally succeeded, where politicians and journalists had failed, in capturing the country's imagination and stirring the nation's desire for expansion and settlement into the Oregon country.

In their desire to convert the Indians to both Christianity and their ideal of a productive life, the missionaries on the Oregon frontier set up training programs to teach the Indians how to farm and raise livestock. Their farms did succeed in convincing a few Indians of the benefits of their agricultural techniques, but more important, they demonstrated to sponsors and observers in the East the great agricultural potential of the region. The soil was fertile and the farms productive. Here, unlike the "Great American Desert," was a vast new area with highly favorable conditions for an agricultural people.

The first of the Oregon country missionaries, Jason Lee, who had founded the mission at French Prairie on behalf of the Methodists in 1834, returned East in 1838 and preached the glories of Oregon from pulpits all over the country. Marcus Whitman, whose greatest ambition was to settle Oregon with Protestant Americans, wrote and talked extensively on the subject. An Oregon Emigration Society was organized in Lynn, Massachusetts, in 1838, and others developed elsewhere. To patriotic and missionary motives were added the pressures of the Panic of 1837, the desire to escape the seemingly unhealthful climate of the Mississippi Valley, the lure of opportunity in a new land, and just plain adventure.

Early in May 1841, the first band of settlers, the Bidwell-Bartleson party—nearly one hundred in all, including a few missionaries—set out from the Missouri frontier. Their guide was the veteran mountain man Thomas Fitzpatrick. Near Soda Springs, in present Idaho, the group divided, with half heading for California and the remainder pushing on to Oregon.

The next year more than one hundred men, women, and children were in the emigrant party. Their leader, Elijah White, who had gone to Oregon as a missionary with Jason Lee, was now returning as an Indian agent. Also in 1842 Lieutenant John C. Frémont led an exploring expedition through the Platte Valley to South Pass. Though Frémont was to go down in history as the Great Pathfinder, he was actually traveling a trail over which hundreds of traders, missionaries, and emigrants had gone before. He found no new trails, but his report, written in part by his wife, Jessie, who was the daughter of Missouri's noted expansionist senator, Thomas Hart Benton, greatly stimulated interest in Oregon and established the Platte Valley–South Pass route as the best way west.

By 1843 the full tide of emigration had set in, and in that year more than a thousand persons went over the trail, taking with them about 120 wagons drawn by six-ox teams and several thousand loose horses and cattle. This great migration was not the result of an organized movement but was simply the coming together of restless and adventurous souls, who assembled at Independence because they had heard that a wagon train would start from there for Oregon as soon as the weather permitted.

In the beginning, some effort was made to travel in one body, but this proved so unwieldy that at the crossing of the Big Blue River the group divided into two columns to proceed separately but within supporting distance of each other. At Independence Rock on the Sweetwater and out of danger from the Indians, they divided further into small parties and proceeded on their individual ways.

The migration of 1843 was only the beginning. Each succeeding year through the 1850s and into the 1860s additional thousands of people headed for Oregon. The Oregon Trail was becoming the high road of American expansion.

The two-thousand-mile trail began at Independence, Missouri. From Independence, the emigrants followed the old Santa Fe Trail for about forty miles (generally a two-day journey) to where a crude sign marked "Road to Oregon" had been placed. Here they angled northwest, crossing the Kansas River and the Blue River. The trail entered present-day Nebraska at about the present line between Gage and Jefferson Counties, followed the Blue Valley across present-day Jefferson, Thayer, Nuckolls,

A wagon train fording the South Platte River some fifteen miles above the forks in the summer of 1866. Courtesy, NSHS, E54:32.

and Adams Counties, and joined the Platte River near the head of the Grand Island in Hall County. It went along the south side of the Platte to a point in Keith County, about seven miles east of Big Springs. There the emigrants crossed the South Platte and went northwest through Ash Hollow to the North Platte, then past Court House and Jail Rocks, Chimney Rock, and Scotts Bluff to Fort Laramie. They crossed the North Platte and went on to the Sweetwater and South Pass.

Initially, the trail swung south of Scotts Bluff, named for Hiram Scott, a fur trader who lost his life there, through Robidoux Pass, rejoining the river to the west of the bluffs. Beginning about 1850, Mitchell Pass, nearer the river, was used. In many places, of course, there was no one trail. Whenever the ruts became too deep for the wagons, the emigrants simply broke out a parallel trail. Certain trails that were used during dry years became impassable in wet years, when the streams were full and the lowlands swampy.

Though the journey across the plains and up the east slope of the mountains was wearisome, it was the easier part of the trip. The Pacific side was much more difficult: the narrow valleys and high passes were almost impassable, and only the most determined could prod their footsore oxen into dragging the worn-out wagons past Fort Bridger, Soda Springs, and Fort Hall, along the Snake River, and down the Columbia River to the Willamette Valley.

THE MORMON TRAIL

Beginning in 1847, the Mormons, writing an additional chapter in the history of American expansion, broke a new trail through the Platte Valley. Driven out of Nauvoo, Illinois, they made their way across Iowa to the Missouri River in the spring of 1846. Here Brigham Young made an agreement with the government to furnish five hundred "volunteers" for the Mexican War in return for the privilege of stopping for the winter in the Indian country just across the river.

Selecting a beautiful tract of land a few miles above Bellevue, the present site of suburban Florence on the northern edge of Omaha, the Mormons busied themselves during the summer and fall in constructing Winter Quarters. More than three thousand of the faithful moved across the Missouri to take up temporary residence there. Others remained in Iowa, and a small detachment spent a miserable winter among the Poncas on the Niobrara, finally abandoning the faith. Those at Winter Quarters had a miserable time of it, too. Some built log houses, but most clung to life in their wagons or in caves dug in the hillsides.

Poorly housed and inadequately fed, the pitiful residents of Winter Quarters fell victim to scurvy, malaria, and just plain cold and starvation. More than six hundred died that winter. Many of them lie in nameless graves in the little Mormon cemetery overlooking Florence. Winter Quarters, however, was more than just a wayside camp. It was the administrative center of a great movement, and through all the suffering and starvation Brigham Young worked relentlessly to organize his followers for the push the following year to some point well beyond the United States where they might create a new Zion.[2]

By early spring, Young's plans were firm. He would lead a small, hand-picked band to point the way and select the site; the others would follow. The pioneer band of 148 persons included three of the leaders' wives, three black servants, and two small children. With seventy-two wagons and a large herd of livestock, they left their appointed rendezvous on the Elkhorn River on April 16.[3]

To keep as far away from non-Mormons as possible, Young chose the north side of the Platte. They crossed the Loup fork, the most substantial barrier along the Platte, on April 23, building two light rafts to carry their supplies and equipment, and fording the empty wagons. By June 1 they reached Fort Laramie, where they halted to rest the animals and build ferryboats. Finding they had to recross the North Platte 124 miles further on, they instructed subsequent emigrations to keep to the north side of the river. By July 24 they had arrived at the valley of the Great Salt Lake and decided that here they would build their new Zion. The pioneer band was followed by some two thousand of the faithful during 1847.

Having established his followers at Salt Lake, Young returned to Winter Quarters, arriving on October 31, to organize the next year's emigration. In what probably was the first example of printing in Nebraska, he issued a call to the Saints, "abroad, dispersed throughout the earth," to gather at Winter Quarters "and, if possible, be ready to start from hence by the first of May next, or as soon as grass is sufficiently grown, and go to the Great Salt Lake City, with bread stuff sufficient to sustain you until you can raise grain the following season." He advised those who could not afford to make the trip to Salt Lake to work the Pottawatomie lands: "In a year or two their young cattle will grow into teams; by interchange of labor they can raise their own grain and provisions, and build their own wagons; and by sale of their improvements, to citizens who will gladly come and occupy, they can replenish their clothing, and thus speedily and comfortably procure an outfit."[4]

Young led some three thousand emigrants to Salt Lake in 1848, more than doubling its population. If Zion were to succeed, however, still more people would be needed. Missionaries were sent throughout the United States and to Europe to convert people to the faith and to persuade them to journey to the promised land. To assist the indigent, a perpetual emigration fund was formed. The lure was great, especially among the impoverished of Europe, and converts continued to come. Winter Quarters was abandoned, but the north bank of the Platte still was recognized as the official trail. Many, however, used the South Platte trail, starting from old Fort Kearny, and after 1856 from Wyoming in Otoe County, which flourished briefly as an outfitting point.

Unfortunately, most of the emigrants were so poor that they needed almost total assistance, and it took all of Young's ingenuity to keep the perpetual emigration fund alive. Finally, in desperation, Young announced in 1855 that the church could no longer provide wagons for the emigrants. Instead, he would make handcarts for them, and they would make the trek on foot. And so he did, setting in motion the most incredible phase of the entire westward emigration.

The new town of Florence, located on the site of old Winter Quarters, was selected as the starting place, but the march actually began in Iowa City, Iowa, adding about three hundred miles to the total trek. The first company, made up of about five hundred persons, set out on July 17, 1856. A traveler coming down the Platte from Oregon described them:

The carts were generally drawn by one man and three women each, though some carts were drawn by women alone. There were about three women to one man, and two-thirds of the women were single. It was the most motley crew I ever beheld. Most of them were Danes, with a sprinkling of Welsh, Swedes, and English, and were generally from the lower classes of their countries. Most could not understand what we said to them. The road was lined for a mile behind the train with the lame, halt, sick, and needy. Many were quite aged, and would be going slowly along, supported by a son or daughter. Some were on crutches; now and then a mother with a child in her arms and two or three hanging hold of her, with a forlorn appearance, would pass slowly along; others, whose condition entitled them to a seat in the carriage, were wending their way through the sand. A few seemed in good spirits.[5]

Altogether, five handcart companies set out in 1856. The last two got caught in the snows, and 150 of 500 in the fifth company perished. Though Young had counted the operation a success, the handcarts were little used after 1856. Two expeditions were made in 1857, one in 1859, and the last two in 1860. Altogether three thousand persons walked across the plains to Salt Lake City. After 1860 Young sent church teams to meet emigrants at the railroad terminal. With the completion of the transcontinental railroad, of course, the Saints could make the entire trip by rail.

THE CALIFORNIA GOLD RUSH

The pioneer Mormons were hardly settled at Salt Lake City before gold was discovered at Captain John A. Sutter's mill on the south fork of the American River in California. Sutter tried to keep the discovery secret, but such news could not be kept. By May 1848, diggings were being worked for thirty miles along the river. That summer rich placers were found on other streams. By autumn the whole world was alive with excitement. By early 1849 hundreds of excited gold-seekers were on the high seas in ships bound for California. Thousands more were making plans to go overland as soon as the grass was green in the spring.

There were various overland routes to California, but the one most heavily used was the Platte Valley–South Pass trail. By early spring of 1849, more than twenty thousand persons were congregated at Independence, Fort Leavenworth, St. Joseph, and Council Bluffs eagerly awaiting the day when they could begin their trek across the plains. A more diverse group would be hard to imagine. As one emigrant wrote his wife from Westport: "It would astonish you to see the number of people going to California. It would be the greatest sight you ever saw. The people are of all kinds, some of the first people in the United States a-going and some of the meanest are also along."[6]

Though thousands had been over the trail before them, many of the Forty-Niners were unable or unwilling to make use of the information that had accumulated over the years. As a result, many started west pre-posterously overloaded; many others tried to walk, carrying their worldly goods on their backs. By the time they reached Fort Kearny, if not before, they were aware of their folly; the trail near that post was literally strewn with abandoned equipment, foodstuffs, and even wagons. Some sold their excess baggage; others left it along the trail for whoever wanted it; still others burned their wagons and mixed turpentine with their sugar and dirt with their flour. Those who started out with too little had to call on the commandant at Fort Kearny for relief, and had not the army come to their rescue, many would have gone no farther.

There were other problems, even more serious. The grass of the Platte Valley was ground and eaten away by the vast throng of animals. Buffalo and other wild game, upon which many planned to depend for food, became scarce, and hunters had to range far from the trail. And if these conditions were not bad enough, cholera struck with a vengeance in 1849. Whether it was an epidemic or the result of contaminated water is unclear. The heterogeneous mass of humanity on the trail provided an ideal medium for its spread. The disease struck quickly and without warning, and the victims often died within twenty-four hours.[7]

Despite hardships, the eager gold-seekers pushed on to California. Estimates place the number who went over the trail in 1849 at about 40,000. The emigration of 1850 was even greater. By August 14, the official register at Fort Laramie had recorded 39,506. Altogether, an estimated 65,000 people went through the Platte Valley that year, most of them headed for California. Again cholera ravaged the trail across the plains. One emigrant wrote: "I had intended to notice in my journal every grave and burying place that we passed, but I have abandoned this part of my plan. . . . Graves are so numerous, that to notice them all would make my narrative tedious."[8]

Another, in sight of Court House Rock, noted: "It is supposed that one-fifth are dying here now with cholera and diarrhoea. Thus far one-tenth of our company have died."[9] There was virtually no letup in 1852, and some 70,000 persons probably crossed the plains that year. By 1853 the gold fever had diminished, and the emigrants who went over the trail in decreasing numbers during the 1850s were primarily seeking new homes.

The gold-seekers generally followed the Oregon Trail across the plains, which after 1849 might more properly be called the California Trail. Many travelers, however, confused the trail names in their journals, and Oregon Trail became the generic designation for their route. Each year an increasing number used the north side of the Platte, coming up the Missouri or across Iowa to Kanesville (present-day Council Bluffs).[10] By 1852 and thereafter this was the principal jumping-off point.[11] The enterprising merchants of Kanesville advertised the merits of their crossing and the North Platte route so effectively that the inadequate ferry service they provided usually was loaded beyond capacity.

LIFE ALONG THE TRAIL

Though no two years and no two trips were quite alike, life on the trail was about the same for all the overland emigrants, whether they were bound for Oregon, California, or Utah, whether they went along the north side of the Platte or the south. Some were better equipped than others, some were wiser, some were simply luckier. All suffered weariness, hardship, and danger, and it should be remembered that even though their experiences, seen in retrospect, appeared to follow a similar pattern, the experience for each traveler was new, exciting, and at times overwhelming. Little wonder that many of them kept diaries and wrote long letters home to their friends and the hometown newspaper. The plains portion of the trail, except perhaps in the cholera years, proved the easiest part of the journey. Anticipation, however, was another matter. That long stretch of "desert" between the Missouri and the mountains was fearful to contemplate. In actuality, the emigrants learned the lessons of overland travel on the plains, and hence that leg of the journey was a time of testing. Even for experienced travelers, nothing could have alleviated the effect of the sudden and violent storms, the dust, and the oppressive monotony of travel across the plains. Those harbingers of the mountains, Chimney Rock and Scotts Bluff, were eagerly watched for and always reached with rejoicing.

By early spring in the peak years thousands of emigrants had congregated at the principal jumping-off places, Independence, Fort Leavenworth, St. Joseph, and Kanesville (Council Bluffs), eagerly awaiting the day when the grass was green enough that it was safe to start. While waiting, the emigrants bought provisions and equipment, perfected their organizations, and eagerly discussed conditions on the trail with anyone who seemed to have information. Guidebooks of various sorts made their appearance, but many of the emigrants apparently did not have access to them, and some of those used were unreliable. Mountain men who could no longer make a living in the declining fur trade occasionally hired out as guides, but anyone who had been over the trail qualified as a veteran and found his services much in demand. The jumping-off places exhibited all the characteristics of frontier boom towns: supplies and equipment were scarce, prices were high, and everything was overcrowded. Particularly overcrowded were the ferries, and human nature exhibited itself at its worst as the emigrants fought for places in line. Occasionally, small parties wearied of the struggle and left the towns to get across the river where they could; in the late 1840s a considerable ferry business developed at old Fort Kearny, largely as overflow from St. Joseph.

By late April or early May the emigrants were on the move, and the trails west of the Missouri were lined as far as the eye could see with the swaying, white-topped wagons, not the Conestoga, which carried an earlier emigration into the eastern Mississippi Valley, but the Murphy, manufactured in St. Louis. For mutual protection and assistance, the emigrants generally organized into companies. The importance of order and discipline was generally accepted, and once chosen, a leader was given broad powers. A leader who became overzealous in the exercise of those powers, however, was apt to be deposed. The rate of travel varied considerably with the size of the company, the obstacles encountered, and the ability of the leadership. Sixteen miles a day with oxen was considered fairly good on the plains. The traveling day was from sunup to sundown, with a long rest at noon. At the end of the day, the wagons would be formed into a circle, the evening meal cooked, and guards posted.

The emigrants brought to the trail all their strengths and weaknesses, along with their hopes, fears, and foibles. If the environment wrought any change, it was generally to intensify characteristics already present: the cowardly had opportunity to show their cowardice, the excitable went to pieces, the calm and brave managed somehow to get along. The strain of the trail frayed tempers and brought on an unusual amount of bickering. A particularly aggravating problem was posed by the loose cattle: the well-to-do might have hundreds along; those who had few or none thought them a great nuisance and complained bitterly of the trouble they caused.

They came from all parts of the country, but most of the adult whites came from a corridor of states in the Old Northwest (Ohio, Indiana, Illinois, and Iowa) or Middle Border states, principally Kentucky, Tennessee, and Missouri. Blacks came, too, although in smaller numbers; a few were brought as slaves, but most came as free persons. The territorial census of Oregon included 58 blacks in 1850 and 154 in 1860.

Except for the year 1849, most travelers on the trails were families. Made up of groups of families, the wagon trains were, in reality, communities on wheels. As such, they experienced much of the support, as well as tension and stress, that existed in more traditional, permanent communities. The organization of tasks and daily routines was quickly established. Likewise, the roles played by men and women were not unlike those of the typical mid-nineteenth-century farm family. Care of the wagons and livestock fell to the men. The men drove the wagons, usually walking beside the oxen, rather than riding on the seat. The average day's travel of fifteen miles was enough to tire the sturdiest. In the evening, the livestock was frequently driven some distance from the campsite to graze and then corralled within the circled wagons. Guard duty was rotated among the men.

Women had a different routine. They were almost solely responsible for the needs of the family. They normally arose before the men to stoke the fire and prepare the breakfast. After breakfast, the women washed the cookware and packed up the wagons. At noon, they served a cold lunch that had been prepared the night before. In the evening, women gathered sagebrush or buffalo chips to prepare the fire and brought water to the camp. Women watched the children and did the milking, sewing, washing, and cooking. It was little different than at home, except perhaps that there were greater obstacles to overcome in doing those same tasks. Yet the demands of trail life added a new dimension to these traditional, nineteenth-century sex roles. Diaries kept by women indicate that they were ready and willing to substitute for men in emergencies. When men fell sick, women tended the stock and filled in where necessary. Many women regularly took a turn at driving the wagon.

Fresh graves along the trail were a constant reminder of the reality of death. It is estimated that approximately 20,000, or about 1 in 17, of the emigrants died between 1842 and 1859. The risk of death on the trail was nearly two and a half times greater than if they had stayed at home.[12] The most dreaded killer, particularly after 1849, was cholera. Estimates indicate that about 750 persons died from the disease in 1849. It struck with even greater force the following year, 1850, and again in 1852.[13]

Disease was the greatest killer, but carelessness also took its toll. The lurching, swaying, jolting wagons provided a hazardous perch for people with firearms and a menace to those in the line of fire. They were a constant threat to those on foot. The wheels often proved fatal to anyone who walked too close and tripped in their path.

Danger from Indians was more anticipated than real. Though the Indians were alarmed and frightened at the long lines of wagons rolling through their country, they generally kept the peace during the period of heavy overland emigration of the 1840s and 1850s. Until the 1860s attacks on wagon trains were rare. The occasional incident was motivated more by a desire for food and goods, particularly sugar, tobacco, and old clothing, than by hatred of whites. The Indians were persistent beggars, and when begging failed they often turned to thievery. From time to time a few braves would attempt to steal a horse or a cow, and the resulting altercation would inevitably end up with fatalities on both sides.

The danger of Indian attack and death was far greater for those traveling alone or in small groups or parties of one or two wagons that separated from the larger caravan to chart their own course. But contrary to the fears of many, even these attacks were not part of any organized effort to drive the white man from the plains, as later efforts were. Nevertheless, emigrants and western congressmen insisted upon military protection along the trail.

The troops at Fort Leavenworth covered the trail in Kansas. To provide additional protection, the army established Fort Kearny on the Missouri at the mouth of Table Creek (on the site of present-day Nebraska City). The army soon found, however, that this position was outside the general stream of overland travel, and in 1848 a new Fort Kearny was established at the southernmost point of the big bend in the Platte River. The next year, the army purchased Fort Laramie, which had served as a fur trading post since 1834, from the American Fur Company. The American Fur Company then moved down to the Scotts Bluff region, where one of the St. Louis Robidoux already was well ensconced, operating a blacksmith shop and trading establishment and taking advantage of the profits to be made from the emigrant traffic. Though troops from Fort Kearny would later provide protection for freighting trains and stagecoaches and Fort Laramie would be the army's headquarters during the Indian wars of the northern plains, they functioned primarily as relief and rest stations during this period. At both places the emigrants usually stopped for a day or two to rest, repair wagons and equipment, write letters, and, if possible, secure additional supplies. And so, summer after summer the

Table 1. Approximate Number of Travelers over Platte Valley Trails, 1841–1866

Year	Estimate	Year	Estimate	Year	Estimate
1841	100	1850	65,000	1859	80,000
1842	200	1851	10,000	1860	20,000
1843	1,000	1852	70,000	1861	10,000
1844	2,000	1853	35,000	1862	20,000
1845	5,000	1854	20,000	1863	20,000
1846	1,000	1855	7,000	1864	40,000
1847	2,000	1856	12,000	1865	20,000
1848	5,000	1857	6,000	1866	25,000
1849	40,000	1858	7,500	TOTAL	500,000

Source: Estimates based on Merrill J. Mattes, *The Great Platte River Road* (Lincoln: Nebraska State Historical Society, 1969), and revisions published in Merrill J. Mattes, *Platte River Road Narratives* (Urbana: University of Illinois Press, 1988).

wagons rolled west, their heavy wheels grinding deep ruts in the Platte Valley, ruts that in places are still visible.

Although there is no official census or record of the numbers who took part in this great migration, estimates suggest that half a million persons traversed the great Platte Valley highway to the West over the California, Mormon, or Oregon Trails after the first organized party in 1841.

Within a decade after those first home-seeking emigrants had pushed west to California and Oregon in 1841, the United States, fulfilling its "manifest destiny," had extended its boundaries to the Pacific, from the forty-ninth parallel on the north to the Rio Grande on the south. By 1850 Texas and California had been admitted to the Union, and Oregon, New Mexico, and Utah had achieved territorial status. The only remaining unorganized territory was the Great American Desert between the Missouri River and the Rockies. Pressures from both the East and the West would soon bring territorial status to most of this area as well.

CHAPTER 6

The Kansas-Nebraska Act

The reports of Pike, Long, and other explorers, describing the plains as an uninhabitable desert, provided Congress with a seemingly easy solution to the problem of the Indians who appeared to stand in the way of the early nineteenth-century American advance into the eastern Mississippi Valley. What could be simpler than removing them to the plains, thus opening the land east of the Mississippi to white settlement while at the same time providing a haven where the Indians would be free from further white encroachment? The process was begun in the South in the 1820s. In 1830 Congress passed a general Indian removal act and, in 1834, the Indian Intercourse Act, which prohibited whites without license from the government from trespassing on Indian lands and provided for the administration of the Indian country.

Though the line of demarcation was intended to define a permanent Indian frontier, the process of shifting it westward began almost as soon as it was established. By the early 1830s, federal officials defined the land between the Platte and Red Rivers as Indian country and in 1833 persuaded the Pawnees, who occupied a vast area north and south of the Platte River, to cede their lands south of the Platte.

An ever-shifting frontier and changing policy made evident almost from the beginning that a permanent Indian frontier was doomed to failure. The eastern semisedentary tribes and the western nomads found it almost impossible to live peaceably together, but, more important, white settlers were not to be stopped at the Mississippi, the Missouri, or any other point short of the Pacific coast. By 1850, the Indian country was no longer beyond but was surrounded by the United States. It had become a barrier that had to be removed.

The Kansas-Nebraska Act signaled the abandonment of the concept of a permanent Indian frontier, set forth less than a generation earlier, and fanned into flame the controversy of expansionist politics that had been smoldering for almost half a century. That act embodied not only the demand of westerners that the territory be organized but also the inflammatory issues of federal internal improvements, particularly transportation, and the extension of the institution of slavery.

THE PACIFIC RAILROAD

Some Americans were agitating for a railroad to the Pacific even before the coast region had become part of the national domain. Chief among them was Asa Whitney, a New York merchant interested in the China trade, who as early as January 1845 submitted a plan to Congress providing for a transcontinental railroad from the Great Lakes to Oregon. Most Americans in and out of Congress considered Whitney's proposals impractical and visionary, but as railroads began to demonstrate their practicality and as settlements developed in the Pacific coast region, interest in a transcontinental railroad was renewed. By the early 1850s, the stumbling block was no longer apathy but rivalry over the proposed route. This was a sectional rivalry between North and South but also among cities vying for selection as the eastern terminus. And the rivalry was intense because not even the wildest visionary believed there would ever be more than one transcontinental railroad.

Initially, the South possessed a distinct advantage. It could provide an all-weather route and, with the annexation of Texas and the organization of New Mexico territory, a southern route that could skirt the Indian country. The Gadsden Purchase of 1853, adding suitable right-of-way south of the Gila River, further strengthened the southern position. Northern routes, however, had their proponents. Whitney advocated his Lake Superior–Oregon route as the shortest and most practical. The thousands of people who had gone over the Platte Valley trail by the early 1850s had demonstrated the practicality of that way west. So much interest and rivalry had developed by 1853 that the army appropriation bill of that year contained a rider authorizing the secretary of war to survey routes that seemed advisable and to determine which indeed was most practical.

Secretary of War Jefferson Davis immediately dispatched engineers to survey four routes: (1) the northern, or Whitney, route, between the

Stephen A. Douglas, architect of the Kansas-Nebraska Act of 1854. Courtesy, NSHS, P853.

forty-seventh and forty-ninth parallels; (2) a route between the thirty-eighth and thirty-ninth parallels, championed by Senator Thomas Hart Benton of Missouri; (3) a route along the thirty-fifth parallel recommended by Senator William McKendree Gwin of California; and (4) the Gila River route along the thirty-second parallel. Oddly enough, the Platte River valley route, deemed by many northerners as the most practical and the one ultimately selected, was not included in the Davis surveys. The surveys did demonstrate that several routes were feasible, thus throwing the question back to Congress.

Northerners were aware that an overriding obstacle in the way of any northern route was that it would have to traverse the Indian country. Territorial organization of the country west of the Missouri, therefore, was a necessary prerequisite to any northern railroad. Many voices were raised in favor of the organization of Nebraska territory, as it was then being called, but the most persistent and effective was that of Stephen A. Douglas of Illinois. Vitally interested in developing Chicago as a great national railroad center, he saw clearly that a transcontinental railroad running west from Chicago through the Platte Valley would be an important aid in that development. While a member of the House of Representatives in 1844, he had introduced a bill to organize Nebraska territory. His bill did not come up for consideration, but he introduced a similar measure in the next session of Congress. The primary purpose of these early bills, Douglas explained, was to serve notice on the secretary of war not to locate any more Indians in the territory.

For the next decade Douglas worked actively to promote the organization of Nebraska territory to provide a route for the Pacific railroad and to forestall commitments to any alternative route. He was elected to the Senate in 1847 and became a member of the Committee on Territories, which widened the scope of his activities and increased his influence. In 1849 he presided over a great railroad convention in St. Louis. That body declared itself in favor of St. Louis as the eastern terminus of the Pacific railroad, but it also favored the South Pass route, which could lead only to a direct connection with Chicago.

The organization of New Mexico Territory in 1850 gave proponents of a southern route a great advantage and caused Douglas to intensify his efforts for Nebraska. The Davis surveys and the Gadsden Purchase in

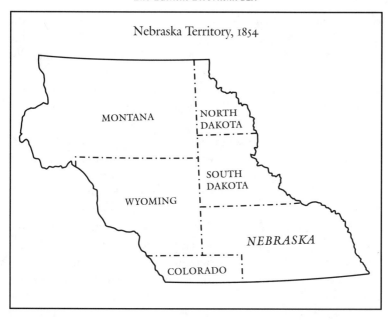

Nebraska Territory, 1854

1853 further emphasized the importance of immediate action if the southerners were to be forestalled. By early 1854, therefore, Douglas was willing to make any reasonable compromise to get a Nebraska bill through Congress, and as chairman of the Senate Committee on Territories he was in a position to exercise great influence. Douglas's primary concern was the Pacific railroad, and he was willing to shape other issues to achieve that goal. One of those other issues was the extension of slavery, which, unfortunately for Douglas and for the nation, would become the overriding, central issue of the Nebraska discussion.

THE SLAVERY CONTROVERSY

From the founding of the republic the slavery question had been an increasingly divisive force in American politics. The issue had strong moral implications, to be sure, but also equally strong economic and political consequences. It was particularly important in connection with territorial expansion, which envisioned the creation of new states and the consequent readjustment of representation in Congress. Throughout the first half of the nineteenth century, a majority in Congress and in the country, primarily concerned with working out the nation's "manifest destiny," sought to compromise the slavery question whenever it impinged upon the central issue. A growing intransigence among extremists both North and South, however, made compromise progressively more difficult.

When the issue came to a head in 1820 in connection with the admission of Missouri and Maine, it was compromised by providing for the admission of Missouri as a slave state in accordance with its constitution, while bringing in Maine as a free state. This way the balance was maintained and a political catastrophe averted. To avoid future political strife over this issue, the act further provided that slavery would be prohibited forever in all the rest of the Louisiana territory north of 36°30'. This concession from the South by no means indicated that southerners had resigned themselves to limiting the expansion of slavery. The admission of Missouri as a slave state was a significant immediate victory, and those who thought beyond short-term goals believed that the area would never be settled. Should that not prove to be the case, there was always the possibility of reinterpreting the word "forever."

The controversy flared again over the organization of the territory acquired from Mexico. Northern extremists generally rallied behind the proviso submitted in August 1846 by Congressman David Wilmot, a Pennsylvania Democrat, that would forever prohibit slavery in the lands obtained from Mexico. Southern extremists insisted that Congress had no power to ban slavery in the territories, though they had agreed to it only a few years earlier. More moderate spirits in the South wanted the Missouri Compromise line extended to the Pacific, which would have given most of the new territory to slavery. Douglas and other westerners suggested that the good western principle of squatter sovereignty be applied to the question, letting the people of the territories decide for themselves whether they would allow slavery. Facts came to the aid of compromise. California already had organized a state government and was clamoring for admission as a free state. The sandy deserts and rocky hills of Utah and New Mexico would never support slavery. The North could surely bend sufficiently to allow the people of the territories to decide the slavery question for themselves when they applied for admission to the Union. And so it was. California was admitted as a free state in 1850, and the territories of Utah and New Mexico were organized with the understanding that they would be admitted as states with or without slavery as their constitutions provided.

Then came Nebraska. Southerners, unenthusiastic about the organization of a territory to make possible a northern route for the Pacific railroad, were downright hostile to setting in motion the machinery that ultimately would grind out more free states. It was clear that to gain southern support for a bill organizing Nebraska as a territory, the Missouri Compromise of 1820 would have to be greatly modified or repealed.

THE WESTERN DEMAND

Almost lost in the flaming controversy over slavery was the growing insistence in Missouri, Iowa, and even the Indian country that Nebraska be organized to provide a route for the Pacific railroad, to legalize settlement already existing in defiance of the law, and to open the way for a further extension of settlement westward. Nebraska boomers roamed the area and wrote glowing accounts of the fertility of the soil, the healthy climate, and the general excellence of the region. Mass meetings were held in Iowa and Missouri demanding that Nebraska be organized as a territory.

Beginning in 1850 Iowa senators Augustus Caesar Dodge and George W. Jones held meetings throughout the western part of their state urging the organization of Nebraska. Missourians were even more active, and the Nebraska question became embroiled in Missouri politics. Senator Thomas Hart Benton, Missouri's old expansionist, had long advocated the organization of Nebraska territory to make possible a central national highway to the Pacific along what he liked to call "the old buffalo trail." When his moderate course on slavery cost him his seat in the Senate in 1851, he tried to make a comeback based on a campaign for a Pacific railroad with St. Louis as its eastern terminus and the organization of Nebraska territory for both railroad and settlement purposes. Although he won election to the House of Representatives, he was unable to unseat

73

Senator David R. Atchison, who was strongly proslavery. Atchison had opposed the organization of Nebraska because of the Missouri Compromise. When it became evident that the Missouri Compromise might be repealed and mounting pressure from home made an anti-Nebraska position untenable for a Missouri politician, Atchison shifted his course to become ardently pro-Nebraska.

A series of mass meetings in northwestern Missouri and southwestern Iowa culminated in the holding of a Nebraska Delegate Convention at St. Joseph, Missouri, on January 9 and 10, 1854, at which strong resolutions protesting further delay in the organization of Nebraska territory were adopted.

Residents of the Indian country were also doing what they could to promote the Nebraska movement. There was some settlement activity at Florence, on the site of the old Mormon Winter Quarters. A growing number of traders and others were congregating around Peter Sarpy's establishment at Bellevue. Hiram P. Downs (a delegate to the St. Joseph convention) operated a ferry at old Fort Kearny. Farther south, civilians gathered around Fort Leavenworth, Fort Riley, and the Shawnee mission. Leadership for the movement was provided by the Wyandotte Indians, who had been removed from Ohio in 1843 and had settled on the west bank of the Missouri River at the mouth of the Kansas River. The Wyandottes had much white blood and many white customs. They appeared to believe that territorial organization would improve their position against the pressures they were sure would be brought against them. In the fall of 1852, they elected Abelard Guthrie as a delegate from the provisional territory of Nebraska and sent him to Washington to urge organization. The next August at "Wyandot City" a convention was held which nominated Guthrie for reelection. In September a second convention convened at Kickapoo and nominated the Reverend Thomas Johnson of the Shawnee mission for the same post. Johnson, supported by the missionaries and Commissioner of Indian Affairs William C. Manypenny, defeated Guthrie for the empty honor.

Meanwhile, in October a group from the vicinity of Council Bluffs went to Bellevue and participated in another independent movement to organize a provisional government. They elected Hadley D. Johnson as delegate to Congress. Both men journeyed to Washington to represent the provisional government of Nebraska territory. Both sat in the House of Representatives for a time, and both were subsequently removed. The two men worked for the organization of Nebraska territory, but it is unclear whether they and the movement they represented had any impact. In any event, they had an opportunity to watch the smooth-functioning Democratic machine push the Nebraska bill through.

LEGISLATIVE HISTORY

Against a backdrop of violently conflicting cross purposes, expansionist politics, and local ambition, the Kansas-Nebraska Act became law. Although Senator Douglas had introduced earlier Nebraska bills, he did not introduce any new ones after 1848, but he continued to work actively for the Nebraska cause. The urgency of northern railroad ambitions increased in the years to come; so, too, did the acrimony of the debate over slavery. The presidential election of 1852 found the leaders of both parties committed to compromise and willing to do anything to prevent sectional discord. After a campaign in which both candidates praised the Compromise of 1850 and urged sectional unity, the Democrats, augmented by the return of many southern Whigs, regained power in a sweeping victory. Having enjoyed a term of power based on the magic of an old-soldier candidate and dissatisfaction with the long-entrenched Democrats, the Whigs were no longer effective. The Democrats had returned to power, but they were by no means united. Any action affecting slavery, as well as any action relating to territorial organization, would require compromise. Although the Democratic Party was deeply divided, compromise was possible with the proper leadership. Stephen A. Douglas, still a senator from Illinois and chairman of the critical Committee on Territories, would provide that leadership.

On February 2, 1853, Representative William A. Richardson of Illinois, chairman of the House Committee on Territories, introduced a bill to organize Nebraska territory. It passed the House 98 to 43 but, despite Douglas's efforts, failed to get through the Senate, largely because of opposition from southern Democrats. The bill made no mention of slavery; presumably the provisions of the Missouri Compromise would apply. Senator Sam Houston of Texas, the hero of San Jacinto, orated against it; Senator Atchison violently opposed it. In short, the South would have none of it.

On December 5, 1853, the opening day of the first session of the Thirty-third Congress, Senator Dodge of Iowa gave notice that he would introduce a bill to organize a territorial government for the Territory of Nebraska. On December 14 Dodge introduced his bill, which proposed that all the territory between the states of Iowa and Missouri on the east and the summit of the Rocky Mountains on the west, the parallel 36°30' on the south and 43°30' on the north, be organized as Nebraska Territory. The bill, however, contained no reference to slavery, so presumably the Missouri Compromise would apply. The Committee on Territories, led by Senator Douglas, reported out a vastly altered bill on January 4. Instead of one territory, two were created: Kansas (after a later boundary adjustment) was to occupy the area between the thirty-seventh and fortieth parallels from Missouri to the crest of the Rockies; Nebraska was to be located between the fortieth and forty-ninth parallels from the Missouri River and Minnesota Territory to the crest of the Rockies. Whereas the Dodge bill had made no mention of slavery, the committee substitute provided "that all questions pertaining to slavery in the Territories, and in the new State to be formed therefrom, are to be left to the decision of the people residing therein, through their appropriate representatives."[1] The eighth section of the Missouri Compromise, which had prohibited slavery in the territories north of 36°30', was explicitly nullified by this act.

The gauntlet was now down. The abolitionists' swords flashed against the repeal of the Missouri Compromise, almost as sacred as the Constitution itself. William H. Seward, Salmon P. Chase, and Charles Sumner led the opposition against Douglas, who used the popular sovereignty formula to hold the Democratic majority together. Their efforts were futile; the bill passed the Senate on March 3 by a vote of 37 to 14. The vote was closer in the House, but on the evening of May 21, the bill was passed by a vote of 113 to 100. As amended by the House, the bill was accepted by the Senate on May 25, and President Franklin Pierce signed it into law on May 30.

The controversy kindled by the congressional debate soon spread across the country. Anti-Nebraska meetings were held throughout the North, particularly in the Northwest. Out of these developed a new organized opposition in the form of the Republican Party, which became a militant substitute for the defunct Whigs. Anti-Nebraska orators charged that Stephen A. Douglas, architect of the territories of Nebraska and Kansas, had sold freedom out to slavery solely to further his own political and financial ambitions. They also charged that he not only had led the repeal of the Missouri Compromise but also had created two territories instead of one to serve his own purposes.

For more than a century following the passage of the Kansas-Nebraska Act, Stephen A. Douglas was maligned by politicians and historians. Largely unfounded charges of the anti-Nebraska forces were treated as an unquestionable, if not regrettable, part of the American past. Yet there is little substance to the charge that Douglas divided the territory to further the interests of slavery in the West. The two delegates who claimed to represent the provisional government, Hadley D. Johnson and the Reverend Thomas Johnson, agreed to the division of the territory so that the people would have two delegates instead of one. Senator Dodge supported division because he believed that the railroad interests of Iowa demanded it. Likewise, Douglas supported division if it would protect Chicago's railroad interests, a natural and perfectly legitimate interest for a senator from Illinois.

There is little question that Douglas was ambitious, but the suggestion that the Kansas-Nebraska bill was designed solely to further his ambition is unwarranted. As the leader of a divided majority party, he was forced to compromise to achieve passage of legislation he believed to be vitally important. And finally, the doctrine of popular sovereignty, inasmuch as it represented local self-government, was not inconsistent with the ideals of American democracy. The sectional strife stirred by the Kansas-Nebraska Act had profound ramifications; yet the important consideration for the history of Nebraska, and for that of the nation, is that it opened to settlement the remainder of the Louisiana territory acquired only a half-century before.

CHAPTER 7

The Nebraska Territory

When President Pierce signed the Kansas-Nebraska Act on May 30, 1854, there were a few squatters' cabins scattered along the Missouri River and a small, vagrant civilian community clustered about Fort Kearny on the Platte River. A few enterprising individuals operated ferries at locations along the Missouri River that would soon become St. Stephen, Nebraska City, Plattsmouth, and Omaha, but the only point that could be described as a settlement was Bellevue. Here possibly as many as fifty persons were gathered about the Indian agency, the Reverend William Hamilton's Presbyterian mission, and Peter A. Sarpy's trading post. Sarpy maintained a ferry across the Missouri and conducted most of his trading activities at St. Mary on the Iowa side.

Anticipating the passage of the Kansas-Nebraska Act, Sarpy and his friends had organized the Bellevue Town Company on February 9, 1854. Once Congress gave the signal for legal settlement, the company feverishly set to work to transform Bellevue into a city. On July 15, it began publication of a newspaper, the *Nebraska Palladium*. Though printed across the river in Iowa, the paper greeted its readers with a triumphant review of progress already made: "Within the last month a large city upon a grand scale has been laid out, with a view of the location of the capital of Nebraska, at this point, and with a view to making it the center of commerce, and the half-way house between the Atlantic and Pacific Oceans. . . . [Prospective settlers could have the word of Colonel Sarpy] that the great line of communication between ocean and ocean must cross the Missouri River at Belleview."[1]

Others disagreed, and all along the river, promoters and land jobbers from western Iowa were busy preempting town sites and laying out cities. Each city, its promoters confidently proclaimed, was destined to become the gateway to the West. Hiram P. Downs, custodian of the government's property at old Fort Kearny and a longtime Nebraska boomer, joined with men from Sidney, Iowa, in laying out Nebraska City. Samuel Martin of Glenwood, who had been operating a ferry across the Missouri below the mouth of the Platte since 1859, established a log trading post on the Nebraska side in the winter of 1853. Shortly after the territory was opened, he began promoting the town of Plattsmouth. James C. Mitchell and others from Council Bluffs had taken over the old Mormon Winter Quarters and as early as 1853 were planning to develop the new town of Florence. In 1854 the first territorial legislature granted charters to seventeen of these would-be cities.

The most successful of the early towns was Omaha City, promoted by ambitious residents of Council Bluffs, and specifically by the Council Bluffs and Nebraska Ferry Company. Beginning with the Mormon activity of 1846–47, there had been settlement at Council Bluffs, first known as Miller's Hollow and later as Kanesville. The California gold rush created new demands for emigrant outfitting points, and as agitation over Nebraska developed, the more enterprising Council Bluffs citizens began to take a keen interest in the prospects of a town immediately across the river. They reasoned that if this town could be developed into the Nebraska territorial capital, Council Bluffs might yet draw a transcontinental railway.

In 1853, William D. Brown, who since 1850 had been operating a ferry business near Council Bluffs known as the Lone Tree Ferry, staked out a claim to a town site on the Nebraska side of the river. Later that same year a group of Council Bluffs promoters organized the Council Bluffs and Nebraska Ferry Company and purchased Brown's ferry business along with his interest in the town site. Though the company acquired a steam ferryboat, the *General Marion*, and thus greatly improved the service, it was more concerned with town development than with the ferry business.

Claims were staked out on the town site as early as November 1853. The company adopted the name Omaha, and in the spring of 1854 a postmaster was appointed through the influence of western Iowa's congressman Bernhart Henn, an ardent advocate for territorial status for Nebraska.

Immediately after the territory was organized, the company set out to develop the town of Omaha. Postmaster A. D. Jones, employed to

This engraving depicting a scene from the Nebraska territorial legislature suggests the highly emotional and chaotic nature of legislative deliberations, which frequently escalated into physical violence. From Sorenson, *Story of Omaha*. Courtesy, NSHS, PCI371:E712.9.

survey the site, laid out the town in 320 blocks, with streets 100 feet wide, except for Capitol Avenue, which was to be 120 feet wide. On July 4, the ferry company organized a picnic on the town site, and a log cabin was partly erected that day. A newspaper, the *Omaha Arrow*, printed in Council Bluffs, made its appearance on July 28. By autumn, Omaha gave promise of being more than a paper town. A. D. Jones still used his hat for a post office, but Omaha City had some twenty houses, two shacks with dirt floors serving as hotels, saloons, stores, and a brickyard. Though it had begun as the progeny of Council Bluffs, Omaha would soon be greater than the parent.

POLITICAL CHAOS

President Pierce appointed forty-seven-year-old Francis Burt, an editor from Pendleton, South Carolina, as governor of Nebraska territory.[2] Burt, son of a South Carolina planter, had been active in politics since early youth. He had served almost twenty years in the South Carolina legislature, as a member of the state's constitutional convention, and as a member of the famous nullification convention of 1832. At the time of his appointment to the Nebraska post, he was serving as third auditor of the United States Treasury.

The Nebraska Territory

A trip from South Carolina to Nebraska was no easy journey in 1854 so by the time Governor Burt arrived at Bellevue on October 7, he had traveled by private conveyance, railroad, stagecoach, steamboat, and wagon. He might have made the journey all the way from St. Louis to Bellevue by steamboat, but the Missouri River was so low in the fall of 1854 that boats could not go above St. Joseph. There he hired a hack to Nebraska City and then went by wagon to Bellevue. Upon his arrival at St. Louis, he spent several days in the care of a physician. He was so weak by the time he got to Bellevue that he sought immediate rest at the mission house of the Reverend William Hamilton. The oath of office was administered at his bedside on October 16; two days later Nebraska's first territorial governor was dead.

Governor Burt's untimely death clouded the territory's political future, particularly in regard to the hotly contested issue of the location of the territorial capital. Always a bitterly fought question in new territories, the issue of Nebraska's capital was intensified by the assumption that the transcontinental railroad would probably go through the territorial capital. Although every town in the territory looked covetously at the plum, the leading contenders were Omaha and Bellevue. Burt appears to have had no fixed notions regarding the permanent territorial capital, although he had apparently planned to convene the first session of the territorial legislature at Bellevue.[3] Whatever Burt's intent, it soon became apparent that territorial secretary Thomas B. Cuming, who took over the reins of government as acting governor, was open to suggestions.

Cuming, the son of a Protestant Episcopal minister and a graduate of the University of Michigan, was only twenty-five years old when President Pierce appointed him secretary of Nebraska Territory. At the time of his appointment he was editing a Democratic weekly in Keokuk, Iowa. In common with all the rest of the politicians descending upon Nebraska, he was deeply concerned with his own political advancement. The hand of fortune had now placed him in control of organizing the territory, and he did not intend to be bound by any commitments expressed or implied by the deceased governor. Moreover, Cuming owed his appointment to Iowa influence, and insofar as Nebraska was concerned, that influence was primarily interested in using the territory to further the ambitions of Council Bluffs.

As a step toward the establishment of civil government, Cuming ordered a territorial census to be taken by November 20. The population was counted, but with difficulty. The line between Kansas and Nebraska had not yet been surveyed, and the permanence of almost every settler was open to question. As finally compiled, the returns showed a total of 2,732 inhabitants of whom 1,818 lived south of the Platte and 914 north of the river.

Even though almost twice as many persons were living south of the river, Cuming assigned the four counties he had created in the North Platte section a total of seven councilmen and fourteen representatives, while giving only six councilmen and twelve representatives to the four counties south of the river.

This flagrant favoring of the northern section caused great indignation south of the river. Bellevue, though north of the Platte, objected strenuously to being included in the same county with Omaha and joined those south of the Platte in suspecting the governor's motives. On December 9 the citizens of Bellevue held a mass meeting as part of their effort to secure the capital and invited Cuming to attend. They charged the acting governor not only with accepting but with exacting bribes from the Omaha town company. It did little good. On December 20, Bellevue's worst fears were realized when Cuming announced that the first session of the territorial legislature would convene at Omaha.

With the gauntlet thus thrown down, Bellevue's politicians joined those from south of the Platte in organizing mass meetings at many places in the South Platte region. Leading the attack on Cuming was twenty-two-year-old J. Sterling Morton, who had arrived from Michigan less than a month earlier. A delegate convention at Nebraska City adopted resolutions written by Morton, denouncing Cuming as "an unprincipled knave . . . [who] seeks rather to control than to consult the people" and demanding his removal as secretary as well as from the post of acting governor of the new territory.[4] The controversy was carried to the legislature, where most of the first session was devoted to an investigation of Cuming and an effort to undo his work in locating the capital at Omaha.

The question of the capital's location agitated territorial politicians for many months to the detriment of more serious legislative business. The

82

Table 2. Representation in the Nebraska Territorial Legislature, 1854

Counties North of Platte River				Counties South of Platte River			
County	Population	Council	House	County	Population	Council	House
Burt	163	1	2	Pierce	614	3	5
Washington		1	2	Forney		1	2
Dodge	106	1	2	Cass	353	1	3
Douglas	645	4	8	Richardson	851	1	2
Total	914	7	14	Total	1,818	6	12

Source: Compiled from data in J. Sterling Morton and Albert Watkins, *Illustrated History of Nebraska* (Lincoln: J. North, 1905–13), 1:180.

struggle was sectional as well as local. The Platte River naturally splits Nebraska into two sections. It was too wide and shallow for ferries, the sandy bottom made it unsuitable for fording, and during territorial times the people were too poor to build bridges. Governor Cuming intensified that natural sectional division by apportioning the territory to favor the North Platte region.

During the fourth legislature both fists and guns flashed in a turbulent row, after which a majority of the members adjourned to Florence to hold a rump session. Though the Florence secession accomplished nothing, it did awaken a slumbering sentiment in the South Platte region for annexation to Kansas.

J. Sterling Morton had moved to Nebraska City following Bellevue's initial defeat and had promptly been elected to the legislature from Otoe County. He had introduced a resolution in the second legislative session memorializing Congress to move the boundary of Kansas north to the Platte River, but the resolution had not been considered. After the Florence fiasco, however, South Platte politicians were ready to pursue the idea with vigor. Mass meetings were held across the region, and delegates were elected to represent the South Platte section at the free state constitutional convention being held in Wyandotte, Kansas. At first there was some sentiment for annexation among the antislavery elements in Kansas, but when they realized that southern Nebraska would not be needed to win control of the territory, most of them lost interest. Kansas, moreover, had its own sectional division: those living south of the Kansas River had no interest in increasing the strength of those living north of the river.

The failure of the annexation movement did not end the sectional controversy. It remained a divisive factor in Nebraska's politics throughout the territorial period and would emerge again with vigor during the controversy over the location of the state capital.

THE FIRST TERRITORIAL LEGISLATURE

In accordance with Cuming's call, the first territorial legislature assembled in Omaha on January 16, 1855. The capitol, a two-story brick building, thirty-three by seventy-five feet, fronting east on Ninth Street between Farnam and Douglas, had been provided by the Council Bluffs and Nebraska Ferry Company "without a cost of one single dollar to the government."[5] The House of Representatives met on the first floor, and the Council, or upper house, on the second. Both chambers were fitted out with school desks, each shared by two members. The windows were curtained with red and green calico. Though unpretentious on the inside, it was the only brick building in Omaha and was as distinct in the landscape of its day as the present monumental structure is today.

J. W. Pattison, editor of the *Omaha Arrow*, as well as local correspondent for the *New York Times*, described the legislature in action:

It is a decidedly rich treat to visit the General Assembly of Nebraska. You see a motley crowd inside of a railing in a small room crowded to overflowing, some behind their little schoolboy desks, some seated on the top of desks, some with their feet perched on the top of their neighbor's chair or desk, some whittling—half a dozen walking about in what little space there is left. The fireman, doorkeeper, sergeant-at-arms, last year's members [he was describing the second session], and almost anyone else become principal characters inside the bar, selecting good seats and making themselves generally at home, no matter how much they may discommode the members. The clerk, if he chooses, jumps up to explain the whys and hows of his journal. A lobby member stalks inside the bar, and from one to the other he goes talking about the advantages of his bill. A row starts up in the secretary's room, or somewhere about the building, and away goes the honorable body to see the fun . . . then a thirsty member moves an adjournment and in a few minutes the drinking saloons are well patronized. . . . Although both bodies have about seven more days to sit, only four bills have been passed. It is one continued personal and local fight—a constant attempt at bargain, sale and argument.[6]

The early days of the session were devoted to an acrimonious struggle over seats and procedure. Bellevue sent three men whom it had elected to represent Douglas County. Though they had received virtually all of Bellevue's votes, Omaha's candidates had received a larger number and were, of course, certified by Governor Cuming. Denied admission, the Bellevue men served notice of contest. Others also tried to contest seats of members certified by the governor. All such contests were referred to a committee dominated by Omaha delegates, and in due course the committee reported that it was inexpedient to investigate further the subject of contested seats. Governor Cuming and Omaha had the situation well in hand.

The principal reason advanced in the notices of contest was that the certified member was not a resident of the territory. With a population as shifting and impermanent as that of early Nebraska, such a charge was almost meaningless. Out of a total membership of thirty-nine, at least five were never residents of the territory, and many of the rest were transients at best. Joseph L. Sharp, for example, represented Richardson County and was elected president of the Council, yet he lived in Glenwood, Iowa, and never became a resident of Nebraska. Indeed, so unsettled were both the population and the geographical divisions of the territory that many of the members were referred to as "from Iowa," "from Michigan," or from some other place outside the territory.

Most of the legislature's time was consumed with investigating and trying to undo Cuming's action in locating the capital at Omaha. Omaha was too well entrenched, however, and the opposition was badly divided so Omaha retained the prize. Cuming had been given control of the territorial government at a critical juncture, and he used that control to advance the interests of his Iowa constituents, who were promoting Omaha to assist in the development of Council Bluffs. His actions were bitterly assailed by Bellevue and South Platte partisans in the press and in the legislature, with the result that his achievements have been over-shadowed by criticism in the historical record. Had his career not been cut short by death in 1858, he might have exercised even greater influence in the development of the territory and state.

On February 20, 1855, Mark W. Izard, Burt's successor, arrived in Omaha. Originally from Arkansas, he had been United States marshal for Nebraska. He had taken the oath as governor on December 23, 1854, in Washington, where he had gone to further his appointment, and hence was not on hand to participate in the initial organization of territorial government. Born in Lexington, Kentucky, on December 25, 1799, Izard was somewhat older than most of the territorial politicians, and although his short term was distinguished more by good intentions than by accomplishment, he provided a badly needed stability in territorial affairs.

In his first address to the legislature the new governor recommended that the laws of Iowa be adopted temporarily because many of Nebraska's residents, having come from Iowa, were already familiar with them. To legislators preoccupied with partisan political squabbles this seemed like a good suggestion. The problem of providing laws for the new territory was thus solved by the simple expedient of adopting in its entirety the civil and criminal code of Iowa. In addition, the first legislature located and established ten territorial roads; defined the boundaries and established the seats of the eight original counties, none of which retained its original form, and created sixteen additional counties; incorporated industrial companies, bridge and ferry companies, and towns; and enacted a series of general laws.

Among the general laws were acts providing for the organization of courts; establishing a free public school system; and, in a curious move for a frontier legislature, prohibiting the manufacture, sale, and consumption of intoxicating beverages. Although there is no evidence of any attempt to enforce it, this incongruous law remained on the books until 1858, when it was replaced by a license law. Indeed, saloons flourished adjacent to the capitol building and enjoyed steady patronage from members of the legislature and other territorial officials.

CHAPTER 8

Territorial Growth and Development

On March 3, 1854, western Iowa's congressman Bernhart Henn, addressing his colleagues on behalf of the Kansas-Nebraska bill, had predicted
that within three days after passage there would be not less than three
thousand people in Nebraska. Like many other hopes for Nebraska expressed by the territory's ebullient Iowa promoters, this prediction fell
short of fulfillment. The census of November 1854 returned a population
of only 2,732, a number that included many transients and some who,
after the Kansas-Nebraska boundary was surveyed, were found to be
living in Kansas.

Though in virtually every instance territorial development fell far short
of advertised expectations, growth was steady. A territorial census taken
the following year, in October 1855, showed a population of 4,494, nearly
double that of the previous year. A year later the population had doubled
again, increasing to 10,716. From 1856 to 1860 it appeared to increase by
nearly threefold when the territorial census of 1860 reported a population of 28,841. By 1867, when Nebraska was admitted as a state, it had
an estimated 50,000 persons. Considering that the territory had been
untried by the pioneer farmer, the backbone of westward expansion, that
much of it was believed unsuited to agriculture, and that thousands of
vacant acres remained in Iowa, where agricultural possibilities had been
demonstrated, Nebraska's territorial growth is remarkable.

LAND AND LAND POLITICS

Land to which Indian tribes held title was unavailable for settlement,
but in the event that such claim or title was extinguished or voided, it
became part of the public domain. Before the Homestead Act of 1862,

title to lands in the public domain could be acquired by purchase under the Pre-Emption Law of 1841, by which a settler could file a claim to 160 acres of the public domain and acquire title by paying $1.25 per acre at the time the land was put up for sale; purchase with military bounty land warrants; or direct purchase, on or after the date on which the land was put up for public auction.

Had procedures in force since 1785 been followed, settlers in Nebraska Territory would not have been able to take up legal residence on the land until it was surveyed. From the beginning, however, the pioneers who pushed the boundaries of the United States ever westward had moved far ahead of the surveys, squatting on desirable tracts of land. In March 1854, Congress, recognizing the futility of trying to hold back the squatters, provided that in certain areas, including the proposed Nebraska territory, individuals could settle on unsurveyed land and, as soon as the surveys were completed, be permitted to select the quarter section whose lines corresponded most closely with the land on which they had settled.

The first surveying contract in Nebraska, dated November 2, 1854, provided that by January 20, 1855, the baseline, or Kansas boundary, was to be established along the fortieth parallel for a distance of 108 miles, or to the sixth principal meridian, the western border of the Omaha cession (the western boundary of present Jefferson County). A second contract, dated April 26, 1855, provided for establishing the guide meridian between ranges eight and nine and the first, second, third, fourth, fifth, sixth, and seventh parallel lines. A third contract provided for the subdivision of the eastern tier of townships in Pawnee County, the southeast corner of Johnson, and the southwest corner of Nemaha by December 1, 1855. Initial subdivisions in Douglas County were to be completed by June 1856. Surveys were done rapidly, and by September 30, 1857, more than 2.4 million acres had been subdivided and staked.[1] By then, however, there were more than ten thousand people in the territory, and virtually all the heads of families had staked out claims on their own.

To protect these presurvey claims, the settlers fell back upon an old frontier device, the claim club. One of the first public meetings in the territory was held under the famous "Lone Tree" near the ferry landing on Omaha's riverfront on July 22, 1854, which in the name of the Omaha Township Claim Association promulgated a set of "laws" and announced

This early 1867 photograph, taken from 18th and Douglas Streets in Omaha, shows the territorial capitol on the eve of statehood. Courtesy, NSHS, 054:2-20.

that "the jurisdiction of the association shall extend north and south of the grade section line in Omaha City three miles and west from the Missouri River six miles."[2] The Belleview Settlers Club announced similar laws and defined the area of its jurisdiction on October 28. Numerous other claim clubs were organized so that by the time the first townships were officially subdivided by survey, claim law was in force for about one hundred miles along the Missouri River and as far back as the settlers thought the land to be of any value. Anyone who dared disregard the land system thus established was visited by a committee from the local club, headed by the "sheriff." Under the persuasion of rifles and a coil of stout rope, even the most incorrigible was likely to see the benefits of cooperation.

Though clearly in defiance of federal law, the claim clubs provided order where there could easily have been chaos, and with the sanction of a vast majority of the settlers, the clubs served as the most practical and effective agency of local government during the early years of settlement.

The first session of the territorial legislature, indifferent to the constitutionality of the situation, passed an act recognizing and defining the authority of the claim clubs. As surveys were completed and valid claims filed in the federal land offices, the need for the claim clubs ceased, and, having served their purpose, they quietly passed out of existence.[3]

From the beginning, land policies were an important factor in territorial politics. By the 1850s westerners were committed to the free homestead as the only satisfactory solution to the problem of disposing of the public domain. The claim clubs had sought to achieve that goal by establishing 320 acres as a valid claim on the theory that after the survey the settler could sell 160 acres to obtain the money with which to purchase the other quarter section. Though this principle was affirmed by the first legislature, it collapsed with the opening of the land offices.

The settlers then turned their attention to the possibility of acquiring at least temporary free homesteads by having local land sales postponed. They found themselves at odds, however, with the federal government and the Buchanan administration, which, in the midst of the depression of 1857, announced that lands in Nebraska would go on sale beginning September 6, 1858. The howl of protest was instantaneous and almost unanimous. Governor Izard attempted to mollify the settlers, but his words were drowned in the chorus of denunciation that poured from mass meetings and newspaper offices in all parts of the territory. If necessary, the settlers would resist the order by force, and mutual protection associations were formed in many communities. Finally, Buchanan was persuaded to postpone the sale dates until the summer of 1859: July 5 and 25 at Omaha, July 10 at Dakota City, August 1 and 29 at Nebraska City, August 8 at Brownville.

The protests against the land sales had been based on the contention that they would throw the settlers into the hands of speculators and moneylenders. That contention was not unfounded. Settlers, frantically trying to salvage their claims, borrowed money at usurious rates, sometimes as high as 60 percent, to pay for their land. Military land warrants were as good as cash, and speculators bought them from needy soldiers and their widows for as low as fifty cents per acre and advanced them to settlers at the full price and at high rates of interest. For those who wanted to speculate in land directly by buying large tracts, the situation was equally favorable. By July 1, 1862, a total of 912,898.86 acres in Nebraska had been entered with land warrants and only 139,898.01 with cash. Looking back in 1872, Robert W. Furnas, who had spearheaded the fight against land sales, wrote:

In '59 the land from the Missouri river for sixty or seventy miles west was offered for sale and immediately after the sale nearly all of the land in Nemaha county was entered by speculators with their land warrants and tens of thousands of acres are to this day unimproved in consequence.

Numbers entered land on credit, with trust deeds for security, and after struggling for several years and paying hundreds of dollars of interest money, walked off and left their farms to the speculator that had sucked the life blood from him for several years in the shape of forty percent interest.[4]

BOOM AND BUST

The frenzied speculation in farmland into which the territory was plunged in 1859 and which continued into the 1870s and 1880s came on the heels of frantic speculation and subsequent panic in many other areas: town lots, banks, business and industrial enterprises.

The Iowa boomers who poured across the Missouri in the summer of 1854 were interested first and foremost in founding towns in the hope of gaining a personal stake in what they believed would become the future gateway to the West. The procedure was simple: a group of enterprising promoters would organize a town company, stake out the 320 acres allowed under the Federal Townsites Act, and then, to enlarge the site, individually preempt adjacent quarter sections; the site was cut up into lots, 125 by 25 feet, and shares were sold usually on the basis of ten lots per share; then at the first opportunity the legislature was petitioned for a special act of incorporation. The first session of the territorial legislature incorporated seventeen such towns, all but three with the word "city" in the name.

Once the organization was set up and the site located, the town company began promoting its property. Local newspapers played a major role, for most of the early territorial newspapers were little more than advertising sheets for their various town companies. The larger part of each edition was sent east to attract prospective settlers. Locally, the editor played politics for the benefit of his employers and advertised the community as the ideal location for the territorial capital. As J. Sterling Morton, who had provided a similar service for the Nebraska City Town Company, later said, the greater part of their time was spent "talking and meditating upon the prospective value of city property. Young Chicagos, increscent New Yorks, precocious Philadelphias, and infant Londons were duly staked out, lithographed, divided into shares, and puffed with becoming unction and complaisance."[5]

All this activity had its effect. In 1857, individual lots on the river landings of some of the towns were valued at $10,000. Three or four blocks back they sold for $2,000, and even those as far distant as half a mile brought $1,200. Actually few, if any, of the early towns developed as their promoters hoped. The map of eastern Nebraska is dotted with the ghosts of once-to-be-great cities long since given over to farming. Even Omaha, which soon worked itself into a position of political and commercial dominance, was characterized by uncertainty and instability. But the optimism continued. In his annual message to the legislature in January 1857, Governor Izard boasted of the prosperity evident in the towns and cities by their buildings, particularly the churches and schools, and busy streets.

The governor should have looked out the window at the Omaha sprawled about him, but like many of his contemporaries, his eyes were only on the future. As Morton expressed it:

We all felt, as they used to print in large letters on every new town plat, that we were "located adjacent to the very finest groves of timber, surrounded by a very rich agricultural country, in prospective, abundantly supplied with building rock of the finest description, beautifully watered, and possessing very fine indications of lead, iron, coal and salt in great abundance." In my opinion we felt richer, better and more millionarish than any poor deluded mortals ever did on the same amount of moonshine and pluck.[6]

Such prosperity was based on hope and supported by an inflated currency. Hard money was even scarcer in Nebraska Territory than in the country at large. All over the nation irresponsible legislatures were creating banks of issue to increase the amount of money in circulation, and Nebraska's lawmakers, working hard to strengthen their prosperity, opened the gates to a flood of paper money. The second territorial legislature created five banks of issue providing that each could begin operations as soon as $50,000 was subscribed, an amount that included the issuance of paper money. In reality, they did not need a cent of cash on hand.

The third legislature passed six more bank bills. Governor Izard vetoed them all, but two were passed over his veto. During the same session the legislature also repealed a law enacted by the second legislature which had made the establishment of banks, except by legislative charter, a criminal offense. As a result, some of the disappointed applicants set up business without the benefit of a legislative charter. After all, they argued, the soundness of any bank depended on the responsibility and integrity of the banker, not on a legislative charter. In reality, it made little difference because neither the second nor the third legislature had seen fit to provide for any control of banks, chartered or not.

The banking boom persisted throughout the spring and early summer of 1857. Wildcat notes issued from the new Nebraska banks were not good in any state and were viewed with suspicion even in the territory. They did provide a medium of exchange, however, and as such they circulated, keeping prices up and appearances prosperous. Appearances were misleading, and there was plenty of evidence had anyone bothered to look. The territorial auditor's report to the second legislature, for example, showed a total assessed valuation of only $617,822, and not a cent of tax had been collected on the meager two-mill levy of that assessment.

Late in the summer of 1857 the territory began to hear news of a financial panic in the East, including the failure of many well-established firms. At first the territorial financiers considered themselves safe from trouble, but by fall the panic had spread to Nebraska. Almost as fast as they had been established, the territorial banks came tumbling down. As they closed their doors, their utter worthlessness became evident. The sheriff of Burt County tried to collect an execution against the Bank of Tekamah, which had $90,000 in paper money outstanding. He reported that the only assets he could find were a shanty used as the banking house, furniture consisting of an old table, and a broken stove. One of two banks in De Soto had an office, safe, and cashier. All the other De Soto bank had to show for its existence was its name engraved on its bills. A sheriff's writ of execution against the closed Bank of Nebraska at Omaha showed as assets "thirteen sacks of flour, one large iron safe, one counter, one desk, one stove drum and pipe, three arm chairs, and one map of Douglas County."[7]

When the banks failed, the territory's financial structure collapsed. Town lots tumbled in value, businesses failed, and money became practically nonexistent. For a time, interest rates soared as high as 10 percent per month. In some places, merchants issued scrip simply to facilitate exchange. In reality, scrip was much better than the paper money it had replaced because it was based on merchandise, rather than on faith and credit.

AGRICULTURAL AND INDUSTRIAL BEGINNINGS

Aside from speculation, there was very little serious interest in agriculture or industry in Nebraska before the Panic of 1857, and speculators were much more excited by commerce and industry than by agriculture. Farming did not seem to be lucrative enough; thus the principal interest in land was for speculation. Pressed by the financial panic in the fall of 1857, however, many turned to farming because they could find nothing else to do. Even so, as late as the fall of 1858 it was still being charged that "scarcely any produce enough to support themselves. Hundreds of acres of land, entered and owned by men who live among us, are allowed to lie idle doing no more good to the community than when the land was owned by the native savages."[8]

In the spring of 1859, however, it was noted that the flour mill of Pollard and Sheldon at Weeping Water Falls was regularly delivering sacks of meal for shipment out of the territory by steamboat. By 1862, editors could exult over the change that had taken place in the territory. Now, they observed, enough agricultural produce was being exported to more than counterbalance goods imported, and exchange for the first time was running in favor of the territory.

Corn had been grown in the region long before the first white settler arrived and, not surprisingly, became the dominant crop in territorial agriculture. Sod corn tended to be the first crop planted on any piece of ground, perhaps because the process was simple. Corn could be planted by cutting holes in the sod with an ax and dropping the kernels beneath the sod. It was simple but laborious. Fortunately, sod corn required little or no cultivation, and if there was a reasonable amount of rain, the yield was good. Wheat, soon to become the second most important crop, was also found to be well suited to much Nebraska land. There was also a good market for wheat, both at home and abroad; hence the territorial press, ever alert to the problems of agriculture, constantly urged readers to plant more and more wheat.

By 1860 farming was proving to be a fairly dependable way to make a living in Nebraska. The United States census that year revealed that there were three thousand farms in Nebraska. The average farm size was slightly over 225 acres with a average value of $5.82 per acre, resulting in an average total value per farm of $1,293. Although 81.8 percent of the land held in farms remained unimproved, the state's farmers produced nearly 1.5 million bushels of corn, 148,000 bushels of wheat, 162,000 bushels of Irish potatoes, and 75,000 bushels of oats.[9]

Farming was not without its hazards, however. Drought, a periodic problem in Nebraska, was much more serious than the territorial promoters would admit. The records are somewhat scanty and perhaps unreliable, but in seven of the thirteen territorial years rainfall appears to have been less than average; and in 1859, 1860, 1863, and 1864 the average annual rainfall was not over sixteen inches. Grasshoppers plagued the territorial farmer periodically. The years 1857, 1860, 1865, and 1866 appear to have been particularly bad grasshopper years. Indeed, with grasshopper years alternating with drought years, farming in territorial Nebraska was a precarious occupation.

Almost from the beginning there was considerable official and editorial interest in agriculture as Nebraska's principal industry. Acting Governor Cuming recommended the formation of industrial societies in every county to develop agricultural and other productive resources. A territorial board of agriculture, established by the legislature in 1858, held the first territorial fair at Nebraska City on September 21 to 23, 1859. The fair was unsuccessful financially and suffered from numerous problems, which is perhaps why such an event would not occur again until 1868, a year after statehood. Even so, it was the first such territorial agricultural fair in the nation and was touted by its promoters as a highly successful event:

The display in the various departments of Agriculture, Manufactures, Arts, stock, &c., was highly creditable; and although limited in number were unsurpassed in quality especially as to Horses, Cattle, Swine, Grain and vegetables. . . . The Board feel flattered, that with the experience now obtained, and the spirit aroused, they will be able, another year, to bring forward such an exhibit of our agricultural products, as well as fuse into our people a spirit of emulation and improvement that cannot fail to result beneficially to an incalculable extent.[10]

Circumstances may have dictated the choice of farming as an economic activity, but Nebraska's early newspaper editors helped to develop it as a way of life. Robert W. Furnas of the *Brownville Advertiser,* J. Sterling Morton of the *Nebraska City News,* and many others were deeply concerned about the problems of agriculture and devoted many columns to advice and encouragement for those engaged in an essentially experimental enterprise. So too did the *Nebraska Deutsche Zeitung,* a German-language newspaper established at Nebraska City in 1861. In addition to its Nebraska subscribers, for whom it offered suggestions for improving farming methods and crop yields, editor Friedrich Renner sent copies to the German-speaking countries and provinces of Europe extolling the virtues of Nebraska, including its climate and soil and the great opportunities to be had there for farmers. Even editors whose primary interests appeared linked to urban growth and development, such as George L. Miller, founder of the *Omaha Herald* and avid booster of Omaha, championed Nebraska agriculture and regularly published articles reporting improved agricultural techniques. In an editorial in 1865 Miller vigorously put forth his philosophy: "If we have one purpose nearer to our hearts than any other, it is to render ourselves useful to the great cause of Agriculture in this Territory."[11]

Government also recognized the vital link between the state's future growth and prosperity and a viable agriculture. Acting Governor Cuming convinced the first legislature that agriculture could be promoted and immigration increased if immigrants could be assured of the availability of timber. Raising forests, he insisted, would provide the necessary timber for homes, fuel, and fences, as well as dispel the notion that Nebraska was unfit for agriculture. The legislature responded by passing an act in 1861 which encouraged tree planting by reducing the taxable value of real estate by $50 for each acre of trees planted and cultivated.

Then, as for years later, farming overshadowed other economic activity. The 1860 census indicates the subordinate role of manufacturing in the territory. There were only 107 manufacturing establishments with a total capital investment of $266,575, employing 336 persons at a total wage of $105,332, and turning out products valued at $607,328. The leading industry was the sawmill, which employed more than half of the labor (155 persons) and turned out more than half of the product. Next in importance was the gristmill, employing 36 persons, and third the shoemaker, accounting for 33 persons.[12] All of the establishments were small, and industrial enterprise as a whole was little more than an expanded home manufacture supplying consumer goods for a local market. Though a committee of the first legislature called attention to the deposits of coal, copper, and granite in the territory and in 1869 Governor David Butler referred to the "rich and apparently inexhaustible supply of pure and easily manufactured" salt in the Lancaster salt basin, the territory simply did not have the raw materials to sustain heavy industry of any kind.[13] It was apparent before the end of the territorial period that Nebraska's industry would consist largely of the processing of agricultural products. Factories that did exist for other purposes were finding it increasingly more difficult to compete with products shipped in from the East, and many soon discontinued operation.

SCHOOLS AND CHURCHES

Among the more important acts of the first territorial legislature was legislation providing for free public schools. The Free Public School Act, passed in March 1855, created the office of territorial superintendent, to be combined with that of territorial librarian, and provided for the selection of county superintendents by popular vote. Each county superintendent was to divide his county into districts and notify the residents to organize schools. To support the schools, the county superintendent was authorized to levy a tax of not less than three or more than five mills on all property in the county and to distribute the proceeds among the various districts on the basis of the number of white children between the ages of five and twenty-one. Most of the control was centered in the local districts, and each was to be governed by a three-member board. Most of the initiative appears to have rested there as well, for the development of public schools varied greatly from place to place in the territory. Everywhere the first schools were very unpretentious, and during the Panic of 1857 many closed down. When this happened, churches or private teachers usually stepped into the breach to provide schooling for the children of parents who were interested enough to pay direct fees. In some cases, private schools preceded the public schools, and when public schools were organized, or reorganized, the first step generally was to grant public funds for the support of the existing private school.

In the early years, many children in the Nebraska Territory were denied the opportunity to attend school. Of the 10,934 school-age children in 1860, only 3,296, or 30.1 percent, attended any school during the year, comparable to the 30.3 percent that was reported for all U.S. territories in 1860. It was half the ratio for the United States as a whole, however, which showed 59.8 percent of school-age children attending school in 1860. There would be considerable improvement in school attendance by the time of the 1870 census, however, when the state of Nebraska could claim that 52.0 percent of its school-age children attended school, a figure very close to the national average of 54.7 percent.[14]

Though effective interest in the public schools lagged at times, many communities appear to have had great enthusiasm for universities, colleges, academies, and seminaries. Part of this, of course, was pure town company promotion. It was impressive to have the distinction, at least on paper, of enjoying higher educational facilities. Within two years after the territory was opened for settlement, the legislature had chartered seven colleges and universities, and by the end of the territorial period twenty-three institutions of higher learning had been chartered. The only one of these remaining today is Peru State College, organized by the Methodists in 1866 as Peru Seminary and College. The first such institution chartered was Simpson University at Omaha. The first to give collegiate work was Fontanelle University, opened in 1858 by the Congregationalists as the nucleus of the little interior settlement of the same name. Within a year, however, it was apparent that Fontanelle University could not flourish, and after a struggling existence it closed its doors in 1873. The fortunes of the town paralleled those of the college, and Fontanelle dwindled from a town of five hundred, which was good-sized for territorial Nebraska, to a crossroads village.

Churches, like schools, faced an uphill struggle to get started and keep going. As the Reverend George W. Barnes, a pioneer Baptist preacher in Omaha, wrote:

There were but few Christians among that varied population, and religion met only a left-handed favor. The great mass seemed in a terrible hurry to build their houses, and push their various enterprises to success and wealth. A very large proportion seemed to have come to make a speedy fortune, then return east and enjoy the same. Everything was made to bend that way. The Sabbath was painfully disregarded. You could hear the whiz of the saw, and the click of the hammer, at all hours of day and night for the whole week. The Lord's day found only a few who honored its claims.[15]

Though Baptists, Presbyterians, and Catholics had been active in the missionary field for two decades, the Methodists were the first to establish organized churches for the benefit of the settlers. The first church in the territory appears to have been the Methodist Church at Nebraska City, which was established in October 1854, with the Reverend W. D. Gage (for whom Gage County later was named) as pastor. The Baptists, Catholics, Christians, Congregationalists, Episcopalians, and Presbyterians soon followed. By 1860, the census showed sixty-three church congregations in the Nebraska Territory, of which a full half (thirty-two) were associated with the Methodists. The Presbyterians claimed nearly a quarter with fourteen congregations. The remaining 27 percent seemed evenly divided among the Congregational, Baptist, Episcopal, Christian, Lutheran, and Roman Catholic, each claiming two to three congregations.[16]

Until a building could be erected, which was likely to be some time, church services were usually held in the homes of members. The Methodists, with their itinerant circuit riders, were particularly well organized to serve the needs of frontier communities and for that reason probably developed more rapidly than other denominations. Moreover, the

Methodists were ardent revivalists, and protracted revivals were much-enjoyed institutions in a frontier community, beginning just after the corn was shucked in the fall and lasting three or four weeks.

Even more popular than revivals were the camp meetings, protracted revivals held in the open during the summer months. The camp meeting combined a vacation with a period of spiritual refreshment, and families who could afford them took tents to the meeting place, usually a grove on the banks of a stream. The prairie camp meetings do not appear to have suffered from the excesses that characterized those held in the Appalachian forests, but the ministers made the prairies ring with a strong emotional gospel.

Churches often formed the nucleus around which territorial settlements developed. St. Johns, for example, an early Dakota County settlement, was established in 1856 by Catholics from Dubuque, Iowa, under the leadership of Father Jeremiah Trecy. This pattern would become even more common in the 1870s, when ministers negotiated with the railroads for tracts of land on which to settle their flocks.

CHAPTER 9

Highway to the West

Nebraska Territory, organized to make possible a Platte River valley route for the transcontinental railroad, was indeed on America's great road west. The great overland migration of the 1840s and early 1850s continued through the 1850s at a much reduced rate, but the summer of 1859 saw the Platte Valley alive once again with gold seekers. This time they were headed for the elusive riches believed to lie buried in the sands of Cherry Creek, where Denver was to arise almost overnight. The military posts, the Colorado mining camps, and even the diggings in far-off Montana created a heavy demand for goods that could best be supplied through the Platte Valley, and overland freighting developed into one of Nebraska Territory's biggest businesses. The western demand for mail and passenger service was exceeded only by the demand for freighted goods, and the territorial years saw exciting developments in faster and more efficient transportation and communication taking place in the Platte Valley: the stagecoach, the Pony Express, and finally the telegraph and the railroad. The technological advances that occurred during Nebraska's territorial and early statehood years made possible the rapid transformation from wagon to railroad on the plains and proved to be pivotal factors in Nebraska's growth and viability.

STEAMBOATS

Technology had already made an impression along the Missouri River by the time the territory was organized. Steam ferries were in operation at Omaha and Bellevue. Steamboats had first been seen on the river as far north as the mouth of the Platte River in 1819, when Major Stephen H. Long brought the *Western Engineer* up to Council Bluffs. In 1831 the *Yellowstone*, owned by the American Fur Company, ascended the river as far as Fort Tecumseh, later known as Fort Pierre, and the next year went as far as Fort Union, three miles above the mouth of the Yellowstone River. The success of these two voyages prompted the American Fur Company to abandon keelboats in favor of steamboats. Though expensive, this decision proved fortuitous, for the steamboat was an important factor in the company's acquisition of a virtual monopoly on the fur trade of the Far West.

Normally the company sent only one vessel upstream each season, but occasionally it had two boats on the river, and until 1846 virtually all those on the upper Missouri River were engaged in the fur trade. The Mormon emigration and the California gold rush resulted in a few non-fur-trade boats penetrating as far as Council Bluffs and Winter Quarters. Council Bluffs remained a port of call, and after 1854 the steamboats touched at the ambitious little settlements springing up on the west side of the river. The Rulo *Western Guide* published with pride a summary of the number of steamboats that had docked at Rulo from the spring through the summer of 1858: March, 8; April, 32; May, 23; June, 26; July, 27; and August, 30.[1]

River traffic increased steadily during the 1850s, reaching its zenith in 1859, the year of the Colorado gold rush. Unfortunately, no comprehensive statistics are available, but scattered figures indicate the traffic's growth. In 1857, 28 steamboats arrived at Sioux City before July 1; by August 11, 1859, 128 steamboats had arrived at Omaha–Council Bluffs.

Unlike the steamboats of Mississippi River fame, some of which were little short of floating palaces, those that plied the upper Missouri River were smaller and lighter draft to enable them to maneuver the snag-filled and often shallow channels. After 1860 they became even more practical in design as stern-wheel architecture increasingly replaced the side wheel. Costing from $20,000 to $25,000 each, these boats were slightly larger than the earlier side-wheelers, ranging from 170 to 215 feet long and 30 to 35 feet wide with a freight capacity of 300 to 500 tons.[2]

It took skill and experience to guide a boat along the treacherous Missouri, and the pilots, who had a tight little union known as the Pilots' Benevolent Association, sometimes drew as much as $1,200 per month. Even with the best pilots, accidents were frequent and losses heavy. All told, more than four hundred vessels were sunk or damaged, resulting in losses of almost $9 million. The extent and variety of the goods carried

"General" Joseph R. Brown's ill-fated steam wagon promised to revolutionize overland freighting and assure Nebraska City's commercial prominence. This copy of a painting of the steam wagon, which broke down just a few miles into its inaugural first voyage, hangs in Arbor Lodge at Nebraska City. Courtesy, NSHS, 5800:3a.

by the Missouri River steamboats was revealed beginning in 1968 when Jesse Pursell and Sam Corbino located the remains of the steamboat *Bertrand*, which had struck a snag and sunk near the DeSoto Landing on April 1, 1865.[3]

The *Bertrand* was typical of the low-draft, stern-wheel "mountain" steamers of the time, 162 feet from bow to stern, approximately 32 feet in width, with a hold approximately 5 feet in depth.[4] En route to Fort Benton, Montana Territory, it carried a cargo of over 10,000 cubic feet.[5] An amazing collection of goods removed from the holds of the *Bertrand* is on display in the museum at DeSoto Bend National Wildlife Refuge on the Iowa side of the Missouri River across from Blair. That the *Bertrand* was carrying food, clothing, and mining supplies was not as surprising as the vast variety of those items, including canned oysters, champagne, horseradish, bolts of wool, tablecloths, ties, slippers, candlesticks, glass goblets, spice grinders, doorknobs, teaspoons, and tobacco. The incredible list of luxury as well as practical items goes on and on.[6]

For the river towns of Nebraska Territory, the steamboats provided an indispensable connection with the outside world. They brought settlers, carried goods to stock the frontier stores and to be shipped across the plains in heavy wagons, and brought mail and newspapers. Little wonder that the first boat up the river in spring provided the occasion for an impromptu celebration, with the entire town population rushing to the river landing to greet debarking passengers and watch the freight being unloaded.

The Missouri River steamboat business enjoyed continued expansion into the 1860s, boosted by the Montana gold rush and the military campaigns during the Civil War. By 1865 the business appeared to have a bright future. The end of the Civil War that year released both men and capital, and business boomed as people rushed west to seek their fortunes in the gold fields.

Yet in the midst of prosperity, signs of approaching decline were already on the horizon. The Hannibal and St. Joseph Railroad had reached the Missouri River by 1859. Prosperity for the steamboat business peaked eight years later, in 1867, the same year that the Chicago and Northwestern Railroad reached the Missouri River. As railroads continued to expand, the steamboats could not meet the competition, and by the 1870s river traffic was confined largely to servicing points not yet reached by the railroads. The arrival of the Great Northern at Helena in 1887 delivered the final blow.

OVERLAND FREIGHTING

The heavy emigration to California, Oregon, and Utah in the 1840s and 1850s, the Colorado gold rush of 1859, and the opening of the Montana diggings in the 1860s created an almost insatiable demand for goods and supplies of all kinds. Adding heavily to the demand were the military posts established throughout the West to protect trails and settlements from the Indians. California and Oregon could be supplied by ship, but the most feasible way to get goods to Colorado, Utah, and Montana was through the Platte Valley, the route of the emigrants. Nebraska's river towns developed into important freighting terminals, where steamboats unloaded goods to be shipped by wagon across the plains. Omaha, in particular, developed as both a freighting point and an important emigrant outfitting post.

Drawn by six to twelve yoke of oxen and loaded with three to five tons of freight, the heavy wagons carried an amazing variety of goods: food, grain, clothing, whiskey, mining machinery, lumber, arms, ammunition, as well as anything for which there was a demand or for which a demand might be created. One freighter took a load of cats to Denver, disposing of them at a good profit to miners who sought companions and mousers. Another filled a wagon box with frozen eggs at Omaha in the fall and hauled them to Denver. Two entrepreneurs loaded a similar wagon with frozen oysters at Omaha, peddling them along the way at $2.50 per quart. Another specialized in hauling apples, which commanded as much as $15 per bushel in Denver. Still others drove flocks of turkeys and sheep and herds of cattle from the Missouri to Denver. The big companies, however, concentrated on grain, food, and military supplies for the army, serving as carriers rather than speculators.

The freighting business embraced everything from the farmer or small merchant who loaded a single wagon with goods and set out for Denver to the large companies that employed hundreds of people and did millions of dollars worth of business each year. Of those regularly engaged in the business, sixty-four have been identified as operating out of Nebraska City at one time or another and twenty-four out of Omaha. Prominent in the Nebraska City trade were Russell, Majors and Waddell; Coe and Carter; the Gilman Brothers; Hosford and Gaynon; John Coad; Ben Holladay; Wells, Fargo and Company; Hawke, Nuckolls and Company; A. and P. Byrum; Moses Stocking; R. M. and D. P. Rolfe; H. T. Clarke and Company; Moses Sydenham; and many others. Among the Omahans were Edward Creighton, William Paxton, and Major Frank North.

By its very nature, however, the freighting business tended to be concentrated in a relatively few large firms. Costs were high; profits, though occasionally large, were speculative; and to bid on government contracts, the most dependable source of income, the freighter needed hundreds of wagons and thousands of oxen. The standard "bull outfit" consisted of a train of twenty-five freight wagons and one mess wagon, representing an investment of from $18,000 to $20,000 and requiring 300 to 320 head of oxen, including extras, and a minimum crew of about thirty men. The wagon boss received about $75 per month and the teamsters about $25 each. In addition, all were rationed, at a cost of about forty-five to fifty cents per day. A freighter had to have considerable financial backing to operate a freighting train—and the big outfits, of course, had several trains on the trail at once.

Largest of all the freighting firms was Russell, Majors and Waddell, which in the late 1850s virtually monopolized military freighting on the plains. Alexander Majors and William H. Russell, both veteran freighters, formed a partnership in 1855 to carry military freight from Fort Leavenworth to the posts of the plains and the mountains. When they secured, in addition, the contract to supply Albert Sidney Johnston's Army of Utah in 1857, they added another partner, William B. Waddell. The new contract necessitated the establishment of an additional terminal upriver from Fort Leavenworth, and the partners chose Nebraska City, transforming it in one season from a struggling frontier settlement to a major river port. Russell, Majors, and Waddell spent over $300,000 developing their Nebraska City terminal, buying 138 lots on which they constructed houses, wagon shops, foundries, boardinghouses, and warehouses. Majors, who was the superintendent of the firm's operations in Nebraska City and on the trail, announced that he would need eight thousand yoke of oxen and about twelve hundred men. Ultimately he advertised for sixteen thousand yoke of oxen and fifteen hundred men. The river landing was soon busy with steamboats unloading huge quantities of freight. The uphill grade of Nebraska City's main street was pulverized by the grinding of heavy wheels.

Initially, the route west from Nebraska City followed what was known as the Ox-Bow Trail, crossing Salt Creek at Ashland and following the Platte River to Fort Kearny. This route was generally unsatisfactory because much of it traversed the indirect eastern Platte River bottoms, impassable for freight wagons when wet.

Before he located at Nebraska City, Majors had demanded that the town agree to lay out and develop a road directly west to Fort Kearny.

Nebraska City failed to keep its promise to do so, and finally, in the spring of 1860, Majors, having invested so heavily in the town that he could not afford to move the terminal, assumed the burden himself, hiring Augustus Harvey to survey a direct route. Harvey found a well-beaten path as far as Olathe, later known as Saltillo, on Salt Creek. From Salt Creek he plowed a furrow due west to Fort Kearny. Wagons, coming along later, straddled the furrow, and before the season was out the Nebraska City–Fort Kearny cutoff was well established. Later the cutoff came to be known as the Steam Wagon Road to commemorate the ill-starred effort of "General" Joseph R. Brown.7 Brown planned to run a wood-burning steam locomotive across the treeless plains to Denver, an effort that ended when the wagon broke down on its maiden run a few miles out of Nebraska City. Brown left for the East to find parts for his machine. Weary of waiting for his return, his associates, whom he had left in Nebraska City, performed some makeshift repairs in 1866 and ran the machine to J. Sterling Morton's farm. Brown finally returned in 1868 but without the necessary parts. He dismantled the machine the following year and died in 1870.

Although the steam wagon experiment ended in failure, Brown indirectly improved the position of Nebraska City in the freighting business. In anticipation of Brown's return to repair his machine, the residents of Otoe County approved a $2,500 bond issue to complete bridges over Salt Creek and the Big Blue River and generally to improve the trail from Nebraska City to Fort Kearny.

The freight wagon, like the steamboat, declined in importance in the wake of the railroad. It would, of course, remain important for local freighting until the advent of the motorized truck. Overland freighting in the history of economic development of Nebraska Territory, however, can hardly be overemphasized. The river towns developed almost in proportion to the amount of steamboat or freight wagon transfer business they were able to secure. Nebraska City's success in this activity established it as the second most important town in the territory. The big operators provided an outlet for crops and livestock produced in the territory and employment for thousands. Small-scale freighting ventures helped many farmers and small merchants to keep going and at times to develop operations of considerable stature. And all along the trail, road ranches developed to provide the freighters with feed for their oxen and food and diversion for themselves. Some of these developed into the large cattle ranches of a later day, and others became towns.

STAGECOACH AND PONY EXPRESS

The West desired mail as much as it did freight service. Almost from the beginning of settlement in California, Oregon, and Utah, the government was bombarded with requests for improved mail service. Inevitably this demand became an issue in the growing sectional controversy over the location of the route of the Pacific railroad. Initially, mail to California came by ocean, but no service was provided to the mountain settlements, and by the 1850s Californians, among others, were demanding overland mail service.

In 1850, United States mail service was established between Independence, Missouri, and Salt Lake City and the next year from Salt Lake City to Sacramento. The service, particularly to the East, was far from satisfactory. The contract provided for a monthly mail, but the contractor, using the same wagon and team for the entire journey, frequently failed to keep the schedule and during the winter virtually suspended operations.

When the government finally established through service to California in 1857, it used the southern route, of no value to the Utah settlements. The bill providing for overland mail service to California, passed by Congress on March 3, 1857, left decisions for implementation in the hands of Postmaster General Aaron V. Brown of Tennessee, who awarded the contract to John Butterfield, an influential director of American Express, a partner of Henry Wells and William Fargo, and a personal friend of President James Buchanan. Some charged that Brown selected the southern route for political purposes, claiming that he was interested in expanding the area of slavery by encouraging settlement in the Southwest.[8]

By 1858, as the result of a generous expansion of postal facilities in the West, the central route had a weekly mail from Independence to Placerville by way of Salt Lake City. It was soon evident that the overland mail service, whatever the route, was an expensive operation, and in 1859 the western service was cut back and that on the central route was reduced to a semimonthly basis.

The West, of course, wanted more, not less mail service, regardless of the cost to the federal government, and in 1859 the newly established mining communities of the Pikes Peak region added to the demand. Responding to this need, William H. Russell conceived the daring idea of a stagecoach express to the Pikes Peak region. Though his partners refused to join what they considered a wild scheme, Russell, with the aid of John S. Jones, proceeded to establish the Leavenworth and Pikes Peak Express along the Republican–Solomon River route. The company was in financial difficulty from the beginning. In an effort to bail out the enterprise, Russell, Majors, and Waddell transferred the route to the Platte Valley so that they could combine it with their own Salt Lake mail service. Further service on the Platte Valley route was provided by the Western Stage Company, which ran a weekly mail over the Military Road from Omaha to Fort Kearny, extending its service to Denver in September 1860.

Meanwhile, Senator William M. Gwin of California had persuaded William H. Russell to launch the Pony Express between St. Joseph and California as a dramatic means of demonstrating the superiority of the central route. Russell's partners, still making up losses for the Pikes Peak Express, were not enthusiastic over this latest brainchild of their overly enthusiastic colleague. Finally, they were induced to agree so that he could make good his pledge to Senator Gwin, who, in turn, had promised to obtain a government mail contract for the Pony Express. Having made their decision, Russell, Majors, and Waddell began preparations to launch the service at the earliest possible date, and on April 3, 1860, to the accompaniment of celebrations at both ends of the line, the first riders set out from Sacramento and St. Joseph. Riders, station keepers, and ponies functioned with brilliant precision to bring the first mail through both ways in the scheduled ten days.

The Pony Express generally followed the route of the Oregon-California Trail, along which stations of logs, stone, or adobe were built at intervals of about fifteen miles. Riders covered seventy-five to a hundred miles, although horses were changed at each station. Both riders and horses were the best obtainable. For the most part the horses were half-breed California mustangs, noted for their dependability, endurance, and speed; the riders were young men hired for their light weight, strength, courage, horsemanship, and marksmanship.

Throughout the summer and fall of 1860, the Pony Express maintained its ten-day schedule fairly well. By autumn, the transcontinental telegraph extended west as far as Fort Kearny and east to Fort Churchill, Nevada, and telegraphic messages carried between these two points by the Pony Express spanned the continent in record time. News of Abraham Lincoln's election in the fall, for example, took only eight days to cross the country; the run between Fort Kearny and Fort Churchill was made in six days. During the winter, when the operations were watched with great interest as a test of the practicality of the central route for year-round use, the schedule was extended to fifteen days between terminals and eleven days between telegraph stations. The schedule, however, was seldom kept. The average time between Forts Kearny and Churchill was 13.8 days. Even so, only one trip was missed altogether, and the Pony Express was able to maintain supremacy over the Butterfield Line, which was operating on the southern route.

Though the Pony Express made improvements in the spring of 1861, its days had been numbered from the beginning. Its function was limited to shuttling messages across the ever-narrowing gap between the termini of the transcontinental telegraph. By October 24, 1861, when the lines were joined at Salt Lake City, the Pony Express ceased to operate. Financially, the Pony Express was never a success. Even at their highest at $5 per half ounce of mail, the rates charged were not high enough to pay the costs of operation. The often-promised government mail contract, which might have offset its losses, failed to materialize. Even when loaded to capacity, the Pony Express could not pay for itself.

The failure of the Pony Express was disastrous for Russell, Majors, and Waddell. It completed their financial destruction, which had begun in the Pikes Peak Express venture. Nationally, however, the experiment was a success. It demonstrated the practicality of the central route at all seasons of the year, it blazed the path for the first transcontinental railroad, and it helped tie California to the Union in the first difficult months of the Civil War. Although in operation slighly more than a year and a half, it remains one of the more colorful acts in the drama of the West.

With the advantages of the Platte Valley route clearly demonstrated, the Butterfield Overland Mail was transferred from the southern to the central route, and in the desire to strengthen the ties between California and the Union, daily service was inaugurated under a contract that was to cost the government a million dollars a year. Letter mail was to go through in twenty days, other mail in thirty-five.

Butterfield could not keep his schedule, however, and the whole operation was soon denounced as a fraud. Ben Holladay purchased the line in 1862 and, despite Indian difficulties in 1864, greatly improved and extended the service. In 1866 Wells Fargo purchased the lines and continued to operate them until the completion of the transcontinental railroad, when the stagecoach, like the freight wagon, was changed from a transcontinental to a local carrier.

Throughout the Civil War, however, the Concord coaches rolled through the Platte Valley on their daily transcontinental schedule. Manufactured by Abbott-Downing of Concord, New Hampshire, the swaying coach, drawn by four to six horses or mules, was as much an institution on the plains as the covered wagon. As many as nine passengers could be accommodated inside, and at times additional passengers rode on top. Mail and express were carried in large leather pouches at the front and rear. Speed varied greatly, although in the Platte Valley a coach could make ten miles per hour. Six miles per hour, including stops, was considered average. Fares increased steadily during the Civil War, and by the end of the conflict in 1865, passage from the Missouri River to Denver cost $175, or nearly twenty-seven cents per mile. Meals were extra. Samuel Bowles, a Massachusetts editor who rode a coach in 1865, described the facilities as follows:

Every ten or fifteen miles is a stable of the stage proprietor, and every other ten or fifteen miles an eating-house; perhaps as often a petty ranch or farm house, whose owner lives by selling hay to the trains of emigrants or freighters; every fifty or one hundred miles you will find a small grocery and blacksmith shop; and about as frequently is a military station with a company or two of United States troops for protection against the Indians. This makes up all the civilization of the plains. The barns and houses are of logs or prairie turf, piled up layer on layer, and smeared over or between with a clayey mud. The turf and mud make the best houses, and the same material is used for military forts and for fences around the cattle and horse yards. Their roofs, where covered, are a foot thickness of turfs, sand, clay, and logs or twigs, with an occasional inside lining of skins or thick cloth. Floors are oftenest such as nature offers only; and, as at some of the Washington hotels, the spoons at the table do not always go around. Mexican terms prevail: an inclosure for animals is called a "corral"; a house of turf and mud is of "adobe"; and a farm-house or farm a "ranch."

Our meals at the stage stations continued very good throughout the ride; the staples were bacon, eggs, hot biscuit, green tea and coffee; dried peaches and apples, and pies were as uniform; beef was occasional, and canned fruits and vegetables were furnished at least half of the time. Each meal was the same; breakfast, dinner and supper were undistinguishable save by the hour; and the price was one dollar or one dollar and a half each. The devastations of the Indians last summer and fall, and the fear of their repetition, form the occasion and excuse for enormous prices for everything now upon the Plains.[9]

More important, Bowles clearly saw the destiny of the Platte Valley:

This valley of the Platte, through these Plains, is the natural highway across the Continent. Other valleys and routes have similar advantages, but in minor degree: this unites the most; for it is central—it is on the line of our great cities and our great industries, East and West, and it is the longest, most continuous. A smooth, hard stage road is made by simply driving over it; a railroad awaits only sleepers and rails.[10]

TALKING WIRES AND THE IRON HORSE

On June 16, 1860, Congress authorized the secretary of the treasury to subsidize a telegraph line from the western border of Missouri to San Francisco at the cost of $40,000 per year for a period of ten years. Hiram Sibley, president of Western Union and principal inspiration for the act, immediately went to work to complete a line and secure the subsidy. W. H. Stebbins was employed to build the telegraph line from St. Joseph, Missouri, to Omaha and westward along the Platte River. By August 29 the line was at Brownville, its first Nebraska station, prompting "a general jollification. . . . Bonfires, illuminations, fire balls, music, burning gunpowder, speeches and toasts were the order of the evening."[11]

By September 5, 1860, the line was open to Omaha, and by November it had been stretched west to Fort Kearny in time to bring news of Lincoln's election to the post and the waiting Pony Express. Meanwhile, on November 18, Edward Creighton, general agent of Western Union, who had built many miles of telegraph lines east of the Mississippi, left Omaha by stage to make plans for extending the line farther west. During the winter of 1860–61 a California company was formed to cooperate with Western Union by building the western end of the transcontinental line. To build the eastern end, Western Union organized the Pacific Telegraph Company under the liberal incorporation laws of Nebraska Territory.

During the spring of 1861, Stebbins completed the line from Fort Kearny to Julesburg, Colorado. Creighton then divided the construction force into two crews. One under Stebbins was to build east from Salt Lake City and the other under Creighton to build west from Julesburg. Creighton completed the line to Salt Lake City by October 20, 1862. The west end was in by October 24, and the wires were joined.

Creighton's greatest problem, of course, was obtaining supplies. Hundreds of wagons were used to transport wire, insulators, tools, and provisions west from the Missouri River. On the treeless plains acquiring wood for poles was also a problem, and in one instance they were hauled 240 miles. Cedar poles from the canyons at Cottonwood Springs near North Platte were used for miles along the line.

Meanwhile, the transcontinental railroad was gradually taking shape. The project languished during the 1850s, largely because of sectional controversies over the route, which were eventually settled by the coming of the Civil War. On July 1, 1862, Congress chartered the Union Pacific Company to build the eastern end of a transcontinental railroad and provided assistance for the Central Pacific Company, organized a year earlier, to build the western end.

Congress had placed the responsibility for establishing the eastern terminus of the transcontinental railroad on the president. Although Lincoln had previously designated Omaha as the site of the eastern terminus, the order was apparently lost, and the second order of December 2, 1863, clearly established it in Iowa.[12] The designated location mattered little, however. Because there was no railroad bridge across the Missouri River and it was necessary to build west from the river, the plum had, for all practical purposes, fallen to Omaha. Groundbreaking ceremonies were held that very day with Nebraska governor Alvin Saunders wielding the ceremonial spade to the accompaniment of guns and cheers. The day's festivities concluded with supper at the Herndon House, served promptly at one-thirty in the morning.

For more than a year after this auspicious beginning, nothing was done. The act of 1862 had provided a grant of ten sections of public land and a government loan for each mile of track laid. The amount of the loan varied according to the land: $16,000 for each mile on the plains, $32,000 for each mile in the foothills, and $48,000 for each mile in the mountains. Generous as this may seem, it was still not enough to attract sufficient capital for building a railroad across the desert wastes to California.

Not until Congress, under heavy pressure from the railroads, doubled the land grant and relegated the loan to the status of a second mortgage in 1864 did enough money become available. Congressman Oakes Ames of Massachusetts and his brother Oliver, prestigious Boston bankers, provided much-needed assistance. Thomas Durant, the Union Pacific's chief executive, devised a scheme, the Credit Mobilier of America, in which company officers, congressmen whose influence was needed, and others could make their fortunes from the construction operation. This move brought in still additional capital—capital that returned annual dividends of about 100 percent. The Credit Mobilier's fantastic operations that enabled the officers of the Union Pacific and their friends to profit at the expense of the railroad, the small stockholders, and even the government, developed into a national scandal that was to be a major factor in antirailroad politics in later years.

By 1865, the Union Pacific was at last ready to move. Money was available, and so was labor. Supplies, however, were difficult to obtain. Tie-cutting crews denuded the Missouri Valley of trees for miles up and down the river from Omaha. When this supply ran out, ties were shipped from the East. Until 1867, when the Chicago and Northwestern Railroad reached Council Bluffs, everything had to be shipped to Omaha by steamboat. Even after the railroad reached the eastern bank of the Missouri, materials had to be ferried across the river. West of Omaha, the railroad could haul its own rails, ties, and other supplies, but the crews who worked ahead of the rails had to be supplied by wagon. And the company faced additional problems in western Nebraska, where Indians periodically looted supply wagons and attacked construction crews. Once construction was under way, however, General Grenville M. Dodge pushed it steadily toward completion. Although only forty miles of track had been laid by the end of 1865, the rails reached Kearney by August 1866 and North Platte by that November.

As the road pushed west, base towns were established at the end of the track to facilitate the handling of supplies, men, and equipment. Such was the origin of places like Fremont, Kearney, North Platte, and Sidney, which became boisterous little towns loaded with prostitutes and gamblers ready to prey on the Irish workmen who came to town on payday. As the end of the track moved on, these places became mere way stations, but all of them ultimately developed into prosperous small cities. Also, as the tracks moved west, many pioneer Platte Valley settlements literally moved from their original location to one along the railroad.

For Omaha too, the railroad was a great boon. The Union Pacific attracted both people and money as investors expanded their activities into freighting as well as fuel, dry goods, restaurants, and bawdy houses. Nowhere was the economic vitality more evident than at the wharf. A visitor to Omaha in 1868 described the activity:

Five steamboats were unloading and the two large Ferryboats were going backwards & forwards crowded with teams & passengers as fast as they could load and unload. The wharf on the Iowa side was covered with some hundreds of cars surrounded by numbers of wagons unloading the coal, freight, grain, iron, etc. out of them and transferring them to this side. On our wharf the railroad has several lines of rails on which were scores of cars & engines & cars passing & repassing all the time. On the wharf were great piles, hills, of corn & oats, iron & railway & government goods & material with scores of men & teams, yelling & screaming . . . we were struck by the bustle & excitement and the amounts of business being done. There was the real life of Omaha.[13]

On November 13, 1867, the rails reached Cheyenne, Wyoming. A year and a half later, on May 10, 1869, they joined those of the Central Pacific at Promontory Point, a few miles west of Ogden, Utah. The nation was united by rail. The Platte Valley, the funnel through which America had been channeled into the West, had become an important link in the iron chain binding East and West and could now provide home sites as well. The technological transformation that would make possible the settlement of the plains west of the Missouri had been completed.

CHAPTER 10

Securing the Land

Supporters of the concept of a permanent Indian country west of the Missouri River had objected vigorously to the passage of the Kansas-Nebraska Act on the grounds that the area had been set aside for the Indians and by treaty guaranteed to them in perpetuity. Their concern was not without substance, for the organization of Nebraska Territory and the beginning of white settlement activity west of the Missouri completely and irrevocably negated the possibility that the area might serve as a permanent Indian territory. Conflict was inevitable in the face of an expanding nation.

THE EASTERN RESERVATIONS

The semisedentary tribes along the Missouri River in what would become eastern Nebraska had never been particularly warlike or aggressive. Already under the influence of white culture, they acquiesced with relatively little resistance and by 1854 had ceded their lands to the U.S. government.

Aside from the Kansas cession of 1825, which included a claim to what is now south-central Nebraska, the earliest cession in Nebraska was that of the Otos and Missourias. At Prairie du Chien in 1830 they had ceded for $3,000 a tract of land, estimated at 128,000 acres, between the Little Nemaha and the Nemaha Rivers, for the benefit of Oto, Iowa, Omaha, Yankton, and Santee mixed-bloods. Provision was made for the allotment of lands in severalty to recognized mixed-blood claimants. It was the first allotment to Indians in the United States and was soon the focus of conflict between the Indians and white settlers as the tract quickly developed into a land-grabber's paradise.

In 1833 the Otos and Missourias ceded additional lands, and on March 15, 1854, by treaty they gave up the remainder of their Nebraska lands, except for a strip of land ten miles wide and twenty-five miles long on the

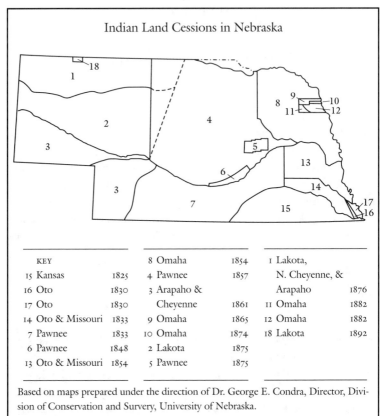

Indian Land Cessions in Nebraska

KEY		8 Omaha	1854	1 Lakota,	
15 Kansas	1825	4 Pawnee	1857	N. Cheyenne, &	
16 Oto	1830	3 Arapaho &		Arapaho	1876
17 Oto	1830	Cheyenne	1861	11 Omaha	1882
14 Oto & Missouri	1833	9 Omaha	1865	12 Omaha	1882
7 Pawnee	1833	10 Omaha	1874	18 Lakota	1892
6 Pawnee	1848	2 Lakota	1875		
13 Oto & Missouri	1854	5 Pawnee	1875		

Based on maps prepared under the direction of Dr. George E. Condra, Director, Division of Conservation and Survery, University of Nebraska.

Big Blue River. Yet the Otos and Missourias, destitute and diminishing in numbers, had neither the ability nor the inclination to develop this remnant of land agriculturally, and settlers began to bring pressure upon their representatives in Congress to reduce the size of the reservation even further or to abandon it altogether. During the 1870s Congress authorized sale of part of the reservation; in 1881 the tribes were removed to Indian Territory (Oklahoma) and the remaining lands were opened to settlement. The Iowa, Sauk, and Fox tribes, related to the Otos and the Missourias, were given a common reservation located primarily in Kansas but extending to the Nemaha River in the southeastern corner of Nebraska. This land ultimately was allotted to the Indians in severalty.

On March 16, 1854, the Omahas ceded all of their lands in eastern Nebraska except for three hundred thousand acres to be set aside as a reserve. The Omahas had claimed the country bounded by the Missouri River on the north and east, Shell Creek on the west, and the Platte River on the south. This was a significant cession, and the government agreed that if the reserve they were first given along the Ayoway River proved unsatisfactory, another location would be sought. It did in fact prove unsatisfactory, and consequently they were given a tract, eighteen by thirty miles, that fronted on the Missouri River in what is now Thurston County.

Though much of their reservation land was hilly and unsuited to farming, the Omahas raised fairly good crops in the river bottoms and managed to survive with government assistance. Their situation looked good to the Winnebagoes, who, starved out and dried out at their reservation on Crow Creek in South Dakota, began in the fall of 1863 to "visit" the Omahas in increasing numbers. Agent Robert W. Furnas, with the consent of the tribe, did what he could to assist the destitute Winnebagoes, but their presence posed a serious problem. In 1865 Furnas took a delegation of Omaha chiefs to Washington, where they agreed to cede part of their reservation to the Winnebagoes.

In 1858 the Poncas had relinquished all the land they owned or claimed except for a small reserve along the Niobrara River. A mistake in the Treaty of Fort Laramie (1851) included these lands among those assigned to the Lakotas, who made annual raids on the unfortunate Poncas, causing them to lose more than a fourth of their population in unsuccessful efforts to defend themselves. In an effort to solve the problem, the government arbitrarily removed the Poncas to Indian Territory in 1877. Within a year after this forced removal from their historic lands, a third of the tribe had died and most of the remainder were sick.

In 1879 Standing Bear, chief of the Poncas, and a group of followers were arrested as they attempted to return to Nebraska to bury the remains of Standing Bear's son. While being detained near Omaha by the U.S. Army, Standing Bear was interviewed by Omaha newspaperman Thomas H. Tibbles. As a result of the ensuing publicity, two of

During this gathering of government representatives and the delegations of several Indian tribes in Washington DC in December 1857, the Pawnee signed a treaty officially surrendering most of their lands in Nebraska. Courtesy, NSHS, PC1782:1-1.

Omaha's best-known lawyers, Andrew J. Poppleton and John L. Webster, offered their services on behalf of the Poncas. In a celebrated ruling on their petition for a writ of habeas corpus, federal judge Elmer S. Dundy declared that "an Indian is a person within the meaning of the law" and that Standing Bear was being held illegally. The noted chief was freed and allowed to return to northeastern Nebraska, where he lived out his life. The plight of the Poncas attracted nationwide attention, and in 1880 President Rutherford B. Hayes appointed a commission to inquire into the matter. The commission worked out an arrangement whereby Poncas who wanted to return to Nebraska (approximately one-fourth of the tribe's 833 members) were allowed to do so and were allotted lands along the Niobrara in severalty.

Of the semisedentary people the Pawnees were the most troublesome for the government. In 1833, the Pawnees ceded all their lands lying south of the Platte. In 1848 they sold an eighty-mile strip along the Platte, including Grand Island. In a treaty negotiated at Table Creek, just north of Nebraska City, on September 24, 1857, they ceded all their remaining lands in Nebraska, except a fifteen- by thirty-mile tract along the Loup River.

Until they went to the reservation in present-day Nance County, the Pawnees had been a source of irritation to the whites. Although not particularly warlike, the Pawnees had a penchant for plunder which resulted in numerous losses by both travelers on the overland trails and settlers. Even after they had accepted reservation status, they continued to waylay travelers. In the spring of 1859 their activities caused general alarm in the Elkhorn River valley and forced many settlers to abandon their cabins. The territorial militia was called out, but the Pawnees gave up the offending braves without a struggle and promised to keep the peace.

At Table Creek, the government had promised to protect the Pawnees from their hereditary enemies, the Lakotas. This protection, however, was soon withdrawn, and by 1860 the Pawnees were again suffering harassment at the hands of their wide-ranging foes. Whites, too, were constantly encroaching on their territory. As a result, agitation developed within the tribe for removal to Indian Territory. The massacre of a hunting party under Sky Chief by Oglalas and Brules in 1873 convinced many Pawnees that it was useless to try to remain in Nebraska, and by 1875 most of them had moved to Indian Territory. In 1876 their Nebraska reservation lands were formally exchanged for lands in Indian Territory.

Finally, the Santee Sioux, whom white explorers had first encountered along the Mississippi River in northern Minnesota in the early 1700s, ultimately came to reside in northern Nebraska when they were assigned a small reservation in Knox County in 1866. After ceding all of their lands east of the Mississippi River in an 1837 treaty, the Santee were to have been given a reservation in southwestern Minnesota. Disagreements between the tribe and the government, however, had led to the Santee uprising of 1862. After the army had quelled the uprising and executed those deemed to be perpetrators, a Minnesota reserve was judged by the government to be no longer feasible. It finally succeeded in obtaining a reservation in northern Nebraska along the Missouri River. The reservation initially consisted of slightly over 115,000 acres. Aside from a few acres set apart for agency buildings, the lands were later assigned to tribal members in severalty.

THE WESTERN TRIBES

The Treaty of Fort Laramie in 1851 was supposed to bring peace for the tribes located in present-day western Nebraska. In return for annuities, the Lakotas, Cheyennes, and Arapahoes had agreed to certain tribal boundaries, to keep the peace, and to permit the government to build roads and forts in their country. The territory assigned the Lakotas included all land in Nebraska north of the North Platte River, whereas the Cheyennes and Arapahoes were given lands south of the North Platte. From the beginning, however, it was an uneasy peace, little honored by the whites and little understood by the Indians. The tribes tried to observe the terms of the treaty even though, as the commissioner of Indian affairs reported in 1852, "The mountain and prairie Indians continue to suffer from the vast number of immigrants who pass through their country, destroying their means of support, and scattering disease and death among them, yet those who were parties to the treaty concluded at Fort Laramie in the fall of 1851 have been true to their obligations, and have remained at peace among themselves and with the whites."[1] Indian officials continued to report that the tribes were generally quiet and peaceable. Yet underneath a seemingly placid surface smoldered an explosive irritation waiting to be touched off. The spark was struck by the hoof of a lame cow.

On August 17, 1854, a footsore cow belonging to a party of Mormons en route to Utah strayed into a Brule camp. The wandering cow was killed and promptly eaten by the hungry Brule, who had been camped along the North Platte River with other Lakotas waiting for promised food and supplies. The next day the Mormons complained to the commandant at Fort Laramie, who immediately sent a detachment of twenty-nine men with two cannon to the Brule camp with orders to bring in the offender. Heading the detachment was twenty-one-year-old Lieutenant John Grattan, fresh from West Point, inexperienced and contemptuous of Indians. Conquering Bear, chief of the Brules, tried to reason with Lieutenant Grattan, explaining that the cow had actually been killed by a

Minneconjou who was a guest in his camp and for that reason he could not turn the offender over to Grattan. Conquering Bear, attempting to speak through Grattan's drunken interpreter, failed to get his point across; and the impatient lieutenant broke off the discussion, withdrew, and opened fire on the encampment, killing Conquering Bear. In the ensuing struggle, Grattan and all but one of his men were also killed. The Brules, now aroused by fear as well as distrust of the whites, went on to raid the nearby trading posts of Bordeaux and Chouteau.

Throughout the next year, the Lakotas terrorized travelers on the Platte Valley trail. In August 1855, General William S. Harney set out from Fort Leavenworth with twelve hundred men and orders to restore peace on the trail. On September 3, Harney came upon Little Thunder's band of Brules camped on Blue Water Creek near Ash Hollow.[2]

Harney parleyed with Little Thunder until his cavalry was in place, then gave orders to attack.[3] Lieutenant Gouverneur Kemble Warren, an engineer with the Pacific Railway Survey who had been assigned to General Harney during the Lakota campaign, recorded his observations of the battle in his journal: "Wounded women and children [were] crying and moaning, horribly mangled by the bullets. Most of this had been occasioned by the creatures taking refuge in holes in the rocks, and armed Indians sheltering themselves in the same places. These latter fired upon our men killing 2 men & wounding another of the Artillery Company. . . . Two Indian men were killed in the hole and two as they came out. 7 women were killed in the hole & 3 children, 2 of them in their mothers' arms."[4] After this needless massacre, which had instilled even greater fear and distrust of whites into the hearts of the Lakotas, Harney took his captives to Fort Kearny.

Although Lieutenant Warren was sympathetic to the Indians living in the Platte Valley, in his reports he urged the government to extinguish Indian title to the area and encourage white settlement because he believed it provided the most favorable route for the Pacific Railroad. "I think there is no route north of the Arkansas by which the barren portions of our Territory between the Missouri and Rocky Mountains can be passed that is so favorable as the valley of the Platte, and a cheap rail road combining both horse and steam power could be built . . . almost without grading."[5]

From Fort Kearny Harney proceeded to Fort Pierre, where he spent the winter. On his own authority, he assembled the Lakotas at Fort Pierre and forced them to agree to a treaty which restated their willingness to permit white travel along the Platte Valley trail and to the establishment of a military road from Fort Laramie to Fort Pierre. Harney then went down the Missouri River to establish Fort Randall across from the mouth of the Niobrara River.

Though Harney's conduct at Ash Hollow was inexcusable by any but the most primitive standards, his Lakota campaign of 1855–56 seemed to have had the desired effect, at least as far as the army was concerned. The military believed that the Indians could be controlled only by the most stringent measures, and because Harney had brought peace to the trail by applying such measures, his actions supported the military contention.

Representatives of the Indian Service, particularly Thomas S. Twiss, Indian agent on the Upper Platte and stationed at Fort Laramie, bitterly opposed Harney's policies. The army was in the saddle, however, and rode roughshod over such objections. Harney even forbade Twiss to have any communication with the Lakotas, Cheyennes, or Arapahoes.

Harney's peace was short-lived. The Indians, though temporarily cowed, bitterly resented the treatment accorded them at the hands of the army. Peace won by the sword would have to be preserved by the sword; and when the demands of the Civil War drained most of the nation's military strength from the plains the consequences of the maxim would be borne out.

THE CIVIL WAR

Settlers in the Nebraska Territory responded willingly to President Lincoln's call for volunteers to put down the southern rebellion, and Nebraska ranked second among the territories in the number of men furnished for the Union cause. The First Nebraska Infantry (later Cavalry), commanded by Brigadier General John M. Thayer, served at Fort Donelson and Shiloh; and the Curtis Horse Cavalry, made up only partly of Nebraskans and later renamed the Fifth Iowa Cavalry, fought in Tennessee and Alabama.

Securing the Land

The real problem in the Nebraska Territory during the Civil War was to protect the exposed frontier against Indian attack. Alarmed by the Minnesota Sioux uprising during the summer of 1862, Nebraskans through their territorial government petitioned the War Department for authority to organize a regiment of cavalry for home defense. Permission was granted, and the Second Nebraska Cavalry was organized under the command of Colonel Robert W. Furnas. Initially, the regiment, made up of twelve companies, was stationed at various points along the Missouri River from Falls City to Dakota City.

In the summer of 1863 Furnas and nine of the companies joined Brigadier General Alfred Sully and the Sixth Iowa Cavalry in a campaign against the Lakotas in Dakota Territory in a punitive expedition designed to prevent repetition of the difficulties in Minnesota of the year before. At White Stone Hills, two hundred miles above Fort Pierre, Sully's force surprised a Lakota encampment on September 3 and in a bloody battle virtually wiped it out. Having thus demonstrated their strength, the two regiments returned southward, and the Second Nebraska was mustered out at Omaha on November 30, 1863.

The success of Union forces at the Battle of Gettysburg in July 1863 relieved some of the pressure in the East and allowed the army to respond to concerns that the Confederates were trying to organize a general Indian uprising on the plains. On September 19, 1863, eight companies of the Seventh Iowa Cavalry arrived in Omaha destined for service on the plains. The Seventh Iowa pushed on to Fort Kearny and then to Cottonwood Springs, an important point on the trail a short distance east of the forks of the Platte River. In addition to its importance as a stopping place for westbound emigrants and freighters, Cottonwood Springs was a great crossing for Indians going north and south. To break up this movement, the Seventh Iowa established a post near the mouth of Cottonwood Canyon, first known as Camp McKean and later as Fort McPherson. In April 1864, the Eleventh Ohio Cavalry, consisting in part of Confederate prisoners who had taken the oath of allegiance to the Union and had enlisted with the understanding that they would be used only to fight Indians on the frontier, was ordered west to be distributed along the trail from Fort Kearny to Fort Laramie.

Securing the Land

Throughout the spring and summer of 1864 incidents along the South Platte River in Colorado signaled an approaching conflict. It came on August 7, when Cheyennes, Arapahoes, and Brules launched attacks on stagecoaches, emigrant trains, freight trains, stations, and ranches all along the central and western stretches of the Platte Valley. For two days they struck every stage station and ranch between Julesburg and Fort Kearny. Because a warning was telegraphed from Plum Creek station, where they first hit, few lives were lost, but as the attacks spread to the valley of the Little Blue River, where there was no telegraph to warn the settlers and station keepers, the loss of life was considerably greater.

The entire Nebraska frontier was thrown into a state of panic, and settlers in the Platte and Little Blue valleys fled eastward. The First Nebraska Cavalry, recently returned from the South, was recalled from furlough and ordered to Fort Kearny. Major General Samuel R. Curtis, commandant of the Department of Kansas, which included Nebraska, came out from Fort Leavenworth with a small force and, with Brigadier General Robert Mitchell, in command of the District of Nebraska, organized an expedition against the Indians. Though Curtis did not have enough men to move against the Indians in force, he provided escorts for stagecoaches and freight wagons traveling west of Fort Kearny and thus reopened traffic along the overland trail. In addition, several companies of the First Nebraska Cavalry were assigned to guard the Union Pacific Railroad at the Plum Creek station between Forts Kearny and McPherson.

The Indians made no more large-scale attacks but confined themselves to small, sporadic hit-and-run raids against isolated points. As one means of combating the Indians, the army in October set the prairie aflame from Fort Kearny to Julesburg and as far south as the Republican River. The Indians were subdued for a while, but by November 1864 they were again launching attacks all along the trail.

Thus, at the end of the Civil War in April 1865, the Indian problem was more critical than it had been at any time since white settlement of the plains had begun. The Indians were further inflamed when, on November 29, 1865, Colonel J. M. Chivington, formerly the presiding elder in the Nebraska Methodist Conference but now in command of the Third Colorado Cavalry, attacked Black Kettle's band of Cheyennes, who were awaiting peace negotiations and camped on Sand Creek in

Colorado. This bloody massacre, launched without warning on Indians who had voluntarily surrendered, ended any hope for early peace on the plains.

The Chivington outrage caused widespread concern throughout the United States and underscored the contention that the army's policies would never pacify the Indians. After an investigation of the Sand Creek affair, in 1866 Congress created a peace commission to remove, if possible, the causes of the Indian wars and to try to persuade the Indians to give up their nomadic ways and accept reservation status.

But the Indians were in no mood for peace. The Cheyennes who had survived the Sand Creek massacre spread the news and invited all plains and mountain tribes to join them in a general war against the whites. Thus the peace commission found only by the sword could peace be brought to the plains.

THE PEACE POLICY

The Lakotas, with memories of Harney, Sibley, and Sully fresh in their minds, had new grievances by the spring of 1865. Whites, drawn by the discovery of gold in Montana, were moving into the area by the thousands in direct violation of the Fort Laramie Treaty of 1851. Early in 1865, the government announced that it would open a road from Fort Laramie to Montana directly through the heart of the Lakota country. Red Cloud, chief of the Oglalas, bitterly protested this latest violation of his people's rights, and when his protests went unheeded, the Lakotas took to the warpath.

To subdue the Lakotas and open the Bozeman Road to Montana, General Patrick E. Connor was sent into the Powder River country during the summer. The Powder River campaign did little but further infuriate the Indians, and early in the fall Connor's troops were recalled for another try at negotiation.

The added responsibility of protecting the Union Pacific Railroad and the telegraph lines, in addition to a continuing stream of freight and emigrant wagon trains, was a major challenge to the army by 1866. In an effort to make more efficient use of troops and provide a safer trail, an order from General John Pope in February 1866 prohibited wagon trains of fewer than twenty wagons and thirty armed men on the trails in Indian country. Smaller groups were to wait at the nearest fort until they could be combined with others and arrange for military escort.

During the fall of 1865 representatives of the peace commission had negotiated a series of treaties with various bands of Lakotas around Fort Sully, and in the spring of 1866 General Grenville M. Dodge, commandant of the Department of Missouri (which now included Nebraska), persuaded the Brules and Oglalas to come into Fort Laramie for another conference. By June 1, peace terms had been worked out. At this juncture, however, Colonel Henry B. Carrington arrived with a large body of troops to open the Bozeman Road. Red Cloud and Man-Afraid-of-His-Horse withdrew from the conference, and once again the Lakota country was engulfed in war. Carrington went on to garrison Fort Reno and establish Forts Phil Kearny and C. F. Smith. The Indians, now thoroughly disillusioned, gave these isolated posts along the Bozeman Road a great deal of trouble. On December 21, 1866, they wiped out the command of Captain W. J. Fetterman that had been sent out from Fort Phil Kearny to relieve a wood train. Further south, the Indians continued to harass travelers in the Platte Valley and particularly the construction crews of the Union Pacific Railroad. To protect the railroad, Sidney Barracks was established on November 19, 1867.

Meanwhile, in September 1867, the peace commission sent runners through Lakota country to invite the Indians to return to Fort Laramie for a conference. Only a few appeared. Red Cloud sent word that there could be no conference as long as the whites maintained the Bozeman Road. He adhered firmly to this position and did not come in until April 1868, after Forts Phil Kearny and C. F. Smith were officially closed. The Lakotas agreed to confine themselves to the country north of Nebraska and west of the Missouri River, with the understanding that they would be permitted to hunt on their old ranges. They also agreed to allow roads and railroads to be built through their country.

The congressional peace commission published its report in January 1868, calling for a "hitherto untried policy [in connection with Indians] of endeavoring to conquer by kindness."[6] The central feature of the peace policy as adopted by the Grant administration in the spring of 1869 was an "enforced reservation plan for all western Indian tribes."[7]

For all practical purposes, U.S. Indian policy had already been moving in that direction. The Oglalas under Red Cloud, who had accepted a restricted hunting area in 1868, had in principle accepted the idea of a fixed reservation.

Early in 1869 the Brules under Spotted Tail were placed on a reservation at the mouth of Whetstone Creek, eighteen miles northwest of Fort Randall. Red Cloud objected strenuously to going so far east, and finally in 1871 the government agreed to establish his agency on the North Platte River, thirty-two miles below Fort Laramie. In 1871 Spotted Tail, dissatisfied with his location on the Missouri River, persuaded the government to relocate the Brules on the White River in northwest Nebraska. The next year Red Cloud also agreed to accept a White River location near present-day Crawford, about fifty miles upstream from the Brules.

While the army was embroiled with the Lakotas in western and northern Nebraska, peace in the Republican River valley of northern Kansas and southern Nebraska was being threatened by conflict between settlers and the Cheyennes under Chief Tall Bull in the spring of 1869. Tall Bull's band had eluded General Philip H. Sheridan's campaign on the southern plains and moved, along with remnants of other Cheyenne and Lakota bands, into the Republican River valley. In the spring of 1869, increasingly pressed by white settlement in the area, the Indians lashed out in a series of raids, terrorizing settlers. In May Tall Bull's band destroyed a German settlement in Kansas, killing thirteen settlers. Nebraska governor Butler wrote to General Christopher Augur, commanding officer of the Military Department of the Platte, asking for the army's help to bring peace to the area. General Augur responded with an offer to supply guns and ammunition to the settlers to defend themselves until a cavalry detachment could be assembled.

Charged with driving the Indians out of the Republican River country, the Republican River Expedition, which was assembled in June 1869 at Fort McPherson under the command of Major General Eugene Carr, included several companies of the Fifth Iowa Cavalry, the Pawnee Scouts led by Major Frank North, and William "Buffalo Bill" Cody. With the assistance of the Pawnee Scouts, Carr tracked Tall Bull's band through the Republican Valley from June 9 until catching up with and surprising him on July 11 at Summit Springs in Colorado Territory. In the ensuing battle, Tall Bull and some fifty of his followers were killed. General Carr's troops did not suffer a single fatality. It had been a relatively brief but highly successful campaign—a complete rout. The Indians who survived fled north.

The Battle of Summit Springs broke the Cheyennes' hold on the Republican Valley. With the removal of both the Cheyenne and Lakota threat to settlers, the pace of settlement quickened, and the army was now able to devote most of its time to patrol and scouting.

CHAPTER II

The Politics of Statehood

Though pallid in comparison to the bloody conflicts raging in Kansas Territory to the south, politics in Nebraska Territory were also characterized by the excesses all too common to frontier society. Many pioneers seem to have come to Nebraska for the express purpose of carving political careers for themselves in the new territory, others to use politics as a means to financial gain. They lost no time in getting down to business. The same issue of the *Nebraska Palladium*, for example, that reported the arrival of Silas Strickland from Tennessee carried a notice that he was announcing his candidacy for election to the territorial House of Representatives; and J. Sterling Morton attended two political meetings and made a political speech before he had been in the territory a week.

PERSONAL AND SECTIONAL POLITICS

The Democratic Party ruled Nebraska's early politics. The territory had been created by a Democratic Congress and a Democratic administration, and the first governors, secretaries, judges, and other appointive officials were all good Democrats, being rewarded by President Pierce for faithful party service or appointed to strengthen the Democratic cause. The initial counties all bore good Democratic names, except for Washington, named to honor the father of his country: Burt, Cass, Dodge, Douglas, Forney, Pierce, and Richardson.

Within the territory, however, party lines were not sharply drawn, and political contests were frequently decided on personal and sectional considerations, particularly the latter. Individual towns struggled for preferment, and counties south of the Platte made common cause against those north of the river. The first legislature contained twenty-seven Democrats and twelve Whigs, but they had not been elected on the basis of political affiliation. Nor had the delegate to Congress been elected because of party strength. Candidates had appealed for sectional rather than party support.

The legislature, however, soon found itself at odds with the executive. This situation was not unique to Nebraska but was common in all the territories. The federally appointed executive represented outside control and was the symbol of an inferior political status which most territorial residents wished to escape. And even though the executive usually tried to act in the best interest of the territory, legislators, elected by the people of the territory, considered themselves the champions of the people against federal authority.

Legislative independence was strengthened by the doctrine of popular sovereignty. Although in the act creating the territory, this doctrine applied only to the institution of slavery, it was popularly construed as a mandate for the widest possible exercise of local self-government. Moreover, the provision in the Kansas-Nebraska Act which permitted laws passed by the territorial legislature to take effect without submission to Congress for approval greatly strengthened the legislative arm in Nebraska.

Squatter sovereignty was good frontier doctrine, and it was easy to rally local public opinion against acts of the executive on the grounds that they encroached on that sovereignty. Thus those who opposed Governor Cuming's selection of Omaha as the territorial capital denounced his act as a denial of popular sovereignty, the basis of government in the territory:

The doctrine of popular sovereignty is a good doctrine, our faith is in it, and we had expected that here in its new home it would be developed properly, and by its benign influence, put down the cant and hypocrisy which has ever opposed it. But our hopes have thus far proved futile. And though the world abroad may envy us our privileges, it cannot know, and if it could, is too incredulous to believe, that by a conspiracy, headed by one rascal, those privileges and rights have been snatched from us.[1]

Later, when Acting Governor J. Sterling Morton assumed the right to appoint the public printer, formerly selected by the legislature, that act too, was denounced as a denial of popular sovereignty.

These black workers loading wagons in Brownville in 1864 were among a very few blacks in the Nebraska territory where the issue of black suffrage should have been no more than an academic question. Nevertheless, the Nebraska constitution submitted to Congress for approval contained a clause restricting the vote to white males, causing the Republican Congress to hold up Nebraska's admission as a state until the restrictive clause was removed. Courtesy, NSHS, B884:283.

So even good men found it difficult to function effectively as territorial executives, and it was perhaps even more difficult to get good men to accept the appointment. The position of governor paid only $2,500 per year. Nebraska was far from the beaten path, and an appointment to serve there was not looked upon as a stepping-stone to greater things. Shortly after his arrival, Judge Edward R. Harden of the territorial supreme court wrote his wife, who had remained at home in Georgia: "I will start for home, on the very first boat that comes up in the Spring . . . and unless my views, and feelings and opinions undergo a great change, I shall not return. It is a poor country no Timber, sickly, and out of the world and settled up with Savages."[2]

Consequently, appointments often went to the young and inexperienced or to political hacks who needed to be rewarded for faithful, if relatively insignificant, service. Cuming and Morton, who served as acting governor, were both young, inexperienced, and hot-tempered. Mark W.

Izard had good intentions but little else. Samuel W. Black was capable, but repeated stories that he was "in his cups," or intoxicated, much of the time reduced his effectiveness. The only man of stature and experience to serve the territory as governor during the period before the Civil War was Senator Douglas's close friend William A. Richardson of Illinois. As an influential congressman, Richardson had played a large part in the struggle to get the Kansas-Nebraska Act through the House, and before his Nebraska appointment he had been the Democratic candidate for governor of Illinois. He served, however, for less than a year (January 12 to December 5, 1858) and resigned in protest against President Buchanan's proslavery policy in Kansas.

PARTY POLITICS AND THE CIVIL WAR

Local dissatisfaction with the acts of federally appointed officials naturally tended to develop into opposition to the party in power. The strong prosouthern, proslavery attitude of the Buchanan administration alienated Douglas and many northern Democrats. It also gave powerful ammunition to the burgeoning Republican Party and provided additional grounds on which to base opposition to the Democrats, particularly in a territory whose settlers were preponderantly from the North. This situation combined with the president's stance on public lands made life difficult for pro-Buchanan Democrats in Nebraska Territory.

The opposition, however, was slow to commit itself to the Republican Party. Those who opposed the Democrats in the election of 1858 organized as the People's Party and carefully avoided use of the word *Republican*. They sought merely to provide a voice for all those who disapproved of the policies of the national government over the previous six years. Their candidate for delegate to Congress was Samuel G. Daily of Peru, a vigorous campaigner.

The Democrats selected Experience Estabrook, prominent Omaha lawyer and former United States attorney for Nebraska Territory, as their candidate for delegate. The Democrats won control of the legislature and by a narrow margin of three hundred votes elected Estabrook to Congress. Daily immediately contested the election on charges of fraud, and the Republican House of Representatives found that there had been fraud on both sides but less on Daily's and allowed him to take over the seat. This was an old story in Nebraska. Almost every delegate had faced a contest. Indeed, as the *Nebraska Advertiser* complained, "One great reason why so little has heretofore been secured for Nebraska is that she has never yet had a delegate so situated that he could work for the territory; he has always devoted the most of his time to watching and defending his seat."[3]

By the election of 1860, the issues were more clearly drawn. The People's Party switched its allegiance to the Republicans and at its convention at Plattsmouth aligned itself enthusiastically behind Abraham Lincoln and Hannibal Hamlin. For delegate, it nominated Samuel G. Daily. The Democrats, meeting in Omaha, nominated J. Sterling Morton, secretary of the territory, who though only twenty-seven years old, was easily one of the most prominent men in Nebraska. Both parties campaigned enthusiastically for federally supported internal improvements in the territory. The Republicans, in addition, insisted that the election of Lincoln was essential to prevent slavery from encroaching further upon freedom.

The Democrats, embarrassed by the national split in their party, contended that since residents of the territory had no vote in the presidential election, local issues were the only ones worth considering. Morton, sensing Buchanan's unpopularity in the territory and his own vulnerability as a Buchanan appointee, early in the campaign declared himself to be a Douglas Democrat. This declaration was vigorously disputed by the Republicans and particularly by Robert W. Furnas, editor of the influential *Brownville Advertiser*, who had initially been a Douglas Democrat but had joined the Republicans by 1860.

This first contest between Republicans and Democrats in Nebraska brought together two of the best stump speakers in the territory. Daily, thirty-seven, a lawyer who also owned a sawmill, had been an active free-soiler in Indiana before moving to Nebraska. He had served a term in the Nebraska territorial legislature and had been a leading spirit in the organization of the Republican Party. Morton, though ten years his opponent's junior, was even better known and was a brilliant speaker and an aggressive debater. According to the custom of the time, the campaign consisted of a series of joint debates, which were followed avidly by the territorial press.

When the returns were in, Morton was declared elected by a vote of 2,957 to 2,943. Daily immediately filed a notice of contest, making twelve specific charges of fraud and irregularity. Morton responded with a vigorous denial and countered his opponent's dozen charges of fraud and irregularity with seventeen of his own. The two men spent the winter collecting evidence to support their charges, and it soon became clear that there was plenty of evidence on both sides.

Territorial elections were conducted in a free and easy manner, and a little manipulation was the rule rather than the exception. To complicate matters further, Governor Black, who had become estranged from Morton both personally and politically, issued Daily a second certificate of election. When the House of Representatives finally got around to considering the matter in May 1862, it was almost impossible to determine who was rightfully entitled to the seat. The House decided the question on purely partisan grounds and gave the seat to Daily.

The Civil War was demoralizing to Democrats in Nebraska, as it was all over the North. Forced to make peace with the Republicans because of the need to preserve the Union, they would only go so far. They refused to forget their differences with the radical elements of the Republican Party and give up the Democratic label. Democratic refusal to disband the party for the sake of unity against the common enemy, the South, was looked upon as giving aid and comfort to the enemy. Because the southerners who were attempting to destroy the Union were Democrats, it was easy to argue that all Democrats were anti-Union and disloyal.

The change in administration robbed Nebraska Democrats of federal patronage. Alvin Saunders of Mount Pleasant, Iowa, was appointed by President Lincoln to replace Governor Black, who went back to Pennsylvania to lead a regiment and was killed in battle. Morton was succeeded as territorial secretary by Algernon S. Paddock, who had immigrated to the territory in 1857 and had been active in the formation of the Republican Party there. Surprisingly, against such odds, the Democrats maintained considerable strength during the Civil War. Not until the area began filling up with Union veterans did the Democrats became a minority party in Nebraska.

The Civil War was not popular in Nebraska, largely because the demands of war reduced the garrisons at Fort Kearny and throughout the plains and exposed the entire frontier to Indian attacks. Led by Morton, the Democrats kept up a steady drumfire of criticism against Lincoln's conduct of the war. Morton skirted close to Copperheadism with his references to "black republicanism," implying that Lincoln and the Republicans perpetuated the war solely for the cause of abolitionism, and the Democratic Party picked up on the slur by referring to the "black flag of Republicanism" in its 1862 platform.[4]

Sometimes political contests were close. In 1862, the Republican candidate, Samuel G. Daily, won reelection as territorial delegate to Congress by a margin of only 136 votes, and Republican David Butler defeated Morton for the governorship in 1866 by only 145 votes. But the tide was running against the Democrats, and these near misses were evidence that most Nebraskans failed to identify with the Democrats' intransigent opposition to Lincoln's program.

Aside from the overriding necessity to preserve the Union, the Republicans in Nebraska were greatly aided by the enactment in 1862 of a free homestead law, a measure the previous Democratic administration under Buchanan had consistently opposed. In 1864, Nebraska Republicans, who had adopted the Union Party label, won an overwhelming victory when Phineas W. Hitchcock defeated Dr. George L. Miller in the race for congressional delegate. Though Miller had been inclined toward a moderate course, he had been saddled with the intransigent anti-Lincoln platform of the Democrats nationally as well as locally. The impressive Republican victory of 1864 convincingly demonstrated that the people of the North were tired of the political sniping about Lincoln's conduct of the war. In the nation the Republicans went on to a successful conclusion of the war and the preservation of the Union; in Nebraska, they turned their attention to bringing the territory into the Union as a state.

THE STRUGGLE OVER STATEHOOD

Nebraskans, schooled in an environment of manifest destiny and expansionism, regarded territorial status as temporary and looked forward to early statehood. Though conscious of this generally popular goal, politicians were aware of the importance of timing in its achievement, an attitude conditioned by an assessment of their own chances of gaining the desired offices that would be created as a result of statehood.

As early as 1858, the *Omaha Times* urged that the question of statehood be submitted to the people, and in 1859 both parties declared their support for immediate statehood. On January 11, 1860, the legislature authorized a special election to be held on March 5 to determine whether a convention should be called to frame a state constitution. Politicians of both parties became suddenly wary of the proposition and so complicated it with sectional and partisan questions that, as election day drew near, it became apparent that obtaining a true expression of public sentiment on the issue of statehood would be impossible. The Republicans won forty of the fifty-two delegate positions to the constitutional convention, but the voters rejected the call for a constitutional convention.

Following this fiasco, the issue of statehood remained dormant for nearly four years. In January 1864 a majority of the legislature, Republicans and Democrats alike, memorialized Congress to pass legislation making statehood possible. On April 19, Congress responded with an act authorizing the people of Nebraska to form a state government. Republicans in Congress, who viewed Nebraska as safe for their party, had promoted the enabling act in the hope of getting partisan reinforcements from west of the Missouri. On June 6, 1864, Governor Saunders ordered an election of delegates to a constitutional convention, which was to meet on July 4.

The dormant Democrats came out strongly against statehood, charging that the real leadership of their party was not in the legislature. They put forth the convincing argument that taxes would be increased, for in addition to those already paid, the people of the state would have to raise the amount currently supplied by the federal government. The argument was effective. An overwhelming majority of the delegates elected were opposed to statehood, and when the convention met in the territorial capitol in Omaha it adjourned immediately without forming a constitution.

The proponents of statehood were not deterred by this surprise defeat. Though the issue had not been debated in the legislative campaign of 1865, Governor Saunders had devoted a considerable portion of his January 9, 1866, message to the eleventh legislature to the advantages of early statehood, declaring that he had "the assurances of many of the most intelligent and influential men of both political parties that the people of the Territory are anxious to have this subject acted upon at as early a day as practical . . . [and that he had] no hesitancy . . . in giving . . . [his] candid opinion that the resources of Nebraska would be sooner developed, and her wealth and population increased by becoming a State, than if she remains a Territory."[5] A constitutional convention was unnecessary, he declared, suggesting instead that the legislature might adopt a constitution and submit it to the people for approval.

Though the legislators appear to have had little initial enthusiasm for statehood, the governor and other Republican territorial officials apparently were determined to push it through. A voluntary committee, the full composition of which is not known, met secretly to draft a constitution. Consisting of both Democrats and Republicans, it probably included Governor Saunders, Secretary Paddock, Chief Justice William Pitt Kellogg, William A. Little, Hadley D. Johnson, Experience Estabrook, and O. P. Mason. When they had completed their work, they turned the document over to J. R. Porter, the only Democrat of any prominence in the legislature who favored statehood. Porter introduced it in the Senate on February 5, 1866. Under pressure from Governor Saunders and other federal officials, the issue became a party matter, and the constitution was pushed through the legislature in a way that would have been unusual for even the most minor, noncontroversial measure.

On the day it was introduced, the constitution was referred to a special committee consisting of Porter and two others, who reported it back favorably later in the day, just in time for the Senate to pass it before adjourning. The vote was seven to six, with President Mason casting the deciding ballot. Four days later the constitution was approved by the House, and on the ninth day Governor Saunders signed the bill. The constitution had not been printed for the use of members of either house, no amendments had been permitted, and in the lower house it was not referred to a committee. Only a few of the legislators had more than a vague notion of the new constitution's provisions.

When the document finally became available for examination, it was found to be simply an instrument to establish a state government, with very little provision for its functioning. Because the argument of expense had been used so effectively in 1864, the goal apparently was to set up as cheap a government as possible. The governor, for example, was limited to a salary of $1,000 per year, and the salaries of other officials were in proportion: auditor, $800; secretary of state, $600; treasurer, $400. The justices of the supreme court were to get $2,000 per year, and members of the legislature $3 per day. The sessions were limited to forty days.

The constitution had been accompanied by a joint resolution providing for a special election on June 9, 1866, to vote on the instrument and for state officers if the constitution were adopted. The Republicans adopted a platform favoring the constitution and nominated a ticket headed by former territorial legislator David Butler of Pawnee City, who had come to the territory from Indiana in 1859.

The Democrats were divided. One faction, headed by J. Sterling Morton, wanted to refuse to nominate a ticket and based their campaign on opposition to the constitution. Others, particularly Dr. George L. Miller, now editor of the newly established, but already powerful *Omaha Herald*, argued that it would be unwise merely to oppose the constitution. Statehood, he argued, could not be delayed for long; the territory was filling up as settlement advanced well beyond the counties along the Missouri River. The people of the territory were becoming wealthier and more numerous, and they wanted the advantages of statehood, including equal representation in Congress. In the end, the Democrats nominated Morton for governor and adopted a platform that was noncommittal on the proposed constitution.

This first campaign for state offices in Nebraska was characterized by all the excitement that had marked territorial political struggles. The press of each side attacked the other in a fury of frenzied partisanship. The opposing candidates denounced each other with unbridled license. In addition to Morton, who was judged by friend and foe to be the most gifted political entertainer in Nebraska, the Democrats had the services of George Francis Train, an eccentric world traveler who was temporarily residing in Omaha. Train stumped the territory in a white suit, perhaps the first ever seen in Nebraska. Butler was a strong debater, and his seemingly unaffected sincerity was more useful in reaching the sensibilities of the majority than was Morton's brilliant wit. Butler combined his favorite expression, "I thank God from my heart of hearts," with an effort to impugn his opponent's loyalty in the late war.[6] Waving the bloody shirt proved to be as effective for the Republicans in Nebraska as elsewhere in the nation.

The election results were close and, like so many times in the past, were ultimately determined by those who counted the votes rather than by those who cast them. The Cass County board of canvassers, for example, threw out the entire vote of Rock Bluffs precinct (107 for Morton, 50 for Butler) on technical grounds but allowed the heavily pro-Butler vote at Plattsmouth to stand even though the same supposed technical irregularity had prevailed. The almost unanimously Republican soldier vote from Fort Kearny was allowed to stand. Once counted, the official returns showed the constitution approved by a vote of 3,938 to 3,838 and Butler elected by a vote of 4,093 to 3,984. The Republican victory was complete. Their entire ticket, except for O. P. Mason, who was running for chief justice, was elected. Ironically, William A. Little, who defeated Mason, died before he could take office and Mason was appointed in his stead.

Nebraska's statehood soon ran into difficulties in Washington. The new Nebraska constitution had restricted suffrage to free white males. This was not an oversight caused by the way the constitution had been rushed through the legislature. The House of Representatives, by the resounding margin of thirty-six to two, had voted down a resolution to strike the restriction.

Black suffrage had been debated by all the territorial legislatures during the war, but Nebraska had few slaves or free blacks so the question was little more than academic. Only four slaves were listed in the Nebraska territorial census of 1854, and from 1855, when Sally Bayne arrived in Omaha, becoming the first free black to settle in Nebraska Territory, the number of black settlers had increased by only twenty-four when the territorial census was taken in 1860. Even so, the Republican Congress was both surprised and disappointed that the Republican position on black suffrage was not affirmed in the constitution of the presumably safe territory of Nebraska.

Senator George Edmunds of Vermont moved to amend Benjamin Wade's bill admitting Nebraska as a state to provide that the act would take effect "with the fundamental and perpetual condition that . . . there shall be no abridgement or denial of the exercise of the elective franchise or of any other right to any person by reason of race or color, excepting Indians not taxed."[7] The Radical Republicans in the Senate, led by Edmunds and Sumner, denounced the constitution as a rebel document, but the moderates, led by Wade and Sherman, did not feel that the restriction was of much importance. After all, twenty of the twenty-six states then constituting the Union had similar restrictions. The more important consideration was that Nebraska be admitted without further delay because its population already exceeded that of most new states, and public lands were rapidly being claimed. Senator Reverdy Johnson of Maryland argued that Congress had no constitutional right to interfere with state suffrage requirements. The moderates, however, gave way to the Radicals, and the bill passed the Senate with the Edmunds amendment. The Senate also accepted a House amendment requiring the Nebraska legislature to be convened and agree to the said "fundamental condition," which was to be considered part of the organic law, and Nebraska should then be admitted without further congressional action. President Andrew Johnson, already at loggerheads with the Radicals, vetoed the bill on constitutional grounds, but Congress promptly passed the bill over his veto on February 9, 1867.

Governor Saunders called both the state and territorial legislatures into special session on February 20 to consider the "fundamental condition." In a two-day session, the legislature promptly passed the necessary act, which negated the restrictive provision in the constitution. Acting as an intermediary between Congress and the territory, General John M. Thayer carried a certified copy of the act back to Washington, and on March 1, 1867, President Johnson reluctantly signed a proclamation admitting Nebraska as the thirty-seventh state.

CHAPTER 12

Establishing the
State Government

When admitted to the Union as a state in 1867 Nebraska consisted of only
a little more than a fifth of the area that had been organized as a territory
in 1854. The territory's 351,558 square miles had included a vast area which
people assumed in 1854 and for several years thereafter would never be
settled. This assumption proved just as erroneous as the earlier belief that
the entire region west of the Missouri could not sustain settlement.

While settlers began occupying the lands along the Missouri River and
in the eastern Platte River valley, others pushed still farther west. On
February 28, 1861, in response to demands from miners and others in the
Rocky Mountain region, Colorado Territory was organized, decreasing
the area of Nebraska Territory by 16,035 square miles. Three days later, in
anticipation of ultimate statehood for the settled portion of Nebraska, the
territory's area was reduced by 228,907 square miles through the creation
of Dakota Territory. In 1863 the organization of Idaho Territory brought
about a further reduction so by the time the state was admitted in 1867
it consisted of 75,995 square miles. The annexation of the Sioux reserve
(now Boyd County) in 1890 and several minor changes increased the total
land and water area of the state to its present 77,355 square miles.

In 1867 the area admitted as a state was on the threshold of the rapid
development of mechanized commercial farming that would transform
it from empty prairie to a settled commonwealth. The almost complete
dependency of the state's economic, political, and social life on agriculture would be reflected in alternate periods of prosperity and depression,
fluctuations that were often violent during the developing years. Moreover, the early years of statehood constituted a period of trial-and-error
experimentation in the development not only of commercial agriculture

143

and the distribution of its products but of agricultural techniques suitable to the plains.

The state government would suffer from having to operate under the hastily drawn and inadequate constitution of 1866 as well as from the demands of an unstable economy. Even more serious, the years in which Nebraska's state government was being established were characterized by gross public immorality in financial matters, especially an all-too-general practice of using public funds for private gain. As a result, the state government soon became engulfed in scandals that sapped its effectiveness and came close to threatening its very existence.

ORGANIZATION

Between the adoption of the constitution on June 2, 1866, and admission to the Union on March 1, 1867, Nebraska had a curious mixture of state and territorial governments. Governor Butler called the first state legislature into session on July 4, 1866. The only business transacted before adjournment on July 11 was the election of two United States senators. As had been the case in the contest over the constitution and the election of general officers, the action of the Cass County board of canvassers in throwing out the heavily pro-Democratic vote of Rock Bluffs Precinct was decisive. The House and Senate upheld this action and seated four Republican representatives and one Republican senator from Cass County instead of the five Democrats who would have been elected if the Rock Bluffs vote had been included. By a straight party vote of twenty-nine to twenty-one, the legislature elected John M. Thayer and Thomas W. Tipton over Andrew J. Poppleton and J. Sterling Morton.

On February 20 and 21, 1867, the state legislature met in special session with the territorial assembly to consider the "fundamental condition" imposed by Congress relative to admission. A second special session convened on May 16, 1867, to enact general laws was actually the third session. Because of the wrangle in Congress over its constitution, Nebraska's transition from territorial status to statehood was more complicated than that of any other Louisiana Purchase state.

In calling the special session of May 16, Governor Butler listed thirty-one subjects for legislative consideration. Among them were selection

When Lancaster, soon to be known as Lincoln, was selected as the site of the new state capital in 1867, it showed little promise as a city. From this 1868 photograph of Lincoln's business district, it is little wonder that critics claimed the new state capital "was destined for isolation and ultimate oblivion." Courtesy, NSHS, L741:38b.

and management of lands the state would get from the federal government; free schools and their support; creation of counties: revision of the general incorporation laws; appropriations; encouragement of immigration; and the location and construction of public buildings. Probably the most important item of business, though by no means given the most attention at the time, was the selection and management of state lands. Nebraska received slightly more than 3.5 million acres from the federal government.

This gift of land was one of the primary arguments in favor of statehood; the fact that good lands in the eastern part of the state were rapidly being taken up was advanced as an imperative for early statehood. By the time the state government got around to locating its lands, the railroads, purchasers, and homesteaders had indeed occupied a large portion of the choicest, most accessible land, and the state had to locate much of its land in the northern and western areas. The lands set aside for the erection of

Table 3. Lands Received by Nebraska from the
Federal Government upon Statehood (acres)

Common school endowment	2,797,520.67
Public buildings at capital	12,751.05
Penitentiary	32,034.01
State university	45,439.93
Agricultural college	89,140.21
Saline lands	48,893.37
Internal improvements	500,812.00
Total	3,526,591.84

public buildings and the penitentiary were among the first selected and sold. The internal improvement lands were almost immediately absorbed by various railroad companies, some of which had been organized solely to get benefits under the act, although grants of a thousand acres each were made to Gage and Saline Counties for the construction of bridges across the Blue River. The disposition of the saline lands was involved and complicated, but most of them were sold to provide an endowment for the normal school at Peru. The state held on to its university and agricultural college lands until about 1880, after which the landed endowment was gradually converted from real estate to cash.

The common school lands, by far the most important part of the gift, became involved in a succession of political disputes that continue to the present day. Initially, the state proposed to build up its school endowment through the sale of these lands, but this plan was beset with so many abuses that in 1897 such a sale was forbidden and a system of leases substituted.

Ranchers in the central and western part of the state, where most of the school lands were located, were dissatisfied with the lease system from the beginning. The legislature, over the veto of Governor Frank B. Morrison, repealed the ban on sale in 1965. By this time it could be argued that investment of the proceeds from sale of the lands in securities would provide a more productive endowment for the common schools than the land itself.

Of more immediate interest to the politicians of the new state was the location of the capital. As had been true in the early years of the territory, this question tended to overshadow all public problems. Actually, there was little need for a change. The territorial capitol at Omaha, constructed in 1857–58, was highly suitable and probably could have been used for some years with only minor repairs. Transportation facilities and the distribution of population also gave Omaha an advantage over any other point that could have been selected. Relocation of the capital, nevertheless, became the first order of business. South Platte legislators were determined almost unanimously that the capital should not remain in Omaha. Omaha newspapers charged that they obtained sufficient votes for their removal scheme by supporting a land grant to the North Nebraska Airline Railroad, whose incorporators were almost all state officials and members of the legislature from north of the Platte.

After a spirited contest, the legislature passed a bill on June 4, 1867, providing that the governor, the secretary of state, and the auditor should constitute a commission to locate the seat of government on a section of land within "the County of Seward, the south half of the counties of Saunders and Butler, and that portion of the county of Lancaster lying north of the south line of township nine."[1] The commissioners were to have the site surveyed and platted and then sell lots at public auction. The proceeds would be held as a state building fund. In the original bill, the seat of government was to be known as Capitol City. This unfortunate name was dropped when Senator J. N. H. Patrick of Omaha, in an effort to draw South Platte Democratic votes away from the measure, moved that it be called Lincoln. The name still was anathema to many Democrats, but sectional loyalty overrode political considerations, and South Platte Democrats promptly approved the new name. The act further provided that the state university and state agricultural college, combined as one institution, as well as the state penitentiary, should also be located at Lincoln.

THE NEW CAPITAL CITY

The bill relocating the seat of government was approved on June 14, 1867, and four days later Governor Butler, Secretary of State Thomas P.

Kennard, and Auditor John Gillespie assembled at Nebraska City to make preparations to examine the area named in the legislation. Having secured an outfit and employed Augustus F. Harvey as surveyor, the commissioners set out on their tour on July 18, 1867. They made a cursory survey of all eligible sites and on July 29 returned to the vicinity of Yankee Hill and Lancaster, on the banks of Salt Creek. At Lancaster "the favorable impressions received at first sight . . . were confirmed." They described it thus:

We found a gently undulating surface, its principal elevation being near the center of the proposed new site. The village already established being in the midst of a thrifty and considerable agricultural population; rock, timber and water power available within short distances. The centre of the great Saline region within two miles, and in addition to all other claims. The especial advantage was that the location was at the center of a circle of about 110 miles in diameter along or near the circumference of which are the Kansas State line, directly south, and the important towns of Pawnee City, Nebraska City, Plattsmouth, Omaha, Fremont, and Columbus.[2]

The removal act had directed the commissioners to locate the capital on state lands, although title to the lands selected by the state had not yet been confirmed by the federal government. Fearing delay or even possible failure to receive title, the commissioners entertained a proposition from various people residing in the vicinity as well as the Lancaster Seminary Association, whose building had burned in 1866, to donate land for the new city. Meeting in the house of W. T. Donavan of Lancaster on the afternoon of the July 29, the commissioners unanimously agreed to accept the proposition.

Sites further south or east might have been preferable, but the commissioners' obsession with the potential value of the saline deposits carried the day for Lancaster so the capital city was located directly within the salt basin. Later inhabitants were not so favorably impressed with the basin, and Lincoln developed almost solely to the south and east, as far away from the salt deposits as possible. Many legends tell about Indians, trappers, and others coming great distances to secure their supply of this precious mineral at the salt basin. From early territorial days there had been an interest in commercial development of the salt deposits, but nothing of substance ever materialized.

Omahans and many others living along the Missouri River and north of the Platte River severely criticized the choice and spoke disparagingly of the new city's prospects. "Nobody will ever go to Lincoln," predicted the *Omaha Republican*, "who does not go to the legislature, the lunatic asylum, the penitentiary, or some of the state institutions."[3] Founded on fiat, with "no river, no railroad, no steam wagon, nothing," the new capital was thought to be destined for isolation and ultimate oblivion.[4]

The capital commissioners, however, went ahead with the building of their paper city. On August 14, 1867, they formally announced their decision. The next day Harvey and A. B. Smith began surveying the site, and by August 17 the commissioners gave notice that the first sale of lots would be held one month later on September 17. Meanwhile, they had reserved twelve acres each for the capitol, the state university, and a city park. Additional lots were set aside for ten different churches, the Lancaster County courthouse, a city hall and market space, a state historical library association, public schools, the Independent Order of Good Templars, the Independent Order of Odd Fellows, and the Ancient Free and Accepted Masons.

Initial lot sales were highly disappointing. The weather on September 17 was cold and rainy, which may have dampened the ardor of bidders already beset by doubts that the enterprise could ever succeed. The first lot offered brought only twenty-five cents on an appraised value of $40, and the entire day's sales amounted to only about one-tenth of the commissioners' expectations. Realizing that something must be done to prevent the project from collapsing, the commissioners arranged secretly with James Sweet and a group from Nebraska City to bid the appraised value for every lot up to $10,000 worth of lots, with the understanding that any party bidding more than the appraised value on any lot should have it. They also agreed that unless $15,000 worth of lots were sold, in addition to the $10,000 held by the Nebraska City Trustees, the auction would be called off. Under the impetus of this forced bidding, the second day was much more successful, and at the end of the five-day sale in Lincoln, $34,342.25 worth of lots had been sold at prices ranging from $40 to $150. Additional sales at Nebraska City and Omaha during the next two weeks produced an additional $19,750.50, and the success of the project seemed assured.

The commissioners now began construction of the capitol. At that time there were no architects in Lincoln, and those in Omaha ignored advertisements for such service. Finally, in response to an advertisement in the *Chicago Tribune*, James Morris of that city prepared a plan for a central structure, with wings to be added. It was not very imposing, but it was the only plan received so it was accepted. The commissioners realized that if they did not have the plans for the capitol building ready when the legislature convened in January 1869, the legislature might never meet in Lincoln. They received only one bid in response to the advertisement for construction, and, again under the pressure of time, they accepted it.

Once the contract was let, the next problem was finding materials. Finally, a limestone quarry near Beatrice was able to provide satisfactory stone, and all of the teams that could be hired were put on the road to haul the building stone to Lincoln. This work was slow at best, but by December 1, 1868, the capitol was ready for occupancy. It had cost $75,000, although it was supposed to have been built for $40,000, and was so poorly constructed that it had to be replaced after a dozen years of service.

With the capitol built and the legislature in session, Lincoln's prospects improved considerably. On the last day of the session, February 15, 1869, the legislature approved the act chartering the University of Nebraska. The beginnings of that institution, which played an important role in the development of Lincoln, were as uncertain and confused as those of the capital city itself. Even before the first day of classes, the new university was subjected to severe criticism. In 1870 the State Teachers Association contended that it was impractical to establish a university and that the state should concentrate its efforts on building preparatory and subordinate schools. Internal wrangling among the regents over the management of the university, as well as the wisdom of its establishment, hampered its chances for success. Sectional jealousy from towns that had wanted the university also worked against it once its location in Lincoln was decided. Nevertheless, construction went ahead, and by the fall of 1871 the university had one building and a faculty of five and was ready to receive students.

The much-desired railroad connection was achieved in the summer of 1870, when the Burlington and Missouri River Railroad, which had been built from Plattsmouth to Lincoln, began striking off in a southwestwardly direction to connect the capital city with the rapidly developing South Platte country. The rail connection and the construction of the capitol, the university, a penitentiary, and an insane asylum seemed to provide evidence that the paper city was going to become a reality. During 1867 investors had been hesitant about risking money in the enterprise. Beginning in 1868, however, confidence increased, and by 1870 the town had a population of 2,500. It was off to a good start, but its future was by no means secure. Scandals in state government, which were associated in the public mind with the Lincoln promoters, threatened the young capital city's existence and, for a time, even the stability of the state government.

SCANDAL AND IMPEACHMENT

In their haste to construct the capitol building and develop the city of Lincoln, the capital commissioners sometimes ignored the law; at other times they proceeded in a highly irregular manner. To begin with, instead of locating the capital on state lands as the law had directed, they accepted a site donated by the people of Lancaster. Then, in their effort to encourage land sales, they allowed certain buyers, including themselves, to speculate in Lincoln town lots without advancing money for them. Finally, the commissioners had refused to turn receipts from lot sales over to the state treasurer, Augustus Kountze, as the law required, on the grounds that Kountze was an Omaha man and probably would not release the money for construction of public buildings in Lincoln. Kountze had, in fact, earlier declared that inasmuch as the commissioners had not filed bonds with him, as required by the law, he would receive money but would not honor their requests for payment.

Though Democratic and anti-Lincoln newspapers hammered away at the commissioners' irregularities, the legislature of 1869, which was meeting in the new capitol building in Lincoln, generally approved their activities. The Lincoln lot sales had brought in much more money than had been expected, the capital city enterprise was an apparent success, and the state was experiencing great growth. The papers credited the success of these ventures to the energetic work of Governor Butler and his associates, all of whom had been reelected in 1868. Most people seemed inclined to ignore the occasions when they had overstepped the law. Even the fact that the capitol building had cost almost twice as much as had been approved was excused by a joint resolution of the House and Senate that the commissioners had "been governed by an honest purpose to subserve the best interests of the state."[5] Unfortunately, the governor and his associates continued to act as though they assumed the people of the state would continue to overlook technical irregularities in appreciation of their great service to the public. They were wrong; the air was soon heavy with charges.

The governor was charged with having entered into a contract that exceeded the amount appropriated for the construction of the university building without the consent of the Board of Regents. In addition, the contract for the insane asylum had been let in excess of the amount appropriated and to a contractor who could not post bond and who was, at the same time, erecting palatial residences for both the governor and the secretary of state. Further, the governor had lent $40,000 of the school funds to friends, with inadequate security, as personal or political favors. These funds were to have been invested only in United States or state securities. Butler had also speculated illegally in Lincoln lots and had profited greatly. All these and other charges, including the acceptance of bribes from contractors, railroads, and private individuals, were freely and openly discussed.

As Governor Butler began campaigning for a third term in 1870, there was strong sentiment in the legislature for impeachment. A joint committee of both houses was appointed to investigate the activities of the commissioners. Butler treated the appointment of the committee solely as the work of his political enemies in an attempt to destroy him both as a private citizen and as a public official. The stories, he declared, were mere gossip. He did not deny that, as governor, he had exceeded instructions, but he declared that the exigencies of the situation demanded that he do so, and he had acted in the best interests of the state. Typical, perhaps, was his response to the charge that he had illegally loaned state funds to private individuals. He argued that United States bonds were depreciating rapidly at that time, and the individuals to whom he had loaned state school fund money provided better security. Besides, it was in the state's interest to circulate the money to keep business flourishing in the state.

While indicating that there was legitimate ground for many of the charges against Butler, the committee's report generally absolved the governor and his associates of any evil intent. Speculation in Lincoln lots, for example, was looked upon as an act of faith in the capital city. Furthermore, the committee reasoned, the commissioners had wisely recognized that not enough money had been appropriated to build public buildings. The people also apparently accepted the governor's explanation. Though his majority was smaller than those of other Republican candidates, Butler was reelected to a third term in 1870 over John R. Croxton by a vote of 11,126 to 8,648.

The governor's many enemies were not so easily satisfied. When the eighth session of the legislature convened in 1871, Edward Rosewater, a Republican from Omaha, introduced an entirely new element in the charges. He asked Butler to account for funds collected from the federal government for school lands sold before the state's admission. The governor replied that he had collected the money, which amounted to $16,881.26, and had deposited it with the state treasurer. When neither the treasurer's nor the auditor's books showed any account of the transaction, the governor was again confronted with the question. This time Butler admitted that he had not deposited the money but instead had borrowed it for his own use. He assured the legislature, however, that it was adequately secured by Pawnee County land mortgages.

The governor's opponents quickly realized that this was a charge they could push effectively. Though influential voices continued to argue that impeachment proceedings would be expensive and would cast great discredit upon the new state, the Nebraska House of Representatives on March 6, 1871, approved eleven articles of impeachment against the governor. The first charge, and the only one on which the Senate would vote to convict, was that Butler had appropriated for his own use school funds that had been collected from the federal government. The remaining ten articles were simply revisions of old charges.

The trial before the Senate revealed an incredible laxity in the handling of the state's financial affairs. Auditor John Gillespie, who by this time had turned against Butler, was impeached for malfeasance in office but was not convicted. James Sweet, who had succeeded Kountze as state treasurer, was severely criticized but not impeached. Sweet and his deputy, Nelson Brock, owned the bank in which all state funds were deposited. Not only had they failed to keep state funds segregated from their private accounts, they did not even identify them as state accounts. State deposits were entered under the name of "John Rix," making it impossible to determine from an examination of the books that there were any state funds in the bank. Much of the money ultimately identified as state funds, the trial brought out, had been lent on real estate mortgages at usurious rates of interest.

On June 1, the Senate voted, nine to three, to convict the governor of having misappropriated state funds. He was acquitted of the remaining charges. The punishment, adopted by a vote of eleven to one, was to remove him from office. Since Nebraska's constitution at that time did not provide for a lieutenant governor, the secretary of state, William H. James, who had been serving as acting governor during the proceedings, completed the remainder of the term. Butler retired to his farm in Pawnee County and resumed his stock raising as successfully as if he had never left it. The legislature authorized a commission, consisting of the governor, secretary of state, and treasurer, to settle the state's claim of $23,633.74 against Butler. In 1874 the commission took a deed for 3,392.16 acres in Pawnee, Jefferson, and Gage Counties, believed to be the amount necessary to settle the total claim. Actually, by 1895, when the last parcel of land from the settlement was sold, the state had recovered a total of $27,635.32.

After several unsuccessful attempts, Butler's friends in the legislature finally got the impeachment proceedings expunged from the record in 1877. They were unsuccessful, however, in getting an appropriation to reimburse him for losses suffered at the hands of the state. In 1882 Butler was elected to the state Senate as an Independent, and in 1888 he ran for governor again, this time as the Union Labor Party's candidate.

A survey of the record of the case and the times suggests that the people generally did not expect rigid honesty in the handling of public affairs and that Nebraska's first governor was as unfortunate as he was malfeasant. Certainly, in the minds of many, David Butler's great service in building the state and its new capital city overrode any irregularities in the performance of his office. These irregularities, however, cast a shadow upon the capital city and all the public institutions located there, which hindered their development for some years.

CHAPTER 13

Years of Settlement

Nebraska was home to approximately 50,000 people when it became a state in 1867. Three years later, the U.S. Census of 1870 would show a population of 122,993. In 1854 2,732 persons had been scattered in small clusters along the Missouri River. By 1867 the population stretched westward one hundred miles south of the Platte River, forming an irregular but almost continuous line running south from Columbus to a point near Fairbury. North of the Platte River the valley was settled from its mouth to Grand Island, with a few homesteaders on the Elkhorn River as far north as Norfolk and a fringe of settlement along the Missouri from Sioux City to the mouth of the Niobrara.

More than three-fourths of the territorial population at the time of the census of 1860 was native-born, and for the most part they represented a stream of migration which had moved out across the Old Northwest from New England and the Middle Atlantic states. The leading native states of the population were, in order, Ohio, New York, Pennsylvania, Illinois, Iowa, Indiana, and Missouri. Of the foreign-born, Germans were the largest group, more than one-fourth of the total, followed by English and Irish, each of which accounted for nearly one-fourth. Many of the foreign-born were concentrated in Omaha, accounting for 60 percent of Douglas County's population, although they made up 51 percent of the population of Platte and Madison Counties, 49 percent of that of Kearney County, 33 percent in Dakota, and 25 percent in Otoe. Hall County, with a population of only 116, was predominantly German.

The years immediately following the Civil War saw the beginning of a flow of immigration into Nebraska, which continued almost unabated for two and a half decades despite political and economic uncertainties. By the 1890s the state had a nearly static population. Population census figures dramatically show both the expansion and the leveling off.

Table 4. Population Growth in Nebraska, 1854–1994

Year	Population	Year	Population	Year	Population
1854	2,732	1890	1,058,910	1950	1,325,510
1856 (est.)	10,716	1900	1,066,910	1960	1,411,330
1860	28,841	1910	1,192,214	1970	1,485,333
1867 (est.)	50,000	1920	1,296,372	1980	1,569,825
1870	122,993	1930	1,377,963	1990	1,578,385
1880	452,405	1940	1,315,834	1994 (est.)	1,623,000

Source: U.S. Bureau of the Census, *Population of the United States in 1860, 1870, . . . 1990* (Washington DC: Government Printing Office, 1862, 1872, . . . 1991). Figures for 1994 are estimates released by the Bureau of the Census as reported in *Lincoln Journal*, December 28, 1994.

The most important impetus for the expansion of the late 1860s, 1870s, and 1880s was the construction of railroads through the state. The railroad made it possible to settle away from the Missouri River, the only navigable stream in the area. As early as August 1866, the Union Pacific was carrying passengers and freight as far west as Kearney. The line was completed to Cheyenne in May 1868, and a year later it joined the Central Pacific to span the continent. The completion of a bridge across the Missouri River at Omaha in 1879 enabled the Union Pacific to make connections with the roads crossing Iowa. The Burlington, starting from Plattsmouth in July 1869, reached Lincoln a year later and in 1872 joined the Union Pacific at Kearney. By the end of 1881 the road had built through the Republican River valley and on to Benkelman, almost at the new state's western border. The Midland Pacific, soon to become part of the Burlington system, connected Nebraska City and Lincoln in 1871 and later built westward through Seward, York, and Aurora to Central City. The St. Joseph and Denver entered Nebraska in 1870 and reached Hastings two years later. The Atchison and Nebraska built through the southeastern corner of the state to Lincoln in the early 1870s. North of the Platte, the Sioux City and Pacific built from Missouri Valley, Iowa, to Fremont; and the Omaha and Northwestern reached Blair. The Fremont, Elkhorn, and Missouri Valley built up the Elkhorn River Valley, and the Union Pacific constructed various branches connecting with its main line.

A second major factor in the settlement of the state was federal land policy, which, theoretically at least, allowed a settler to acquire a landed estate solely by demonstrating the willingness and ability to provide the personal labor to improve it. Expressed through the Homestead Act and related legislation, this policy made available the land the railroads had made accessible. A third significant factor was the colonization activity of the railroads, combined with an intensive advertising campaign conducted by both private and public agencies.

Nebraska land, made accessible, available, and known, was a strong impelling force; combined with expelling forces at work in the East and in Europe, particularly unemployment, lack of opportunity, and just plain restlessness, it brought about the great expansion of the late 1860s, 1870s, and 1880s.

THE LAND LAWS

When President Lincoln signed the Homestead Act on May 20, 1862, it was applauded by Nebraskans, who had promoted the legislation since the organization of the territory. In his message to the legislature in 1864, Governor Saunders spoke exultantly of the nation's future under the act: "What a blessing this wise and humane legislation will bring to many a poor, but honest and industrious family. Its benefits can never be estimated in dollars and cents. The very thought, to such people, that they can now have a tract of land that they can call their own, has a soul-inspiring effect upon them, and makes them feel thankful that their lots have been cast under a government that is so liberal to its people."[1]

The act provided that "any person who is the head of a family, or who has arrived at the age of twenty-one years, and is a citizen of the United States, or who shall have filed his declaration of intention to become such . . . and who has never borne arms against the United States government or given aid and comfort to its enemies"[2] could, upon the payment of a ten dollar fee, file a claim upon as much as a quarter section of unappropriated public land and that after having "resided upon or cultivated the same for the term of five years immediately succeeding the time of filing," and "if at that time a citizen of the United States," the claimant could receive a final patent from the government.[3]

A quarter section of land on the prairie could be a lonely place, as evidenced by this photograph of a Nebraska homestead near McCook. Courtesy NSHS, C689:46.

Although amended many times, principally to extend its privileges, the Homestead Act remained in force substantially as passed and was looked upon as the cornerstone of the nation's public land policy. The Pre-Emption Act of 1841, under which many of Nebraska's early territorial pioneers had secured their land, also remained in force. The Pre-Emption Act, however, was relegated to a position of supplemental importance and was ultimately repealed in 1891. Why would a person pay $1.25 per acre for land that could be secured free of charge? Its only importance now was the opportunity it provided for individuals to add an additional quarter section to their homestead at the minimum price.

Another supplemental land law was the Timber Culture Act, approved on March 3, 1873, which provided that the same class of persons who could homestead could acquire an additional quarter section by planting it to trees and tending them for ten years. The time was later reduced to eight years and the required acreage of trees to ten. This act, introduced by Nebraska's Senator Phineas W. Hitchcock, was primarily designed to encourage planting of trees on the plains and was closely associated with other similar efforts in Nebraska: Arbor Day had been established the year before; in 1869 the legislature had exempted one hundred dollars worth of property from taxation for every acre of forest trees planted and kept in cultivation.

The nation's first entry under the Homestead Act was made by Daniel Freeman, a soldier in the Union army home on furlough, to a quarter section lying along Cub Creek northwest of Beatrice. The story of that filing has been somewhat confused in the frequent retelling. Freeman's military service has never been documented, but according to the folklore, he had selected the land a few days earlier and persuaded the register of the land office at Brownville to open up shortly after midnight on January 1, 1863, the date the law went into effect, and receive his entry before he had to leave early on New Year's Day to join his regiment.[4]

Freeman was followed by many others. The *Brownville Advertiser* remarked on January 3, 1863, that since the Homestead Law had gone into effect, there had been "a rush to take advantage of its benefits." The extent and nature of the "rush" can perhaps best be shown statistically.

An examination of the figures in Table 5 reveals that of 131,561 persons who filed original homestead entries on 18,393,541 acres of the public domain in Nebraska between 1863 and 1895, only 68,862 had received final patents by 1900, and the total acreage that had been transferred to individual homesteaders up to that time amounted to only 9,609,922 acres. In other words, only about 52 percent of the original homestead entries were carried through to the final patent. Moreover, including the Kinkaid homesteads of the early twentieth century, only a little more than half of the original land in the public domain in Nebraska actually passed to settlers.

Why did the public land policies, and particularly the Homestead Act, fall so short of expectations? Historians of the era have suggested a variety of reasons. First, the Homestead and Timber Culture Acts frequently were perverted from their original purposes. The provision in the Homestead Act allowing commutation for cash was used by speculators and other large operators to acquire vast tracts to which they were not entitled in the spirit of the law. The process was simple: hirelings would file homestead claims, then after six months commute or purchase them for the minimum price of $1.25 per acre ($2.50 per acre in the railroad areas); title would then pass to the employer who had put up the money. Further

Table 5. Homestead Entries in Nebraska, 1863–1900

Year	Original Number	Original Acres	Final Number	Final Acres
1863	349	50,775		
1864	769	114,649		
1865	812	114,875		
1866	1,456	203,980		
1867	1,628	225,856		
1868	2,844	325,459		
1869	3,596	376,860	277	41,687
1870	4,583	509,062	285	42,134
1871	6,021	713,306	437	61,465
1872	5,970	696,620	649	91,466
1873	6,189	742,884	1,658	220,420
1874	5,165	615,424	2,818	321,743
1875	2,281	265,548	2,828	344,345
1876	1,984	237,786	3,590	418,962
1877	1,345	163,312	3,507	422,147
1878	3,015	407,949	3,897	456,075
1879	4,905	703,750	2,960	349,373
1880	5,648	827,112	2,559	315,501
1881	2,545	365,922	1,611	202,241
1882	3,223	471,939	1,925	258,393
1883	4,728	716,509	1,768	241,511
1884	8,887	1,362,186	2,595	375,128
1885	11,293	1,748,841	2,658	393,239
1886	10,269	1,590,410	2,121	328,968
1887	7,120	1,098,636	1,949	292,874
1888	5,439	839,675	2,184	331,409
1889	4,105	622,626	3,017	467,373
1890	3,141	475,183	4,207	651,732
1891	1,969	288,480	3,918	611,116
1892	3,999	604,320	2,770	431,590
1893	3,270	484,357	2,900	451,773
1894	1,712	245,477	2,204	342,155
1895	1,301	183,773	1,671	255,845

Continued

	Original		Final	
Year	*Number*	*Acres*	*Number*	*Acres*
1896	1,101	154,930	1,227	185,245
1897	1,309	191,701	1,000	153,094
1898	1,882	271,725	1,205	181,246
1899	2,452	351,449	1,189	178,092
1900	3,141	456,855	1,278	191,580
Total	141,446	19,820,201	68,862	9,609,922

Source: Annual Reports of the Commissioner of the General Land Office.

compounding the evil, repeated filings were made in violation of the provision in the law which limited each person to one entry. In Nebraska, 2,634,240 acres were commuted for cash, and most of those for speculative purposes. The Timber Culture Act, under which final patents were issued for 2,456,969 out of 8,876,351 acres on which original entries were filed, was subject to even more flagrant abuse. To be sure, in many areas it was impossible to grow trees even with the best of care; but in many more instances the act was used simply to increase holdings with little effort to produce timber. In his annual report for 1883, the commissioner of the General Land Office wrote: "My information leads me to the conclusion that a majority of the entries under the timber-culture act are made for speculative purposes, and not for the cultivation of timber. Compliance with the law in these cases is a mere pretense. . . . My information is that no trees are to be seen over vast regions of country where timber culture entries have been most numerous."[5] Again, in 1885, he quoted from a field inspector as follows: "I have traveled over hundreds of miles of land in western Kansas, Nebraska, and central Dakota, nearly one-fourth of which had been taken under the 'timber culture Act,' without seeing an artificial grove even in incipience, and can scarcely recall an instance in any one day's travel where the ground had been more than scratched with the plow for the purpose of planting trees."[6]

In addition, the homestead and other related acts designed to provide farms for settlers suffered from being added to an already incongruous land system that sought to use the public domain to further a variety of social purposes: the provision of bounties for those who had served in the nation's wars, the construction of railroads and other internal improvements, and the furtherance of education. Whether by accident or design, legislation enacted toward these ends resulted in the transfer of vast quantities of the public domain to large, monopolistic, and speculative holders. Thus the homestead and related acts did not play the central role expected of them to attract settlers to Nebraska and other plains states. The state, like the territory before it, continued to be a paradise for land speculators.

More important, the assumptions underlying the Homestead Act were spurious or, at best, more optimistic than realistic. A "free farm" in itself by no means assured the success of the farmer. A successful farm operation required both capital and experience. Although many who homesteaded were experienced farmers, they generally had very little capital, and much of their farming experience had been in Europe or in the more humid regions of the United States and was of little use on the plains. Moreover, the Homestead Act lured many settlers into areas where a quarter section could not support a family. Even in areas where a quarter section might have been sufficient, the homesteaders seem to have been particularly unfortunate in the land they acquired. In Wayne County, for example, 33.11 percent of the land settled by homesteads and timber entries was poorer land; no other group received such a high percentage of inferior land. It is little wonder that so many failed in the venture.

That some did succeed is testimony to their courage, fortitude, and sheer determination to triumph against the odds. And for all its problems, the Homestead Act held out hope for those who sought a chance to start over. This was true for women as well as men, as was the case with Esther Carter Griswold-Warner, who, after losing two husbands, came to Nebraska with three young children and filed a homestead claim in 1864 near Roca in Lancaster Country. Not only did she survive the hardships of pioneer life, but she succeeded as a farmer. From 1870 until her death in 1901, she was also an avid spokesperson for the cause of women's suffrage in Nebraska.

RAILROAD COLONIZATION

Approximately 16.6 percent of Nebraska's total acreage was given to various railroad companies, either by the federal government or by the state. The state's two major railroads, the Union Pacific and the Burlington,

Table 6. Nebraska Land Given to Railroad Companies

From the United States	Acres
Union Pacific	4,846,108.18
Burlington and Missouri River	2,374,090.77
Sioux City and Pacific	38,227.84
Central Branch Union Pacific	2,560.03
St. Joseph and Grand Island	380,768.96
Total	7,641,755.78
From the State (Internal Improvement Lands)	
Fremont, Elkhorn, and Missouri Valley	100,030.32
Midland Pacific	100,384.08
Brownville and Fort Kearney	19,989.12
Sioux City and Pacific	47,327.10
Burlington and Missouri River	40,104.77
Omaha and Southwestern	100,010.00
Omaha and Northwestern	80,416.24
Burlington and Southwestern	20,000.00
Atchison and Nebraska	12,841.54
Total	531,103.17
Grand Total	8,172,858.95

Source: Addison E. Sheldon, *Land Systems and Land Policies in Nebraska* (Lincoln: State Historical Society, 1936), 87; and *Report of the Commissioner of the General Land Office* (Washington DC: Government Printing Office, 1906), 109.

were each given alternate sections, which extended back twenty miles on both sides of the track, or a total of twenty sections of land for each mile of road constructed. Except in the area along the Missouri River and a few isolated places elsewhere, the Union Pacific was generally able to locate its lands in the forty-mile strip along its tracks. Had the Burlington done this, however, its grant would have overlapped that of the Union Pacific, so the Burlington secured a ruling that enabled it to locate land elsewhere in lieu of that along the road itself, which meant that its land as finally located lay north and south of the Union Pacific grant.

Once the railroads had located and patented their land, they were, of course, anxious to dispose of it as quickly as possible and at the highest possible price. The problem was somewhat complicated, however, by the realization that the development of farms and towns upon which a profitable carrying trade could be based was of even greater significance than the immediate returns from land sales. The land departments, therefore, tried to establish prices and terms that would produce as much immediate revenue as possible and, at the same time, encourage settlement on the railroad lands. In their pricing policies, they were aided because homesteaders could acquire only eighty acres within the area of a railroad grant and preemptions and commutations within the same area were at a minimum price of $2.50 per acre rather than the $1.25 that applied elsewhere. During the thirteen years 1871 to 1883, the Burlington received an average of $6.05 per acre for its land and the Union Pacific $4.27 per acre.[7] Both roads also made long-term credit available to buyers.

The land departments of both roads conducted vigorous promotional campaigns. Immigration agents were stationed in the principal cities of the East and in the countries of northern and central Europe, where they distributed brochures by the millions describing the beauties and prospects of Nebraska. Lecturers were sent around the country extolling the virtues of the state, and the State Board of Agriculture and other agencies cooperated to exhibit Nebraska's products at fairs and expositions. Special land-seeking excursions were conducted with the understanding that if the excursionist decided to buy land, the fare could be applied to the purchase price. Indeed, almost every device known to the advertising trade of the nineteenth century was used in the promotion of the railroads' Nebraska land.

The land departments also encouraged groups to move to Nebraska, and many of the state's communities were settled that way. The Union Pacific, for example, located a large group of people of Swedish descent on its lands in Saunders and Polk Counties in 1869–70, and in 1870 sixty families from Nova Scotia came to Colfax County. The Burlington likewise located large group settlements on its lands, many from foreign countries, among them the Russian-Germans who settled in and around Sutton in 1873.[8] Frequently groups were organized around a church, particularly the Lutheran and Roman Catholic, and their emigration was directed by the pastor. Other communities such as Gibbon were organized by individuals as business enterprises. The Burlington, through its subsidiary the Lincoln Land Company, also carried on systematic town development, particularly along its line through the Republican River valley. By 1905, all of the Burlington's lands in Nebraska had been sold and paid for. The Union Pacific had 12,307 acres remaining unsold in the state in 1921, of which 1,335 remained on the company's books as late as 1994.[9] The two railroads had disposed of more than 7 million acres to private purchasers, almost 75 percent as much as was obtained free of charge under the Homestead Act. The railroads did not altogether abandon their interest in their land and its purchasers upon sale, however, but continued to carry on agricultural improvement programs by working closely with the University of Nebraska and various agencies of both the state and federal governments. George W. Holdrege, general manager of the Burlington's Lines West, was particularly active in agricultural development work and supported the revolutionary experiments of Hardy W. Campbell in dry farming.

THE GREAT ADVERTISING CAMPAIGN

The state government joined the railroads in promoting settlement. In his message to the legislature in 1869, Governor Butler urged the establishment of an immigration bureau, and in 1870 the lawmakers established the Board of Immigration with five members who were to be chosen by the legislature to serve two-year terms. The board was given $15,000 and authority to appoint four immigration agents who were to serve both in the United States and abroad. After an initial burst of enthusiasm, support for the work of the Board of Immigration sharply declined, and it was abolished in 1877.

More effective, and for a longer time, was the work of the State Board of Agriculture. Under the leadership of Robert W. Furnas, the board developed the State Fair into an effective annual agricultural exposition. The State Board of Agriculture and the State Horticultural Society cooperated to send exhibits of Nebraska fruit and grains to expositions throughout the East. The railroads provided free transportation. J. Sterling Morton, a member of both boards, an agriculturist of wide reputation, as well as the paid publicist of the Burlington, performed particularly effective liaison work between the railroads and the state boards.

A major obstacle to the settlement of the state was the widely held belief that much of the trans–Missouri River region was unsuited to agriculture. Descriptions by explorers and others of the Great American Desert lying east of the Rockies had found their way into periodical and newspaper literature and had created a generally unfavorable impression of the plains. The promotional activity of the railroads and various state agencies was designed primarily to counter this impression. The exhibits, the brochures, and the lectures demonstrated by statistics and examples that the desert concept was myth.

In addition, Samuel Aughey, professor of natural sciences at the University of Nebraska, declared that the state's rainfall was adequate and actually increasing. Before joining the first faculty of the university in 1871, Aughey had combined his scientific studies with the ministry and land speculation. In 1880 he published his views in a book entitled *Sketches of the Physical Geography and Geology of Nebraska*. He had been in the state since 1864, and from his own experience as an old settler, as well as from the experience of others, he was sure that rainfall in Nebraska was increasing. There were many phenomena to demonstrate the validity of this assertion: the appearance of new springs, the appearance of water in old creekbeds, the increasing size of the streams of the state, and the changing vegetation. From experiments conducted on a farm about a mile east of Lincoln, Aughey concluded that the reason for the increased rainfall was to be found in "the great increase in the absorptive power of the soil, wrought by cultivation." He wrote:

Anyone who examines a piece of raw prairie closely, must observe how compact it is. Everyone who opens up a new farm, soon finds that it requires an extra force to break it. There is nothing extraordinary about this. For vast ages the prairies have been pelted by the elements and trodden by millions of buffalo and other wild animals, until the naturally rich soil became as compact as a floor. When rain falls on a primitive soil of this character, the greater part runs off into the canyons, creeks and rivers, and is soon through the Missouri on its way to the Gulf. Observe now the change which cultivation makes. After the soil is broken, the rain as it falls is absorbed by the soil like a huge sponge. The soil gives this absorbed moisture slowly back to the atmosphere by evaporation. Thus year by year as cultivation of the soil is extended, more of the rain that falls

is absorbed and retained to be given off by evaporation, or to produce springs.
This, of course, must give increasing moisture and rainfall.[10]

The theory that rainfall follows the plow was indeed provocative. C. D. Wilber popularized it in *The Great Valleys and Prairies of Nebraska and the Northwest* (Omaha, 1881), a book that was widely circulated by the railroads. Orange Judd, the well-known and highly respected editor of the *Prairie Farmer*, published in Chicago, expounded on it further in an address at the Nebraska State Fair on September 16, 1883. Speaking from a platform of baled hay, Judd extolled the virtues of Nebraska as an agricultural state. An important feature of the state's climate, he declared, was that its rainfall was increasing annually as a result of the extension of agriculture westward.

Agriculture, then, would provide its own solution to the problem of the plains. Those who disagreed were promptly shouted down. When, for example, the Department of the Interior in 1879 published Major John Wesley Powell's report, *Lands of the Arid Region*, in which the hundredth meridian was designated as the western limit of agriculture, Nebraskans' indignation knew no bounds. The state agricultural and horticultural societies requested Professors Aughey and Wilber to draft a reply. This they did, suggesting that the condemnation of the western part of the state was inspired by cattlemen who wanted to keep farmers out. The soil of the area was as productive as any in the country, they declared. The only element lacking for successful agriculture was an adequate supply of moisture, which soon would be remedied. If rainfall continued to increase at the current rate, they predicted confidently, even the western part of the state would soon support agriculture without irrigation.

The proponents of the increased rainfall theory were aided immeasurably by the fact that during the early 1880s Nebraska experienced a series of comparatively wet years. As a result, many were willing to take a chance at homesteading the relatively subhumid lands of the central part of the state. Unfortunately, bitter experience demonstrated that these lands could not be farmed by the methods applied to the humid regions east of the Missouri, and that experience became a major factor in Nebraska's economic and political history.

CHAPTER 14

The 1870s: Growing Pains

The forces of settlement that were at work in the West brought profound changes to Nebraska in the decade immediately following the close of the Civil War. Population, which had been only 28,841 in 1861, at the beginning of the war, increased to 122,993 by 1870 and was estimated at 250,000 in 1874. During the same time, thirty-seven new counties were organized, thirty-one of them in the years 1870–73. With the exception of omnibus Lincoln County at the forks of the Platte River and a strip along the north side of the Platte to Grand Island, county government before the end of the war did not extend much beyond seventy-five miles west of the Missouri River. By 1874 the entire region south of the Platte River was solidly organized through Frontier and Hitchcock Counties. Organization north of the Platte, except for the Indian reservations, had been extended to the eastern edge of the Sand Hills. Keith County had been organized west of Lincoln County, and the southern portion of the Panhandle was established as Cheyenne County.

Except in the range country, this growth generally represented the westward extension of conventional, humid-region, diversified agriculture. Much of the land occupied during the period was submarginal for this activity, even in good years, and the middle 1870s saw serious distress that brought the experiment near the brink of failure. The depression that hit during those years almost pushed it over completely. Moreover, agriculture on the prairie-plains was not "corn and 'tater patch" subsistence farming but a commercial enterprise employing an increasing amount of machinery and requiring a corresponding increase in capital. Each time the farmer substituted a machine for a hand tool he usually went further into debt. The land was free, but the question was whether it could produce enough to pay the cost of farming it.

Political instability, growing out of the scandals of the Butler administration and the inadequacies of the constitution, combined with economic instability, produced a period of grave uncertainty in the middle 1870s. Particularly distressing to the farmer who lived in his soddy and worked his parched fields for little or no return was the apparent collusion between the politicians and the groups to which he was constantly in debt: the railroads, the banks, and the commercial classes. Though it would be a decade before Nebraska farmers would rise in organized rebellion against these "oppressing" forces, they were willing to lend an ear to those who denounced the government, the railroads, the bankers, and the "middlemen."

Attitudes formed in the 1870s tended to become more rigid as the years wore on. As Addison E. Sheldon, who during those years was growing up on a Seward County farm, later wrote: "In these years was created the Soul of Nebraska—characteristic mind, vision and form of action. Soil and sun and wind, hardship and conflict, spirit, institutions, debates and experiences shaped the type of man who still lives upon these prairies. The blendings of different racial stocks, begun then, still goes on. But the Nebraska type was created in the '70s. . . . The soul of Nebraska remains in dominant feature the product of the pioneer '70s."[1]

INITIAL GROWTH

Approximately half of Nebraska's population increase during the 1870s resulted from the growth of counties that had been established earlier. Homesteads and railroad lands were still available in these counties, and in some, notably Dodge, Douglas, Gage, and Lancaster, small cities were developing. Yet, to those with little or no capital, the more significant opportunities seemed to lie further west, with the result that nearly half of those living in the state by 1880 resided in the counties created during the decade before.

Particularly noteworthy in these years was the extension of population up the Republican River valley. Before 1870 the region had been little affected by white contact or settlement. It lay outside the mainstream of the overland migration. While providing an easy route, it seemed to lead nowhere. Trappers and traders visited the region but generally moved on to more profitable fields. In addition, the Indians, driven out of the other great valleys on the plains, stubbornly resisted white efforts to

This Czech-language brochure prepared by the Burlington Railroad is an example of advertisements developed by the railroads in many different languages for promotion throughout Europe promising cheap land and bountiful harvests and success within six years to entice immigration to Nebraska. Courtesy, NSHS, A245:10.

171

penetrate this last haven, where the buffalo and other wild game were still plentiful. In 1870, however, exploratory and settlement expeditions into the Republican Valley were being organized in several Missouri River towns.

The first in the field was the Rankin Colony, organized in Omaha in the fall of 1869. They established themselves at Guide Rock and began to build a house, but before the house was completed an Indian scare drove all but two of the colony members away. The first permanent settlement in the valley was Red Cloud, which was established in the summer of 1870 by a party from Beatrice, led by Silas Garber, who would later become governor. In the fall of 1870 another Omaha group, known as the Thompson Colony, explored the valley and returned the next spring to found Riverton. A branch of the Rankin Colony known as the Republican Valley Land Claim Association settled at Franklin City in the fall of 1870, but the town never materialized. Present-day Franklin grew out of the town of Waterloo and was established by the Plattsmouth Town Company. Another Plattsmouth company was organized in 1872 to found Bloomington.

Also in 1870, Victor Vifquain, the first Nebraskan ever to receive the Medal of Honor, led a party west from Nebraska City. Most of them quit in disgust, but a few remained and erected Melrose Stockade. In February 1871, a group of Union Pacific laborers from Cheyenne explored the valley, returned to Cheyenne, and recruited settlers to establish Alma. Later in the year, a group led by Dr. John McPherson, a wealthy Brownville doctor, established Republican City.

One of the best known of the colonizing companies was the Red Willow Colony, also known as the Republican Valley Land Company, which was organized in the fall of 1871 at Nebraska City. This colony sent out an exploring party under Royal Buck. After encountering difficult weather and even more difficult Indians, they pushed on to Red Willow Creek and organized the town of Red Willow in December 1871. The company, capitalized at $100,000, had visions of organizing a large city in the valley. Based on the plan used to plat Lincoln, the town had streets one hundred feet wide. A newspaper was started, and the company worked feverishly to promote its new city. For a variety of reasons, however, the venture failed. The same land company was also active in the establishment of

Indianola and Bartley, but in these ventures it ran up against competition from the Lincoln Land Company, which would be incorporated in 1880 as a subsidiary of the Burlington Railroad. The Lincoln Land Company, with its powerful railroad backing, would become an important force in the urban real estate boom of the next decade.

The prospect of a railroad in the Republican River valley provided a significant impetus to the settlement of the region. This prospect did not materialize, however, until the Burlington Railroad built along the river in 1878–82. Earlier settlers had to make the long trip overland to the Union Pacific or, after 1873, to the Burlington at Lowell. The area along this South Platte extension of the Burlington was developed by the Eastern Land Associates, which had been organized by Burlington officials in 1870 to develop the lands along its main line. The Associates were primarily responsible for the development of the railroad's "alphabetical towns" west of Lincoln: Crete, Dorchester, Exeter, Fairmont, Grafton, Harvard, Inland, Juniata, Kenesaw, and Lowell.

In the Republican Valley as elsewhere, individual settlers pushed out ahead of the colonies and the railroads. In the fall of 1870, Galen James went out from the Melrose Stockade to live at the junction of the Beaver and Sappa Rivers. Cambridge's first settler was Hiram Doing, who arrived in 1871. In 1872 George Hunter and E. S. Hill settled on the site of Indianola. The village of Culbertson was settled in 1873 as a headquarters for cattlemen.

Meanwhile, the Union Pacific continued to develop its lands in the Platte Valley. By 1873 it had settled forty groups, or 2,113 families, in its land grant as far west as the eastern edge of Buffalo County. The larger groups concentrated on the cheaper lands south of the Platte River or the area west of Colfax County. Settlement activity was uneven, however. A group of 348 families of Swedes from Illinois, who occupied a large tract in Phelps and Kearney Counties, represented the only significant settlement on Union Pacific lands for the next four years, although smaller groups took up the lands east of Central City. By 1878 group settlement did not extend much beyond the Cozad settlement of 1873.

Farther north, Norfolk, which had been founded in 1866 by a group of Germans from Wisconsin, began to develop as a trading center for growing settlements along the Elkhorn River, particularly after the Fremont,

The 1870s: Growing Pains

Missouri Valley and Elkhorn Railroad built up the valley to Wisner in 1871 and to Neligh in 1880. Farther up the valley, General John J. O'Neill, an eccentric Irish leader who had served a term in prison for participating in the Fenian invasion of Canada, founded a community bearing his name as an Irish colony in 1874. He later established similar colonies at Atkinson and in Greeley County.

Religious groups were also active in the settlement process of the early 1870s. Many Scandinavian groups were led by Lutheran pastors. The Catholics were active in Platte and Cedar Counties. York was founded by Congregationalists. A group of Seventh Day Baptists established a colony in the Loup Valley. Large Mennonite colonies were founded south and west of Lincoln, particularly under the leadership of Peter Jansen. An English Methodist pastor, Richard Wake, promoted English immigration and settlement with a series of articles published in the London *Christian World*, encouraging English farmers, and particularly farm laborers, who were experiencing economic hardships at home to form colonizing companies to settle in Nebraska. In 1866 he returned to England to lead the first such group of 115 men, women, and children to Otoe County, where they settled in Palmyra precinct near the present-day community of Palmyra.

Although Nebraska had a mixed population, communities were frequently dominated by a particular national group. Many of these groups had little contact with people in other sections of the state and as a result continued to maintain their ethnic and national customs and traditions. Official state papers were printed in a variety of languages. By 1880, the federal census estimated that over half the people in Nebraska were either foreign-born (97,414 or 21.5 percent) or born in the United States of at least one foreign-born parent (168,538 or 37.2 percent).[2]

Although European immigration became a dominant factor in the settlement of the state by the 1870s, others came to homestead or form communities, contributing to the polyglot nature of Nebraska's population throughout the remainder of the decade and into the next. The state's history is replete with unique stories and experiences such as those of the prominent Jewish leader Samuel Wolbach, for whom the community of Wolbach is named, who settled in 1874 and became active in the Democratic Party in the late 1880s, serving in both the lower house of

Table 7. Birthplaces of Nebraskans, 1880

Germany	31,125
Sweden	10,164
Ireland	10,133
Bohemia	8,858
England and Wales	8,831
British America	8,678
Denmark	4,511
Russia	3,281
Austria	2,346
Scotland	2,230
Norway	2,010
Switzerland	1,579
Poland	1,128
Holland	753
France	749
Wales	624

Source: U.S. Department of the Interior, Bureau of the Census, *Population of the United States at the Tenth Census: 1880.* (Washington DC: Government Printing Office, 1883), 492–95.

the legislature and the state Senate. Unique also is the experience of black homesteaders beginning with Robert Anderson, a former slave who in 1870 became the first black to homestead in Nebraska, or the experiences of black homesteader Charles Meehan, who formed the black colony at Overton in Dawson County in 1885, which was followed by the formation of other black communities in Cherry County: Brownlee in 1905 and DeWitty in 1907.

DISTRESS AND DOUBT

Hope ran high in Nebraska during the first decade after statehood. Thousands of settlers poured across the Missouri River to claim farms for themselves. New towns staked out on the plains vied with each other for preferment, and almost every one of the thirty-one counties organized during those years had a fight over location of the county seat in its history. The various local struggles were somewhat reminiscent of the territorial struggle for the location of the capital city that had occurred almost two decades earlier. The struggle was all the more intense because of a general feeling of optimism. In almost every instance, the first year's crops were good enough to convince those who had planted them that their future in the new land was assured. Even in the regions beyond the railroad, where marketing absorbed almost all of the profit, those who had pioneered in the experiment were optimistic. It was only a matter of time until the railroads came and their investment paid off.

Then in September 1873, the New York City investment house of Jay Cooke and Company failed, precipitating a panic that swept across the country like a prairie fire. Agricultural prices tumbled, and many Nebraska farmers were unable to find a market for their wheat and corn. In July of the following year the plains from Canada to Texas were overrun by vast hordes of Rocky Mountain locusts, which descended in ominous black clouds upon the pioneer farms and literally ate everything in sight. Almost every pioneer story of the period has its account of the grasshopper infestation. Addison E. Sheldon's is typical:

In a clear, hot July (July 26) day a haze came over the sun. The haze deepened into a gray cloud. Suddenly the cloud resolved itself into billions of gray grasshoppers sweeping down upon the earth. The vibration of their wings filled the ear with a roaring sound like a rushing storm. As far as the eye could reach in every direction the air was filled with them. Where they alighted they covered the ground like a heavy crawling carpet. Growing crops disappeared in a single day. Trees were stripped of leaves. Potatoes, turnips and onions were pursued into the earth. Clothing and harness were cut into shreds if left exposed. Wheat and oats were mostly in the shock, but the grasshoppers covered the shocks, cut the bands and gnawed the grain.

Everywhere the earth was covered with a gray mass of struggling, biting grasshoppers. Turkeys and chickens feasted on them. Dogs and swine learned to eat them—the latter making them their chief food for many days. It was hard to drive a team across a field because the swarm of grasshoppers flew up in front, striking the horses in the face with a force that made them wild.

We thought when they were filled they would fly away. Not at all. . . . Each one laid about one hundred eggs. Then they died and the ground was covered with their dead bodies.[3]

The 1870s: Growing Pains

Though weather records for the years before 1876 are incomplete, the grasshoppers apparently delivered the final attack on crops already withering under the effects of a serious drought. The hard times were bad enough before the drought and the grasshoppers, but as long as the farmers had their sod corn and gardens, they could at least feed themselves and their livestock. With these gone, however, the situation became desperate, and the future was made more hopeless by the knowledge that the soil was filled with eggs that would hatch a hundred times as many grasshoppers the next spring. Farmers who were trying to raise their first crop were particularly discouraged. Many sold or gave away their claims and returned east. On the tattered covers of their wagons they scrawled:

Eaten out by grasshoppers
Going back East to live with wife's folks.[4]

At first, public officials and newspapers, concerned with promoting settlement, minimized the seriousness of the situation. On August 21, 1874, Governor Robert W. Furnas issued a report to the public acknowledging that crop production was down from previous years and that there was apparent need for help in some locations. Information derived from correspondence with county officials and from personal observation had not convinced him that the situation constituted failure or was grounds for panic or alarm. And J. Sterling Morton was confident that exhibits of Nebraska's products at the State Fair and at eastern expositions would soon allay rumors of starvation in Nebraska.

But as reports of destitution began to pile up from all parts of the state, it became apparent that something had to be done, and quickly. To avoid calling a special session of the legislature, Governor Furnas asked a number of well-known citizens to meet with him in Lincoln on September 18, 1874, to find a means of dealing with the situation. The Nebraska Relief and Aid Society was incorporated to collect money, provisions, clothing, seeds, and other supplies for distribution among the needy of the state. Various Nebraskans also toured the eastern states soliciting aid and, despite competition from Kansans on the same mission, were able to secure cash donations amounting to $74,000, 28 percent of which went for expenses and freight charges. In addition, the society collected and distributed supplies valued at from $350,000 to $400,000. Most of these supplies were carried free of charge by the railroads. General E. O. C. Ord, commanding the Department of the Platte and acting on his own authority (later legalized by Congress), issued large quantities of damaged and unserviceable army clothing and equipment to destitute settlers. In the spring of 1875 the federal government, through the army, distributed rations valued at $41,316.72 to 49,817 persons. The Grange tried to provide relief for its members, concentrating on the purchase of seed in the spring of 1875. Churches and other groups also tried to relieve the destitute.

Grasshoppers continued to menace prairie-plains agriculture through 1876. Various devices and techniques, including grasshopper traps, were brought forth to control them, and in the fall of 1876 the governors of ten western states met in Omaha to consider the problem. This convention called upon the federal government to take action to eliminate pests and urged the states to offer bounties, modify game laws to prevent the destruction of insect-eating birds, prevent prairie fires, and encourage tree culture, the latter as a means of holding moisture and attracting birds. The grasshopper problem, however, solved itself, at least partially and temporarily. So, too, did the drought; from 1877 through the remainder of the decade the state got more than the mean of 22.84 inches of annual rainfall and enjoyed a wet cycle that continued through the 1880s. Immigration, which had all but ceased during the grasshopper-drought years, resumed. The production of corn, which had fallen from seven million bushels in 1873 to three and a half million bushels a year later, jumped to twenty-eight million bushels the next year and by 1879 had reached sixty-two million bushels. Wheat, which ranked second in production, had not been as seriously affected by the drought and grasshoppers. Annual wheat production remained between three and four million bushels through the middle 1870s and then increased markedly to over thirteen million bushels by 1878. This increase was largely the result of extending wheat production into the southwestern counties.

Through it all, however, the farmer's relative economic position steadily worsened. Production costs rose and farm prices generally declined during the decade. The decline in farm prices was reflected in assessed values, which also declined during the decade, slipping from $4.79 per acre in 1870 to $2.86 per acre by the end of the decade. Farmers seemed to be at a disadvantage at every turn. High freight rates reduced the price of their products and increased the cost of farm machinery and other necessary commodities. The shortage of cash meant that purchases had to supported with mortgages on crops or land. At best, farmers had to sell their crops immediately after harvest at any price the local speculators were willing to pay. Should the crops fail, they were likely to find themselves confronted with judgments against their land which could absorb their entire equity. Even in good years, farmers were fortunate if both bills and debts could be met and they could still retain title to their land.

Some farmers made an effort to alleviate their condition through the Patrons of Husbandry, or the Grange, which had been established in 1869 as a social and educational institution and was organized in Nebraska three years later, in 1872. The Grange grew rapidly, and by the end of 1872 fifty local Granges had been organized. By the early part of 1874 the Grange reported twenty thousand members in Nebraska. Grange meetings soon developed into forums for the discussion of social and economic questions, and before long the organization was combining action with discussion. Because direct participation in business seemed to promise the greatest benefits, the Nebraska Grange adopted methods of cooperative buying which were being used by Grange organizations in other states. For a while, it even attempted to manufacture farm machinery. A state purchasing agent for the Grange was appointed, with an office in Lincoln. County Granges formed cooperatives to buy and sell farm products and deal in farm machinery, lumber, and coal. Local Granges even established some cooperative stores. A Grange Plow Factory was established at Plattsmouth, and headers, which were widely used before the development of the self-binder, were manufactured at Fremont.

All these enterprises failed. The reasons were many and varied: inadequate resources, mismanagement, and an unwillingness on the part of members to give them sustained support. Many were perfectly willing to buy from the dealer who was underselling the Grange store simply to drive it out of business. But even if those problems could have been solved, the agricultural depression left the farmers unable to buy, even at the low prices and favorable terms offered by the Grange. With the failure of its economic enterprises, the Grange went into a decline. After

1875 few local Granges were organized, and by 1876 the order was on the wane throughout Nebraska.

In spite of its problems, the Grange had achieved one of its major political objectives by 1876 and in so doing may also have contributed to its own decline. That objective was a provision in the new state constitution concerning the regulation of railroads, which by the middle 1870s were considered by many farmers to be the principal oppressor of the farm population.

POLITICAL REFORM: THE CONSTITUTION OF 1875

The scandals culminating in Governor Butler's impeachment left an ugly stain on the opening pages of the new state's political history. It was a penetrating stain and would cast its blot on the record for some time even after the governor had been removed from office. Butler's irregular methods seemed to permeate all the state's fiscal affairs, and the public buildings at Lincoln stood out as stark monuments to the slipshod way he had handled the public's business. All had cost more to build than had been appropriated, and all were so poorly built that they began falling apart almost as soon as they were occupied. The insane asylum burned to the ground on April 17, 1871, at the same time a legislative committee was recommending repairs to correct its bulging walls. The only university building was in need of a new foundation and extensive repairs on its superstructure six years after it was opened.

All this, many outstate politicians and editors argued, was the work of what they liked to call the Lincoln ring. This group, whose membership was unidentified, was generally assumed to include the principal state officials and the leading businessmen of the new capital city. The most radical of the critics contended that the only adequate solution to the problem was to remove the capital and all state institutions from Lincoln. For a time this climate of criticism retarded the growth of the state's institutions, particularly the university. In addition to its internal difficulties, the university was under constant fire from a wide variety of groups within the state, including certain religious groups who considered it a godless institution.

Designed to provide as cheap a government as possible, the hastily drawn constitution of 1866 came close to providing no government at all. Although there was little agreement about the nature of the reforms needed, almost all groups in the state were certain that the basic law should be overhauled. Under the constitution, the governor was limited to a salary of $1,000 per year, and many politicians argued that ridiculously low salaries made it difficult to attract good men for public office. Lincoln interests felt that the capital should be permanently located by a constitutional provision. A substantial and influential group felt that more encouragement should be given railroads and other business projects. A growing number were insistent that taxpayers be given constitutional protection against exploitation by reckless public officials, both state and local. Still others wanted the constitution to provide for women's suffrage, prohibition, and compulsory education.

All these objectives and others were represented among the fifty-two delegates to the constitutional convention who assembled in the jerry-built state capitol on June 13, 1871, less than two weeks after Governor Butler had been removed from office. Soon it became evident that no agreement could be secured on many of the issues that had emerged before the convention. Debate was heated, and many issues were decided by a bare majority. Throughout the proceedings, partisan politics reigned triumphant, and valuable time was occupied with the question of whether the impeached governor should be given, as were current members of the legislative bodies, "the privileges of the floor of the convention," and with such matters as an investigation of the management of the insane asylum, an inquiry into the selection of state lands, and an investigation of the expenditures of the State Board of Agriculture. Although allowing the impeached, and thus defamed, Governor Butler a voice in the deliberations seemed incomprehensible to some, others had different sympathies for it was defeated by only twenty-eight to fifteen. Floor privilege for members of the legislature, however, was adopted during the opening debate on convention rules.[5]

After two months of wrangling, the convention adjourned on August 19. The new constitution was modeled after the Illinois constitution of 1870, a Granger document affirming the right of the legislature to regulate railroads and seriously restricting the right of local governments to provide financial aid to corporations. In addition, the governor's salary was increased to $3,000 per year and other salaries were raised accordingly, with a provision for adjustment after five years. Lincoln was to remain the capital until 1880 or until "otherwise provided by a law designating some other place therefore, which shall be submitted to, and be approved by a majority of the electors voting thereon." Settling all these issues took days of discussion and debate.[6] Five proposals were separately submitted to the voters and were to become a part of the constitution only if specifically approved: a definition of the liability of stockholders in a corporation as twice the amount of stock held; prohibition of county and municipal aid to corporations; compulsory education; a provision requiring the legislature to submit the question of prohibition to the voters; and women's suffrage.

Opposition to the proposed constitution surfaced almost immediately and from a variety of quarters. The railroads, which were already a dominant force in the state, were absolutely opposed to the regulatory features of the constitution and were able to line up an imposing array of leading politicians of both parties against it. A "sleeper" providing for the taxation of church property valued in excess of $5,000, which had been inserted at the insistence of certain Protestant groups who were irritated by the fine church buildings being constructed by the Catholics in Omaha and elsewhere, provoked widespread opposition among the state's considerable Catholic population. There was also a general fear that the constitution, which raised salaries and created the offices of lieutenant governor and attorney general, would create a government that was too expensive.

At the special election called for the purpose, the constitution was turned down, 8,627 to 7,986. Only 48 percent of the voters had approved of the new constitution; none of the separate proposals fared as well. Liability to stockholders received the greatest support with 46 percent, followed by prohibition of aid to corporations (41 percent), compulsory education (39 percent), submission of prohibition to the voters (37 percent), and women's suffrage (22 percent). The work of the convention had been totally rejected.

Rejection of the revised constitution only intensified the problems facing the new state. The legislature, which had provided for the constitutional convention and removed the governor, finally adjourned on June 7, 1871, to reconvene on January 9, 1872. Because there was some question about the authority of the legislature to reconvene itself in this way, Acting Governor William H. James attempted to settle the question by declaring that the legislature did not have the authority to reconvene itself and had simply adjourned sine die. As a result, part of the body refused to adjourn and stayed on, occupying itself with an effort to impeach the acting governor. James responded by shutting off the coal supply to the legislative chambers, forcing the session to end. The battle, however, was not over, and it resumed later when Isaac Hascall, president of the Senate, took advantage of Governor James's absence from the state on a trip to Washington to reconvene the legislature. The acting governor hurried home and issued a counterproclamation, but some of the members assembled in accordance with Hascall's call, only to find that the doors of the legislative chambers had been barricaded.

Meanwhile, government, both state and local, continued to provide evidence of the need for basic change. In the fall of 1872 Robert W. Furnas was elected governor in reaction to an incipient "liberal Republican" movement. Furnas was soon involved in a spectacular libel suit against the *Omaha Herald*, which had charged him with accepting a bribe. Taxes were delinquent to the point that the state's entire revenue system was imperiled. Local governments continued recklessly to vote bonds for railroads. Nearly $4.5 million of local debt was outstanding in 1874, and many of the bonds were virtually unsalable. The newspapers were full of charges of bribery and corruption leveled against many of the state's leading political figures. All this plus increasing agitation from the new counties in the west for additional representation in the legislature, contributed to the growing demand for another constitutional convention.

In 1874, the Republicans acceded to western demands by nominating Silas Garber as their candidate for governor. Garber, who three years earlier had helped establish the settlement of Red Cloud, was a proponent of a constitutional convention. Garber won easily; the Republicans enjoyed such a strong position in the state at that time that nomination by the party was tantamount to election.

In his inaugural message, Governor Garber urged the legislature to act quickly on the voters' approval of the ballot issue calling for a constitutional convention. The legislature provided for the election of delegates, and on May 11, 1875, sixty-nine delegates assembled in the crumbling capitol building to draft a new constitution.

The delegates met in an atmosphere of gloom. Hard times were everywhere. As they assembled, the principal item of news was the hatching of grasshoppers across the state. Economy was the watchword. A resolution requiring the secretary of state to furnish each delegate with three dollars worth of postage stamps was immediately voted down. In lieu of hiring a chaplain, the convention decided to ask ministers from Lincoln churches to open the daily sessions with prayer. They even decided that a shorthand report of the proceedings was too expensive; hence there is no verbatim report of the convention.

The convention adjourned on June 12, 1875, after adopting another constitution modeled closely on the Illinois constitution of 1870 and closely paralleling the rejected Nebraska constitution of 1871. The clause providing for church taxation was dropped, as was the railroad right-of-way restriction. Both had been major factors in the defeat of the earlier constitution. Other provisions gave the right of appeal to the supreme court in every lawsuit, separated the supreme court and the district courts, and enlarged the legislature to eighty-four members in the House and thirty in the Senate, with a stipulation for further enlargement after 1880. The executive department was enlarged by the creation of the offices of lieutenant governor and attorney general. The constitution provided for increased salaries, included a section on education, provided limitations on county taxes, and limited state debt to $100,000.

The new Nebraska constitution retained the Illinois provision giving the legislature power to regulate the railroads. Even though the constitution was bitterly opposed by the railroad interests of the state, the people adopted it by the overwhelming margin of 30,332 to 5,474. Two separate propositions, one providing for the location of the capital in Lincoln and the second for a preference vote for United States senators, were also approved.

The adoption of the constitution of 1875 signaled an end to the era of uncertainty in the state's affairs. Fortunately, too, economic conditions improved in the late 1870s and early 1880s, giving the new state government a fighting chance. Farmers, who were reasonably satisfied with the constitution's regulatory provisions, seemed content for a time to expand their holdings and vote the Republican ticket. Within a decade, however, they would find that authorization to regulate railroads was a far cry from the achievement of effective regulation. That, combined with a growing discontent over general economic conditions, would cause the state's agricultural population to develop a spirit of rebellion more aggressive than anything witnessed previously.

CHAPTER 15

The Range Cattle Industry

While the grangers settled the valleys and uplands of the eastern and central parts of Nebraska, cattlemen occupied the wide expanse of the western areas. Except where grangers and cattlemen came in conflict, the development of the range cattle industry was far removed from the general agricultural development of the state. Yet the cattle industry was to become Nebraska's most important economic activity.

The establishment of the range cattle industry on the plains was co-incident with the extermination of the bison. As long as these shaggy beasts occupied the plains, there was no room for cattle. Moreover, while bison remained plentiful, the Indians had the wherewithal to maintain resistance against white encroachment.

The bison were exterminated after the discovery in the early 1870s that their hides could be used in the manufacture of harness, belting, shoes, and other leather goods. To satisfy the demand thus created, commercial hunters went out on the plains in gangs, armed with high-caliber, long-range rifles. In a few short years they literally wiped the bison off the face of the earth. Conservative estimates place the kill on the plains at more than ten million during the years 1870–85. Moreover, this was simple, wanton destruction. Whereas the Indians had used virtually all of the animal, the commercial hunters took only the hide, leaving the carcass to rot where it fell. Before the commercial hunters wiped them out, the bison had furnished great sport for big-game hunters. A particularly celebrated hunting excursion took place south of Fort McPherson in 1872, arranged by General Sheridan for the Grand Duke Alexis of Russia.

With the bison gone and the Indians forced onto reservations where they could not menace white occupation of the range, the rich grasses of the plains were available for cattle. Small herds of cattle had developed along the Platte Valley trails before, during, and immediately after the Civil War. Strategically located operators of road ranches developed a substantial business exchanging fresh cattle for trail-worn animals. The large-scale postwar range cattle industry, however, had its origins in Texas. As Professor Edward Everett Dale put it: "Any history of the cattle industry in the West must begin with Texas since that state was the original home of ranching on a large scale in the United States, and from its vast herds were drawn most of the cattle for the first stocking of the central and northern plains."[1]

Almost from the days of its earliest settlement, Texas had been cattle country. The long-horned cattle brought in by the Spanish thrived under the climate and range conditions of Texas, and in addition to those in herds, many ran wild. Almost as much as the physical factors, the land system of both Spain and Mexico, involving large grants to individuals and groups, fostered cattle raising. Although it was easy to raise cattle in Texas, the problem was finding a market for them. This problem was partially solved in the prewar years by driving them to New Orleans, Galveston, and other Gulf ports and to northern markets such as Chicago and Cincinnati. The Civil War cut off the established markets and disrupted the industry. The cattle, however, continued to thrive; and by the end of the war thousands of wild cattle roamed the Texas plains. At the same time, a brisk demand for beef in the North and in Europe made it possible to get forty or fifty dollars in Chicago for a fat beef that would bring only six or seven dollars in Texas. The problem was getting the beef to market. Even before the war there had been great opposition in Missouri and Illinois to the cattle drives. After the war that opposition extended to eastern Kansas and Nebraska. The solution was found in driving cattle to shipping points along the westward-moving rails of the Kansas Pacific and the Union Pacific Railroads, ultimately resulting in the development of ranches on the northern plains, which were much closer to the markets.

THE LONG DRIVE

Before 1870 only a few of the cattle from Texas were driven as far north as Nebraska. In 1866, for example, the number amounted to approximately 15,000 out of 260,000, or less than 6 percent. A few cattle were ferried across the Missouri River at Brownville, Nebraska City, or Omaha for

The Sand Hills proved ideal for cattle raising, as evidenced by this photograph taken around 1900 on the Lee Brothers Ranch in Cherry County. Courtesy, NSHS Butcher Collection, B983:1837.

points east, but most were bought by the government to feed the Indians on Nebraska reservations. The Union Pacific did not have adequate shipping facilities, and most of the cattle destined for rail shipment stopped at Abilene, Kansas, on the Kansas Pacific. During the winter of 1869–70, however, Union Pacific officials became interested in the possibility of shipping Texas cattle from some point along their line in Nebraska. Drovers dissatisfied with both the rates and the service on the Kansas Pacific were definitely interested. When the Union Pacific was able to work out a uniform rate with the Burlington and Rock Island Railroad for the haul from Omaha to Chicago, which was about 25 percent less than the rate from Abilene to Chicago, the way was opened for the southern drovers to move into Nebraska. The next question was the location of the shipping point. Both Schuyler and Columbus pressed hard for it, but Schuyler, at the upper end of the Blue River Trail, won, and the sleepy little frontier village was transformed into the first of Nebraska's cow towns.

During the summer of 1870, between forty and fifty thousand head of Texas cattle were sold at Schuyler, causing the town's population to jump from less than a hundred people to approximately six hundred. Plattsmouth, with its direct connection via the Burlington Railroad to Chicago, competed with Schuyler for the Texas trade. Although Plattsmouth's location on the Missouri River offered the cowboys more in the way of diversion, the trail to Plattsmouth was not as good as the Blue River Trail. Fewer than five thousand longhorns were shipped from there in 1870, and by 1871 heavy settlement in the lower Platte River valley disrupted easy access to Plattsmouth, and it faded as a cattle market. Schuyler's boom was also short-lived. As the Blue River valley filled with settlers who were quick to invoke Nebraska's herd law to keep the drovers out, the trail shifted westward to Kearney by 1871. Two years later it had moved still farther west to Ogallala, which became Nebraska's cowboy capital for more than a decade.

Originally established as a way station by the Union Pacific, Ogallala seemed destined to be little more than a section house and water tank in the vast emptiness of western Nebraska. By 1873, however, Louis Aufdengarten was doing a thriving business supplying professional hide hunters and a few ranchers at his Drover's Store. As his advertisement in the *North Platte Enterprise* put it, he sold "Groceries, Dry Goods, Provisions, Cigars, and Liquors." That same year in Ogallala, the Lonergan brothers opened a men's store and L. M. Stone opened a hotel. In 1873 these men and a few others organized Keith County and moved a small frame house from Brule to Ogallala to serve as the courthouse.

The future of the endeavor seemed uncertain at first, but Aufdengarten, the Lonergans, and Stone had faith in their enterprise. In the summer of 1874 that faith seemed well on the way to being justified when the Union Pacific built a cattle pen and loading chute just west of town in an effort to maintain the profitable trade the railroad had enjoyed at Schuyler, Kearney, and other eastern points. Between sixty and seventy-five thousand Texas cattle were driven into Ogallala in 1875. By 1876 the number had jumped to over one hundred thousand, where it remained until the middle 1880s. Schuyler and Kearney never became boisterous cow towns, but Ogallala helped to establish the tradition of the wild and wooly West. As Norbert Mahnken put it, "Gold flowed freely across the

189

tables, liquor across the bar, and occasionally blood across the floor as a smoking gun in the hands of a jealous rival or an angered gambler brought an end to the trail of some unfortunate cowhand on the stained boards of Tuck's Saloon."[2]

The trail into Ogallala was an extension northward from Dodge City, Kansas, and was known as the Western Trail. As settlement had moved west in Kansas, the Western Trail replaced the old Chisholm Trail, which had run from San Antonio, Texas, to Abilene, Kansas. The Western Trail started at Bandera, Texas, crossed the Red River at a point known as Doan's Store, then pushed on to Dodge City, Kansas, located on the Arkansas River and on the Santa Fe Railroad. Some of the older longhorns were sold there, but most of the younger animals were driven on to Ogallala. From Dodge City the trail angled north and west to Buffalo Station, about sixty miles west of Hays, Kansas, and on to Ogallala. The last leg of the journey was the most difficult, principally because of the lack of water. Streams were few and far between at best, and the drovers frequently found that many of the smaller streams on which they were depending had dried up. For the trail-weary cowhands, the last day's drive, some thirty miles from Stinking Water Creek to the South Platte River, was almost the worst of the whole journey.

The long drives came to an abrupt end in the middle 1880s when settlers in northwestern Kansas and southwestern Nebraska invoked herd laws to keep the cattle out. New quarantine laws, passed at the insistence of the northern cattlemen against the spread of Texas fever, also blocked off the longhorns from the South. By the time this happened, however, western Nebraska and eastern Wyoming were experiencing a new industry, which had literally come up the trails from Texas.

OCCUPYING THE NEBRASKA RANGE

Early Nebraska cattlemen such as James E. Boyd near Kearney and Jack Morrow near the forks of the Platte River had also become the operators of road ranches along the Platte River and dealt in working oxen. The early beef cattle industry also developed between the North and South Platte Rivers, between the Platte and the Republican Rivers, and in the Platte River valley near Fort Kearny, on the islands in the Platte River itself, and in the valley of the South Loup River, now southern Custer County. All of these areas had good pastures; and they were protected from the Indians by Forts Kearny, McPherson, Mitchell, and Laramie, as well as by the patrols along the line of the Union Pacific Railroad. They were also near the terminals of the Texas trails, and they were readily accessible to markets in the region, including the Indian agencies and the Union Pacific.

By the early 1860s J. W. Iliff was ranging cattle in the western Platte River valley, and Edward Creighton, the builder of the transcontinental telegraph and Omaha's pioneer millionaire, was ranging working oxen on the western plains. In 1867 Creighton drove three thousand head of beef cattle from Schuyler to the western part of the state. Another early operator was R. C. Keith of North Platte, who began stock raising in the autumn of 1867 with five cows. Two years later he purchased one thousand head of Texas cows. John Bratt, who had run cattle near Cheyenne in 1868, brought twenty-five hundred Texas cattle to the Platte Valley near Fort Kearny in 1869. There were many others: Texans who had driven cattle up the trail; freighters who turned to the cattle business when competition from the Union Pacific ruined their business; eastern farmers who turned to ranching when they found that grazing was more profitable than general farming; scouts, hunters, and army men; eastern-ers and Europeans out for a fling and a quick killing. Their names were woven securely into the fabric of the old West, names like John Bratt, William F. Cody (Buffalo Bill), Captain James H. Cook, the Newman brothers, Frank and Luther North, and Colonel James H. Pratt.

As the initial range areas filled up, the industry spread elsewhere, im-pinging in places on the settled part of the state. When settlement, which had pushed up the Republican River valley into Furnas, Red Willow, and Hitchcock Counties, receded somewhat during the drought and grasshopper years of the middle 1870s, the cattlemen moved in and es-tablished ranches in parts of the area extending westward into Dundy County. To the north, cattlemen established themselves on the upper stretches of the Elkhorn River, particularly in Holt County.

For several years the cattlemen avoided the Sand Hills. To be sure, they had occupied the Loup River valleys in the eastern part of the hills in the early 1870s; and from North Platte west, John Bratt, the Keystone Cattle

Company, and the Bosler brothers had penetrated the region from the south. The interior, however, remained little known and greatly feared until 1879. In the spring of that year, Frank North decided to take a herd straight through the hills from the roundup on Blue Creek to his home ranch on the Dismal River. After going about thirty-five miles through supposedly dry country, he came upon a lake, around which were about seven hundred head of cattle in much better shape than those he had gathered on the roundup. At about the same time, the Newman brothers had a similar experience. A blizzard in March 1879 had driven about six thousand head past their line riders into the hills so the manager decided to make a desperate attempt to save some of them. When the snow melted in April, he sent a roundup into the hills, and after working for five weeks the crew brought out about eight thousand head of Newman cattle and an additional thousand head of unbranded cattle, descendants of animals that had drifted into the hills in previous years. If these experiences were not enough to convince cattlemen that they were overlooking the best range in the West, the winter of 1880–81 provided conclusive proof. During the heavy storms of that season, thousands of cattle died in the Platte Valley, but the Cody-North ranch lost only a few on its range back in the Sand Hills.

By the middle 1880s the Sand Hills developed into an important segment of the cattle country. The big organizations were not responsible for this growth; they generally remained out of the hills. Rather, it was small operators like Thomas Lynch, "Dad" Abbott and his son Arthur J., the Haney brothers, J. M. Gentry, James Forbes, J. H. Minor, Sidney Manning, and R. M. "Bud" Moran, who came in with only a few cattle and developed their herds over time and helped establish the political structures as well. Grant County was organized in 1887 to meet the demands of cattle owners for local law enforcement. Originally, the only accessible market to Sand Hills ranchers was provided by the Indian agencies in northwest Nebraska and southwest Dakota, but the extension of the Burlington Railroad through the area in 1887–88 opened up new markets to the east.

Stories of the easy money to be made in the range cattle business circulated widely in the eastern United States and Europe. These stories described the possibility of parlaying an investment of $5,000 into a net gain of $40,000-$50,000 in four years. General James S. Brisbin's *The Beef Bonanza; or, How to Get Rich on the Plains* set forth facts, figures, and directions as to how the neophyte could quadruple an investment in a few years, making an annual return of as much as 25 percent.[3] Brisbin's chapter headings such as "Estimated Fortunes," "Millions in Beef," "The Money to be Made," "Great Land and Great Owners," combined with stories of large profits and tales of high adventure, provided an irresistible lure. Millions of dollars were poured onto the plains by easterners and Europeans who wanted to set themselves up as cattle barons.

An early collapse was inevitable, however. Unsound financing combined with overstocking of the range created a precarious situation in which even the slightest adversity could have drastic consequences. When adversity came, it was not slight. Great blizzards roared across the plains during the winters of 1885–86 and 1886–87 and literally wiped out many of the newly established herds, along with the fortunes of their owners. Again, the Sand Hills was hit less severely than the rest of the country. Moreover, most of the Sand Hill ranchers were seasoned westerners who understood the limitations of both their range and their money. And it was in the Sand Hills that the revival of the cattle industry was based in the early 1890s, a revival that was to continue relatively unchecked for more than half a century.

But when it revived, the cattle industry of the 1890s was not the old range industry. Blooded stock, like Shorthorns, Herefords, and Angus, replaced the now unsatisfactory Texas longhorn. Fenced land replaced the open range. Supplemental feed was added to grass, which produced more and better beef and also helped herds survive the hard winters. Haying became as much a part of the cowhand's regular activity as riding the range, and the great flatlands interspersed among the Sand Hills came to be dotted with stacks of wild hay.

FENCING THE OPEN RANGE

Although almost every Nebraska farmer raised a few cattle, the cattle industry, in the strictest sense, generally was carried on by large-scale operators. By 1900, for example, the Sand Hills, which initially had been occupied by small, one-owner ranches, had come to be dominated by large organizations. Some big companies, such as the Spade, 101, and UBI (British), had come in; and many of the early settlers had developed into large-scale cattlemen: the Haney brothers, G. G. "Dad" and Arthur Abbott, James Forbes, Thomas Lynch, and P. A. Yeast, to name a few. By the 1930s, Sand Hills ranches constituted as many as sixty thousand acres; a medium-large ranch included from ten to twenty thousand acres, with herds running from twelve to fifteen hundred head.

Although the term "cattlemen" has become one of the enduring symbols of the western range, cattle ranching was not an exclusively male domain, as is illustrated by the career of Essie Buchanan Davis, who had married Cherry County rancher Albert Thane Davis in 1913. Widowed just two years later, she was left with an infant son, 3,650 acres, and a herd of cattle. She resisted the advice of many who urged her to sell and, over the next two decades, expanded the ranch to over 30,000 acres and 2,500 head of Hereford cattle. The OLO ranch became one of the most impressive cattle operations in the state, and before her death in 1966, Davis was one of the most powerful figures in Democratic politics in Nebraska and the nation.

Initially, the ranchers simply ran their cattle on public domain land, on which they paid neither taxes nor rent. This range, of course, was theoretically open to all. By mutual agreement and through friendly local governments as well as the influence of their associations, the ranchers generally were able to control the range and keep out any who tried to encroach upon it.

Particularly obnoxious to the ranchers were the "nesters" who ventured into the range country to take quarter-section homesteads to build their little soddies and fence their land, breaking up the open range. Wire cutters became standard equipment for cowhands, and when harassment failed to drive the homesteaders away, some ranchers resorted to stronger methods, even outright murder. One of the most notorious incidents in the homesteader-cattlemen conflict in Nebraska was the hanging and subsequent burning of Luther Mitchell and Ami Ketchum, Custer County homesteaders, in 1878 by a gang led by I. P. (Print) Olive, one of the wealthiest ranchers in the state.[4]

Except in the Sand Hills and certain smaller areas elsewhere, the homesteaders gained the ascendancy by persistence and sheer force of numbers.

From county to county they extended the provisions of the herd law, which had been adopted in 1871 and made it mandatory to restrain cattle from wandering at will over the prairie. The herd law, however, contained a provision allowing county officials to suspend it. Even so, it was not sufficient to maintain open ranges in the face of advancing settlement. Frontier County provides a good example.

Frontier County was organized by cattlemen in 1872 for the express purpose of making stock country out of the region south of the Platte River and north of the Republican River. The county seat was even given the appropriate name Stockville. A decade later, however, the cattlemen of Frontier County gave up on the open range and were willing to do some political horse-trading with the Grangers, supporting the herd law in exchange for Granger support of their choices for sheriff, judge, and other county offices.

Further strengthening the homesteaders' hand was federal legislation, adopted in 1885, that made it illegal to enclose lands in the public domain. Cattlemen in western Nebraska and elsewhere had fenced in large tracts of the public land to keep homesteaders from occupying it. The Brighton ranch in Keith County, for example, had fenced in 125,000 acres. The Coad brothers had also fenced in huge tracts; when they sold their ranch in 1883, they listed four enclosed pastures, the largest of which was 143,000 acres.

The government made no serious effort to enforce the law against illegal fencing until the administration of President Theodore Roosevelt in the early 1900s. Typical of his approach in fighting what he considered injustice or abuse, Roosevelt ordered action against two of the largest offenders in the country, Bartlett Richards and William G. Comstock, president and vice-president of the Nebraska Land and Feeding Company, which operated the Spade, Bar C, and Overton ranches, occupying more than five hundred thousand acres in Cherry, Sheridan, and Box Butte Counties.

In November 1905, Richards and Comstock pleaded guilty before Federal Judge William H. Munger in Omaha to the charge of having illegally fenced 212,000 acres of government land but asked for leniency because they were removing the fences. Judge Munger fined them each $300 and costs and sentenced them to six hours in the custody of the United States

The Range Cattle Industry

marshal. Because approximately six hours remained before their train was scheduled to arrive to take them home, the marshal turned them over to their attorney, who let them return to their hotel and then eat dinner at the Omaha Club before catching their train.

When Secretary of the Interior Ethan Hitchcock received the news of the trial and its outcome, he was indignant. He knew, too, that President Roosevelt would be furious. Indeed he was; Roosevelt removed the district attorney and the United States marshal and expressed regret that he did not have the power to remove Judge Munger. Richards and Comstock had, perhaps, received too much leniency, but the two men were later indicted and convicted of conspiring to secure title to public land through fraudulent entries. For this conviction both were fined $1,500 and received a year in prison.[5]

THE ROUNDUP

Brand inspection and the roundup ultimately provided a reasonable means of controlling the range cattle industry. At first, the cattlemen's associations registered and inspected the brands; in 1877 it was made a function of state government. The Nebraska Brand Committee, which was created by the legislature in 1941, consists today of the secretary of state as chairman and four active cattlemen as members.

In the days of the open range, the roundup was essential to control of the industry. Carefully supervised by the cattlemen's associations, a spring roundup was held for the purpose of branding calves and a fall roundup for gathering cattle for shipment to market. The roundup was a great social institution as well as an economic necessity, bringing the ranch hands together and giving them opportunities to exhibit their skills while competing with one another in sporting and daring feats. As the open range disappeared, so did the roundups, and by World War I they were a thing of the past.

THE KINKAIDERS

Much range country was not suited to general farming. Originally shunned even by ranchers, the Sand Hills and high tablelands had proven unsuitable for farming on the basis of the standard, quarter-section homestead. The homestead law was used in the area only by cattlemen to secure stream fronts and water holes. The Public Lands Commission of 1879 had recommended a free homestead on grazing lands of four square miles, but the cattlemen were satisfied with conditions as they were. If there were to be any change, they wanted unlimited sale or leasing, and so nothing happened. In 1901 Congressman William Neville of North Platte introduced a bill to provide a two-square-mile homestead, but it was killed in committee.

Agitation continued, however, for enlarged homesteads as a means of effecting more general distribution of grazing land, and in 1902 President Theodore Roosevelt called attention to the inadequacy of the quarter-section homestead for much of the West. Roosevelt made no specific recommendations, but Moses P. Kinkaid of O'Neill, who had been elected to Congress from the sixth district in 1902, decided to try to change the land laws for the benefit of homesteaders in his area. Despite opposition from the General Land Office and from many congressmen who expressed the fear that the proposal was simply another means for cattlemen to secure additional fraudulent landholdings, Kinkaid, with some support from Senator Charles H. Dietrich, was able to push his bill through, and President Roosevelt signed it on April 28, 1904.

The Kinkaid Act provided for homestead units up to 640 acres in thirty-seven counties of northwestern Nebraska. Irrigable lands were not eligible for entry under the act. After five years, homesteaders could receive patents for their land if they could prove that they had improved them by $1.25 per acre. Many were skeptical, but the *Alliance Times*, published in the principal town in the area, reported that "the majority of citizens are hopefully waiting and sanguine that the outcome will be advantageous to this section."[6]

The General Land Office has no precise record of the number of Kinkaid patents granted before November 1910, although some 1,600 patents were granted for approximately 800,000 acres in the Kinkaid area by that date. Part of these were probably taken under the original Homestead Act, which also applied to the area. Between November 1910 and July 1917, a total of 18,919 patents were issued for 8,933,527 acres.

Afterward the acreage patented declined each year, although as late as 1941 one Kinkaid patent was issued for a 40-acre additional entry.

In 1900 the population of the thirty-seven counties affected by the Kinkaid Act was 136,615. By 1910 it had jumped to 199,676 and in 1920 to 251,830. Production of principal crops increased as well, with corn production nearly doubling from 13.5 million bushels in 1900 to 24.7 million bushels in 1910. Wheat production experienced a fourfold increase from 3.3 million bushels to nearly 13 million bushels over the same time period.

Unfortunately, no figures are available to indicate what percentage of original claimants carried through to final patent and continued to live on their Kinkaid homesteads. It is clear, however, that many found even a 640-acre homestead too small for successful farming in the Sand Hills and in certain parts of the high plains. Nor did a section of land provide enough acreage for successful cattle ranching in an area where each animal required from fifteen to twenty acres.

The average size of farms in the area increased steadily, and the average went well beyond the section, indicating that the Kinkaiders either added to their holdings or, more probably, sold out to others who used the Kinkaid homesteads to add to their already large holdings. Generally the Kinkaiders, existing in their tar-paper shacks and little soddies, had a hard time, repeating the experience of other pioneers in the central portion of the state two decades earlier. They seemed to be a hardy lot, however, proud of their new country and willing to make the best of it. Dry farming techniques helped a good deal on the high tablelands, and in years when wheat both yielded well and sold well life was fairly good. At least enough were sufficiently impressed with the law to send Moses P. Kinkaid back to Congress again and again. He died in office in 1922 while serving his tenth consecutive term.

CHAPTER 16

The 1880s: Progress and Prosperity

The 1880s were good years in Nebraska; the decade was one of unparalleled progress and prosperity. Rain, so essential to survival in Nebraska, fell in relative abundance: the average annual rainfall for the whole state during the decade was 24.18 inches, compared with the mean of 22.84 inches; for the eastern section, 28.83 inches, compared with a mean of 27.74 inches; and for the central portion, 25.00 inches, compared with a mean of 22.28 inches.[1] Rainfall seemed particularly abundant in the central section where most of the new lands were being opened. The theory that "rainfall follows the plow" appeared to be demonstrating its validity.

Under the impetus of favorable conditions and aggressive promotion, settlers poured in by the thousands, increasing the state's population from 452,402 in 1880 to 1,058,910 in 1890.[2] Twenty-six counties were organized, extending county government to virtually all parts of the state, leaving only Boyd, Thurston, Garden, and Arthur Counties yet to be organized.[3] Both reflecting and making possible the growth of settlement was the great increase in railroad mileage from 1,868.40 miles in 1880 to 5,144.48 miles in 1890. The extension of the Burlington line through the Republican River valley and the Sand Hills accounted for a major portion of that increase.

In summarizing the progress of the decade, Addison E. Sheldon wrote:

In it came the largest addition to our population; the greatest increase in our production; the furthest extension of railway mileage; the greatest change in the physical aspects of our state. More land was taken by settlers in this period, more livestock added, larger increase in crops of all kinds, more new towns were founded, more postoffices were established, more schools were created, more churches built, more homes constructed than in any other decade of Nebraska history.[4]

AGRICULTURAL DEVELOPMENT

Farming may have become established as a way of life in the decade of the 1870s, but in the 1880s it turned Nebraska into a major food producer. A total of 19,585,382 acres of the public land was taken during the decade, leaving only about 11 million acres, mostly in the Sand Hills, still unclaimed. The Burlington sold 937,100 acres of its land, most of it in the first four years of the decade; and the Union Pacific sold 6,913,539 acres, including over 4 million in 1884. Much of this activity was purely speculative. Even so, the total number of farms increased by 80 percent from around 63,000 in 1880 to over 113,000 by 1890. The improved acreage nearly tripled from 5.2 million to 15.2 million; so too did valuation, increasing from $147.2 million to $511.8 million.[5] Agricultural settlement, except in the Republican River valley, had not extended much west of Grand Island in 1880, and there was still considerable land available east of that point. By 1890 agricultural settlement had pushed clear across the state. Though the pioneer settlers were not yet aware of it, virtually all of the free arable land had been occupied.

While the population doubled during the decade, the number of cattle and hogs tripled, as did production of many of the crops raised on Nebraska farms. The first crop planted by the pioneers continued to be the state's most important crop, and from 1879 to 1889 the amount of corn produced increased more than threefold from 65.5 to 215.9 million bushels. Nebraska jumped from eighth to fourth place among the corn states of the Union by producing in the latter year 10.2 percent of the nation's entire crop.

Corn maintained its ascendancy even though its relative purchasing power was lower than that of wheat, oats, or barley. During the 1880s farmers increased the number of acres planted to corn from 1.6 million to 5.5 million. Acreage in oats also increased, from about 250,000 to 1.5 million acres, and wheat production declined from 1.5 million to approximately 800,000 acres.[6] The production factors mentioned above account in part for these changes, but also important was the belief that corn fed

Anton Smock stands before his farmstead near Oconto. For Anton and many others, a frame house was a sign of progress and prosperity. Courtesy, NSHS Butcher Collection, B983:1764a.

to livestock would yield a good return. It was noted that a bushel of corn would make ten to twelve pounds of pig, and it became an empiric rule that hogs at five dollars a hundred could be grown profitably on fifty-cent corn. The price ratio was almost always satisfactory. Agricultural journals and farm spokesmen constantly talked about the corn-hog ratio and the importance of hogs that could be marketed at two hundred pounds at the age of six to eight months; J. Sterling Morton called them "mortgage lifters." Morton was an avid hog-corn enthusiast. As president of the State Board of Agriculture, he encouraged farmers in this direction with numerous quotable statements as "Corn is King, Swine Heir Apparent" and "A mother swine is an inter-convertible bond, her family, annual coupons serving as farmers' 'mortgage lifters.'"[7] In his last report as president of the State Board of Agriculture, in 1876, Morton wrote:

We cannot raise too much corn. No matter what corn may be worth as corn in the market. It may be worth five cents or nothing at all. But transmuted

to beef, pork, or mutton, it will always pay the husbandman a handsome and
satisfactory return. This should be, and must be, if it will grow prosperous, a
stock-feeding state. Wheat growing for exportation will not pay. It wears out the
soil, the men who till it, and the reputation of the State; the first by taking away
part of its productive power each year; the second by hard work and fretting over
poor compensation; and the last by the pronounced and unyielding poverty of
its citizens.[8]

Wheat found little favor among Nebraska farmers until about the turn
of the century. The soil and climate of Nebraska seemed to be unsuitable
for spring wheat and for the varieties of winter wheat most farmers were
willing to plant. The Mennonites who came to the south-central part of
the state in the 1870s and 1880s produced good yields from the Turkey
Red winter wheat they brought with them from Russia, but most farmers
were slow to adopt it. Moreover, the millers looked with disfavor upon
hard winter wheat because their equipment was designed for processing
soft spring wheat.

The development of new milling processes and of other varieties of
hard winter wheat by the University of Nebraska's College of Agriculture
helped create an appreciation for winter wheat. Yet it would take two
more decades for winter wheat to come into its own. By the beginning
years of the twentieth century, when farmers and agricultural leaders alike
began to appreciate the need for diversification, winter wheat would
almost universally be viewed as a strong second crop.[9] By 1899, for example, J. Sterling Morton, who had severely criticized wheat two decades
earlier, was writing of winter wheat: "The success which has come to the
farmers, within the last five years of its cultivation, leaves no room for
speculation upon the problems of wheat culture on these vast and rich
areas. The fact arms our people for a new advancement and the advantage
of diversifying production as a measure of both profit and safety, whose
probable benefits it would be impossible to estimate."[10]

The 1880s saw Nebraska farmers taking advantage of the general improvement in farm machinery that had been occurring in the United
States since the Civil War. Horses replaced oxen as motive power, and in
the 1880s the sulky plow was introduced. Although the disc harrow was
not in general use in Nebraska until after 1900, spike-toothed harrows

began to come into the state in the late 1870s and early 1880s. There were improvements in planting as well. The end-gate seeder replaced the sowing sack and was itself later replaced by the force-feed drill. For corn, walking one-row markers and single-row planters were introduced in the late 1870s, replacing the hand planter and the crude homemade marker; and by the late 1880s the two-row marker became available.

The cultivator also contributed greatly to the expansion of corn production. First there was the one-horse, two-shovel cultivator, which could cover only one side of the row at a time, but by the late 1870s the shovels were arranged so that the row could be straddled. Although some of the most prosperous farmers used riding cultivators as early as 1880, this convenience was not in general use until after 1900. Indeed, many of the older farmers looked askance at the riding cultivator. Given the work ethic of the day, it is not surprising that some felt sitting down to work was evidence of laziness.

Reapers had been used in Nebraska in territorial times, but they only cut the grain and laid it on a platform from which it had to be raked by hand. Later a self-rake was added, but still the grain had to be picked up from the ground and tied into bundles by hand. Twine binders came into use in Nebraska in the early 1880s. Threshers began to appear in the state in the early 1870s. The first ones knocked the grain from the straw but did not separate it. Later, separators and a winnowing device that separated the grain from the chaff were developed. The early separators were horse-powered; the most common type was the sweep power drawn by five teams of horses. Threshing was done from a stack or from racks, although the early machines had to be hand-fed, one bundle at a time. Threshing under these conditions was hard work at best. To the joy of the hired hands and the irritation of the owners, however, the routine was frequently interrupted by breakdowns. By the middle 1880s steam began to replace horses as the motive power for threshing. An even greater improvement was the development of the traction engine, which could move the separator from place to place as well as power its operations.

Most of the corn in the state was harvested by hand from standing stalks in the field. Nebraska's pioneer farmers generally used a device known as a husking peg, a small, round piece of hard wood sharpened at one end, approximately six inches in length. This device was held in the hollow of the right hand and kept in place by a loop of buckskin or soft leather. Even so, husking corn remained an unpleasant and seemingly never-ending task in the late fall and winter months.

Throughout the period, Nebraska's leading agriculturalists continued their program of popular education. In large part through the efforts of J. Sterling Morton, they continued to place great stress on the importance of tree culture, both fruit and forest. Morton presented a resolution to the State Board of Agriculture on April 4, 1872, urging that April 10 be designated Arbor Day. The idea of encouraging all Nebraskans to plant trees on that day was well received, and in 1874 the board sought to make it an annual occurrence, designating the second Wednesday in April for the celebration. In 1885 Morton's birthday, April 22, was designated Arbor Day and made a legal holiday by the state legislature. To be so honored while in the prime of life and by a legislature composed largely of his political opponents was an indication of the unusual esteem in which the people of Nebraska held the founder of Arbor Day. In a sense, the state also honored his wife, Carolyn, or "Carrie," who had died in 1881. Carrie Morton had taken great pride in their home and grounds in Nebraska City and supervised much of the work, including the planting of most of the trees at Arbor Lodge.[11]

Even though the University of Nebraska's College of Agriculture had opened in 1882, much of the early popular education in farming was conducted by the State Board of Agriculture and its affiliated organizations, particularly the State Horticultural Society. In 1884, when Charles E. Bessey arrived from Iowa State College to begin a long and distinguished career as professor of botany at the University of Nebraska, he began a statewide investigation of plant life and instituted a program of scientific and popular experiments. In 1886, the Board of Regents authorized the establishment of an Agricultural Experiment Station and appointed Frank S. Billings as its first director.

THE URBAN BOOM

Measured in product value, Nebraska's manufactures increased sevenfold from $12.6 in 1880 to $93 million in 1890. Most of the industry, however, was related to agriculture and was concentrated in Omaha, which

Table 8. Nebraska's Manufactures, 1880–1890

	1880	1890	% Change
Establishments	1,403	3,014	114.8
Capital	$4,881,150	$37,569,508	669.9
Employees	4,793	23,876	398.1
Wages	$1,742,311	$12,984,571	645.2
Materials	$8,208,478	$67,334,532	720.3
Product value	$12,627,336	$93,037,794	636.8

Source: Department of the Interior, Bureau of the Census, *Manufacturing Industries in the United States at the Eleventh Census: 1890.* (Washington DC: Government Printing Office, 1895), 68.

accounted for 61 percent of manufacturing capital. Lincoln ran a distant second with 8.6 percent of the state's manufacturing capital. Already Omaha was beginning to assume a metropolitan flavor that set it off from the rest of the state.

The meatpacking industry paced Omaha's industrial development; indeed, meat products counted for more than one-fourth of the state's entire manufactured products in 1890. Omaha had had commercial stockyards since 1867. Beginning in 1871, small packinghouses were established, the most important of which was that of James E. Boyd, organized in 1872.

The modern large-scale packing industry dates from the establishment of the Union Stock Yards Company in 1884. At first, skeptics were inclined to doubt that the Omaha yards could ever become more than transit and feeding places for stock en route to Chicago. The railroads, preferring the longer haul, discouraged the packing industry in Omaha. Yet Omaha was located in the center of the corn belt and had direct communication to the great grazing regions of the West. The energy with which John A. McShane, president of the Stock Yards Company, set out to develop a packing industry also helped make Omaha a significant center. The first big packer to locate in Omaha was George P. Hammond of Detroit, who opened a plant near the yards on May 19, 1885. It was a great day for Omaha; and many of the city's leading citizens rode out in their carriages to see McShane kill the first steer and hog.

In 1886 the Anglo-American Provision Company began operations in a plant built by the Stock Yards Company. McShane had aggressively recruited the company, offering a $200,000 subsidy and a promise of free use of the stockyards for five years. In addition, McShane had personally given Anglo-American Provision $25,000 worth of stock in the Omaha Land Company. That same year, Sir Thomas Lipton made a brief foray into the Omaha packing business but was soon bought out by the Armour-Cudahy Packing Company. In 1890 the Cudahys bought the Armour interests, and Armour did not reenter the Omaha field until 1898. In 1888 Swift and Company opened an Omaha plant after the Stock Yards Company offered it $100,000 in stock, $100,000 in cash, and eleven acres of land.

Accompanying the growing packing industry was the revitalization of some of the city's older industries and the organization of a variety of new ones. The old Omaha and Grant Smelting Company, which had been organized in 1870, consolidated with a Denver company in 1882, which greatly increased its business. By 1892 it had a thousand employees and turned out products valued at more than $21 million annually. It was drawing ore from as far away as Canada and Mexico and was reputed to be the largest plant of its kind in the world. The Carter White Lead Works, using the pig lead of the Omaha smelter, increased its capital 500 percent from 1880 to 1889. Also during the decade, a linseed oil company reached an annual production valued at $1.5 million, and a pioneer soap factory expanded its operations tenfold. In addition, there were many new establishments, including brickyards, clothing factories, food processing plants, breweries, and distilleries.

In short, Omaha was booming. Its population of thirty thousand in 1880 increased to sixty-one thousand in 1885 and doubled again in the next three years. Real estate additions were platted for miles on all sides of the city. A 614-acre farm that once sold for $2.50 per acre brought $1,000 per acre. Eastern capitalists made highly publicized visits to the city, and many seemed convinced that the very dirt of Omaha's streets had a magnetic charm.

Omaha was not alone. Lincoln, too, enjoyed a boom during the 1880s. As an enthusiastic contemporary writer put it: "Day by day it [Lincoln] has grown and thriven, adding some new industry or social element, until the winter of 1886–1887, when like a mountain stream, bounding free from its frozen embrace, and leaping with mad delight to meet the warm sunshine, has this capital city sprung into national fame and great prosperity."[12] In 1885 Lincoln's population stood at twenty thousand; two years later it had doubled, and enthusiastic residents prophesied a population of one hundred thousand by 1890. New additions were laid out, and the city began to assume a metropolitan air, with an electric light plant, a water system, street railways, and a few blocks of paved streets. Its citizens, however, still used the University of Nebraska's campus as a pasture for their livestock.

The boom spread to the smaller cities. Beatrice, envisioning itself as a city of fifty thousand, extended its city limits and promoted a street railway to carry residents into town from the new subdivisions. In Norfolk, the Elkhorn Valley Investment Company employed all the methods of professional boomers, with parades, celebrations, conventions, and advertisements to attract new industry and new population. Kearney, under the leadership of H. D. Watson, founder of the famed Watson ranch, enjoyed perhaps the most spectacular growth of any of the smaller cities. Hastings, trying hard to outdo Grand Island, manufactured a short-lived but exciting boom. Even the small towns, each aspiring to have a canning factory, a flour mill, or a creamery, were affected with the boom spirit.

Indeed, that spirit was highly reminiscent of the speculative mood of the middle 1850s. Progress was in the air. Good crops, expanding railroads, and a growing population all suggested a great future. Any town could become a commercial center or a great railway metropolis or both. A score of villages coveted the state capital, and more than a few believed that in time the greatness of the new West would necessitate the abandonment of Washington DC for a national headquarters on the plains.[13]

Everywhere, however, the dreams of greatness were implemented with borrowed money. Counties and towns issued bonds to assist railroads and other enterprises; corporations issued stock; individuals assumed mortgages. There was a great demand in the East for western mortgages, and many companies sent out solicitors and paid large commissions on the new loans they made. As the manager of one large investment company, which ultimately failed with liabilities of over $10 million, testified: "It is a fact that during many months of 1886 and 1887, we were unable to get enough mortgages for the people of the East, who wished to invest in that kind of security. My desk was piled high every morning with hundreds of letters, each enclosing a draft, and asking me to send a farm mortgage from Nebraska."[14]

The fever was not confined to Nebraska but spread throughout the West. A contemporary observer wrote:

During the years from 1880 to 1887, and in some cases 1890, the date of the climax, varying in different sections, there developed in Minnesota, the Dakotas, Nebraska, Kansas, Texas, in all the states and territories farther West, and in some parts of Iowa, Wisconsin, and Missouri, a fever of speculation in real estate, which affected the whole population, destroyed all true sense of value, created an enormous volume of fictitious wealth, infected with its poison all the veins and arteries of business, and swelled the cities to abnormal proportions.[15]

When the bubble burst in the late 1880s, its repercussions were felt all over the country. Moneylenders took over the properties that had secured their mortgages, but their hope of profit was gone. Farmers were forced to take out chattel mortgages, if indeed they could get mortgages at all, to protect their land. In cities everywhere were crumbling derelicts that stood as stark monuments to the speculative spree. There had been prosperity, but who had become prosperous?

LIFE ON THE SOD HOUSE FRONTIER

While city dwellers were beginning to enjoy modern conveniences and prosperous farmers in the eastern counties constructed comfortable frame houses in pleasant groves, most of the newer settlers, who occupied the central and western portions of the state, eked out a precarious existence under the most primitive conditions. Many of the difficulties they experienced in day-to-day living stemmed from the shortage of those two basic commodities, wood and water, which permeated all of life. Efforts to overcome their lack provided unique experiences for the westward-moving people of the United States as they modified their ways of living to meet the demands of the country.

First, there was a basic change in housing. Pioneers in the wooded regions found it a simple matter to get together enough logs for a rude cabin or even a comfortable dwelling. On the plains, however, it took great ingenuity or considerable expense to gather enough timbers for the basic supports. Many found the solution under their feet, in the prairie sod. Alternately baked at temperatures of over 100 degrees by the intense, dry heat of the summers and frozen to subzero temperatures by the long winters, and dried by the ever-present winds, "prairie brick" or "Nebraska marble," as the early settlers liked to call it, and the sod houses constructed from it, became enduring symbols of the new frontier.

Sod houses varied from dugouts that were little more than caves to rather pretentious, two-story affairs, although the typical sod house was a simple one-room, frame-supported structure. The more prosperous pioneers shingled their roofs or covered them with tar paper, but most sod houses were roofed with earth or sod. The hard-packed earth usually served as the floor. Occasionally the inside walls were whitewashed or covered with old newspapers and a cloth was stretched across the top to provide a ceiling. Dark, damp, and inhabited by fleas, mice, and other vermin, it was far from an ideal place in which to live. Yet the sod house was fairly cool in summer and warm in winter, and thus it frequently was more satisfactory than the poorly insulated frame house with which settlers replaced it as soon as they could afford to make the transition.

Another problem posed by the shortage of wood was that of providing fuel for cooking and for heating during the severe winters. The search for an adequate substitute for wood was constant. Buffalo chips and later cow chips, as the dried dung was called, provided an easy, although somewhat unsavory, answer. Coal was available in the railroad towns, but few if any of the homesteaders could afford to purchase it. The wild prairie hay, seemingly the only abundant commodity, offered some possibilities, and soon hay-burning stoves were developed to facilitate its use. Hay, however, was far from satisfactory. It burned too rapidly to provide a steady fire and the great quantities required to keep a stove going for a day posed a fire hazard if kept inside the house.

Corncobs and cornstalks were also used for fuel. At times the price of corn went so low that throwing the ears into a fire seemed the best use for them. Sunflowers were also considered as a substitute for wood. One advocate argued that enough sunflowers could be grown on an acre to provide sufficient fuel for an ordinary family to cook for a year and that two acres would produce enough sunflower stalks to furnish any family with all of its fuel requirements for a year, provided they had a "tight house."

The shortage of wood also made fencing difficult. The rail fence of the eastern pioneer was, of course, out of the question. Osage orange hedges were found to be a fairly satisfactory substitute in the eastern counties, but they would not grow in the central and western portions of the state. A sod fence was reasonably satisfactory for a small yard or corral, but it was unsightly and difficult to construct. When barbed wire was developed in the 1870s, it provided the long-sought solution and became an important technological factor in the occupation of the plains.

Procuring water for domestic use as well as for stock was in many respects a more acute problem than that of securing wood for fuel and construction. Except for cooking, fuel was not needed during the summer, but water was a daily necessity throughout the year. Until a homesteader could sink a well, water had to be hauled from the nearest source of supply, often several miles away. In some favored localities an adequate supply could be found at depths from twenty to forty feet, but on the high plains, away from the streams, it was necessary to dig down three to six hundred feet to reach water. Frequently, this was too costly so the homesteader managed to get along on water hauled in barrels, supplemented by the little that could be caught during the infrequent rains. Well digging was expensive because it was dangerous and laborious, and well diggers occasionally became noted characters on the plains.[16]

Combined with these difficulties were the hot, dry winds in summer and icy blasts in winter. These climatic extremes taxed the endurance of even the most resolute settlers. The exposed soddies were particularly vulnerable to the blizzards that roared across the barren plains with unrelenting fury. The great blizzard of January 12, 1888, which took a heavy toll of both animal and human life in all the northern plains states, is still remembered as a major catastrophe.

CHAPTER 17

The 1880s: Whose Prosperity?

Before the decade was out, the speculative prosperity of the middle 1880s had collapsed, leaving in its wake a trail of empty buildings and foreclosed farms. Even during the height of the boom it was apparent that not everyone was sharing in the general prosperity. For farmers, in particular, the decline had begun in the 1870s and continued through the 1880s with a sharp downward spiral in the later years of that decade. To be sure, land was available, money was easy, and crops were plentiful, but prices remained low. For a time the farmers, preoccupied with breaking new sod and encouraged by increasing production, failed to voice any effective organized protest against their worsening economic position. By the end of the decade, however, they were fully aroused and prepared to set the prairies afire with a far-reaching political revolt.

POLITICS AS USUAL

As in most northern states, the Republicans had dominated Nebraska politics since the Civil War. The stigma of being the party of rebellion was too much for the Democrats to overcome among an electorate dominated by Union veterans. Republican orators exploited that dominance and admonished the people to vote as they had shot. Moreover, Nebraska Republicans could point with pride to substantial national achievements that also had great local significance. The Republicans had enacted the free homestead law after Democratic administrations had consistently opposed it. Republicans had also made possible the Pacific railway and other railroads that made the land accessible to homesteaders and opened the way for settlement of the state.

The Democratic Party in Nebraska was also far from united. A violent personal feud between J. Sterling Morton and Dr. George L. Miller, two of its most prominent leaders, split the party into two factions. Those who wanted to combine with the Greenbackers, Anti-Monopolists, and other activist movements found themselves pitted against those who insisted that the only salvation of the country lay in getting back to the simple, fundamental principles of Jefferson and Jackson.

With the Democrats so divided, the Republicans were able to stay in power even during the Butler scandals and the failure of the constitution of 1871. The adoption of a new constitution in 1875 seemed to assure their continued success. They regularly elected the governor and other state officers, most of the congressmen, and large majorities in the legislature, who in turn regularly sent Republicans to the United States Senate.

For governor, the Republicans usually chose bright young men with an obvious future or faithful old aldermen who deserved recognition for their previous service. Albinus Nance, who served as governor from 1879 to 1883, was one of those bright young men. He had come to Nebraska in 1871 from Illinois, where he had attended Knox College and been admitted to the bar. He was only twenty-three when he arrived in the state and settled on a homestead near Osceola. In 1874 he was elected to the legislature, and when he was reelected in 1876, he was chosen Speaker of the House of Representatives. In the same year he was also selected as chairman of the Nebraska delegation to the Republican National Convention. In 1878, at the age of thirty, he won the Republican nomination for governor and was elected. Unfortunately, Nance left the state shortly after he had completed his second term and moved to Chicago to spend the rest of his life dealing in railroad securities.

James W. Dawes, who succeeded Nance, was only thirty-seven years old when elected governor in 1882. Dawes, also a lawyer, came to Nebraska from Wisconsin in 1871, the same year as Nance. He settled at Crete and immediately began combining his law practice with politics. After serving as a member of the constitutional convention in 1875, Dawes was elected to the state Senate and also to the chairmanship of the Republican State Central Committee. In 1880 he became Nebraska's representative on the Republican National Committee. Though a machine politician, Dawes was a good campaigner and an able orator, so capable that in both 1882 and 1884 he defeated J. Sterling Morton, the ablest and best-known candidate the Democrats could have put forward. As in the case

The railroads became the symbol of progress and success for many communities on the plains, as evidenced by this photograph of the Burlington Depot at McCook in the mid-1890s. Courtesy, NSHS, C689:4.

of Nance, however, Dawes's service as governor ended his active participation in state politics. He continued to practice law in Crete until 1898, when he left the state to spend the rest of his professional life as an army officer.

In John M. Thayer, the Republican candidate for governor in 1886, the party swung from youth to old age. Sixty-six when elected, General Thayer, a hero of Shiloh and Fort Donelson, had been a United States senator and state commander of the Grand Army of the Republic and had also served four years as governor of Wyoming Territory before becoming governor of Nebraska.

The United States senatorships, distributed by the legislature, usually went to men of more standing in the party than those selected for governor. Phineas W. Hitchcock (1871–77), Algernon S. Paddock (1875–81, 1887–93), Alvin Saunders (1877–83), C. H. Van Wyck (1881–87), and Charles F. Manderson (1883–95) had all been prominent in territorial politics. Hitchcock, Paddock, and Saunders were also territorial pioneers. Hitchcock had served as delegate to Congress; Paddock and Saunders had served as secretary and governor of the territory, respectively, from their appointment by President Lincoln in 1861 to the admission of the state in 1867. General Van Wyck did not settle in Nebraska until 1874, although he had previously had property interests in the state, and he had a distinguished Civil War record and eleven years of service as a congressman from New York. He had large interests in Otoe County and was a friend of Edward Rosewater, editor of the powerful *Omaha Bee*. Manderson was also a relative latecomer, moving to Omaha from Ohio in 1869. He had commanded an Ohio regiment in the Civil War, however, and was a lawyer of prominence and means.

Senatorial contests were protracted affairs and often occupied the attention of the legislature for weeks at a time. On occasion, the Democrats and Anti-Monopolists could have elected a United States senator by uniting on one candidate, but they were never able to resolve their differences. Indeed, the Democrats could not even agree among themselves. The Republicans were able to prevail by agreeing finally on one candidate, although it usually took many ballots for one candidate to develop sufficient strength to cause his opponents to withdraw.

The atmosphere of the capital city during a senatorial contest was usually oppressive and marked with intrigue. The leading candidates ensconced themselves in hotel suites at twenty dollars a day. Board bills of the hangers-on, paid by the candidates, often ran to five hundred dollars a day. Hotels and saloons reeked with the smoke of free cigars distributed by the generous candidates. It seemed that each train brought a fresh pack of politicians, all of whom wanted to have some part in the selection of a senator.

The hotels were filled to overflowing. The overflow, if important enough, spilled into the twenty-dollar suites or, if unimportant, into the lobbies. One reporter declared that during the heated contest of 1883, the lobby of the Commercial Hotel usually was so full that if one wanted to invite a man to have a drink, he did it in a whisper or his invitation would get a dozen takers instead of one.

RUMBLINGS OF DISCONTENT

It was generally conceded that the officers of the two large railroads serving the state, the Union Pacific and the Burlington, wielded much influence in the election of senators from Nebraska. The extent of this influence was never demonstrated, nor was its presence absolutely confirmed, yet it undoubtedly existed. All politicians in the state acted in senatorial matters with an eye to the two railroads, and no one was elected to the Senate during this period over the opposition of the railroads. In the case of Van Wyck, however, the railroads and the more conservative elements of the Republican Party soon came to realize that they had put their money on the wrong candidate. Though Van Wyck was known as "a Burlington man" at the time of his election, he soon developed maverick tendencies by aligning himself with the opposition on all the major issues of the day. As a result, the regular Republicans developed an intense hatred for him.

POLITICS AND PROHIBITION

The prohibition issue intruded itself into local politics with considerable vigor. The voters had decisively turned down a proposal to submit the prohibition question to the people in 1871, but by the late 1870s, widespread agitation for abstinence prevailed under the leadership of John B. Finch, who brought prohibition to the fore as a political issue. In 1886 the Prohibition Party nominated candidates for governor and other principal offices. Its gubernatorial candidate, H. W. Hardy, a prominent businessman who had earlier served as mayor of Lincoln, polled 8,175 votes out of a total 138,209. Even though it took all night to defeat a prohibition plank in the Republican platform in 1888, the Prohibition candidate for governor got only about 4.5 percent of the vote compared to Hardy's approximately 6 percent of two years before. Although the Prohibition Party never had a chance, prohibition sentiment grew steadily and by the 1890s became inextricably interwoven with the politics of both major parties.

WOMEN'S SUFFRAGE

The vote for women had been a recurring issue in Nebraska from the territorial days and reemerged with vigor in the early 1870s, when supporters succeeded in getting it attached to the revised constitution which was submitted to the voters at a special election in 1871. The constitution, as well as the proposals for women's suffrage, submitting prohibition to the voters, compulsory education, and liability for stockholders went down to a resounding defeat. Women's suffrage fared the least well, receiving only 22 percent of the vote.

Women's suffrage as an issue was far from dead, however, and was kept alive by a young Canadian immigrant who had moved to Hebron in 1869. Erasmus Correll founded the *Hebron Journal* in 1871. He and his wife, Lucy, both became strong advocates for equal rights for women and provided space on the front page of their paper for women who wished to make their voices heard on the issue. Both also wrote regular columns supporting feminist causes, and in 1877 Correll invited Susan B. Anthony to Hebron to speak on behalf of women's rights. Two years later, in April 1879, Elizabeth Cady Stanton came to Hebron to lend support to the women's cause.

In 1880 Correll was elected to the Nebraska House of Representatives, and the following year he introduced a women's suffrage bill. It was defeated, but by then some thirty-nine local women's suffrage organizations had been formed in Nebraska, as well as a State Women's Suffrage Association. Others had joined the crusade, including Clara Bewick Colby of Beatrice, who would soon become Nebraska's leading female crusader for women's suffrage.

In 1882 Correll was elected to the Nebraska Senate, where he introduced yet another bill, this time to submit the question of women's suffrage to the voters. Clara Colby, who made numerous speeches before both houses of the legislature, was credited with convincing the representatives to pass the bill, which was ultimately defeated by the voters. Women would have to wait until the 1920s to acquire the vote, but Correll and Colby were instrumental in keeping the issue of women's suffrage alive in Nebraska.

THE FARM ECONOMY

Although the organization of the Prohibition Party and the activities of women's suffrage organizations indicated some discontent with the political status quo in Nebraska, the major issues arose out of the unfavorable economic position of the farmers of the state. The West, including Nebraska, was consistently a debtor region. The area's meager capital had been strained to the limit to establish commercial farming, and the additional capital required to keep it going had been secured by wholesale mortgaging, both public and private. Agriculture was the state's only basic industry. Even though Omaha, and Lincoln to a lesser extent, had developed into urban centers with some industry, they too were dependent on agriculture and their leaders' points of view remained agricultural. Furthermore, agriculture in Nebraska was being conducted on a shoestring, and any deviation from full production or minimum prices could throw the whole industry, and also the state, into a debtor's position. Unfortunately, those deviations occurred with ominous regularity, with the result that the wolf, in the form of a mortgage or bond holder, seemed always to be lurking just outside the door. Nebraskans, then, were fair game for anyone who had a proposal that might benefit debtors.

Moreover, the farmers had become convinced that they worked longer hours, under more adverse conditions, and with smaller compensation for their labor than any other group on earth. Their difficulty, they were sure, lay basically in the low prices received for the products they had to sell. The cause was believed to be overproduction, but most farmers refused to admit that they were overproducing. Their newspapers were filled regularly with stories of mass starvation all over the world so it was illogical to suspect that overproduction was the culprit. Instead, they felt, the trouble must lay in underconsumption or conditions that stood in the way of consumption.

Chief among these barriers were the railroads. Railroad construction had made settlement possible in many parts of the state, and the survival of those settlements was, to a large degree, dependent on the railroads. Possibly it was this dependence that made farmers so sensitive to any signs that the railroads were being operated for other interests than their own. To be sure, there were plenty of signs, the most obvious being high freight rates. It cost a Nebraska farmer a bushel of wheat to send another bushel to market. Local rates were particularly high, and farmers recognized discrimination against short hauls and themselves in favor of large, long-distance shippers.

The farmers believed that the railroads' monopoly was the principal cause of high rates. Each town usually had only one railroad, and its monopolistic character was self-evident; in areas served by two or more railroads, business was divided and rates were maintained by mutual agreement. Corollary causes of the high rates, according to the agrarian argument, were the high dividends paid on "watered" or inflated stock and the natural tendency of the railroads to discriminate in favor of other monopolies and against farmers. Added to high freight rates were the taxes levied to pay off construction subsidies that had been granted to the railroads, which seemed to benefit only the railroads themselves. J. Sterling Morton, for example, declared that the Brownville, Fort Kearney and Pacific Railroad was organized for the sole purpose of "public plunder through Brownville bonds."[1]

The railroads successfully resisted local government efforts to tax the lands given them by the federal government. Much of the state benefited as a result of those gifts, but in northeastern Nebraska the Burlington located thousands of acres of "lieu lands," which removed them from the homestead lists without providing any transportation advantages. Moreover, farmers throughout the state felt the federal land grant system had given the railroads the state's best agricultural lands at the expense of the homesteaders.

The charges against the railroads were buttressed by their political activity. Their voice in the selection of United States senators was freely discussed, and they lobbied openly and effectively against legislative efforts to implement the provision in the constitution of 1875 providing for railroad regulation. Particularly objectionable was the "free pass bribery system," the practice of issuing free passes to every public official from dog catcher to governor. As one antirailroad author characterized it,

For thirty years the politics of Nebraska has been policed and the government of the state controlled by railroads. This railroad control of politics and state government is procured through a conspiracy. The conspiracy is between the railroad managers and the politicians. The purpose of the conspiracy is to procure for the railroads, through the politicians, control over the state government. The price paid to the politicians for their part in the conspiracy is the free pass.[2]

Though the railroads epitomized all that was wrong with politics and the economic system, farmers also directed complaints against other groups. The elevators, usually operated as monopolies, often acted in a highhanded fashion by downgrading grain and shading prices to their own advantage. They had very close arrangements with the railroads, too, as farm groups that tried to operate elevators of their own found when they attempted to get trackage and cars.

Bankers and mortgage holders were another obvious source of oppression, particularly in the lean years. To many farmers, however, they were simply the instruments of an inadequate currency and credit system. Interest payments on mortgages often drained off cash needed for immediate activities, and short-term loans were virtually unavailable. Closely allied was the supply of circulating money, and a significant segment of farm opinion in the post–Civil War years advocated measures that seemed to promise an increase in the amount of currency available. There was some feeling, too, that the protective tariff worked to the advantage of the corporations at the expense of the farmer, although the tariff never became an overriding issue in Nebraska politics.

The railroads as the basic political issue came to the fore in the legislative session of 1881. The Nebraska State Board of Equalization, in response to a legislative recital of the problem in 1879, had issued a long report to show that many of the railroads were operating at a net loss and thus needed their taxes reduced. A special Senate committee on railroads came out with a strong report calling attention to rebates, pooling, and rate discrimination. All the legislature managed to do was to memorialize Congress to enact laws to correct unjust discrimination and excessive charges on the part of interstate railroads. Actually, of course, the federal approach to railroad regulation ultimately was found to be the only satisfactory one in many respects, but at this time the legislative memorial seemed like little more than passing responsibility from the state to the federal government.

The Nebraska constitution of 1875 gave the legislature power to regulate railroad rates, and demand that the lawmakers exercise that power was growing. Lawmakers were reluctant to do so, however. Moreover, if rates were to be regulated, a commission would have to be set up, and the constitution specifically prohibited the creation of additional salaried offices. A legislative committee to which the problem was referred in 1883 concluded that the constitution would have to be amended, and the legislature submitted an amendment authorizing the creation of a railroad commission at the same time it memorialized the U.S. Congress to take action to regulate the railroads.

The people, feeling that the problem could be solved without the creation of additional boards and salaries, turned down this proposal, two to one. The legislature then attempted to solve the problem within the limitations of the constitution by creating a railroad commission consisting of the attorney general, secretary of state, and auditor, with the understanding that secretaries or deputies authorized by the constitution could be appointed to do the work. The commission was given the authority to regulate the railroads in a general but innocuous manner. Opponents of the act charged that it was a farce designed solely to forestall significant regulation. The three deputies, appointed for political reasons, had little knowledge of the problem. They were not inclined to do anything that might provoke the railroads to test the constitutionality of their offices, which might put them out of their $2,000-per-year jobs, a comfortable salary in Nebraska at that time.

Other signs of discontent were visible. Omaha had developed into an industrial community and was beginning to feel the stress of labor troubles. In 1882 a strike for higher wages on a large grading enterprise in the Burlington's yards (the "Camp Dump Strike") spread rapidly to other industries. The strikers attempted to maintain a picket line, and the resultant riot was quelled only after the National Guard was called out.

Throughout the decade of the 1880s there were strong signs of discontent with the "regular" Republican approach to the problems facing the state, but, though this unrest weakened the party's hold on state politics, it never developed into effective opposition. Within the party, mavericks such as Senator Van Wyck, editor Rosewater, and Attorney General William Leese were either shouted down at meetings or ignored. Outside the party, there seemed to be no organization around which an effective opposition could develop.

The Democrats were still badly divided, and their leaders seemed even less sympathetic to the problems of farmers and laborers than were the

Republicans. Remnants of the Greenback Party, which had polled almost a fifth of the total vote in 1878, joined with dissident Republicans and other independent spirits to form the Anti-Monopoly Party. It mustered nearly a fifth of the vote in 1882 but suffered from lack of leadership and soon collapsed.

In 1882 the Republicans faced the strongest challenge in the decade when Morton, the Democratic candidate for governor, and E. P. Ingersoll, the Anti-Monopolist, together received more votes than did the victorious Dawes. P. D. Sturdevant, on whom the Democrats and Anti-Monopolists agreed, was elected treasurer, the first Democrat to win an office since statehood (except for Chief Justice William A. Little, who had died before he could take office). Together the two parties won control of the Senate and came within four seats of getting control of the House.

In 1884 the Anti-Monopolists joined with the Democrats to nominate Morton for governor, but the Sage of Arbor Lodge could develop little enthusiasm among the rank and file of the Anti-Monops so the incumbent Dawes easily won reelection. The only other time the GOP armor was pierced was in 1886, when Democrat John A. McShane, founder of the Omaha stockyards and a prominent Catholic layman, was elected to Congress.

THE FARMERS' ALLIANCE

The opposition to Republican control was soon to find an effective voice in the Farmers' Alliance. That organization, founded in Illinois in 1879, was first established in Nebraska in 1880 near Filley in Gage County. Later that year, another Alliance chapter was formed at Alda in Hall County. The early history of the organization in Nebraska is difficult to trace. A state Alliance convention was held in Lincoln in 1881 and elected E. P. Ingersoll of Johnson County as president and Jay Burrows, who had been instrumental in organizing the Filley Alliance, as secretary. The stated purpose of the Alliance was to secure cheaper transportation for farmers and, in general, to wage war on capital. The convention adopted resolutions urging the legislature to pass laws to enforce the constitutional provisions permitting railroad regulation.

At first, the Alliance did not flourish. A second state convention was called for August 3, 1882, but it had not been well advertised and, because it was in the midst of the harvest season, only fifteen persons attended. The meeting adjourned and reconvened in a joint session with the Anti-Monopoly League at Hastings on September 27. At this meeting the Anti-Monopoly state ticket, headed by E. P. Ingersoll, was chosen. By this time the Alliance had begun to decline nationally as well. At the time of the convention in 1881 the Alliance claimed 24,500 members, with Nebraska leading in membership figures. By 1882 the Alliance claimed a membership of over 100,000, but by the following year so few attended the annual convention that the group decided not to meet in 1884.

Interest in the Alliance revived in the mid-1880s. A national convention was held in 1886; that same year more than two hundred local Alliances were chartered in Nebraska. Custer County led with fifty-seven, Frontier came second with eighteen, Hamilton and York had sixteen each, followed by Antelope, Holt, Sherman, Hall, Hitchcock, Buffalo, Saunders, and others. In 1887 the Nebraska State Alliance was reorganized as a secret society with rituals and objectives somewhat similar to those of the earlier Patrons of Husbandry.

Although there was much activity throughout 1888, only fourteen counties were represented by about a hundred delegates at the annual meeting of the state Alliance in January 1889. The state organization authorized its officers to do field work to increase the membership, and under the leadership of J. H. Powers of Trenton, the new president, five hundred locals were chartered.

The state Alliance also authorized the establishment of a newspaper at Lincoln. Jay Burrows, who was serving as chairman of the state Executive Committee as well as president of the national Alliance since 1887, left his farm near Filley and moved to the capital city to develop the *Alliance* (later changed to the *Farmers' Alliance*) into a dynamic and influential paper. The Alliance was supported by a growing number of newspapers all over the state. In 1888 approximately 18 out of 499 weekly newspapers were friendly to the movement, and a year later the number had risen to 113.

Although the stated objectives of the Alliance as reorganized in 1887 were educational and philanthropic, the organization could not avoid political issues. Local meetings held in homes and country schoolhouses throughout the state inevitably developed into political forums. Senator Van Wyck urged independent political action. So menacing had the Alliance become that the old guard in the state Senate was moved to pass a resolution refusing to recognize the right of the Farmers' Alliance to represent or speak for Nebraska farmers, but this action convinced some Alliance members that the organization must play an independent political role.

In its declaration of principles the Alliance pledged to "labor for the education of the agricultural classes in the science of economical government in a strictly non-partisan spirit." Many of the leaders, particularly Burrows, argued that they could succeed only by working through the old parties.[3] Many members, however, disagreed, feeling that neither of the old parties offered any hope. The Democrats were still the party of rebellion; they were dominated by Catholics and opposed to prohibition, which many of the Protestant farmers favored. Cooperation with the Republicans, who were openly antagonistic to progressive ideas, was even less possible.

The only hope for political action thus lay in an independent movement, and many people joined the Alliance precisely because they expected it to take independent action. As early as 1889, the Alliance in several counties had run independent tickets and in some instances had succeeded in electing its candidates. Accordingly, when a state convention of Alliance county presidents and organizers was held in Lincoln on April 22, 1890, it decided that if the strength of the Alliance increased sufficiently statewide, independent action would be justified. And its strength did increase. By July 1, 1890, Alliance authorities estimated that the organization included about fifteen hundred locals with a membership of over fifty thousand. With a total of 174 newspapers on its side, the time was ripe for independent action.

CHAPTER 18

The Populist Revolt

The *Omaha Bee* noted in January 1890:

The remarkable growth of the State Farmers' Alliance during the last year is a gratifying evidence of an awakening among the producers. . . . Organization among the farmers has become an urgent necessity. Confronted on every side by combines and trusts, they are forced to unite to protect themselves from the grasping greed of corporations. It is to be hoped that strong, conservative men will be placed at the helm of the alliance—men who know the right of the producers and who will demand and secure just treatment from the transportation companies of the state.[1]

The Alliance was headed by strong men, but they were not conservative. They were radicals, and by 1890 their difficulties appeared to call for heroic action. For almost a decade, a bountiful nature had given the farmers of Nebraska and other plains states good crops, but as their crops increased, their prosperity decreased. The great crop of 1889, the best in a decade, was met by some of the lowest prices the farmers of Nebraska had ever received. After a winter spent pondering the problem of fifty-cent wheat, ten- to twenty-cent corn, and fifteen-cent oats, a sizable portion of Nebraska's farmers were willing to believe what Alliance orators had been saying for years: the root of their difficulty lay in the human barriers interposed between producer and consumer for the benefit of eastern capitalists. This conclusion determined elections and shaped legislation throughout the decade.

The situation was made all the more urgent in 1890 because nature added to the farmers' burdens. Nebraska received only 17.15 inches of rain that year, well below the minimum required for even reasonably good crops and the lowest since 1864. The drought affected every section of the state but was at its worst in the central division, which received only 16.1 inches, and the western division, which received 13.6 inches.

Even the eastern division, where precipitation was usually the greatest, received only 21.7 inches, a full 6 inches below the mean. Normally, the farmers could deal philosophically with adversity brought on by nature, but the hot, dry winds that parched Nebraska's crops in the summer of 1890 came on the heels of a depression and served to increase the farmers' desperation. They were powerless over nature, but they could attempt to control their own political and economic destiny.

Although the resulting political movement found much of its support and many of its leaders in Nebraska, it spread throughout the states and even into the older Middle West. American society had been completely changed by the post–Civil War technological transformation, and commercial agriculture, created in part by that transformation, was making a serious effort to adapt to an increasingly industrialized society.

THE ELECTION OF 1890

Although leaders of the Farmers' Alliance had initially rejected independent political action as folly, they were increasingly pushed in that direction. Fears that political action would destroy the effectiveness of their organization subsided in the face of mounting pressure from the growing number who joined the organization because the leadership of the old parties offered no hope. Alliance leaders not only gave in to these demands but soon assumed control of the new movement.

A meeting of county presidents and organizers on April 22, 1890, was followed by another meeting in Lincoln in May attended by state officers and county representatives. Some of the leaders still believed that their best course was to work through the existing political parties, but the desire for a new party was so strong that the assembly decided to test sentiment by issuing a call for a people's convention. In a move expressing unity between farmers and laborers, the call signed by the president of the State Farmers' Alliance and the head of the Knights of Labor was accompanied by a Declaration of Principles, which supporters were invited to sign. The declaration, written by Jay Burrows, called for the free coinage of silver, abolition of the land monopoly, government ownership of railroads and telegraph lines, and an adjustment of taxation so that "our laboring interests will be fostered and wealth bear its

Orem Kem, shown here with his family in front of his sod house near Broken Bow, was the Populist Party's successful candidate for Congress from the third district in 1890. Courtesy, NSHS Butcher Collection, B983:200.

just burdens."[2] Within thirty days, more than fifteen thousand voters had signed the petition. There could be no doubt now about sentiment, and a formal call was issued for a People's State Independent Convention to meet on July 29 in Lincoln to nominate candidates.

More than eight hundred delegates from seventy-nine counties assembled at Bohanan's Hall in Lincoln. Hundreds of visitors were also there to witness the launching of the new party, soon to be known as the Populist Party. The convention adopted a party platform, which closely paralleled the Declaration of Principles but had added planks calling for an increase in the amount of money in circulation to fifty dollars per capita, a law allowing freight rates to be no higher than those in Iowa, a liberal service pension for old soldiers, the adoption of the Australian ballot, and an eight-hour day for all except agricultural labor. The Knights of Labor were primarily interested in the eight-hour day, but the farmers insisted that it should not apply to farms.

The only serious division in the convention occurred over the nominee for governor. A considerable block of delegates wanted former Republican senator Charles H. Van Wyck, who had been defeated for reelection by the corporations and party regulars. Alliance leaders, however, led by Burrows, opposed Van Wyck as being too wealthy and too much of a professional politician to be the leader of a common people's movement. They promoted John H. Powers of Trenton, president of the Farmers' Alliance, a Civil War veteran, and a modest man who lived in a sod house on his homestead in Hitchcock County. It was not the most politically advantageous move, but as Addison E. Sheldon, one of the Populist movement's most sympathetic chroniclers, assessed it, Powers's nomination was "a victory of the idealists in the convention over the opportunists."[3] Van Wyck was a tested politician and undoubtedly a stronger vote-getter, "but John H. Powers more accurately represented the spirit of the new political movement than Senator Van Wyck."[4] First district Populists nominated Van Wyck for Congress, but he refused to run. Most of the other nominees on the state ticket were old Anti-Monopoly war horses who had spent their political years leading lost causes but whose reputations for fidelity to the principles of the new movement had been tested in many Anti-Monopoly campaigns.

The cause being hatched in Bohanan's Hall, however, was not lost. The convention had numbers, strength of purpose, and confidence. As the *Nebraska State Journal*, the new movement's most vitriolic newspaper critic, wrote, "A more sanguine lot of politicians one could never dream of meeting. Each individual delegate is endowed with the belief to a degree of dead moral certainty that the political world is his oyster."[5]

Republican as well as Democratic leaders were disturbed. They could refer sarcastically, as the *Journal* did, to "horny handed sons of toil" and "venerable hay seeds," but they were in trouble and they knew it.[6] In January 1890, Governor Thayer had made a blundering attempt to solve the state's transportation problem by sending a letter to the railroads calling attention to the corn piled on the ground that could not be moved because of the high freight rates and pleading with them to lower rates as an experiment. This move increased Alliance certainty that the Republicans were completely captive to the railroads, and when the letter failed to produce results, Thayer compounded his troubles by issuing a call for a special session of the legislature to consider a maximum-rate law, only to revoke the call in the face of a flood of opposition.

Republicans, who met in Lincoln a week before the People's, or Populist, convention, had wrestled with the problem posed by the rising agrarian tide. As Church Howe put it in opening the convention, "the old ship is leaking and men are wanted to man the pumps."[7] Yet despite their sincerity, they failed to produce convincing answers. Their platform made a few concessions to Populist demands by supporting the Australian (secret) ballot, which a Republican majority had voted down in the preceding legislative session; a reduction in freight and passenger rates; abolition of free passes; legislation defining the duty of corporations to employees; the prohibition of illegitimate increases in stock or capital by corporations; abolition of railroad and elevator discrimination in handling grain; more rigid usury laws; recognition of the right of labor to organize; a noncommittal tariff plank; the remonetization of silver; opposition to land monopoly; establishment of a system of postal telegraphy; a more liberal pension system; and a denunciation of trusts. After an all-night session, the party chose as its candidate for governor L. D. Richards, prominent Fremont banker and longtime leader in the Grand Army of the Republic.

The Democrats, who met in Omaha on August 14, 1890, joined the other two parties in denouncing the trusts. Their special fire, however, was reserved for the Republicans, whom they charged with squandering the public domain and perverting the results of victory in the Civil War. The Democrats also favored the Australian ballot, the remonetization of silver, bigger pensions, and the right of labor to organize. They demanded the repeal of laws that enabled the governor to call out the militia in the event of labor troubles and a constitutional amendment to provide for the direct election of United States senators. They nominated as their candidate for governor prominent Omaha meatpacker James E. Boyd, an arch-conservative.

The Democrats also came to grips with an issue that both the Republicans and Populists tried to duck—prohibition. Constant agitation throughout the 1880s had greatly increased sentiment for prohibition, and the legislature by only one vote in the House and two in the Senate had placed a prohibition amendment on the general election ballot in 1890. The Prohibition Party, which had been on the ballot in every election since 1884, emerged again in 1890 with B. L. Paine, a prominent Lincoln merchant, as its candidate for governor.

Many of the Populists were dry, but their convention decided that the prohibition issue was too controversial for the party's initial campaign. They also argued that any effort to make prohibition an issue in the campaign would play into the hands of the railroads and other corporate interests. Many Republicans likewise were prohibitionists, but party leaders recognized that they needed the votes of Germans and Bohemians, who were strongly against the amendment. Although their gubernatorial candidate, Richards, personally sided with the drys, the party refused to take a stand on the issue and as a result lost votes from both wets and drys. The Democrats' stand against prohibition was unchanged, and their gubernatorial candidate was well-known as an anti-prohibitionist.

The campaign produced excitement such as the state had never seen. After the hot winds had withered away the crops, energy that normally would have been spent in harvesting was directed into politics. As the more outspoken Alliance orators were fond of proclaiming, "We farmers raised no crops, so we'll just raise hell."[8] Thousands thronged to hear fiery Populist orators proclaim farm grievances and point the way to victory. A Populist picnic at Cushman Park in Lincoln, on September 1, drew twenty thousand people; on September 23, at Wymore, 1,050 farmer's wagons were counted in the parade; at Hastings on the same day, 1,600 were counted. While waiting for the orators to begin, the assembled throngs sang rousing campaign songs, usually set to familiar tunes like "Goodbye, Old Party, Goodbye," "A Mortgage Has Taken the Farm, Mary." A good example was "The Hayseed," sung to the tune of "Save a Poor Sinner Like Me."[9]

I was once a tool of oppression
And as green as a sucker could be
And monopolies banded together
To beat a poor hayseed like me.

The railroads and old party bosses
Together did sweetly agree;

And they thought there would be little trouble
In working a hayseed like me.

But now I've roused up a little
And their greed and corruption I see,
And the ticket we vote next November
Will be made up of hayseeds like me.

Many Alliance songs were written or adapted by Luna Kellie of Kearney County, who became one of the prominent women leaders in the Farmers' Alliance. One of her more popular contributions and one that caught the antiparty spirit of the Alliance was "The Independent Man," adapted to the tune of "The Girl I Left Behind Me:"[10]

I was a party man one time
The party would not mind me
So now I'm working for myself,
The party's left behind me.

A true and independent man
you ever more shall find me —
I work and vote, and ne'er regret
The party left behind me.

Faced with falling crop prices, high freight rates, a mortgage, and the ultimate loss of their homestead in 1884, Luna and her husband, James Thompson Kellie, were convinced that their problems were not the result of their own failings but rather that they and many others like them were victims of the "system."[11] Both became increasingly active in the Alliance movement, and Luna was elected secretary of the Nebraska Alliance in 1894. The following year she began publishing the *Prairie Home* newspaper, which provided a voice for the Alliance movement in the hope of keeping it viable in Nebraska politics.

Though in some local areas Democrats and Populists allied and supported a common (fusion) candidate, on the state level Democratic leaders joined the Republicans in sneering at the Populists. While Democrats talked the tariff and Republicans waved the bloody shirt before small audiences, their ridicule of the third party movement only served to aid the Populist cause. The *Omaha Bee* could call the Populists "political thugs," and the *Lincoln Journal* could refer to Populist candidates as "hogs in the parlor," but such vilification only drew new converts to the Populist cause and became rallying slogans for its members.[12]

When the election returns came in, the Republicans found that they had been cast aside for the first time since statehood. The Populists had secured clear control of the Senate, with eighteen members to eight Democrats and seven Republicans. In the House there were fifty-four Populists, twenty-five Democrats, and twenty-one Republicans. Not a single Republican was sent to Congress. The first district sent William Jennings Bryan, a young Lincoln lawyer, who had been given the Democratic nomination simply as a gesture of goodwill with no hope that he could be elected. The second district elected William A. McKeighan, the fiery Red Cloud orator who had received both Populist and Democratic nominations. The third district was represented by Omar M. Kem, a Populist from Custer County.

For state offices below governor, Republican candidates generally struggled back into office. In the gubernatorial race, however, Democrat James E. Boyd eked out a narrow 71,331 to 70,187 victory over Populist candidate Powers. The Republican Richards ran third with 68,878, and the Prohibitionist candidate, Paine, received a mere 3,676 votes. Boyd's victory resulted largely because he piled up an overwhelming lead in Douglas County, where opposition to prohibition had outweighed all other issues in the campaign. The Omaha Business Men's Association, which included Omaha's leading businessmen, had organized largely to oppose the amendment. Omaha newspapers, the *World-Herald* and the *Bee*, had both opposed prohibition; indeed, because of its clear stand against prohibition, the *Bee* lost much of its effectiveness as a Republican paper during the campaign. On the prohibition amendment, the wets were victorious, 111,728 to 88,292. The victory, however, would have been much narrower without the Douglas County vote of 23,918 against the amendment to 1,555 for it.

VICTORY AND FRUSTRATION

Republicans and Populists immediately raised a cry that Boyd had been elected by fraudulent votes in Omaha. The Populists contested the election on the basis of those votes, but unfortunately they got trapped into the tactical error of contesting both Republican and Democratic votes in Douglas County, which united the two older parties against them. When a joint session of both houses of the legislature was called to canvass the election returns, the new party's leaders were outmaneuvered, and the returns were officially approved as they had been initially reported.

While the election was being contested, Boyd proceeded to take the oath of office as governor in a notary's office, but Governor Thayer refused to surrender his office. Thayer surrounded himself with policemen to guard him in his office and called out the state militia for the purpose, he said, of preserving order and saving the legislature from the annoyance of noise in the corridors. The Republican Thayer was going to hang on as long as possible; not until the contested election was finally decided in Boyd's favor was the new governor permitted to deliver his message to the legislature.

Boyd's message to the legislature on February 6, 1891, did not end the political trouble, however. Although Thayer had surrendered his office, he had filed a writ of *quo warranto* in the state supreme court to challenge Boyd's citizenship and remove him from office. After emigrating from Ireland, Boyd's father filed first naturalization papers for his son, who was a minor, but took no further steps to complete the citizenship process until 1890, long after his son had reached the age of majority. Thayer argued that naturalization of the father did not give automatic citizenship to the son, who was no longer a minor. On May 5, 1891, the state supreme court sustained Thayer's contention and he was reinstated in office. Boyd immediately appealed to the United States Supreme Court, and on February 1, 1892, that tribunal reversed the Nebraska court and declared Boyd a citizen. One week later he resumed the governorship.

If Independents were frustrated over the citizenship issue, they became even more frustrated when Governor Boyd opposed Populist efforts to regulate the railroads. Those efforts took the form of a bill, which was introduced by Representative Fred Newberry of Hamilton County, to reduce rates on most of the goods shipped on Nebraska railroads to the level of those generally enforced in Iowa. Backed by a solid Independent vote and with the help of a few Democrats and Republicans, the bill passed the House by a vote of seventy-eight to seventeen. In the Senate the contest was much closer. Independent senator W. M. Taylor of Loup

County was induced by railroad lobbyists, for a fee, it was charged, to vacate his position and leave the state, thus reducing the Populist vote by one. And in an effort to wear down the supporters of the bill, the opponents called for roll calls and points of order that kept the Senate in continuous session for seventy-five hours. The bill finally passed by a vote of twenty-three to seven, but Governor Boyd promptly vetoed it on the grounds that it would bankrupt every railroad in the state if Nebraska rates were reduced to the level of those in Iowa, where the tonnage was more than four times greater. The supporters of the bill were unable to gather the necessary three-fifths majority to pass it over the governor's veto. Boyd's action, of course, only served to intensify the Populists' insistence that their sole hope lay in independent action. The Democrats were as much friends of monopoly as were the Republicans.

Though frustrated in their efforts to regulate railroads, the Populists did enact other measures in which they had considerable interest: the Australian ballot, a free textbook law, a public fund deposit law, mutual insurance acts, and a repeal of the sugar bounty law ending state subsidies for the beet sugar industry. They also succeeded in reducing state expenditures, but the reduction largely corresponded to the reduced income of the state's taxpayers. An act establishing eight hours as a legal day's work, except on farms, was also passed but subsequently held invalid by the supreme court.

The U.S. presidential election year of 1892 found the Populists full of fire and ready for victory. Third-party successes throughout the West had greatly heartened Independents everywhere, and they were determined to put together a national ticket. Their national convention in Omaha was attended by approximately thirteen hundred enthusiastic delegates. A platform was adopted, which reiterated traditional Populist demands. They also nominated General James B. Weaver of Iowa, an old Anti-Monopoly, Greenback war horse, as their candidate for president.

To head their state ticket, Nebraska Populists chose Senator Charles H. Van Wyck, whom they had passed over two years earlier. The selection of Van Wyck represented a change in the direction of the Populist Party. As a radical agrarian organization, it had failed to get enough of the farm vote to capture the governor's office; now party leaders were bidding for the support of middle-class business and professional men.

The Republicans nominated Lorenzo Crounse, who was currently serving as assistant secretary of the treasury in Washington and who had earlier served as a member of Congress and on the state supreme court. Crounse was nominated against his wishes, but party leaders believed he was a good compromise candidate who could unite the warring factions within the party and get the G.O.P. back on the victory trail. The Democrats, more badly split than ever, nominated conservative J. Sterling Morton, who had denounced Boyd's veto of the Newberry railroad rate reduction bill as bad politics. More ominous than the personal squabble between Morton and Boyd was the rift in the party over monetary issues. A sizable portion of Democrats were now coming to believe that the steady decline in prices could be halted only by the remonetization of silver. Morton, however, stood firmly against any departure from the gold standard and on this issue stood solidly behind the party's national standard-bearer, Grover Cleveland.

Somehow the momentum generated by Nebraska Democrats in 1890 failed to carry over into 1892; nor were Populist orators able to stir up the same enthusiasm they had created for issues in 1890. In the national election, Benjamin Harrison carried Nebraska, winning a narrow victory over Weaver. Cleveland ran a poor third. In state elections, Republicans took the governorship, with Crounse getting 78,426 votes to Van Wyck's 68,617. Morton, who had campaigned almost solely against Van Wyck and greatly aided the Republicans in the process, ran a poor third. Democrats Bryan, McKeighan, and Kem were all returned to Congress, but Republicans won in each of the three new districts created as a result of the reapportionment that followed the census of 1890. Republicans also won control of both houses in the legislature, although their numbers were less than those of the Democrats and Populists combined. Republican vulnerability was soon evident when the Democrats and Populists combined to elect William V. Allen, a Populist judge from Madison County, to the United States Senate, as well as to pass the Newberry rate bill.

THE POPULISTS ELECT A GOVERNOR

Drought and low farm prices combined in the early 1890s to increase agrarian unrest. By 1893, the country fell into the grip of a paralyzing, worldwide depression. President Cleveland's answer to the problem of the depression was to negotiate with Wall Street bankers to maintain the price of gold and repeal of the Sherman Silver Purchase Act, which had committed the U.S. Treasury to purchase four and a half million ounces of silver each month. The nation's most ardent advocate of the president's position was J. Sterling Morton, whom Cleveland had appointed U.S. secretary of agriculture. Throughout the West, however, and particularly in Nebraska, the rank and file of the farmers had long since come to the conclusion that one of their basic problems was the gold standard and that the free coinage of silver offered their only hope for getting out of their economic morass.

The silver issue split the already divided Democratic Party in Nebraska even further. While Secretary Morton plugged for the gold standard, Congressman William Jennings Bryan, whose oratory had already won him a large following in Nebraska and beyond, emerged as a major leader in the fight against Cleveland's monetary policies. Initially, the Democratic Party in Nebraska remained in the hands of the conservative supporters of Morton and the administration, and in the off-year convention of 1893, Nebraska Democrats enthusiastically endorsed the Cleveland administration and demanded the repeal of the Sherman Silver Purchase Act. During the campaign Bryan had warned Democrats that he would leave the party if it supported the gold standard.

Although Bryan did not make good on his threat to leave the party, he went back to Washington asserting that he had been sacrificed upon the altar of gold and greed. He remained a Democrat, hoping to bring enough Populists into the party to enable him to defeat the administration's supporters. On September 1, 1894, he took a major step toward securing control of the party when he became editor of the *Omaha World-Herald*, the state's most powerful Democratic paper. This move, the administration's bungling in the matter of patronage, the continuing depression, and the almost total crop failures of 1893 and 1894 (the state got only 16.26 inches of rainfall in 1893 and 13.54 inches in 1894) ultimately enabled him to take control of the party in 1894. Under his leadership, the Democratic convention that year fused with the Populists to nominate Silas A. Holcomb for governor, as well as the entire Populist state ticket; it also endorsed Populist congressmen Omar C. Kem and William McKeighan. The only Democrat of prominence approved by the convention was Bryan, whose record in the House of Representatives was praised and who was endorsed as their candidate for the United States Senate. In response, Cleveland Democrats bolted the convention and nominated a ticket of their own, headed by Phelps D. Sturdevant, but from the outset there was little hope that they would make a significant showing.

The Republicans rode roughshod over National Committeeman Edward Rosewater to nominate a slate of party stalwarts, headed by Thomas J. Majors, pioneer soldier and a farmer from Nemaha County, who had long been an active force in Republican politics. In a letter branding Majors as "the pliant tool of the railroads . . . whose nomination was procured by the combined influence of corporation cappers, professional bribe givers, jury fixers and impeached state house officials," Rosewater indignantly resigned his place as national committeeman and placed the *Bee* behind Holcomb.[13] With the combined support of the *Bee* and the *World-Herald*, as well as the Populists and the Democrats, Holcomb defeated Majors 97,815 to 94,613; Sturdevant got a mere 6,985 votes, and the Prohibition candidate followed with 4,440. The Republicans won all other state offices, however, and, with the exception of the sixth district, where the now Demo-Pop Kem was reelected, succeeded in electing all their candidates to Congress. The Republicans also won complete control of the legislature, which on the first ballot sent John M. Thurston, general solicitor of the Union Pacific Railroad, to the Senate.

Although Holcomb was reelected in 1896 and William A. Poynter, a Boone County Populist, was chosen governor in 1898, the Populists, as an independent third party, were never able to win complete control of the state government. Their two successful gubernatorial candidates were also the nominees of the Democratic Party. Moreover, even in 1897, the only time when the Republicans lost control of both the legislature and the executive office, Populist victories were the result of fusion with the Democrats. This was bitterly disappointing to many inveterate Populists who fervently believed that the farmers' only hope lay in independent, third-party action, but they were unable to prevail against the realities of American political tradition or the magnetic personality of William Jennings Bryan.

CHAPTER 19

The Fading Frontier

In what has long been considered one of the most significant papers ever presented by an American historian, Frederick Jackson Turner, addressing a meeting of the American Historical Association being held in connection with the World's Columbian Exposition in Chicago in 1893, called attention to a statement in the reports of the superintendent of the census for 1890 that "the unsettled area has been so broken into by isolated bodies of settlement that there can hardly be said to be a frontier line."[1] He noted that it marked "the closing of a great historic movement . . . the colonization of the great unoccupied West."[2] Although an unsettled area of considerable extent in northwestern Nebraska was not to be filled in until after the turn of a century, by 1890 the settlement period in the history of the state was, in many respects, over. Certainly the years between 1890 and the outbreak of World War I saw the passing of frontier conditions as they had existed during the pioneer years.

THE INDIAN DISPOSSESSED

The Fort Laramie Treaty of 1868 and President Ulysses S. Grant's Peace Policy of 1869, which implemented an enforced, fixed reservation plan for western tribes and also created a Board of Indian Commissioners to help resolve local problems, did quell the fears of whites in eastern and central Nebraska long enough for them to get on with the business of establishing the state government and expanding both settlement and institutions over the next two decades. The Indian problem, however, was far from settled, particularly in the western part of the state, where many younger Indians refused to recognize the proceedings at Fort Laramie and were contemptuous of the reservation idea.

Nontreaty Lakotas, under the leadership of Crazy Horse and Sitting Bull, and the Northern Cheyennes roamed their former ranges at will, causing great concern to the military, who felt that a new Indian war could develop around them unless they were brought under control. But displeasure with the treaty arrangements was not limited to Indians; whites too were impatient with the terms of the Fort Laramie Treaty, particularly after gold was found in the Black Hills.

For a while, the army tried to keep prospectors out of the Black Hills, but with little success. By the middle 1870s a steady stream of fortune seekers was pouring into this last sacred hunting ground of the Lakotas. The nontreaty Lakotas moved further into the hills; those on the reservations became increasingly more sullen and restless. Trouble, indeed, seemed inevitable.

In 1874, while General George A. Custer was "exploring" the Black Hills, General Sheridan was moving troops into the Lakota country of northwestern Nebraska and establishing encampments at both the Spotted Tail and Red Cloud agencies. Camp Sheridan at Spotted Tail was only temporary, but Camp Robinson at Red Cloud became a permanent installation and after 1878 was designated Fort Robinson. At the same time, Fort Hartsuff was established on the Loup River northwest of Grand Island to quiet the fears of settlers in the Loup Valley. Further efforts were made to restrict the Lakotas. In 1875 the Brules and Oglalas agreed to relinquish their hunting rights south of the divide between the Niobrara and Platte Rivers, but they steadfastly refused to cede any part of the Black Hills or to lease mining rights therein. Following this refusal, the government served notice on the Lakotas in Nebraska, Wyoming, and Montana that they must come into the reservations. A notice sent from Washington on December 6, 1875, stated that those who did not comply by January 31, 1876, would be considered hostile. The time allowed was so ridiculously short that even those who might have wanted to comply could not possibly have done so. As anticipated, the nonreservation bands refused to comply, and on January 31, all Lakotas, nonreservation and reservation alike, were turned over to the War Department, and plans were promptly prepared to crush them by force.

And great force was required. General Sheridan, in charge of the campaign, first attempted to move against the Lakotas in winter but was driven back by snow and cold winds. In spring his troops finally advanced, but the Lakotas had had time to prepare and offered bloody

Indian students and their white teachers at the Genoa Indian Industrial School in 1904. The Genoa school, on the site of the former Pawnee Agency, was one of twenty-six off-reservation schools that sought to steep Indian children in the values of white society. Courtesy, Genoa Historical Museum and the Genoa U.S. Indian School Foundation.

resistance. Bands of Cheyennes and Oglalas under Crazy Horse forced General George Crook's troops to retire after a bloody battle at the mouth of the Rosebud River on June 17. Eight days later, on June 25, combined bands of Lakotas and Northern Cheyennes annihilated Custer's command on the Little Big Horn. For two months the Lakotas eluded the forces sent out to bring them in, thwarting the efforts of Generals George Crook and Alfred Terry, who were in immediate command of the campaign.

With dwindling strength and diminishing supplies of food, clothing, and arms, however, the Lakotas could not keep up the unequal contest, and by October 1876, General Nelson A. Miles, who had come out from Fort Leavenworth to rejuvenate the flagging campaign, was able to force about three thousand Lakotas to surrender. Later others came in, surrendered their arms, and accepted reservation status. Crazy Horse, who finally brought nearly two thousand of his Oglala followers the next spring, was killed at Fort Robinson on September 7, 1877. The official report of the incident claimed he was killed while resisting arrest on suspicion of trying to foment another war.

Meanwhile, the Northern Cheyennes had surrendered after a serious defeat at the hands of Colonel R. S. MacKenzie on November 25, 1876, and had been sent south to Indian Territory. In 1878 a small band under Dull Knife broke away from the reservation and headed north. They were captured and confined at Fort Robinson, and when on the night of January 9, 1879, they tried to escape, most of them were killed.

And so the Indian resistance was crushed, and all their great war chiefs were dead or broken in spirit. The Brule and Oglala reservations in Nebraska had been abandoned, and the tribes were concentrated at Pine Ridge and Rosebud Reservations in South Dakota. Troops from Fort Robinson kept them under surveillance, and Fort Niobrara was established near Valentine in 1880 to protect settlers in northeastern Nebraska. The settlers, however, hardly needed protection from the broken people who were trying to farm the barren, arid lands of western South Dakota.

The Peace Policy solved some problems, but it was not without critics, many of whom were associated with humanitarian movements in the East. Of these, the Friends of the Indian found the reservation aspects of the Peace Policy anything but peaceful. Indeed, the reservation system was fraught with inhumanity, as evidenced by press reports of the saga of Chief Standing Bear and his following of Poncas attempting to reach their old homeland on the Niobrara.

The Board of Indian Commissioners, which had been established as part of the Peace Policy, was to be made up of nominees from Protestant denominations, and part of their responsibility was to spread Christian, family values among the Indians. Those critical of the government's reservation policy thus had an avenue on which to focus their concerns.

The attention of those looking for practical as well as humane solutions to the Indian "problem" was soon drawn to the work being done with the Indians by Richard Pratt. Between 1875 and 1878 Pratt, who had trained and led Indian scouts for the army on the southern plains in the years after the Civil War, was given charge of seventy-two Kiowa, Comanche, Cheyenne, and Arapaho prisoners, who were to be exiled for inciting uprisings. Pratt had a deep concern for his charges, and during their exile at Fort Marion, near St. Augustine, Florida, he launched a program to educate them to exist in a "modern," white world. So successful was Pratt's educational experiment that the Board of Indian Commissioners convinced Congress to allow him to establish a school for Indian children on an abandoned military post at Carlisle, Pennsylvania.

Pratt believed that the solution to the Indian problem was to remove Indian children from the influence of their families, the tribe, and the reservation and to educate them in the ways of white society. Teaching them to read and write in English and instructing them in a useful skill or craft would lead them to think like whites in the increasingly industrial society around them and allow them to blend into the white world. The end result would be the disappearance of Indian peoples and cultures.

The Carlisle Indian School opened its doors in 1879, and within three years, Pratt had been so successful in convincing Congress of the merits of his approach that funding was appropriated for four additional schools: Salem in Oregon, Chilocco in Indian Territory, Haskell in Lawrence, Kansas, and the Genoa Indian Industrial School in Genoa, Nebraska. The Genoa school was established and opened in 1884 at the site of the former Pawnee agency on the Loup River in Nance County, left vacant by the final removal of the Pawnees to Indian Territory in 1875.

The school at Genoa was part of a nationwide effort to assimilate the Indians into the mainstream of society, which by 1903 would include twenty-six similar institutions, all federally funded. The Genoa school was the largest. At its peak it was a campus of thirty buildings on 640 acres to the east of the town of Genoa. Like the other schools in the system, it was a boarding school to which students came and lived, away from the negative influences of their past. They worked for half a day performing chores and tasks that contributed to the operation of the school and spent the other half day in classes learning arithmetic and to read and write in English. They dressed, worked, and interacted according to societal standards established by whites. They lived in a semimilitary environment, complete with uniforms, units, and drills, so they would learn the importance of discipline and order. They learned to react to the bells and whistles that sounded at regular intervals to order their days, similar to those that ordered the days of laborers in the industrial factories.

From the 1870s to the 1930s, assimilation of Native Americans was the foundation of virtually all government policy toward the Indians. At about the same time that Pratt began his work in Indian education, the Women's National Indian Association was organized, followed by the Indian Rights Association. Both organizations advocated for humane treatment of American Indians in assimilation-based programs. The central focus of their attack was the reservation system. The Dawes Severalty Act of 1882 was one of results of this pressure.

The Dawes Act provided that individual Indians who would willingly "sever" their ties or associations with their tribe would receive a grant of 160 acres of land. It was, in effect, an Indian Homestead Act. Presumably, Indians could become farmers, lose their Indian identity, and blend into the larger society. The Dawes Act, the Indian Industrial School Movement, and other assimilationist programs such as the Field Matrons all ended in 1934, when Congress passed the Indian Reorganization Act as part of a shift in government policy which attempted to restore a measure of tribal autonomy in matters of organization and education.

BRIDGING TWO CULTURES

Assimilationist efforts met with varied responses from whites and Indians alike. Assessment of the success of assimilation is made more difficult by a lack of agreement on the objectives underlying the initiatives and the motives of those who fostered them. At the extremes were outright cultural annihilation and a genuine desire for the future well-being of Indian people. Some who attended Indian industrial boarding schools did not succeed in the white world and returned to the reservation to meet with rejection there as well. Historians have shown that the Dawes program resulted in the separation of Indians from millions of acres of their allotted lands and helped to contribute to many of the social problems experienced on the reservations today. The stories of tragedy abound.

Yet there were those who were successful in bridging the two cultures and inculcating the values of the dominant white culture among the

Indians. The children of Joseph LaFlesche, "Iron Eyes," the last recognized chief of the Omaha people, succeeded in establishing themselves in the white world. Five of his seven children enrolled in Hampton Normal and Agricultural Institute in Virginia. Hampton was a school for blacks, where Richard Pratt, before establishing his school at Carlisle, had first attempted to provide educational opportunities for Indians.

Susan LaFlesche Picotte, the youngest daughter of Iron Eyes, not only graduated from Hampton but went on to medical school in Philadelphia and became the first Indian woman to graduate from medical school. She then returned to Nebraska in 1889 to serve as a physician to her people. The eldest daughter, Susette, also known as Bright Eyes, became a nationally renowned advocate for Indian rights. She married journalist Thomas Tibbles of the *Omaha World Herald*, who had been an outspoken defender of Ponca chief Standing Bear. Rosalie and Carey became tribal leaders. Carey served an invaluable role in her tribe in public relations, and Rosalie became a strong advocate of education, as well as a successful stock raiser and businesswoman. Marguerite and Lucy became teachers and community leaders. Francis made his career as an ethnologist with the Bureau of American Ethnology and became a well-known lecturer and author.

Winnebago artist and teacher Angel DeCora serves as a similar example from the Winnebago people. Angel's grandfather was chief of the Winnebagoes at the time of their removal to South Dakota and Nebraska. Angel was born in 1871 on the Winnebago reservation in Nebraska. At the age of twelve, she entered Hampton Institute in Virginia. A return to Nebraska interrupted her studies, but after she graduated in 1891 she went on to Smith College to continue her study of art and later to Drexel Institute in Philadelphia to learn the art of illustration. After a distinguished career as an art illustrator, she joined Pratt's Carlisle Indian School as an art teacher in 1906 and served there until 1915.

WOUNDED KNEE

During the high tide of assimilationist thinking, fears of Indian uprisings arose once again, especially in the northwestern part of Nebraska, when the ghost dance, a ritualistic worship of the prophet Wovoka, who had come to restore the game and drive out whites, spread through the reservations. Civilian authorities became alarmed in the fall of 1890 and called for military protection. General Nelson Miles came out from Chicago to take command of the situation, and the Nebraska National Guard was ordered to the northwestern part of the state. Sitting Bull, who earlier had fled to Canada but had finally agreed to come back to the United States and accept reservation status, was believed to be responsible for the ghost dance disturbance. True or not, he was killed in a melee that grew out of an attempt to arrest him at Standing Rock. As a result, the entire frontier was thrown into a state of alarm that culminated in the wanton massacre of a band of Lakotas at Wounded Knee Creek, northeast of Fort Robinson, on December 29, 1890. The "battle" of Wounded Knee was the last armed conflict between the army and Indians in Nebraska or surrounding territory. By the time it occurred, the state had been almost completely settled. The army had crushed the spirit of the Indian, and the settlers had spread over the land; the Indian, who had once been one with land, had honored and cared for it, was now completely dispossessed and began to recede into the background just as surely as the frontier.

POPULATION REDISTRIBUTION

The state's population increased only 12.7 percent (1,058,910 to 1,192,214) from 1890 to 1910. The period was characterized by redistribution rather than growth of population. A trend toward the cities began that has continued slowly but steadily to the present time. Virtually all of the population increase went to the cities. The number of places with more than 2,500 hundred inhabitants increased from sixteen to twenty-seven, and the percent of total population classified as rural decreased from 59.2 to 53.5 in these years. Total wealth during the period increased by more than 200 percent, from $1.3 billion in 1890 to $3.8 billion in 1912, a per capita increase of from $174.49 to $375.77.

The initial phase of the experiment in occupying the prairie-plains of Nebraska had been completed. The lack of any great political upheaval during the hard times of the 1870s may be explained in part because those hard times were viewed as difficulties besetting any new country. By contrast, the great political changes that accompanied the depression of the 1890s may be partly explained by the fact that the state's population had assumed some degree of permanence and had began to realize that it would have to work out its destiny with the resources it had. As Willa Cather put it:

These years of trial, as everyone now realizes, had a salutary effect upon the new state. They winnowed out the settlers with a purpose from the drifting malcontents who are ever seeking a land where man does not live by the sweat of his brow. The slack farmer moved on. Superfluous banks failed, and money-lenders who drove hard bargains with desperate men came to grief. The strongest stock survived, and within ten years those who had weathered the storm came into their reward.[3]

ON THE FARMS

Despite a trend to the towns, Nebraska remained preponderantly an agricultural state, and agriculture during this period, particularly after the turn of the century, was characterized by great growth and the development of a degree of stability.

A part of the story is reflected in the increase in farm acreage and values. Although the number of farms increased by only 14.1 percent from 1890 to 1910, the number of acres of farmland increased by 78.9 percent. More significantly, the average farm size increased by over 100 acres (from 190.1 to 297.8) and the per acre value increased 165 percent from $18.63 to $49.95. At the same time, total farm value in the state jumped from approximately $750 million to over $2 billion. Moreover, it appeared that the old bugaboo, the mortgage, was no longer so great a problem. The amount of mortgage debt increased 65.5 percent from $37.7 million in 1890 to $62.4 million in 1910, but the percent of debt to value decreased from 32.4 to 21.8. Offsetting that somewhat and reflecting the heavy loss of farms during the depression of the 1890s was an increase in tenancy from 24.7 percent in 1890 to 38.1 percent in 1910.

Some of the great increase in farm values, and particularly land values, was the result of an increased number of acres in farms, but most of it was brought about through an increase in both production and price. Rainfall was relatively abundant during the first ten years of the twentieth century. Except for 1907, when the state received 20.1 inches, annual rainfall over the two decades exceeded the state's mean average of 22.84 inches. Indeed, the average for the entire period was 25.54 inches, which resulted in correspondingly good crop yields. To be sure, not all crops were uniformly good every year, but no part of the state suffered from prolonged drought or repeated ravages of insect pests.

In addition to favorable climatic conditions, a general price increase accompanied the good yields. Between 1899 and 1910 the price of wheat increased 67 percent, oats 78 percent, corn 140 percent, and hogs 133 percent. Fortunately, too, at least part of this price increase represented a net gain in agriculture's economic position, for the price of goods purchased by farmers increased only about 30 percent during these same years.

New discoveries, labor-saving inventions, and improved varieties and strains of crops and livestock also contributed to increased productivity. Horses and mules still provided the motive power, except for the steam engines that pulled the grain separators, but farmers generally began to use riding implements. The gang plow replaced the walking plow and the one-bottom sulky. The riding cultivator came into general use. New barns made it easier to care for livestock. The blow stacker, manure spreader, and other labor-saving equipment took a great deal of the drudgery out of farm life, and larger machinery reduced the hours of labor. Though some farm homes could boast an oil stove, carpet sweeper, sinks, and running water, the farmer's wife generally had to do much of her work in the same old way. The family had moved from a soddy into a frame house, but water was still drawn from a well, and long hours were spent over the kitchen range preparing food for the family and hired help.

There was some improvement in existing crops, such as the replacement of late-maturing oats with early-maturing varieties. The most notable developments were the introduction of new crops, especially winter wheat and alfalfa. Winter wheat had a particularly marked effect on the state's agricultural economy. Although spring wheat had never yielded very well, Nebraska farmers generally had been slow to adopt the winter varieties. The Mennonites had had good success with Turkey Red brought with them from Russia, but most of the farmers refused to accept it until its superiority was demonstrated. Newspapermen such as George L. Miller and J. Sterling Morton actively promoted the production of winter wheat. George W. Holdrege of the Burlington Railroad encouraged experimental planting of the new varieties.

Beginning in 1902, the state agricultural experiment station worked to produce varieties of Turkey Red that were well adapted to conditions in various sections of the state. The milling industry had become interested in winter wheat in the late 1890s and began to adjust its equipment to take care of the increased quantities being marketed. Other factors, particularly the introduction of the press drill, made it possible to plant the seed deeper so it could get a good growth before winter came. All this activity resulted in a steady increase in the production of winter wheat, and the Department of Agriculture in 1901 changed Nebraska's classification from a spring wheat state to a winter wheat state. That same year Nebraska was exceeded only by Kansas as a winter wheat producer. When the shift came, it came rapidly. In 1899 spring wheat acreage constituted 96.86 percent of total wheat acreage; by 1909 winter wheat accounted for 91.25 percent of the total. Likewise, the total wheat acreage increased. The number of acres in corn remained relatively constant at about 7.3 million from 1899 to 1902, but farmers were planting an additional 450,000 additional acres in wheat by 1902.

Another development of great significance was the introduction of alfalfa. This crop had been brought to Nebraska in 1875 from Utah and was first grown in 1876 by S. P. Baker of Curtis in Frontier County. During the 1880s it was also raised in some of the southwestern counties, and in the 1890s H. D. Watson pioneered the large-scale raising of alfalfa on his huge ranch west of Kearney. Watson, the father of Kearney's short-lived urban real estate boom, not only planted thousands of acres to alfalfa but also encouraged other farmers to raise it because of its value as a forage crop. In 1894 the Agricultural Experiment Station issued a bulletin expounding alfalfa as a forage crop and as a soil-building plant. This bulletin was widely distributed and induced many farmers to try alfalfa. As farmers began to experiment with it, they readily realized its value in filling an important need in the cropping system of the state. It enabled farmers to readjust their crop system to maintain soil fertility and engage in livestock production on a larger scale than ever before. No other plant except Turkey Red wheat changed the agriculture of the state in so short a time.

Sugar beets, which had met with alternate enthusiasm and disgust, began to make some impression on the agricultural economy of the irrigated North Platte River valley. Interest in sugar beets as a means of diversifying the agriculture and increasing the industrial potential of the state had been evident since the late 1880s. The state had even offered bounties to encourage the production of beet sugar. A sugar factory had been established in Grand Island in 1890, and a few years later other factories were located at Ames and Norfolk. Generally, however, they had been unsuccessful because raising sugar beets was a tiresome job and required much hard labor.

The livestock industry recovered rapidly from the depression of the 1890s. The development of a serum for hog cholera, long the bane of the swine industry, had greatly reduced the ravages of that disease, and the number of hogs on Nebraska farms increased from 1.3 million in 1895 to a high of 2.4 million in 1907. The cattle industry likewise developed rapidly during the early years of the twentieth century, reaching a peak of over 3 million cattle on the farms of Nebraska during the three years 1907–9. The growth in alfalfa greatly influenced the cattle industry, and the alfalfa counties located in the Platte Valley became extensive cattle feeding centers. Likewise, under the leadership of the university's agricultural college, considerable attention was given to the cattle industry as a means of building up the soil. Dairying also increased markedly with the introduction of the hand cream separator and the Babcock tester. During the decade of the 1890s, the number of milk cows in the state increased 61 percent from approximately 556,000 to 897,000.

But most significant of all during this period of farm prosperity was the growing realization that Nebraska had certain limitations as an agricultural state and that farmers needed to apply their best brains to the problems facing them. As early as 1895, William Gunn Whitmore, president of the Improved Stock-Breeders Association, delivered addresses across the state warning farmers that they could no longer assume that common sense and hard work were sufficient to succeed in agriculture. The time had come, he declared, when farmers must start mixing brains with their soil or fail.[4]

And there were many who were mixing brains with the soil. Hardy W. Campbell, encouraged by George W. Holdrege, conducted successful dry farming experiments in the western part of the state. Under the leadership of Robert W. Furnas, who was the state's leading agricultural spokesman until his death in 1905, the State Board of Agriculture continued to urge farmers to try new methods. Both the University of Nebraska's College of Agriculture and its experiment station produced scientific studies of the principal factors entering into the development of agriculture. Geologist Erwin H. Barbour and botanist Charles E. Bessey, who persuaded President Roosevelt to establish a national forest in the Sand Hills, worked ceaselessly to convince their fellow Nebraskans of the importance of scientific farming. Under the university's leadership, farmers' institutes were held in many counties until they were superseded after 1914 by agricultural extension work, which was carried on with both federal and state funds.

As Nebraska agriculture moved into the boom years of the mid-1910s, some farmers still disdained the assistance of the agricultural college and the county agent; yet most of them had accepted the warning they had better mix brains with their soil.

CHAPTER 20

Emerging Awareness:
Cultural Expressions

The depression of the 1890s caught the cities and towns in a paralyzing grip. Symptomatic of the paralysis was the condition of banking. Bank deposits decreased nearly 50 percent (from $53.7 million to $27.3 million) between 1892 and 1896, and creditors of Nebraska banks had over $5 million tied up in 101 failed institutions. Spectacular failures destroyed confidence not only in the banking system but in the men who operated it. Factory buildings stood empty, store windows showed dismal "for rent" signs, street railway tracks built to the new subdivisions rusted from lack of use. Population, which had skyrocketed in the 1880s, came to a standstill or declined. There was very little urban growth during the 1890s, and towns such as Beatrice, Plattsmouth, and Nebraska City declined.

Omaha's major links with the industrial world, the railroads and the big packers, became restive under federal restrictions, and in the hot summer of 1892 its streets echoed with fearful Populist oratory. Nevertheless, Omaha set about to rebuild its fallen fortunes. The suburbs of Dundee and Benson were founded, and South Omaha, home of the great packing industry, increased markedly in population. The businessmen formed a Chamber of Commerce, and the Knights of Ak-Sar-Ben was organized to foster a sense of pride and community spirit.

Under the leadership of Gurdon W. Wattles, a former Iowa banker who had come to Omaha on the eve of the financial panic of 1893, the Knights set out to lick the depression by demonstrating to all the world that it did not exist. Out of this effort grew the Trans-Mississippi and International Exposition of 1898. When incorporated in 1896, it seemed like one of those hopeless gestures that could bring nothing but defeat and disappointment. Yet under Wattles the organization went ahead. Congress was persuaded to appropriate $200,000 when the association raised a like amount. Nebraska appropriated $100,000 and other states provided another $138,000. Out on the Kountze tract a group of glittering white buildings, representing a mixture of classic and Renaissance architecture, which had no relation whatever to the life of the plains, arose to house the exposition. From Little Egypt to Cass Gilbert's monument to agriculture and the huge plaster warrior in a chariot drawn by four lions and inscribed simply OMAHA, the exposition bravely described the bright new future.

On June 1, 1898, President William McKinley opened the exposition by pushing a button in Washington that sent electric current flowing across the nation to set the machinery in operation. Later the president came out to view the wonder, which was attended by approximately ninety-eight thousand midwesterners. The exposition was a great success, even financially, and helped to convince Omaha at least that the depression was over.

The early years of the twentieth century saw another flurry of prosperity in Nebraska's metropolis. Fancy new residential districts, such as Happy Hollow and Fairacres, were platted and occupied. The Omaha Grain Exchange was organized to develop the city into an important grain market. Stockyard receipts, which had become an important barometer of the city's economic activity, increased from nearly 2.5 million head of livestock in 1890 to 4.4 million in 1900 and 6.1 million by 1910, with a total value of $100 million by 1910. Although the number of cattle doubled over the same period, the greatest gains were in sheep, which increased from around 154,000 head in 1880 to nearly 3 million head in 1910, slightly more than a nineteenfold increase.[1]

Although Omaha experienced dramatic economic progress in these years, in some ways it remained as wild and wide open as it had been during the days when it was a jumping-off place for the West. Sporting bloods no longer raced their horses up and down Farnam Street, but there was plenty of entertainment for the farmers and others from small towns who came to have a look at city life.

Known affectionately as "Mayor Jim," Omaha mayor Jim Dahlman was a colorful former cowboy from western Nebraska. Elected again and again, Mayor Jim was an avowed friend of personal liberty, which translated into the open saloon. He had made his way into politics with

The Grand Court and Lagoon at Omaha's Trans-Mississippi Exposition of 1898, located at present 24th and Pratt Streets. An imitation of Chicago's Columbian Exposition of 1893, Omaha's fair was a pronouncement that Nebraska was no longer part of the frontier. Courtesy, NSHS, T772:SIFI.

the support of William Jennings Bryan, but the friendship ended when Dahlman ran for governor on the Democratic ticket and denounced prohibition. Dahlman was not the only politician who contributed to Omaha's reputation for "wildness"; it was assisted as well by Tom Dennison, a gambler driven into politics to protect his business, who became the city's political boss.

Lincoln, too, came out of its doldrums in this era. There was still very little industry in the city, but its growing wholesale houses and retail stores served an ever-widening territory. It was not only the capital but the site of other state institutions as well. With these firmly established, the university flourishing, and small communities developing north, east, and south, Lincoln's prospects looked good.

Life in the capital city was considerably different from that in Omaha. Under the leadership of men such as E. Benjamin Andrews, Roscoe Pound, Charles E. Bessey, Erwin H. Barbour, and George E. Howard the University of Nebraska was developing into one of the major institutions of the West. Lincoln also was home to several church schools, including Nebraska Wesleyan, Cotner University, and Union College. Along with the university, these institutions added an air of intellectual sophistication to the capital city.

Lincoln's social life centered around discussion clubs, literary societies, an opera house, which was proclaimed the most ornate Romanesque building west of Chicago, thirty-eight churches, and thirteen temperance societies. Though his political views disturbed many of the more conservative citizens, William Jennings Bryan occupied a place of prominence in the city's life. He had built a grand farm home east of the city and was frequently asked to speak at local church gatherings, picnics, and banquets. Young lieutenant John J. Pershing, commandant of cadets at the university, also added sparkle to the city's social life. Among the students at the university Willa Cather was making an impression both on her peers and on her teachers with her brilliant pen, sharp tongue, and pronounced views.

MANUFACTURING

Capital invested in manufactures nearly tripled from $37.5 million to almost $1 billion in the years between 1890 and 1910. Fully two-thirds of all manufacturing, however, arose directly from the processing of agricultural products and contributed less to the creation of new jobs than heavy industry might have. The number of employees increased only 23 percent from 23,876 to 29,444 over the two decades, and salaries increased only 50 percent from $12.9 million to $19.4 million. Manufacturing still played a relatively unimportant part in the state's economy.

Transportation was a different matter. Railroad mileage increased from 5,685.13 in 1900 to 7,879.19 in 1910. Double tracks had been laid on the main line of the Union Pacific and part of the Burlington. Most people now depended on the railroad for transportation between towns and horse-drawn vehicles for local travel. An automobile first appeared on the streets of Lincoln about 1902, but by 1905 the noisy, expensive, unpredictable horseless carriages had become such a nuisance that the legislature passed a law requiring the operator of an automobile to halt on the highway until the driver of any frightened horse could get past. Between 1906 and 1908 the number of automobiles registered with the secretary of state increased nearly fourfold from 1,087 to 4,200, and in 1910 the number had jumped to 15,000.

CULTURAL DEVELOPMENTS

If the frontier was fading because of increasing adaptation to new technologies and forms of transportation, it was also fading because of the expansion of cultural institutions such as schools and churches. In one sense the diffusion of culture, expressed in a proliferation of art, music, and literature, was remarkable in a country so young and so often beset with the struggle for mere survival. As Willa Cather expressed it:

Even as late as 1885 the central part of the State, and everything to the westward, was, in the main, raw prairie. The cultivated fields and broken land seemed mere scratches in the brown, running steppe that never stopped until it broke against the foothills of the rockies. The dugouts and sod farm houses were three or four miles apart, and the only means of communication was the heavy farm wagon, drawn by heavy work horses.[2]

Yet in another sense, if the photographs of frontier photographer Solomon Butcher are any indication, cultural and social institutions arrived with the settlers. So, too, the artistic expression of the people was apparent from the beginning. Butcher's collection is replete with pictures of families in front of their sod houses displaying the accoutrements of cultural appreciation: the piano, the organ, the quilts and coverlets with their intricate designs and blends of colors.[3] It is little wonder that the agencies that gave institutional form to culture would also be welcomed, indeed encouraged, even on the "raw prairie."

CHURCHES

The territorial experience of church building was repeated in virtually every community as settlement moved west, except that the sod house replaced the log cabin as the structure in which the first worship services were held. The Methodists, with their itinerant ministry and strong emotional gospel, continued to lead the way, although they were by no means the only group active on the frontier. The United Brethren had an itinerant ministry and also held camp meetings, which were popular in frontier communities. The Seventh Day Adventists were active on the frontier, moving their gospel tents from place to place. The Congregational Church, although not particularly organized for frontier work, was also established early in many communities and soon became an influential body. The Baptist Church found many adherents in all parts of the state. The Catholic and Episcopal Churches actively engaged in missionary work, and Episcopal Bishop George Allen Beecher was particularly effective in western Nebraska. The American Sunday School Union was another active force in carrying religion to western Nebraska.

Many immigrants brought their religion with them from Europe, which accounts for the state's substantial Catholic and Lutheran groups. Frequently entire towns were established under the auspices of one of these groups, although other church groups, notably the Congregationalists, were also active. In these communities the voice of the founding religious group was likely to be dominant for many years. In 1906, when the first census of religious bodies in the United States was taken, approximately one-third of all Nebraskans indicated that they were church members.

The churches had a far greater influence on Nebraska life than the percentage of the population they claimed as members, especially in respect to the major social questions of the time, notably the prohibition controversies of the late nineteenth and early twentieth centuries, and the customs prevailing in many communities. The church was an important center for social interaction for members and nonmembers alike, particularly in the days before the automobile and widespread commercial entertainment. The church provided people with one of their most important opportunities to enjoy the company of others. And those churches that conducted services in the native language of their people played a significant role in maintaining the patterns of thought and life of the homeland.

Table 9. Religious Affiliations of Nebraskans in 1906

	Number	Percent
Roman Catholic	118,545	32.6
Methodist	62,586	17.2
Lutheran	39,375	10.8
Presbyterian	20,926	5.8
Disciples of Christ	19,121	5.3
Baptist	17,386	4.8
Congregational and Christian	16,798	4.6
Protestant Episcopal	6,903	1.9
Evangelical	6,192	1.7
United Brethren	6,045	1.6
Evangelical and Reformed	5,498	1.5
Other (Groups of Less than 1%)	44,210	12.2
Total	363,585	

Source: Bureau of the Census, *Religious Bodies:* 1906 (Washington DC: Government Printing Office, 1910), 226–30.

SCHOOLS

The first territorial legislature had provided for a system of free public schools and a large measure of both local support and local control. This system was carried over into the statehood period, although the quality of the schools varied greatly from community to community, depending on the district's desire as well as ability, actual or assumed, to support education. Most of the pioneers seem to have believed that education, at least in the "fundamentals," was a good thing and a proper object of public support. Beyond that, however, opinion diverged widely as to the extent of the public's responsibility. In 1869–70 only 39 percent of the state's school-age children were enrolled in school. The constitution of 1875 provided for a complete system of public schools, from the elementary level to the university, but the implementation of that provision was left largely to the local districts. As late as 1890 there were only 250 graded school districts in the state and approximately 16 percent of all children between the ages of eight and fourteen attended no school at all.

Compulsory education was rejected by a resounding majority in 1871, and as late as 1883 the legislature showed little interest in education. The Populist legislature of 1891, however, enacted a compulsory school law which guaranteed all young Nebraskans the opportunity for a common school education. For most of Nebraska it meant a one-room, single-teacher school, and this was the most numerous type of school in the state even when it began its second century in 1967. From a record number of 7,655 schools at the end of World War I, the number still exceeded 7,000 in 1950. Consolidation efforts would eventually reduce that number to around 1,400 school districts by 1990.

Before the automobile and the development of an all-weather rural road system, the little sod and frame schools that dotted the countryside not only provided education for farm children but also served as social centers for the rural communities. Frequently on winter evenings the stoves were fired and the lamps lighted for a debate, a meeting of the literary society, a spelling bee, a sing, a box social, a meeting of the Grange or the Farmers' Alliance. Frequently church services were held in the school.[4]

There was considerable interest in higher education. Some of it, to be sure, was motivated by commercial considerations; it was good propaganda if a town could boast of a "college" or "university." But the desire to provide opportunities for higher learning seems to have been genuine. The flurry of activity during territorial times was largely prompted by various church groups, which continued to be interested in higher education. Many of the early efforts failed for lack of support, but a resurgence of activity began with the establishment of Doane College in Crete by the Congregationalists in 1872. From the late 1870s through the early 1890s, other church bodies renewed their efforts. Creighton University was founded in Omaha by the Jesuits in 1878; Hastings College in 1882 by the Presbyterians; Luther College in Wahoo in 1883 by the Lutherans, later part of Midland Lutheran College in Fremont; Dana College, originally founded as Trinity Seminary, in 1884 in Blair by Danish Lutheran immigrants; Nebraska Wesleyan University, founded by the Methodists in 1887 in Lincoln; Union College, founded by the Seventh Day Adventists in Lincoln in 1891; York College, founded in 1890 and later associated with the Church of Christ; and Concordia College in

Seward, founded in 1894 by the Lutheran Church–Missouri Synod. The University of Omaha was founded as a private university in 1908, later to become a municipal university in 1931, and was maintained by the city of Omaha until 1968, when it became part of the University of Nebraska system.

The state's major public university, the University of Nebraska, was chartered on February 15, 1869, and opened in the fall of 1871. Organized as a land grant institution under the Morrill Act of 1862, the university initially was provided for in state legislation passed in 1867, which also resulted in the creation of Lincoln as the state capital. Founded in years of distress and doubt, the university in its early years suffered not only financial vicissitudes but harassment from various forces across the state.

Some people thought that the state was wasting its money in trying to establish and operate a university when so few opportunities existed for secondary education, and the preponderance of students in the preparatory department caused the university to be dubbed derisively "the Lincoln high school." Others opposed the establishment of professional schools and colleges as an unwarranted extension of publicly supported education. Still others looked with skepticism on the activities of the professors. They doubted, for example, that the theoreticians at the agricultural college, or "state farm" as it was universally called, had much to offer the practical farmers of the state.

Various religious groups opposed the university as a godless institution, and, indeed, this charge vexed the school for many years. Initially, there was fear that the university would fall under the domination of one particular religious group. To allay that fear, the regents were careful to employ not more than one person from any denomination in the first faculty. In its early days the faculty was occasionally torn by religious controversies. In later years university administrations interpreted the constitutional provision separating church and state so rigidly that they often offended certain groups. The institution that later became Cotner College was originally established to provide a Christian university in the capital city to counteract the influence of the state university.

Despite vicissitude and controversy, the University of Nebraska continued to develop both the teaching and research aspects of its mission as understood by the faculty, and by the turn of the century it was recognized as one of the great institutions in the West. Faculty members had won wide renown, and the products of its laboratories were finding acceptance among an ever-growing group of the state's citizens.

One of the primary missions of the university, as well as the denominational colleges, was to provide teachers for the public and parochial schools. The lure of teaching school was so weak, however, that many college graduates chose careers in business and the professions instead. Even if all of them had gone into teaching, they could hardly have filled the demand created by the ever-expanding number of schools within the state.

In 1867 the state had acquired Mount Vernon Seminary and College, a Methodist institution located at Peru, and reestablished it as the Nebraska State Normal School. The school helped to provide needed education for teachers, but most who taught in the rural schools did so without the benefit of college training. To remedy this deficiency, "teachers' institutes," short courses conducted under the auspices of the state superintendent of public instruction and the county superintendents, were begun. Occasionally private normal schools developed, and one owned by J. M. Pile at Wayne was taken over by the state and reestablished as Wayne State Teachers College. Another state teachers college was established at Kearney in 1903, followed by one at Chadron in 1911.

THE ARTS

The press provided the first outlet for literary expression during the territorial period and continued to do so into the early years of statehood. A number of the early editors were conscious of the literary aspects of their calling, and some of their work may properly be considered a contribution to the literature of the region. Their primary interests, however, were progress and politics. They were a vigorous breed, never at a loss for words and never without an opinion. They often described political opponents in terms that would bring libel suits today, and they seemed to have an inexhaustible store of adjectives with which to describe the present condition and future prospects of their state and community.

One of the first and most vigorous editors was Joseph E. Johnson, a Mormon who had made the trek to Utah but who reappeared in Council Bluffs, Iowa, in 1852, as publisher of the *Bugle*. An ardent advocate of the organization of Nebraska Territory, he began publishing a paper in Omaha, the *Arrow*, a few weeks after the Kansas-Nebraska bill was signed. In 1859, he moved out to Wood River to start one of the earliest papers in central Nebraska, the *Huntsman's Echo*, "Independent in Everything—Neutral in Nothing." In 1855, J. Sterling Morton began to impress his vigorous personality upon the *Nebraska City News*, and the next year at Brownville, Robert W. Furnas started the *Nebraska Advertiser*, a folksy, influential paper that played a significant role in promoting the Republican Party in the territory. In 1865, Dr. George L. Miller began a quarter-century of editorial service which transformed the *Omaha Herald* from a struggling frontier paper to one of national importance. Others who became influential during the early years of statehood were C. H. Gere, who established the *Nebraska State Journal* at Lincoln in 1869, and Edward Rosewater, who founded the *Omaha Bee* in 1871. These papers were in many ways diametrically opposed to each other, and yet both soon became the principal editorial voices for the Republican Party in the state.

William Jennings Bryan is usually thought of as an orator and politician, but he was also a writer and editor. In 1894, he became editor of the *Omaha World-Herald* and later, in 1901 in Lincoln, he started the *Commoner*, a national weekly devoted primarily to political and religious subjects. Bryan modeled the *Commoner* after the *Conservative*, which was edited by J. Sterling Morton from 1898 to 1902.

Early newspapers frequently gave space in their columns to poems and essays written by their readers. Particularly during the Populist period, a spate of both poetry and prose gave voice to the grievances, the demands, and the aspirations of the embattled farmers. New verses were frequently set to old, familiar tunes, often well-known hymns, and sung at political rallies. The *Nebraska State Journal* had two popular writers: A. L. "Doc" Bixby, whose comments on life, death, and politics were couched in doggerel always ending in "BIX," and Walt Mason, who used a doubtful verse form known as the prose poem.

Other aspects of pioneer literary activity were promotional and historical writing, at times difficult to separate. In 1880 Samuel Aughey published his extensive description of Nebraska's geology, climate, and plant life entitled *Sketches of the Physical Geography and Geology of Nebraska*, and Harrison Johnson wrote the state's first extended history, *Johnson's History of Nebraska*, a work that has much in common with contemporary promotional literature. In 1881 Charles Dana Wilber published a lengthy Nebraska booster work, *The Great Valleys and Prairies of Nebraska and the Northwest*, and the following year Alfred T. Andreas published his monumental *History of the State of Nebraska*, containing a general sketch of the state, followed by an extended account of the history of each county, including biographical sketches of prominent pioneers. It remains an invaluable source of local history. The well-known Morton-Watkins *Illustrated History of Nebraska* was a subscription history originally projected by J. Sterling Morton and completed in 1913 by Albert Watkins with the assistance of Clarence S. Paine.

The newspapermen, the promoters, and even the early historians made little effort to interpret the life of the state. For the most part, they were simply chroniclers. Some of the obscure poets were trying to interpret the region, but their audiences were limited and their impact small. The first substantial effort to interpret Nebraska life through the medium of literature is probably Orasmus C. Dake's *Nebraska Legends and Other Poems* (1871). In this volume Dake, who was the first professor of English literature at the University of Nebraska, created the Indian legends of Weeping Water and the Raw Hide. Ethnologists can find no Indian equivalent for these legends.

The first significant literature dealing with Nebraska appeared in 1913 when Willa Cather published *O Pioneers!*, a memorable regional story that was told simply and spontaneously. The next few years brought an intensive literary outpouring. Willa Cather published *Song of the Lark* in 1915 and *My Antonia* in 1917. John G. Neihardt published the first of his epic cycle, *The Song of Hugh Glass*, in 1915. The same year saw publication of *Barbed Wire and Other Poems* by Edwin Ford Piper and Louise Pound's *Folk-Song of Nebraska and the Central West*. Hartley Burr Alexander's *Pageant of Lincoln* was presented in 1917.

CHAPTER 21

Nebraska Politics and Progressivism

Although the farmers, through the People's, or Populist, Party, had changed the pattern of politics and had achieved some voice in state government, they had not improved their economic position. Indeed, the farmers in the early 1890s were worse off than they had been in the 1870s, when they had been hit by grasshoppers, drought, and depression, or in the 1880s, when bountiful crops brought steadily lower prices. In the early 1890s, the state suffered from protracted drought, and farm prices fell to new lows. There was some improvement in both prices and production in the late years of the decade, but conditions remained so unfavorable that immigration, which had more than doubled the state's population in the 1880s, virtually ceased, and population increased only from 1,058,910 in 1890 to 1,066,300 in 1900.

In the central part of the state, the amount of rainfall decreased even more than it did in the state as a whole, which may help to explain why that section became the center of Populist activity. Agricultural statistics tell part of the story, but not the stories of individual farmers attempting to work their way out from under a crushing burden of debt contracted during the relatively flush times of the 1880s. Charles H. Morrill, for example, a prominent pioneer who both experienced and witnessed the hard times of the period, describes them as follows:

In the year of 1893 crops in Nebraska were almost totally destroyed by drought and hot winds. Then came the panic and financial stress, which paralyzed business. In 1894 Nebraska was doomed to have another crop failure. Farmers were obliged to ship in grain and even hay to feed their stock; many sacrificed their livestock by selling at very low prices. Some farmers shot their stock hogs to prevent their starving. Financial conditions grew worse and the entire state was almost in the grip of actual famine. In Lincoln all banks with the exception *of three went out of business or failed. Farmers could not pay interest on their mortgages; land could not be sold at any price. . . . One eastern loan company offered to sell me forty quarter sections at $200.00 each.*[1]

Labor also had benefited little from the independent political action in which it had participated. The Supreme Court had held invalid a Populist law declaring eight hours as a legal day's work in Nebraska, but for many the question was purely academic. The real problem was finding any work. The financial depression growing out of the worldwide panic of 1893 threw many people out of work and depressed the wages of those who were fortunate enough to find jobs. Because agriculture undergirded most business and industry in the towns and cities of Nebraska, employment opportunities were further lessened by the already depressed agrarian economy of the late 1880s and early 1890s.

It was in this context that William Jennings Bryan appeared, using the full force of his magnetic personality. By taking for his own the coinage issue, which had been paramount in Populist thinking since 1890, Bryan captured the Democratic Party in Nebraska in 1894 and, at the same time, brought many Populists into the Democratic fold. In 1896 he did the same thing nationally. Bryanism thus replaced Populism as the voice of agrarian discontent. The Democratic Party, in Nebraska and the nation, was thus transformed from an organization of conservatives who looked with horror upon the expanding role of government under the Republicans to an organization that accepted not only the reality but the desirability of this expanded governmental role. They insisted, however, that government must act on behalf of different groups than it had since the Civil War under the Republicans.

Within the Republican Party, too, there was a growing insistence that government assist the farmer and the laborer at least as much as it did the capitalist. In Nebraska and other northern plains states, the Populists had secured many of their adherents from dissident elements in the Republican Party. Although they could support a third party, many of them found it virtually impossible to join the Democrats. Instead, they went back to the old party and tried to reform it from within. The result was a growing progressivism within the G.O.P. paralleling Bryanism in the Democratic Party.

THE REPUBLICANS RECOVER CONTROL

Bryan's nomination for the presidency in 1896 created great excitement in Nebraska. The ultraconservative *Lincoln Journal*, for example, greeted the news with the first two-column headline in its history. The presidential nomination secured Bryan's control of the Democratic Party in Nebraska. He was even more the darling of the Populists than he was of the Democrats, and it was easy for him to promote fusion again in 1896 as he had in 1894. This fusion extended in a limited degree to the national campaign as well. The Populists also named Bryan as their standard-bearer, but they could not tolerate conservative Arthur Sewall of Maine for vice-president so they confused the issue by naming Thomas E. Watson of Georgia as their candidate for the vice-presidency. Joining in the fusion, at least informally, were many silver Republicans who could not accept the nomination of William McKinley for president or that of J. H. McColl of Dawson County, regarded as extremely friendly to the Union Pacific, for governor.

With this strength behind him, Governor Silas Holcomb easily won reelection. And though Bryan failed to capture a majority of the electoral votes nationally, he did defeat McKinley in Nebraska, 115,999 to 103,064, thus bringing Nebraska's four electoral votes into the Democratic column for the first time in history. Also for the first time, the Republicans lost all the state offices. In the congressional races, fusionists won four seats and Republicans two. The fusionists gained an overwhelming majority in both houses of the legislature, twenty-six of thirty-three seats in the Senate and seventy-two of one hundred seats in the House.

The destruction of Republican control, begun in 1890, was complete by 1896, but the G.O.P. was not destined to stay out of power long. The fusionist legislature of 1897 passed a variety of reform measures: an act providing for the use of initiative and referendum (the first in the United States), acts regulating stockyards and telephone and telegraph companies; a law forbidding corporations to contribute to political campaign funds and another against grain elevator combinations; and an act forbidding further sale of the state school lands and providing that they should be leased forever, the income to be used for the annual support of the schools. They failed, however, to deal effectively with railroads,

William Jennings Bryan. Courtesy, NSHS, A427:364.

against which so much fusion oratory had been directed, and bills to abolish free passes and reduce passenger rates to two cents per mile were sidetracked or defeated.

Again in 1899, the fusionists elected a state ticket headed by Populist William A. Poynter, but the Republicans controlled the legislature, and the fusionists were unable to abolish the hated free pass system. Indeed, it seemed that politicians' attitudes toward the free pass were determined by whether they were in or out of office. The *Omaha Bee*, which continued to argue that the farmers' only hope lay in the reform of the Republican Party, commented:

Never in the history of Nebraska has the State House been filled by such a rapacious free pass brigade as since the offices were occupied by the Popocrats. According to the authority of the recognized organ of the populist party, there is but one official on the state pay roll who does not ride on free railway passes, and it is notorious that popocratic officeholders high and low have not only been taking pleasure junkets at the expense of the railroads, but have traveled about on public business on free passes and charged up mileage in the expense accounts turned into the state treasury.[2]

There were signs, too, that the economic depression was passing. The rains came again, but despite good crops, prices improved only a little. Unemployment declined, and hope stirred once more throughout the nation. Whether this improvement represented, as the Republicans claimed, the McKinley administration's stabilization of the economy and the saving of the country from the horrors of Bryanarchy, or whether it represented, as some of the fusionists maintained, the completion of a process of liquidation by which most of the heavily mortgaged people had been sold out at panic prices to start life over again, made little difference. The period of stress was over, and many people fell once again into their old habits, which politically in Nebraska meant voting Republican.

Moreover, war occupied the nation's attention. Though Union veterans were still around, albeit in dwindling numbers, the war with Spain was the first international conflict in half a century. The war took on something of the aspect of a great crusade, and though Nebraskans who served in the Philippines or in the disease-ridden training camps of Chickamauga Park soon became disillusioned, McKinley's position as a national leader was greatly strengthened. The war posed a particular problem for Bryan. Struggling hard to keep himself in the limelight and thus retain control of both the Democrats and the Populists, Bryan offered his services to the government. When these were declined by his erstwhile opponent, he persuaded Governor Holcomb to appoint him colonel of the Third Nebraska Regiment, which saw service in Florida and Cuba. Bryan's military career did little to enhance his reputation. He was constantly overshadowed by Theodore Roosevelt. Bryan turned his attention from the silver issue to imperialism, but while most Nebraskans had little enthusiasm for bearing the white man's burden and the conservative Democrats generally agreed with the Great Commoner's anti-imperialist views, he could not stir up much vocal support for his program of anti-imperialism either in Nebraska or in the nation.

The Republicans, who had regained control of the legislature in 1898, fought hard to restore themselves completely to power in 1900. Nebraska was a key state. Bryan easily secured the Democratic presidential nomination again in 1900. In addition, the seats of both of Nebraska's United States senators were at stake. M. L. Hayward of Nebraska City, who had been defeated by Governor Poynter in 1898, had been elected senator over William V. Allen in 1899, only to die before he could qualify. Both Democrats and Populists were devoted to Bryan, but neither group was willing to surrender its party organization to the other. As a result, they went along with a fusion ticket that had within it the seeds of its own destruction. The fusionists had not distinguished themselves for their ability to work together in the legislature; they had never been able to agree to hold a single convention; and they had always argued about candidates. Only the magic of Bryan's name held them together.

Though their victory was far from complete, the Republicans were able to rejoice when the returns for 1900 came in. McKinley defeated Bryan 121,835 to 114,013; Charles H. Dietrich, a Hastings banker, defeated Poynter by the narrow margin of 861 votes; and the Republican candidates for other state offices won by similarly narrow margins. The fusionists retained four of the six congressional seats, but the Republicans secured a considerable majority in the legislature. In the Senate there were nineteen Republicans, twelve fusionists, and two Democrats. In the House there were fifty-three Republicans, thirty fusionists, ten Democrats, and three Populists.

In the joint convention that would choose the two senators, the Republicans had a margin of nine, even if the fusionists, Democrats, and

Populists could have worked together, which appeared impossible. The Republicans would also find it difficult to create a united front. There were simply too many strong candidates. Among the leading contenders were John M. Thurston, seeking reelection; D. E. Thompson, Lincoln millionaire and superintendent of the Burlington lines west of the Missouri; the redoubtable Edward Rosewater; and former governor Lorenzo Crounse. In addition, there was a host of others, each hoping that lightning would strike him should a compromise candidate be necessary. On the fusion side the leading contenders were Senator Allen, who had been appointed by Governor Poynter to fill out Hayward's term, and Gilbert M. Hitchcock, a son of Republican senator Phineas W. Hitchcock, now editor of the Democratic *Omaha World-Herald*. Much of the struggle centered around D. E. Thompson, who had secured almost absolute control of Republican politics in the capital city but who was bitterly opposed by Charles H. Gere, editor of the powerful *Lincoln Journal*. The balloting, which began on January 5, did not end until March 29, providing those who urged the popular election of senators one of their strongest arguments. The struggle was finally ended when Thompson withdrew in favor of Governor Dietrich, and the opposition forces agreed on J. H. Millard, prominent Omaha banker put forth by Thompson, as their other candidate.

Lieutenant Governor Ezra P. Savage, who became governor when Dietrich went to the Senate, immediately got his party in trouble by pardoning Joseph S. Bartley, former state treasurer, who had been found in default in the sum of $555,790.66 and had been sentenced to twenty years in the state penitentiary and fined $303,768.90. But the Republicans themselves took care of Savage. They indignantly refused to renominate him, even though his most ardent critic, the *Lincoln Journal*, admitted that "outside this unpopular and perhaps premature exercise of the pardoning power, the Governor has been the chief of one of the most upright and certainly the most efficient body of state officers that Nebraska has had for years."[3] They selected instead John H. Mickey, a farmer and banker from Osceola, who generally was looked upon as opposed to the Republican machine, an able and public-spirited citizen.

Fusion was even more difficult for the Democrats and Populists in 1902 than it had been in previous years. They met in separate halls in Lincoln on the same day, and though Bryan addressed both conventions, counseling a fraternal spirit and united effort in a common cause, it was clear from the outset that unity would be difficult to achieve. The Democrats demanded as the price of fusion the head of the ticket, inasmuch as they had supported Populists since 1894. Specifically, they wanted C. J. Smyth, who had served as attorney general and had been well liked by the Populists. The Populists, for their part, wanted M. F. Harrington of O'Neill, who had been a Democrat before he became a Populist and who generally was looked upon as one of the ablest lawyers and stump speakers in the state. Bryan apparently wanted William H. Thompson of Grand Island, and after a stormy all-night session in a conference committee from the two conventions, his desire prevailed, as it had in the past.

Thompson conducted a vigorous campaign, but he could not divert the drift back to the Republican Party. Many Republicans who had supported the Populists now felt that the independent movement had been taken over completely by Bryan and the Democrats; and with a candidate of the caliber of Mickey at the head of the ticket they found it easy to return to the fold. Even so, the vote was close, attesting somewhat to the fusion candidate's personal popularity. Mickey received 96,471 votes; Thompson, 91,116; Prohibition and Socialist candidates received 3,396 and 3,157 votes respectively, making the total against Mickey a little larger than the vote cast for him. The Republicans elected their entire state ticket, all but one of their congressional candidates, and gained a comfortable majority in both houses of the legislature. In the second district, Gilbert M. Hitchcock defeated Congressman David H. Mercer, in part because the former got the support of his journalistic rival, Edward Rosewater of the *Omaha Bee*. Rosewater had tried unsuccessfully to prevent Mercer's renomination in the Republican primary and refused to support him in the general election, largely because Mercer had tried to intrude himself as a compromise candidate against Rosewater in the heated senatorial struggle of the year before.

PROGRESSIVISM AND THE G.O.P.

The Populists' influence as an independent party in Nebraska or the nation declined rapidly after 1892. Nationally, they had fused with the Democrats to nominate Bryan in 1896 and again in 1900. They could not accept Alton B. Parker, the Democratic nominee in 1904, however, and by 1908 they had become somewhat disillusioned with Bryan's leadership. They put their own candidates in the field in both those years, but their disappointing showing in 1908 (about twenty-nine thousand votes) resulted in their dissolution as an independent party. In Nebraska, their only victories had been those they shared, through fusion, with the Democrats. In Nebraska as in the nation, fusion spelled disaster for those who hoped to maintain the Populists as an independent third party. As one of their newspaper supporters, John C. Sprecher of the *Schuyler Free Lance*, who had been a Populist state senator in 1901, observed in 1904: "Fusion killed the populist party, because fusion with democrats meant in reality the endorsement of the democratic party which was an older and stronger party. . . . If the democratic party was right there was no room for a populist party and if it was wrong it was clearly a case of combining forces for the sake of spoils."[4]

For their off-year convention in 1905, they could assemble only about fifty delegates in a dingy little room on East O Street in Lincoln. But though they died out as an independent party, their ideas lived on in both of the old parties, which in the early years of the twentieth century seemed to be vying with each other to implement the Populist assumption that the government should be truly representative of the people and that long-established control of politics and economics by the few should be broken. As the great historian of the frontier, Frederick Jackson Turner, once phrased it, "Mr. Bryan's democracy, Mr. Debs's socialism, and Mr. Roosevelt's Republicanism all had in common the emphasis on the need of governmental regulation of industrial tendencies in the interests of the common man; the checking of the power of those business titans who emerged successful out of the competitive individualism of pioneer America."[5]

In Nebraska, Bryan not only took over the Populists, he changed the Democratic Party from an organization dominated by ultraconservatives like Morton, Miller, and Boyd to an organization in which all but the most ardent agrarian reformers could feel at home. The Republicans, too, began to feel the impact of Populist doctrine, as old-timers who had joined the Populists began to drift back and youngsters, nursed on the heady debates of the Populist period, began to make their voices heard in the party's councils. The presence of Theodore Roosevelt in the White House naturally strengthened the hands of the progressives within the state, but the logic of events locally also demonstrated forcibly that if the Republicans were to maintain their control they would have to move toward the progressive position. In 1904, George W. Berge, author of the celebrated *Free Pass Bribery System* and fusion candidate for governor, almost defeated Mickey's bid for reelection despite Roosevelt's landslide majority over Parker.

The Republican progressives clearly saw that if they were to achieve control of the party they must break railroad domination of its affairs. Railroads, the principal big business in the state, had long been the target of reformers. Despite their oratory, however, the fusionists had been unable to do much to curb railroad influence. The roads kept issuing free passes to politicians, watching over the sessions of the legislature through the agency of highly paid and skillful lobbyists, and keeping local politics in order by retaining influential attorneys at all the county seats.

Ironically, the railroads themselves did more to hurt their cause than did their attackers. Many citizens had been greatly irritated when in 1901 the Union Pacific and the Burlington, instead of dividing the two United States senatorships, decided to fight it out for control of both, fore-shadowing a breakup of the railroad machine. That incident also was an important factor in the demand for a change in the method of electing senators. Governor Dietrich, who had been looked upon as the Burling-ton's senator, got involved in a nasty difficulty resulting from his removal of the Hastings post office into a building of his own and his collection from the state of the governor's salary for a few weeks while he was also United States senator. He was hauled into district court on both counts, and though he was acquitted on technicalities, it was clear that Dietrich and railroad influence would do the party no good. His was the short term, and when it ended the Republican state convention endorsed Elmer J. Burkett for his seat over the opposition of the railroads. The elec-torate approved the choice in the preferential ballot, and the Republican-controlled legislature of 1905 elected Burkett without so much as the formality of a caucus. The next year, through the influence of Senator Burkett, the state convention adopted an anti–free pass resolution, de-spite railroad efforts to defeat it.

By the summer of 1906, progressivism was sweeping over Nebraska like a prairie fire. On June 16, Senator George L. Sheldon of Nehawka, who had declared, "You can trust the representatives of the people to deal fairly with the railroads, but you cannot trust the representatives of the railroads to deal fairly with the people,"[6] and Attorney General Norris Brown of Kearney, who had been carrying on an active campaign against lumber dealers' associations, line elevators, and other large business groups, announced that they would seek the Republican nomination for governor and United States senator respectively. They made a series of public addresses which sounded more like old-time Populist fireworks than anything that had been heard in the state for more than a decade, uniting in their attack on the railroad machine and the free pass system. With Roosevelt carrying on an aggressive campaign against millionaire land-grabbers and corporation consolidations and the *Lincoln Journal*, which in former years had been the faithful supporter of party machine and railroad rule, carrying the torch for the aggressive anti-railroad Republicans, the progressives carried the day. The state convention nominated Sheldon for governor and endorsed Brown for the Senate. Their platform, very similar to that of the Democrats, embodied many of the early Populist doctrines and was strong in its opposition to railroads and corporations.

The Democrats also came out strongly for reform, but they nominated Ashton C. Shallenberger of Alma, an old-line machine Democrat generally looked upon as being under the railroad influence, as their candidate for governor. The Populists were persuaded to endorse Shallenberger only after an impassioned speech by George W. Berge in his favor. The Democratic convention also connived with Gilbert M. Hitchcock, who was running for Congress but who wanted to be United States senator in case the Democrats should take over the legislature, to refrain from endorsing anyone for the Senate. Sheldon defeated Shallenberger 97,858 to 84,885; all Republican candidates for state offices were elected by large majorities; and the Republicans got a majority of both houses of the legislature and elected all congressmen, except in the second district, where Hitchcock, largely because of his great local popularity, defeated John L. Kennedy, who had beaten him two years earlier.

On December 12, 1906, W. B. Rose, chairman of the Republican State Committee, addressed a letter to the Republican members of the incoming legislature warning them of the tricky manipulations by which the railroad and corporation lobbies might be expected to attempt to block the reform measures promised in the Republican state platform. Whether they needed the warning or not, the members of the legislature went ahead to redeem their campaign promises with the result that the legislative acts of 1907 marked more important and permanent changes in the political structure of the state than those of any other session. In a very real sense, they brought to fruition the revolution in public thought which began in 1890. Among the major items entered in the statute books were a statewide direct primary law, a child labor law, an anti-free-pass law, a two-cent passenger fare law, and an anti-discrimination law. They also created and defined the power of a state railway commission, established a state bureau for the investigation of insect pests and plant diseases, created a board of pardons, prohibited brewers from holding any interests in saloons, and memorialized Congress to amend the Constitution to provide for the popular election of the United States senators.

Possibly the most important in the long run was the direct primary law. There had been primaries of sorts since the 1870s, but they were purely voluntary. The senatorial fiasco of 1901 had aroused great interest in primary legislation. Adam McMullen of Beatrice had led a fight for a direct primary in the session of 1905, but nothing had been accomplished. Both parties were committed to the primary in 1907, however, and the act was easily passed. In 1909 presidential electors were added to the primary system, and in 1911, delegates to the national conventions, national committeemen, and a presidential preference. The primary, however, was not the great cure-all its proponents had promised it would be, and the system would be revised frequently over the years by the Nebraska legislature.

DEMOCRATIC ASCENDANCY

The campaign of 1908 went forward in an atmosphere of reform, albeit a rather confused and confusing atmosphere. Nationally, the Republicans, led by the relatively conservative William Howard Taft, were victorious over the Democrats, who once again had staked their political fortunes on William Jennings Bryan. In Nebraska, Governor George L. Sheldon, perhaps the most liberal chief executive in the history of the state, was defeated for reelection by the relatively conservative Ashton C. Shallenberger. There were several reasons for this reversal of the trend back to the Republicans. In the first place, Bryan at the head of the ticket was favored over Taft. Then, on two local issues, bank guarantee and county liquor option, Shallenberger campaigned much more effectively than Sheldon.

The panic of 1907 had spotlighted the importance of guaranteeing bank deposits. Oklahoma territory had had such a law since 1903, and under the leadership of Bryan, the Democratic national convention adopted a plank favoring national bank guarantee. Similarly, the Democratic state platform favored a state guarantee law, and Shallenberger, who got the Democratic nomination again, campaigned vigorously in its behalf. Sheldon had also declared himself in favor of a bank guarantee law, but his position was greatly weakened when the Republican state convention voted down the proposal by a resounding three-to-one majority.

Sheldon also got himself in trouble on the liquor issue. He had tried to push a county option law through the legislature in 1907, but it failed. He continued his fight for county option into the election campaign with the result that he lost many wet votes that might normally have been expected to go to the Republican candidate. Shallenberger straddled the issue, letting wets think he opposed county option and the dry Populists think he favored it. As a result, he unseated Sheldon, 132,960 to 125,976. While the Republicans generally won other state offices, Bryan secured the state's electoral votes; the Democrats elected three congressmen and secured a clear majority in the legislature.

The Democrats in the legislature of 1909, assisted by some progressive Republicans, set out to redeem their campaign promises. They passed a bank guarantee law, changed the primary from a closed to an open election, provided for the election of judges and educational officers on nonpartisan tickets, and enacted the Oregon Pledge Law, which required candidates for the legislature to pledge that if elected they would vote for the candidate for United States senator receiving the highest preferential vote. The liquor issue intruded itself into the session in an unusual and unexpected way. County option was defeated in the House and did not come to a vote in the Senate. The real fireworks arose over an eight o'clock closing law which got through both houses and, despite great pressure from the liquor interests who had supported him, received the signature of Governor Shallenberger.

Shallenberger's approval of the eight o'clock law cost him renomination in 1910. Mayor James C. Dahlman of Omaha, colorful former cowhand and a well-known opponent of any sumptuary legislation on the liquor question, entered the lists against him, and with the support of wet Republicans who were able to move into the Democratic primary as a result of the open primary law passed in 1909, squeezed out a five-hundred-vote victory over the governor. The Republicans, meanwhile, nominated Chester H. Aldrich, a David City lawyer and a former state senator, who campaigned as the advocate of county option and had the full support of the Anti-Saloon League.

"Mayor Jim" made an aggressive, colorful campaign, promising to serve his supporters free beer on the statehouse grounds on the day of his inauguration. With the tide generally running toward the Democrats, he confidently expected election. He failed to take into account, however, that many of the Populists were ardent prohibitionists and let their views on that issue overcome any other Democratic predilections. Moreover, the most powerful man in the party, William Jennings Bryan, refused to support Dahlman for governor.

Bryan, personally a dry, had long compromised the prohibition issue with his predominantly wet colleagues, but by 1910 he had come out strongly in favor of the Anti–Saloon League position. As a result, while Gilbert M. Hitchcock defeated Elmer J. Burkett in the senatorial preference vote and the Democrats elected three congressmen and the majority of both houses of the legislature, Aldrich and the Republican state ticket went in by handy majorities.

The Democratic legislature ignored Aldrich's demand for a county option law, concentrating instead on other issues. Perhaps the most important achievements of the legislature of 1911 were the submission of an amendment providing for the initiative and referendum and another providing for a nonpartisan Board of Control with powers of government over seventeen state institutions, thus removing them from the spoils system.

Meanwhile, the fight between the insurgent progressives and the regulars for the control of the Republican Party seriously threatened its position in Nebraska. Representative George W. Norris of McCook had led the insurgent Republican fight against Speaker Joe Cannon. The national prominence he attained as a result of that struggle enabled him to move into a position of leadership among the insurgent Republicans of the state. The Roosevelt bolt from Taft further complicated the Republican position.

By nominating progressive candidates, Norris for the Senate, and Aldrich, who had been one of the governors who had urged Roosevelt to make the independent race for reelection, the Republicans were able to hold their state ticket together. They could not keep Roosevelt off the ballot on the national ticket, however, and the Republican vote for president was so badly split that Woodrow Wilson easily carried the state. John H. Morehead, a relatively conservative Democrat from Falls City, defeated Richard L. Metcalfe, Bryan's candidate, in the Democratic primary for governor, and former governor Shallenberger beat W. H. Thompson, another Bryan candidate, for senator. Bryan's advocacy of county option and his long association with lost causes nationally had cost him much of his former influence in the Democratic Party of the state. The anti-Bryan forces were marshaled under Arthur Mullen of Omaha, a former Populist and one of the state's ablest lawyers.

While Wilson was winning the state's electoral votes and Morehead the governorship, George W. Norris, already proving his ability to attract Democratic votes, ran comfortably ahead of Shallenberger in the senatorial preference; and in compliance with the Oregon Pledge Law the legislature, which had a strong Democratic majority in the House— the Republicans had a small majority in the Senate—went through the formality of electing him.

The Democratic tide continued to roll. Though Morehead was opposed for renomination by Metcalfe and Berge, the state convention made a great show of loyalty. Morehead, who had developed into a strong administrator and, despite his conservative tendencies, had worked earnestly for the initiative and referendum and the Board of Control, easily defeated R. B. Howell, his Republican opponent, and carried with him the lieutenant governor, secretary of state, auditor, treasurer, and attorney general. The Democrats elected three congressmen and a sizable majority in both houses of the legislature.

It was clear now that the Democrats, who had come to power on the shoulders of William Jennings Bryan, were maintaining at least a precarious control of state affairs without his assistance. Bryan, who had alienated a large portion of the party in 1910 on the county option issue, further alienated many of the regulars when he split with Woodrow Wilson over policy toward the European war and resigned as secretary of state. The dominant forces in the party now were Hitchcock, Mullen, and Morehead. The extent of this group's control is perhaps best shown in the primary campaign of 1916. Prohibition was now a burning issue. A prohibition amendment to the constitution was before the voters of the state, and Bryan was doing everything in his power to turn the Democratic Party from its former habits. Yet the antiprohibition forces easily took over the Democratic primaries, renominating Senator Hitchcock, and nominating for governor Keith Neville, thirty-two-year-old rancher and banker from North Platte, over Charles W. Bryan, the Great Commoner's brother. Surprisingly, Hitchcock and Neville were elected by comfortable margins although prohibition was adopted by an even greater margin. Prohibition was an issue, but it was only a side issue.

Wilson, by virtue of his New Freedom, which embodied many of the ideas for which Nebraska liberals had been fighting for years, and of his record of having "kept us out of the war," which appealed to the state's large German population, carried the day again for the Democrats in Nebraska. The Democrats got their usual three congressmen and an overwhelming majority in the legislature. Though Governor Neville had opposed prohibition, he had promised to enforce such a law to the best of his ability if one were adopted, and he urged his brethren in the legislature to enact a law implementing the new amendment without delay.

But Nebraska's attention, like that of the nation, was being turned to other than domestic issues. Wilson had kept us out of the war, but he could not prevent the war cloud hovering on the horizon from engulfing the nation.

Nebraska and World War I

During the fateful months between August 4, 1914, and American entry into the war on April 6, 1917, the issues of preparedness, peace, and war were fought out in Nebraska as vigorously and with as much bitterness as perhaps anywhere in the nation. Many of Nebraska's citizens were either born in one of the combatant nations or had relatives and friends in war-torn Europe and reacted, at least in part, as European nationalists to the struggle across the Atlantic. Although the dominant sympathy was with the Allies from the beginning, Nebraska had a strong German element numbering about two hundred thousand. Of these about thirty thousand were born in Germany and over sixty thousand were children of parents born there, and this group sympathized to a large degree with the cause of the Fatherland. This was particularly true of the more influential Germans in the state: clergy, the editors of some forty German-language newspapers, and German leaders in other phases of Nebraska society who made an effort to counteract influences favoring the Allies by presenting the German version of the origin of the war.

On the other side of the issue were the Czechs, second only to the Germans in numbers and equally vigorously opposed to the Germans. The sympathy of the Poles was also strongly against the Germans. These groups were counteracted somewhat by the Irish, who were strongly anti-British in their views but not particularly sympathetic to Germany.

In addition to these groups, many of the old Populist progressives believed that no good could come of war and that the nation's best interest lay in remaining aloof from the struggle in Europe. Typifying this group were William Jennings Bryan, who resigned as secretary of state on June 7, 1915, in protest against Wilson's stiffening attitude toward the Germans and increasing involvement with the Allies, and Senator George W. Norris, who participated in the filibuster against Wilson's armed ship bill and voted against American entry into the war.

Although some Nebraskans openly rejoiced at the sinking of the *Lusitania*, public opinion in the state was heavily influenced by anti-German press coverage, which painted an increasingly disturbing picture of the nature of the German military machine, and generally supported President Wilson's leadership. In fact, Bryan's break with Wilson was a major factor in Bryan's loss of leadership in the Democratic Party of the state. And Norris's filibuster against the armed ship bill and vote against the war resolution seriously reduced his popularity in the Republican Party. Indeed, had his opponents been able to agree on a candidate, Norris, who won with a plurality of only 35.6 percent, would likely have been defeated in the primary election of 1918.[1] The campaign cry that Wilson "kept us out of war" was an important factor in the Democratic victory in November 1916; but when, a few months later, the president led the nation into war, most Nebraskans were prepared to follow him.

THE HOME FRONT

Peaceful, prosperous America, which, except for a brief interlude in 1898, had gone its own way relatively unconcerned with the problems of the world, was in many respects psychologically unprepared for the worldwide struggle, which, it soon became apparent, would require all the nation's vast resources. Whether from inexperience with international conflict or the naivete and rhetoric of untested idealism, Nebraska, like the nation as a whole, was temporarily thrown off balance to the point that it seemed the only way a democratic nation could save the world for democracy was to negate much of the democratic tradition of individual liberty at home. In Nebraska, this lack of psychological preparation for the role of a democratic nation in a worldwide military struggle, the vigor of the prewar debate, and the presence of many whose pro-German views were widely known resulted in excesses on the home front of which few would later be proud.

Under authorization from the legislature, Governor Neville immediately organized the State Council of Defense as an auxiliary of the federal Council of Defense "to assist the Governor and the State Militia in doing all things necessary to bring about the highest effectiveness within our state in the crisis now existing and to coordinate all efforts with those

Everyone could make a contribution to the war effort. War gardens like this tended by children were common during World War I. Courtesy, NSHS, A545:251.

of the federal government and with those of the other states."[2] Councils of defense were organized at the county level throughout the state; and council leadership was active in virtually every county. The legislature appropriated $25,000 to support the state council, which was given broad authority to carry on investigations, subpoena witnesses and records, and punish offending persons for contempt.

The State Council of Defense saw the large German population as an immediate threat. Not all Germans were sympathetic to the Fatherland, but many who were continued their prewar opposition to the struggle against Germany. They were equipped with a substantial German-language press and used the German language in everyday business and in religious exercises. Antiwar sentiment was not limited to Germans. Some Nebraskans opposed the war because they hated war in all its forms and some because they believed it was not America's fight. Many of these, reared in an atmosphere of fierce independence and almost violent political discussion, were unwilling or unable to keep their views to themselves.

With taxes and the draft taking a heavy toll of the state's wealth and manpower, opposition in any form was unthinkable. The state and local councils of defense made every effort to whip the citizenry into line.

Although the State Council of Defense brought heavy pressure to promote the sale of liberty bonds, enforce food and fuel rationing, and generally stamp out dissent, most of the wartime excesses on the home front seem to have been the work of overly eager individuals. Some perhaps compensated for their own failure to be in uniform by calling attention to their neighbors' shortcomings. In addition, the atmosphere was favorable for the settlement of personal grudges. It was often easy to charge an annoying neighbor with being a slacker, and self-appointed patriots found a new use for yellow paint, liberally applying it to the houses and property of those they so labeled.

Probably the most celebrated incident in the "battle of the home front" was the "trial" of various members of the faculty of the University of Nebraska before the Board of Regents on charges of failing to support the war. In response to complaints from various sources that certain members of the faculty were not in sympathy with the war, the Board of Regents held an open public hearing, inviting all citizens who had any knowledge of un-American utterances or actions on the part of members of the university faculty to appear. These hearings lasted over a period of two weeks and were reported at length in the press. Much testimony, both relevant and irrelevant, was brought before the board, and that body found that though a majority of those reportedly attacked supported the war, two members of the faculty, G. W. A. Luckey and C. E. Persinger, had been so frank in their criticism that their usefulness at the institution was damaged to the extent that their resignations were required.

Though the State Council of Defense could not be held officially responsible for many individual outrages against the American system, its adamant insistence upon the necessity of absolute conformity in thought and action to win the war on the home front inspired a vigilante spirit. The state council's special whipping boy was the Non-Partisan League, imported from North Dakota, where it had achieved spectacular success in May 1917, the same month that the state council had been organized.

The Non-Partisan League's platform, embodying much of the old Populist spirit, went a great deal further than the Populists had gone in demanding state action for the benefit of the farmers. Whereas the Populists had been content to call for the nationalization of railroads and telegraph lines, the Non-Partisan League demanded state stockyards, packinghouses, cold storage plants, elevators, flour mills, creameries, beet sugar factories, and telephones. It also called for exemption from taxation of farm improvements, state hail insurance, rural credit banks operated at cost, and state inspection of dockage and grading of grain. The league developed much influence among the members of the powerful Farmers' Union and in many predominantly German rural communities and within a few weeks was engaged in a bitter conflict with the State Council of Defense.

Though the Non-Partisan League strongly supported the war, its program was anathema to most of the men in the state council, and that body made strenuous efforts to brand the league as unpatriotic. It curtly rejected the league's offer to promote the sale of liberty bonds; it got the attorney general to issue an opinion that league organizers were not engaged in useful occupations; and it branded as treasonable and seditious a book being circulated by the league in Nebraska, *The New Freedom* by Woodrow Wilson.

The attorney general's opinion brought the struggle to a head. With the assistance of attorneys C. A. Sorensen and C. C. Flansburg, the league brought an injunction suit against the State Council of Defense to prevent it from interfering with league meetings. A compromise was finally reached when the Non-Partisan League agreed to withdraw the circulation of its controversial war aims pamphlet and to hire only Nebraska organizers; and the State Council of Defense agreed to permit Non-Partisan League meetings and to suspend the application of its regulation declaring the league's organizers to be engaged in other than useful occupations.

Governor Neville called the legislature into special session on March 26, 1918, to pass legislation which he felt was necessitated by the war. The governor's program called for a plan to allow soldiers to vote; protection of persons in military and naval service from collection of debts or mortgages during the war; acts defining sedition and sabotage and prescribing penalties; provision for a home guard militia; repeal of the Mockett Foreign Language Law; and submission of a constitutional amendment limiting the ballot to full citizens. The governor's program passed quickly, although many in his own party felt that the repeal of the Mockett Foreign Language Law was particularly unfortunate. This law, passed at the insistence of the German-American Alliance, of which

Speaker John Mattes was a prominent member, provided that when a petition with fifty signatures was presented to the board of a school district, any foreign language designated in the petition must be established as a course of study. Governor Neville called it "vicious, undemocratic, and un-American."[3] Many Democrats also thought the sedition law as prescribed by the Council of Defense was entirely too severe, and ten Democratic senators signed a remonstrance against it.

The campaign of 1918 found the Democrats in serious trouble. The German voters, feeling that they had been swindled by the Democratic cry that Wilson had kept the nation out of war and bitterly resentful of the persecution they had suffered under Governor Neville's State Council of Defense, turned solidly against the party in power. The Non-Partisan League saw in the election an excellent opportunity to get even with the State Council of Defense and strongly supported Republican candidates. There was much complaint about war profiteering, and the Democrats, being the party in power, bore the brunt of that complaint. As a result, Samuel R. McKelvie, thirty-four-year-old publisher of the *Nebraska Farmer*, the state's most widely read agricultural journal, and a former lieutenant governor, easily defeated Neville. Except for the senatorial seat, which Norris retained because anti-Norris Republicans lacked a strong alternative, Republicans were satisfied. They won all state offices, all congressional seats, and an overwhelming majority in the legislature. The voters also ratified an amendment to the federal Constitution providing for women's suffrage and approved the calling of a constitutional convention to revise the state's organic law. The prohibition question was another factor in the Democratic defeat. Long able to draw wet Republican votes as the party of personal liberty, the Democrats inexplicably had endorsed national prohibition in 1918. Though the special war session of the legislature had refused to ratify the national prohibition amendment, the legislature of 1919 quickly added Nebraska's name to a list of states ratifying the amendment.

NEBRASKANS IN THE ARMED FORCES

Although the Nebraska National Guard served as a unit on the Mexican border in 1916, Nebraskans in the armed forces during World War I did not serve in state-organized and controlled units as their fathers and grandfathers had in the Spanish-American and Civil Wars. Because the armed forces were federalized, there was no assurance that state-based National Guard units would be kept intact when activated. The 34th Division, for example, was composed of National Guard units from Nebraska and other midwestern states, but its members were used as replacements in other divisions where needed. As a result, Nebraskans were scattered throughout the army up to the 89th Division.

Although Nebraskans did not all serve in the same division, there were some distinct Nebraska units in the war: the 355th Infantry Regiment, called "Nebraska's own," the 314th Ammunition Train, both part of the 89th Division, and Nebraska Field Hospital No. 1, a historic and war-tried unit that had first been organized on January 24, 1903, and was reorganized in 1917 as the 117th Sanitary Train with the 42nd, or famous "Rainbow," Division.[4] The 89th Division was organized at Camp Funston in September and October 1917. Composed of men from Kansas, Missouri, Colorado, South Dakota, Arizona, New Mexico, and Nebraska, it was known both as the "Middlewest Division" and the "Fighting Farmers." Most of the eight thousand men from Nebraska who entered the division were assigned to the 355th Infantry, the 314th Ammunition Train, and the three machine gun battalions organized with the division. Commanded by Major General Leonard Wood, the 89th Division arrived in France in June 1918 and played an important part in the final push ending the war.

Base Hospital No. 49 at Allereye in France was financed by Nebraskans. Organized at Omaha by the University of Nebraska College of Medicine, its personnel were drawn largely from faculty and alumni. Its staff of four hundred men and women began work on September 12, 1918, doing an average of twenty surgical operations a day until the armistice was signed. Nebraskans took pride in the fact that of all the American hospitals in Europe, this unit had the best record for saving lives.

Nebraskans also were proud that the two men leading the military effort for the United States had close Nebraska relationships. General John J. Pershing, named commander in chief of the American Expeditionary Forces (AEF), had been commandant of cadets at the University of Nebraska and had studied at the university's College of Law. General Pershing considered Lincoln his home, and his sister, Mae Pershing, continued to live there. Charles G. Dawes, purchasing agent for the AEF, was also a Lincolnite. Though living in Chicago at the time of his appointment, he had begun his law practice in Lincoln and retained financial interests in the capital city.

Contrary to the image that the Council of Defense may have suggested about slackers and detractors, Nebraska and Nebraskans made considerable contributions to the war effort. While 47,976 Nebraskans served in the army during the war, 6,973 served in the navy, and 547 in the marines. In addition, 375 served as nurses. Fort Robinson saw service as a cavalry training center, and Fort Omaha was used as a balloon school. In all 1,566 Nebraskans were counted among the casualties. Nebraskans also supported the war financially, greatly exceeding the state's quota by purchasing $240 million in liberty bonds and purchasing more war saving stamps per capita than any other state in the Union.

WARTIME PROSPERITY

Nebraska's primary contribution to the war, however, was the production of food for the armed forces and the Allies, and in fulfilling that function the state prospered greatly. Indeed, aside from those who had close friends or relatives in the service or who had felt the ire of the State Council of Defense, the war years were primarily distinguished by their great prosperity.

Farm prices, already higher than Nebraska farmers had previously experienced, increased spectacularly during the war. The value of Nebraska's total harvest, which had sunk from a record high of $103 million in 1891 to a fifteen-year low of $42.7 million in 1895, reached a new record high of $123.8 million by 1902 and continued to increase, reaching a decade high of $195.7 million in 1909. By the outbreak of the war in 1914, the annual harvest was valued at $241.6 million, doubled to $478.5 million in 1917, and reached a new record by 1919 of $507.4, a level that would not be seen again until 1945. The purchasing power of the farmer's dollar was greater than it had ever been before. The year 1916 was the only one of the war years in which the index of Nebraska farm prices fell below that of prices paid by farmers for manufactured goods.

Under the stimulus of high prices and the patriotic necessity to produce food to win the war, Nebraska farmers expanded both their acreage
and production to unprecedented heights. The average number of acres
harvested in 1895 was 11.9 million. This figure increased to 13 million acres
in 1902, 14 million in 1909, 18.1 million in 1914, and peaked at 19.5 million
acres by the end of the war. Farmers would continue to increase acreages
in production through the 1920s in an effort to maintain income levels.
After the depression of the 1930s, production would level out to between
18 million and 19 million acres harvested annually until the 1990s.[5]

The greatest increase in cultivated acreage during the first decades of
the twentieth century occurred in the western part of the state, where the
number of cultivated acres doubled during the war. Most of this land was
planted in wheat, although there was some extension of corn westward
into the marginal corn belt area of the central sections. The great increase
in wheat was accounted for by its relatively high price, the discovery that
the flatlands of the southwest and the high plains west of the Sand Hills
were excellent wheat-producing areas, and the continued improvement of
winter wheat strains adapted to western Nebraska. It was at this time that
the southwestern counties of Cheyenne, Deuel, Kimball, and Perkins and
parts of Banner, Garden, and Keith developed into a specialized wheat-
producing area. As a result, wheat statistics showed a dramatic change
between 1909 and 1919. Although yield remained relatively stable at about
16 bushels per acre, the number of harvested acres in wheat increased from
2.7 million to 4.4 million, prices increased from 90 cents per bushel to
$2.07 per bushel, and the total harvest value of wheat jumped from $42.9
million to $120.7 million.[6]

Increased acreage was not the only factor in increased production.
Except for 1916, when excessive summer rains seriously interfered with
the harvest of small grain, climatic conditions during the war were favorable. Irrigation greatly stimulated the production of sugar beets, potatoes, and alfalfa in the North Platte Valley. Larger and improved farm
machinery enabled the individual farmer to care for more acres than
in the past. New breeds, strains, and methods were developed by scientists at the university's College of Agriculture. Practical education,
greatly stimulated by the Smith-Lever Act and the development of the

county agent system, provided additional information for the average farmer.

Nebraska's farmers were riding high, but they were sowing the seeds of their own destruction. With prices steadily rising, it was axiomatic that the more land that could be put under cultivation, the greater would be the profits.[7] Profits during the war years were not used to pay off existing mortgages or to improve existing holdings but were plowed into more land under the assumption that once the wartime demand eased off, so would farm prices.

When prices in 1919 exceeded those of 1918, however, many persons came to believe that farm prices had reached a new high plateau, and land values rose rapidly in 1919 and 1920. In seven southeastern counties, for example, land sold by warranty deed in 1915 brought $106 per acre; in 1916, $109; in 1917, $119; in 1918, $128; in 1919, $152; and in 1920, $180. The same conditions seem to have existed throughout the state. Land values in Nebraska increased 76 percent, and the average value of farms more than doubled, from $16,038 to $33,771, between 1910 and 1920.

Aside from high prices, an important reason for increased land values was the liberalization of credit available to farmers for the purchase of land. Local banks extended credit more readily on farm mortgages; and farm loan associations, established under the Federal Farm Loan Act of 1916, made loans available at 5 to 6 percent on a long-term basis.

Mortgage debt increased 170.2 percent from 1910 to 1920. Part of this increase was justified by increased production, but a great part was wholly speculative, dependent on the permanent maintenance of wartime farm prices. When those prices were not maintained, Nebraska agriculture went into a tailspin from which it could not recover throughout the entire decade of the 1920s and which so weakened it that the depression of the 1930s reduced the state's basic industry to its most desperate plight in history.

Proportionately, manufactures increased greatly. From 1910 to 1920, the number of manufacturing establishments increased 15.4 percent, from 2,500 to 2,884; the number of wage earners increased 50 percent, from 24,336 to 36,521; wages increased 230 percent, from $13.9 million to $46.1 million; the value of products increased 200 percent, from $199 million to $596 million; and value added by manufacture increased 140 percent, from $47.9 million to $115.3 million.[8] Manufacturing, however, continued to be a relatively unimportant part of the state's economy and largely consisted of the processing of agricultural products. Meatpacking remained the state's leading industry. The great demand for potash during the war and the discovery that some of the alkali lakes in the Sand Hills could produce potash resulted in a brief flurry in that industry, and Antioch boomed to a bustling town of twenty-five hundred, with five factories working twenty-four hours a day. When hostilities ended, however, the boom collapsed and a few dilapidated houses, ruins of five factories with rusting retorts, boilers, and steel skeletons were all that remained to remind the Sand Hills of its short-lived industrial boom.

CHAPTER 23

The 1920s: Adapting to Change

The end of the war and the sudden dismantling of government wartime controls and economic restrictions left the nation in an uneasy period of transition. Nebraskans, like the rest of the nation, experienced many of the same problems adjusting to peacetime: widespread inflation, spiraling prices, particularly for food and housing, and job shortages caused by the rapid reentry into the labor force by returning soldiers. Tension between labor and management increased, and the lifting of the no-strike ban, which had been imposed to assure continued production of vital materials and commodities during the war, left labor organizations free to employ their most effective weapon to make their demands heard, the strike. The uneasy economic climate also heightened racial tension, particularly in the nation's northern cities, where blacks had migrated in increasing numbers during the war to seek employment opportunities. That tension was made more volatile, perhaps, by the patriotic and anti-German "hate" rhetoric that had been encouraged during the war.

In 1919 more than four million workers participated in 3,600 strikes across the nation. Nebraska's largest city, Omaha, also experienced several strikes during the summer of 1919, including a major strike by livestock handlers at the Union Stockyards in South Omaha. In most cases, agreements on basic terms had been reached through mediation, and violence was minimal.

Racial issues emerged in each strike, caused by the arrival of black as well as white strikebreakers from outside the community. While small by comparison to other northern cities, the black community in Omaha had grown significantly during the war. From 1909 to 1919 Omaha's black population had increased 133 percent to approximately ten thousand concentrated on the city's near north side.

Racial tension, which had been kept at bay through most of the labor turmoil of the preceding summer, erupted in late September, when a middle-aged black man was accused of raping a young white woman. In the subsequent manhunt, a forty-one-year-old black packinghouse worker, Will Brown, was arrested and transported to the courthouse, where a crowd of nearly six thousand persons assembled and demanded immediate justice. According to accounts, "The mob took over and charged the courthouse, set it afire, and raided the jail. Frightened prisoners turned Brown over to the mob which stripped him of his clothing, severely beat him, dragged him to the street, hanged him, riddled his body with bullets and burned it."[1]

Mayor Edward P. Smith tried to intervene, but the mob overpowered him and hanged him from a light pole, where he would have died had it not been for the quick response of police officers who cut him down. The crowd continued its rampage through the city until brought under control by some eight hundred federal and state troops under the command of General Leonard Wood, who had been called to the city to quell the riot.

Race as well as ethnic hatred was also apparent in the post-war years in Nebraska as the Ku Klux Klan launched major membership drives throughout the Midwest. The first Nebraska Klavern was founded in Omaha in 1921, and by the end of the year the number of local organizations was estimated at twenty-four. In 1922 Klan membership was estimated at eleven hundred, but by 1923 the Atlanta headquarters of the Klan announced that Nebraska had some forty-five thousand members. According to the *Lincoln Star*, the Klan was "active in Lincoln, Omaha, Fremont, York, Grand Island, Hastings, North Platte, and Scottsbluff."[2]

The Klan enjoyed increasing growth and success in Nebraska through the mid-1920s. Its appeal lay in its insistence that, unlike the prewar Klan, it stood for law and order, morality and civic improvement. Although many Protestant churches, seeking the same goals, supported the Klan, others, including black and Jewish leaders, influential state leaders such as University of Nebraska chancellor Samuel Avery, and Nebraska newspapers, including the Omaha *World-Herald*, Nebraska City *News*, and many others, warned the public about the Klan's historic association with vigilante justice, intimidation, and violence. And though the murder of Will Brown in Omaha had taken place two years before the first Klan organization had been founded there, Omaha's black leaders were insistent that the public not forget the racism and intense hatred that had precipitated it.

After the elections of 1926 the Klan began to lose favor with the public, in Nebraska as elsewhere. News of public scandals nationally involving leading Klansmen convinced many that the Klan was corrupt, if not degenerate. Charges that the Klan was involved in political collusion and that it promoted violence and was more interested in making money than improving society lessened Nebraskans' enthusiasm for it, and it soon faded from the scene.

STREAMLINING GOVERNMENT

Progressive elements intermittently controlled both the Democratic and Republican Parties, and the early years of the twentieth century saw the enactment of much legislation designed to give the people a greater voice in government, to give the government greater authority over the large corporations that had come to control the economic life of the state and nation, and to extend the functions of government for the benefit of the individual. The expectations, as well as the functions, of government had been greatly expanded in the states where much of the reform impulse had originated, particularly those in the Midwest.

For Nebraska, where a half-century earlier, politicians had sought to "contain" government, this was no small problem. The Constitution of 1875 forbade the creation of any new executive offices. The situation was remedied somewhat by a constitutional amendment, adopted in 1912, that provided for a Board of Control of state penal, reformatory, and charitable institutions. Partisan administration of these institutions by the governor's office was greatly decreased and their administration concentrated in a bipartisan three-member board. To overhaul state government further, the legislature of 1917 had submitted a proposal to the voters for calling a constitutional convention, and that proposal had been endorsed by the people in the general election of 1918.

In 1918 the Republicans had pledged to enact a civil administrative code to streamline the cumbersome governmental structure that had resulted from the necessity of adding new functions to already existing offices with the understanding that the actual administrative work would

The Omaha race riot of 1919. Emotions ran high in the aftermath of World War I. Antiblack sentiment erupted in Omaha in September 1919 after a black man, Will Brown, allegedly attacked a white woman and her escort. A mob of nearly four thousand rioters descended on the Douglas County courthouse to take the law into their own hands and execute Brown. Pictured here is the south side of the courthouse, September 28, 1919. Courtesy, NSHS, M936:72.

be done by deputies. Governor McKelvie interpreted the Republican landslide of 1918 as a mandate to enact the civil administrative code in advance of the constitutional convention and urged his party in the legislature to make it the first order of business. In his inaugural message, the Governor said:

Circumscribed by the restrictions of an antiquated fundamental law, we have sought to meet the constantly increasing needs of administration through the creation of boards, commissions, and additional offices. This has resulted in a system of government that reeks with divided responsibility, loose ends and overlapping functions.

This condition may be overcome through the application of a cabinet form of civil government, which centralizes responsibility and eliminates the large number of useless boards, commissions, and unnecessary offices. It is fashioned after our National administration, in which the various duties of law enforcement and control are grouped under common heads known as "Departments." These departments are presided over by heads who are known as "Secretaries," to be appointed by the Chief Executive, and confirmed by the Senate.[3]

The code, McKelvie argued, was well within the present constitution and was simply another way of administering the state's civil affairs. To counter the argument of those who would wait for the constitutional convention, the governor said, "If the plan is practical, why wait for the constitutional convention to initiate it? . . . If the exercise of legislative functions is to await the action of the forthcoming Constitutional Convention, there is little for this legislature to do but adjourn."[4] Though there had been bipartisan agreement that the state's administrative affairs needed overhauling and Democratic governors had repeatedly urged the centralization and consolidation of governmental functions, the Democrats vigorously opposed the code, partly because McKelvie made his particular plan a partisan issue and partly because they were searching for an issue after their overwhelming defeat of 1918. It was Republicans of progressive persuasion, however, who led the fight against the bill in the legislature.

In spite of this combined opposition, the bulky, 430-page bill finally passed on the last day of the session. It had been introduced and ably fostered by Senator C. Petrus Peterson of Lincoln. It eliminated eleven boards and commissions and ten other subdivisions of various existing departments. It created six administrative departments: Finance, Agriculture, Trade and Commerce, Labor, Public Works, and Public Welfare.

Led by Charles W. Bryan, the Democrats continued to fire away at the code, and "The code, repeal it" was to be a campaign slogan of the Democratic Party for the next ten years. Despite opposition, however, the administrative code continued to provide the format for the administration of those functions of state government not otherwise provided for by the constitution. In 1929 the Department of Finance was abolished and its duties given to the state tax commissioner. The code was further amended that year by the provision that the secretary of labor should be ex-officio secretary of public welfare. In 1931, Governor Bryan, long the outstanding opponent of the code, decided to operate the activities of the Departments of Agriculture, Labor and Public Welfare without the appointment of secretaries. In 1933, the legislature complied with Bryan's recommendation that the administrative agencies under the code be rearranged into the following six departments: Agriculture and Inspection, Labor, Health, Roads and Irrigation, Banking, and Insurance. This rearrangement did not materially change the duties of the several agencies. In 1945 the Department of Aeronautics was established as one of the administrative departments, and in 1947 the Department of Veterans Affairs was likewise designated.

Further changes in the 1950s and 1960s reflected the growing complexity of state government. In 1957 the Department of Roads and Irrigation was split into the Department of Roads and the Department of Water Resources, and the Division of Motor Vehicles was elevated to the status of an administrative department. In 1961, the legislature, following the mandate of a constitutional amendment adopted in 1958, replaced the Board of Control, which had functioned since 1912, with a Department of Public Institutions, which was given the management of all state charitable, mental, reformatory, and penal institutions. In 1963 the state penitentiary and the state reformatory were combined into the Nebraska Penal and Correctional Complex, and in 1965 the Department of Administrative Services was established to coordinate the state's purchasing and accounting procedures.

THE CONSTITUTIONAL CONVENTION OF 1919–20

Though the administrative code had to a degree reorganized state government, a constitutional convention was still needed. In addition to the prohibition against the creation of additional executive offices, the constitution limited the legislature in raising revenue to the general property tax, fixed rigid rules for legislative business, severely limited state salaries, and above all prescribed a virtually impossible amending procedure. To be adopted, an amendment had to receive a majority of all the votes cast at the election in which it was considered.

Only eleven of forty amendments submitted to the voters between 1875 and 1918 were adopted; many of those that failed did so not because of opposition but simply because too few had voted on them to provide the requisite majority of all ballots cast. That requirement was circumvented with the adoption of the "party circle" law in 1901 and the primary law in 1907, which allowed all straight party votes to be counted in favor of an amendment if the amendment had been endorsed by the party at the primaries. This was typical of other schemes to get around the restrictions imposed by the constitution of 1875 and create a more efficient government, yet most of these subterfuges only compounded the already cumbersome procedures of government.

In accordance with procedures adopted by the legislature of 1919, one hundred delegates to the constitutional convention were chosen at a special election on November 4, 1919. They were elected without party designation from the same districts and on the same basis as members were chosen for the state House of Representatives. The issues in the campaign were not clear, but in the main the contest seems to have been between the progressive and conservative elements. In some districts, the Non-Partisan League endorsed candidates and the New Nebraska Federation, an organization of business groups, endorsed others. Conservatives expressed some fear that certain progressive elements, who were urging the adoption of a one-house legislature or the establishment of a mere framework of government leaving the rest to the legislature, would prevail. These fears were relieved when the election returns came in. The general spirit of the convention was distinctly conservative. The members included forty-five lawyers, among them some of the most conservative members of the old order in Nebraska politics.

Under the leadership of Falls City farmer and attorney Arthur J. Weaver, who was chosen president, the convention confined itself generally to the consideration of amendments designed to remedy the procedural defects in the constitution of 1875. The convention met from December 2, 1919, until March 25, 1920, at which time it recessed until October 19, when it reconvened to adopt forty-one amendments that had been approved by the voters at a special election on September 21 and incorporated into the constitution by a committee appointed for that purpose.

All forty-one amendments were adopted by margins of three or four to one by approximately one-sixth of the qualified electors voting. Among the amendments were those providing that the constitution could be amended by a majority voting on each amendment if the affirmative vote was equal to 35 percent of the total vote cast; that the salaries of state officers and judges could be increased no more often than once every eight years; and that no increase would be effective during the term of office in which it was voted. There were amendments providing for an increase in legislative salaries and for uniform and proportional taxes on tangible property, permitting classification of other property, and taxes other than on property. Other amendments provided for the creation of new executive offices by two-thirds vote of the legislature, for an executive budget, a Board of Pardons, and the office of state tax commissioner; for women's suffrage and soldier suffrage; for the election of university regents by districts; and for an increase in the number of state senators from thirty-three to fifty.

The state still operates under the constitution of 1875, but since 1920 the legislature has periodically overhauled it through the amendment process. No amendments were approved during the 1920s, but beginning in 1930 through the economic crisis of the depression, 15 amendments were introduced, 3 of which were by initiative, and 7 were adopted. Since 1920 a total of 221 amendments have been submitted, twenty of which were by initiative, and 153 have been adopted. Activity in this area has tended to serve both as a barometer of changing times and the need to make government more responsive to them. Table 10 indicates the variation in amendment activity since 1920.

ADJUSTING TO THE AUTOMOBILE

One of the most pressing problems facing the state government in the postwar years was that of providing a road system to meet the needs of the automobile. When automobiles began to appear on Nebraska's city streets in the early years of the twentieth century, few people thought that the imperfect, noisy, expensive mechanism would ever be more than a rich man's city toy; indeed, the legislature's first action in connection with the automobile was an effort to reduce its nuisance characteristics. By 1920, however, there were 205,000 automobiles registered in the state, and they were no longer isolated to the urban areas. Though the western

Table 10. Amendments to the Nebraska Constitution, 1922–1992

Year Voted On	Total Number Submitted	Number Submitted (by Legislature/by Initiative)	Number Adopted
1922	—	—	—
1924	1	(0/1)	0
1926	—	—	—
1928[a]	1	(0/1)	0
1930	2	(2/0)	1
1932	—	—	—
1934	3	(1/2)	3
1936	2	(2/0)	1
1938	6	(5/1)	1
1940	2	(2/0)	1
1942	1	(1/0)	0
1944	1	(0/1)	0
1946	2	(0/2)	1
1948	1	(1/0)	0
1950	1	(1/0)	0
1952	6	(6/0)	5
1954	8	(8/0)	4
1956	5	(5/0)	3
1958	9	(7/2)	7
1960	9	(8/1)	8
1962	7	(7/0)	7
1964	7	(6/1)	6
1966	19	(17/2)	14
1968	17	(16/1)	13
1970	17	(17/0)	10
1972[b]	34	(33/1)	30
1974	5	(5/0)	3
1976	9	(9/0)	2
1978	7	(7/0)	4
1980[b]	6	(6/0)	3
1982[b]	7	(6/1)	3
1984	4	(4/0)	4

Continued

Year Voted On	Total Number Submitted	Number Submitted (by Legislature/by Initiative)	Number Adopted
1986[b]	6	(6/0)	5
1988[b]	5	(5/0)	5
1990	6	(4/2)	5
1992[b]	5	(4/1)	4

Source: *The Nebraska Blue Book*, 1992–93 (Lincoln: State Printing Office, 1994), 217–31.
[a]The amendment in 1928 passed, but the state supreme court declared the election invalid.
[b]Years in which amendments were considered in both primary and general elections.

counties continued to rely heavily on the horse as a means of transportation, the farming counties of the eastern and central portion of the state exceeded the two principal urban counties, Douglas and Lancaster, in the ratio of automobiles per person.

It is not difficult to understand why the farmer eagerly embraced the automobile. It represented individually owned rolling stock, it reduced rural isolation, and it contributed to the well-being of farmers and their families. It was much more expensive than the horse, but it was infinitely more satisfactory, and the chores connected with its maintenance were fewer and less burdensome. In short, it opened up a whole new world for the farmer.

Even during the years of readjustment from the wartime boom, the number of motor vehicles registered continued to increase. By 1925 there were 301,716, and by 1930, there were 367,410. Registrations declined slightly during the depths of the depression in the early 1930s, but beginning in 1933 the trend started upward again and reached 500,000 in the early 1950s and a million vehicles by the state's centennial in 1967. In 1995 1.67 million vehicles were registered.

The demand for good roads developed in direct ratio to the increase in the number of automobiles registered. Anyone who became the owner of an automobile was an easy prospect for a good-roads association. In 1904 Nebraska had designated public roads totaling 79,462 miles (compared with approximately 100,000 in 1995),[5] but most of these were little more than unimproved trails running along the section lines or wandering off from railroad points to fertile valleys. Only 17 miles were improved with stone, and only 6 miles were surfaced with sand-clay. By 1909, total road mileage had increased to 80,338, but seventy-seven counties reported no improved roads, twelve had less than 100 miles, and only one (Cedar) had more than 100 miles of improved roads.

In horse and buggy days, road improvement and maintenance were largely township affairs, with the work generally being done by men of the neighborhood who came together to work out their $3 road tax at $1.50 per day. Interest in good roads rarely extended beyond the township, and was seriously affected by the desire to keep local taxes as low as possible. When the automobile made possible easy travel from township to township, the discrepancy in roads was quickly noted and loudly complained about.

The first legislation resulting from agitation for good roads was the State Aid Bridge Act of 1911 which provided for the State Board of Irrigation, Highways, and Drainage to contribute 10 percent of the expenditures for roads and bridges within the various counties. To finance the expenditure, the legislature passed a statewide fifth-mill levy. In addition to the 10 percent general contribution, the state paid one-half of the cost of construction and maintenance of all bridges more than 175 feet long. The law also gave county commissioners greater power over roads and allowed them to use the proceeds from property taxes, inheritance taxes, and license fees for road purposes.

Local taxes also increased from $.82 per capita in 1904 to $1.51 by 1919 largely as a result of the demand for improved roads. By 1914 the state had 1,204.54 miles of improved roads, of which 94 percent were sand-clay. This was only 1.5 percent of the total mileage, however, and good-roads advocates were far from satisfied. In particular, they argued that local control of road building was inimical to the development of a sound highway system. Insisting that roads ought to be built from crushed rock and concrete rather than politics, the Lincoln Highway Association became the leading organized advocate of good roads. The Lincoln Highway Association, urging a transcontinental highway, sought to develop sentiment in favor of good roads by demonstrating just what good roads could do. To further its program, it secured from cement manufacturers an offer to supply three thousand barrels of cement free to any community that appropriated adequate funds to construct an improved section of the Lincoln Highway in its region. The offer had been quickly accepted in Grand Island, Kearney, and Fremont, and by 1919, when the program was discontinued, it had created a popular demand for better highways in Nebraska.

Building good roads clearly was not only too big a job for the counties but for the states as well, and the federal government was called upon for both direction and financing in the development of the nation's highway system. The Federal Aid Road Act of July 11, 1916, provided federal funds on a matching basis for use in a construction of "post roads," meaning certain designated roads forming part of an interstate system.

By 1921, 5,619.04 miles of road within the state had been selected as post roads. They were part of the following major systems: U.S. 20, extending west from Sioux City through O'Neill, Valentine, and Chadron; U.S. 30, or the old Lincoln Highway, extending west from Omaha through Grand Island, North Platte, and Sidney; U.S. 26, running from U.S. 30 at Ogallala to Scottsbluff and the west line of the state; U.S. 38 (now U.S. 6), extending from Omaha through Lincoln, Hastings, and McCook to Colorado; U.S. 77, from Sioux City through Fremont, Lincoln, and Beatrice to the Kansas line; and U.S. 81, from Yankton through Norfolk, Columbus, York, and Hebron to the Kansas border.

By 1930, the Department of Roads and Irrigation had graveled 5,000 miles and graded 3,300 more miles, although only 368 miles of the state highway system had been paved. Though travelers could complain about the bad roads across Nebraska, a start had been made toward improving the road system, and fairly good "all-weather" roads connected the county seats and ran across the state.

The initial 0.65 mill levy established by the legislature for state road development in 1917 had been increased to 3 mills in 1919. On the theory that motorists not only could pay for roads but were willing to do so, a two-cent gasoline tax was instituted in 1925 and raised to four cents in 1930. By 1930 the state was receiving over $9 million annually from the gasoline tax. Local governments likewise increased the amount spent on roads, devoting much of the property tax and bond issues to local road construction.

With the depression of the 1930s construction slowed because states were unable to generate the matching funds necessary to continue receiving federal monies. To alleviate this burden on the states, the federal government in 1931 made emergency funds available to the states to use as their matching funds so they could continue to receive monies from the regular federal aid program. Nebraska received $4.25 million from the emergency fund in 1931–32, which not only allowed construction activities in the state to continue but gave the state more monies than it had previously been able to match.

Early New Deal legislation in 1933 also helped to further road building in Nebraska and the nation. Nebraska received $7.8 million under the National Industrial Recovery Act which did not require matching state funds. Nebraska's employment problems, as well as road-building efforts, were also aided by the Civil Works Administration, which made monies available to hire laborers. Nebraska was able to hire more than thirty-six thousand persons in 1934 with these monies, which would not have been available from state sources.

Relief and pump-priming activities of the federal government enabled Nebraska to make significant advances in highway construction, but when the government reinstituted matching fund requirements in 1936, the state again faced the difficulty of appropriating sufficient dollars to match the total federal dollars for which it was qualified. Committed to the "pay as you go" philosophy in highway construction, Nebraska was unable to obtain some $2 million in federal highway funds.[6]

Though costs of government increased following World War I, highway costs were the largest single item in state and county budgets. The automobile thus had a terrific impact on the state's public economy, and its impact was felt in many other areas as well. Small towns began to decline in population and importance because neighboring farmers and the residents of the towns could drive to the county seats and regional cities to purchase everything from staples to luxuries. Local railroad passenger traffic almost halted, and local railroad freight felt the inroads of the motor truck. As a result, railroads began to abandon branch lines and significantly cut back service on others, a trend that has continued to the present.

POLITICAL ADJUSTMENT

Because of the enactment of many reforms fomented during the Populist-Progressive period and the growing costs of state government as a result of expanded government functions, as well as the growing realization that many additional social concerns were beyond state control, state politics in the postwar period tended to revolve around the question of expenditures and taxes and the exercise of regulatory powers. Though aware of national issues and candidates, particularly in presidential years, Nebraskans continued to exercise the independent spirit that had been evident since 1890 by frequently crossing party lines and voting on state issues in a manner somewhat divorced from national politics.

The executive budget system provided a means for holding the governor responsible, to a degree, for state expenditures; and though state expenditures accounted for only a relatively small portion of total taxes paid by the people, they served as a convenient political whipping boy. Governor McKelvie, who was reelected in the Republican landslide of 1920, presented the state's first executive budget to the legislature in 1921, and that body passed a law requiring the governor to submit a budget to the legislature each biennium.

In 1922, Charles W. Bryan, the Great Commoner's brother, defeated Republican Charles H. Randall for governor in face of a general Republican victory which resulted in the defeat of Senator Gilbert M. Hitchcock by R. B. Howell. The Democrats won three congressional seats, but state offices and a strong majority in both houses of the legislature were taken by the Republicans. Bryan's victory was due in part to his name, which was always good for a substantial block of votes in Nebraska, but also in part to his ability to pin responsibility on his opponent for the Revenue Law of 1921, which exempted intangible property from full taxation, and his successful campaign against increased state expenditures that had resulted from McKelvie's budget. Bryan also had campaigned vigorously for the repeal of the administrative code. McKelvie was well aware of these factors when he called the legislature into special session in 1922 to reduce appropriations for the second half of the biennium.

Bryan, who perhaps more than any other man helped to develop the budget into a political issue, presented the Republican legislature of 1923 with a document recommending a reduction of more than $8 million from the budget presented by outgoing Governor McKelvie. Characteristically, Bryan had based his budget on different figures from those used by McKelvie and on the adoption of certain basic changes, including the repeal of the administrative code. After a winter in which the governor and Republican members of the legislature tried to outdo each other in name-calling, the legislature surpassed Governor Bryan in the matter of economy by appropriating $1.6 million less than he had asked for. In his outgoing message, however, the governor, who had temporarily abandoned state politics in 1924 to accept the Democratic nomination for vice-president, came up with a set of figures to show that the legislature actually had appropriated $1.2 million more than he had recommended. He charged further that, despite the failure of the Republican legislature to cooperate by reducing the number of state employees in the departments directly under his control from 610 to 272, he had saved the taxpayers nearly $1 million. He recommended expenditures of $17 million for the next biennium. Governor Adam McMullen of Beatrice, who had defeated J. N. Norton in 1924, ignored Bryan's budget altogether and submitted a request for nearly $27.5 million. The legislature, in turn, increased this by about $2.5 million.

Bryan, who ran unsuccessfully for governor in 1926 and 1928, kept the questions of taxation and governmental economy in a constant state of agitation. That agitation failed at election time in part because the Republicans enjoyed popular support during the 1920s in Nebraska, although the Democrats usually managed to pick up two or three congressmen in each election. In addition, however, Bryan's failure resulted in part from his refusal to use figures other than his own and from the Republicans' ability to demonstrate that some of his more spectacular economies during the years 1923–25 were simply book juggling and not real economies or actions that seriously crippled state services and state institutions. The Republicans stayed in power in part because they recognized the demand for increased state services, particularly highway building, and were willing to accept the responsibility for making increased appropriations for these services.

CHAPTER 24

The Great Depression

Nebraska, like the nation, seemed anxious to return to "normalcy" after the war. Though Wilson had received a 41,000 majority in Nebraska in 1916, the Republican Warren G. Harding rolled over James M. Cox in 1920 by a majority of almost 128,000 votes. Though the *Lincoln Journal* assured its readers after the election that the nation was closer to entering the League of Nations than it had been before Harding's victory, a general dissatisfaction with continued involvement in Europe's affairs, implicit in the desire for normalcy, played an important part in the Republican victory. There were other factors as well, including a general desire for a change; German-American resentment of the war after having voted for Wilson in 1916 on the ground that he had kept the nation out of war; dissatisfaction with the Democrats, blamed for many of the infringements on personal liberty during the conflict; and the ability of the Republicans to cement together the most conservative elements of their party and the radical elements in Nebraska society represented by Non-Partisan League votes. In light of Senator Hitchcock's leadership of the pro-League campaign in the Senate, it is not surprising that Nebraska voters in 1922 could elect the Republican challenger for his Senate seat while electing the Democrat Charles W. Bryan governor in the same election.

Nebraskans joined the nation in a desire to forget Old World difficulties and get on with the enjoyment of the material benefits being made available by the wonders of twentieth-century technology. The old frontier was gone and all but forgotten. The automobile had brought the farms closer together and closer to town. Main Street on Saturday night was lined with cars of farmers who had brought their families to town to shop and see a movie. Cornhusker football became front-page news and the businessmen of Lincoln decided to memorialize those who had died in the war by building a stadium that would hold thirty-five thousand spectators. The old saloon was gone, but the ease with which youngsters, as well as oldsters, could obtain vile bootleg beverages caused many to wonder about the efficacy of the "noble experiment." To many of the oldsters who had built the state, the younger generation seemed completely pleasure-mad. Others were fearful of the impact of the new materialism on the state's future. As Willa Cather put it:

> Too much prosperity, too many moving picture shows, too much gaudy fiction
> • have colored the taste and manners of so many of these Nebraskans of the future.
> There, as elsewhere, one finds the frenzy to be showy; farmer boys who wish to
> be spenders before they are earners, girls who try to look like the heroines of the
> cinema screen; a coming generation which tries to cheat its aesthetic sense by
> buying things instead of making anything. There is even danger that that fine
> institution, the University of Nebraska, may become a gigantic trade school.
> The men who control its destiny, the regents and the lawmakers, wish their
> sons and daughters to study machines, mercantile processes, "the principles of
> business"; everything that has to do with the game of getting on in the world—
> and nothing else.[1]

Throughout the decade of the 1920s, the state exhibited many aspects of material prosperity; its citizens continued to buy automobiles, telephones, radios, and other modern conveniences; cities increased in population and new buildings began to appear on their skylines. For agriculture, however, the 1920s were years of depression rather than prosperity, and because the state was almost wholly agricultural, the depression in that sector of the economy ultimately dominated and overshadowed all else. These years so weakened the state's economy that when the crash came in 1929, followed by drought and deep depression in the early 1930s, the economy came closer to complete collapse than it had even during the beginning years of the 1870s and the bitter years of the 1890s.

THEOS: DEPRESSION IN THE MIDST OF PLENTY

During the war the demand for food to feed the armed services and the Allies had caused farm prices to skyrocket to heights beyond anything old-time farmers had believed possible. When prices maintained their high levels after the shooting stopped, many farmers rubbed their eyes incredulously but then decided that a plateau had been reached and prices

Jobless and without resources, many availed themselves of the charity provided by breadlines and soup kitchens like this one in Beatrice. Courtesy, NSHS, F234:26.

would be maintained more or less permanently at wartime levels. In the rush to cash in on the new prosperity, many mortgaged themselves to secure additional high-priced land on which to plant still larger acreages. By mid-1920, however, foreign demand for U.S. agricultural products fell off sharply, and government price guarantees for wheat expired. The effect was startling. Wheat, which had sold for $2.02 per bushel on December 1, 1919, brought only $1.31 per bushel on December 1, 1920. During the same period corn dropped from $1.22 to $.41, oats from $.65 to $.37, barley from $1.00 to $.50, potatoes from $1.90 to $1.20. Most farmers, pressed for interest payments on their mortgages and on loans many of them had taken to put out their crops, had to market their 1920 crop in this climate of suddenly declining prices and suffered heavy losses. Those who held on to their grain in the hope that the recession was only temporary suffered even greater losses. By December 1, 1921, wheat was down to $.83 per bushel, corn $.27, oats $.21, and barley $.28. Livestock prices also tumbled: beef cattle that had brought $9.53 per hundred in 1920 brought only $6.13 in 1921, hogs fell from $12.62 to $7.52, lambs from $13.39 to $7.68. Though there was some recovery during the decade and prices generally were above the 1910–14 level, they did not regain their wartime heights.[2]

More relevant, perhaps, than the comparison prices is the impact farm prices had on the purchasing power of the average farmer. From 1922 to 1929 the average farm price index in Nebraska was slightly less than 35 percent above the prewar level. During the same time, however, the wholesale price index averaged slightly more than 44 percent above the prewar level. The high tax schedule also affected the farmer's economic position. Most farm taxes were paid in the form of the general property tax, and at no time in the 1920s did levies fall below 122 percent of the 1913 levy. In 1927 the levy was 184 percent higher than that of 1913. Expressed another way, taxes that took 5.63 percent of average net farm income in 1914 absorbed 20.41 percent in 1922, 13.48 percent in 1924, 10.59 percent in 1928, and 8.69 percent in 1929.

Although gross farm income recovered somewhat in the latter years of the decade, studies available indicate that the net income per farm, after operating expenses had been deducted, averaged only $1,795, compared with an average of $3,087 for the years 1914–19. There was a corresponding decrease in farm values, which dropped about 31 percent from $4.2 billion in 1920 to $2.9 billion in 1930. The value of land and buildings decreased more than 48 percent. There was a general decline in land prices: in seven southeastern counties land that sold by warranty deed at an average of $165 per acre in 1921 was selling for $115 in 1930, a decrease of 30.3 percent; in two east-central counties the average price fell from $134 to $114, a decrease of 14.6 percent; in one Sand Hills county it dropped from $29 to $10, a decrease of 65.5 percent.

Hardest hit of all were the farmers who were trying to pay off mortgages on land purchased at high prices during the war and immediate postwar years. Many tried to refinance their mortgages by borrowing from individuals, banks, or the farm loan banks, but though considerable credit was extended, it became increasingly more difficult for farmers to obtain loans. As a result, many either deeded their farms to mortgage holders or let them be foreclosed. In the seven southeastern counties referred to above, there were 315 foreclosure sales from 1921 to 1930; in the two east-central counties, 156; in the one Sand Hills county, 108. In addition, there were many token transfers, which indicated hard times for the farmer. As H. C. Filley put it, "The large number of foreclosure sales and token transfers in 1922 and later years is an excellent index of the severity of the effects of the deflation upon Nebraska farmers."[3]

Though some businesses remained prosperous, agriculture's distress was reflected in all aspects of the state's economy. Particularly hard hit were state banks that had assets tied up in real estate and crop mortgages, which they found increasingly difficult to collect. Nearly 100 banks were forced to close their doors during 1924, 23 in 1926, 19 in 1927, 400 in 1928, and 106 in 1929. Most of these were state banks whose deposits were covered by the Bank Guaranty Fund, created by the legislature in 1911. During years of prosperity, the Guaranty Fund provided a measure of security for the state banks, but in the 1920s payments into the fund by member banks to guarantee the deposits of failed banks resulted in such a strain on the state banking system that the law was repealed in 1930. The Guaranty Fund Commission, created in 1923, operated a number of banks that would have closed under ordinary circumstances.

Manufactures, likewise, showed signs of decline during the period. Census figures from the 1920 and 1930 enumerations show a 48.3 percent decrease in the number of manufacturing establishments, from 2,884 to 1,491 during the decade. The number of employees decreased by only half that amount, dropping 22.8 percent from 36,521 to 28,212; and wages declined by 20 percent, from $46.1 million to $36.9 million. The value of products decreased 29.5 percent, from $596 million to $420.3 million.[4]

Further reflecting the state's basic difficulty was that population increased by only 81,591, or 6.3 percent, during the decade. There was heavy emigration from the state, particularly to the west coast, and virtually all the meager increase went to the cities, continuing the trend toward urbanization begun in the first decade of the twentieth century. As a result, Nebraska's population, which had been 68.7 percent rural in 1920, was only 64.7 rural by 1930.

In spite of great prosperity nationally, at least on paper, of reasonably adequate rainfall, of average or better than average crop yields, and of higher prices than at any period in history except during the war, the state's economic picture was bleak. If Nebraska was in depression in the midst of prosperity, it was clear that the state's economy would be unable to withstand any worsening of conditions, either natural or man-made.

THE COLLAPSE

For Nebraska, the major implication of the stock market crash of October 1929 was not the huge individual fortunes lost, although that did occur, but rather the sudden collapse of farm prices to which the state's entire economy was connected in one way or another. Nebraska's farm income was greater in 1929 than it had been in any year since the end of the war, but prices started to sag in the last quarter and continued to fall until December, 1932, when they were the lowest in the state's history—lower even than those of the middle 1890s.

Although the most drastic decline was in the price of corn, at 80.6 percent, total cash receipts from crop and livestock marketing declined 65.9 percent from $489.1 million in 1929 to $166.7 million in 1932. The distress was compounded because the farmer's relative price position in the economy as a whole became even worse than it had been during the 1920s. Based on market prices received, the income of Nebraska farmers in the 1920s was 12.8 percent less than it had been during the years 1910 to 1914; 17 percent less in 1930; 35 percent less in 1931; and 46 percent less in 1932. The prices farmers had to pay for goods, however, declined

Table 11. December Farm Prices, 1929–1932

	1929	1930	1931	1932	% Decline 1929–32
Corn (bu.)	$.67	$.52	$.36	$.13	80.6
Wheat (bu.)	1.00	.54	.39	.27	73.0
Oats (bu.)	.38	.27	.23	.10	73.7
Sorghum (cwt.)	1.79	1.43	1.16	.50	72.1
Barley (bu.)	.49	.33	.27	.13	73.5
Rye (bu.)	.76	.33	.31	.17	77.6
Hay (ton)	8.00	6.90	6.90	4.10	48.8
Potatoes (bu.)	1.20	.75	.50	.31	74.2
Beef Cattle (cwt.)	10.50	39.00	24.00	18.80	79.0
Hogs (cwt.)	8.20	7.10	3.30	2.30	72.0
Chickens (lb.)	.148	.122	.112	.065	56.1
Eggs (doz.)	.380	.200	.229	.246	35.2
Milk (cwt.)	2.30	2.00	1.45	.95	58.7

Source: Nebraska Department of Agriculture and Inspection, *Nebraska Agricultural Statistics: Historical Record, 1866–1954* (Chicago: State-Federal Division of Agricultural Statistics, 1957).

much less rapidly and in 1932 were still 7 percent greater than during the years 1910 to 1914.

Government support programs helped prices edge up a bit during the 1930s. The depression, however, was far from over. Drought, the periodic enemy of the Nebraska farmer, added its blows to an industry already reeling under the impact of worldwide financial distress. Although Nebraska did not suffer from the general drought of 1930, rainfall was below normal in 1931, 1932, and 1933, and in 1934 the state received only 14.31 inches of annual rainfall—the lowest since 1864. Rainfall was normal in 1935, but again in 1936 it dipped down to 14.42 inches and in 1937 was only 17.66 inches. The dry, powdered soil began to blow, as Nebraska and all the plains states experienced a series of heavy dust storms that blotted out both sun and hope. This disaster took care of the surplus problem. There was a good corn crop in 1932, but corn yielded only 3.2 bushels per acre in 1934 and 3.5 bushels in 1936, compared with an average of

24 bushels per acre for the years 1923 to 1932. Whereas production had averaged 224 million bushels from 1928 to 1932, it was only 21.3 million in 1934 and 26.0 million in 1936. Wheat, the second most important crop, exhibited a similar though less drastic pattern. The yield per acre in 1934 was 7.8 bushels and in 1936, 14.2 bushels, compared with an average of 15.4 bushels. Growing conditions for wheat were actually better in 1936 than in either 1935 or 1937. Total production amounted to 17.5 million bushels in 1934 and 47.3 million bushels in 1936, compared to the average of 56.5 million bushels. Part of the lower total production may be accounted for by reduced acreage under government programs, but most of the disparity between the drought years and the average for the five preceding years resulted from the low yield per acre.

Though the government ultimately stepped in to enable farmers to renew thousands of farm mortgages at lower rates of interest in the hope of saving their farms, many lost their farms before that action was taken. Complete data are not available, but certain statistics indicate the nature of the tragedy. From 1930 to 1935 the percent of total farms mortgaged decreased from 52.5 to 43.6, and farm mortgage debt decreased from $545.5 million to $448.3 million. In eleven southeastern counties there were 136 farm mortgage foreclosures in 1932, representing 8.2 percent of the total number of farm land transfers during the year. In addition, there were 691 token transfers, most of them made because of fear of foreclosure, accounting for 41.5 percent of all transfers. The percentage of farms operated by tenants, which had increased by 4.2 percent during the 1920s, increased an additional 5.7 percent during the 1930s.

The agricultural depression affected all other activities in this primarily agricultural state. The number of manufacturing establishments declined 22.1 percent, from 1,491 in 1929 to 1,161 in 1939; the number of wage earners 20.4 percent, from 28,212 to 22,449; and manufacturing wages 23.8 percent, from $36.9 million to $28.1 million.[5]

Though the number of wholesale trade establishments increased 17 percent, from 2,886 in 1929 to 3,378 in 1939, their net sales decreased 46.3 percent, from $1.1 billion to $565 million. In retail trade the situation was the same. The number of stores increased 15.9 percent, from 16,682 in 1929 to 19,330 in 1939, but net sales dropped from $554 million to $397 million, a decrease of 28 percent.[6]

Table 12. Nebraska Farms, by Ownership and Tenancy, 1920–1945

	Farms Operated by						
Year	Owners		Managers		Tenants		Total
	Number	Percent	Number	Percent	Number	Percent	
1920	69,672	56.0	1,315	1.1	53,430	42.9	124,417
1925	67,766	53.1	669	0.5	59,299	46.4	127,734
1930	67,418	52.1	1,020	0.8	61,020	47.1	129,458
1935	67,013	50.2	795	0.6	65,808	49.3	133,616
1940	56,561	46.7	554	0.5	63,947	52.8	121,062
1945	58,225	52.1	432	0.4	53,099	47.5	111,756

Source: Nebraska Department of Agriculture and Inspection, *Nebraska Agricultural Statistics: Historical Record, 1866–1954* (Chicago: State-Federal Division of Agricultural Statistics, 1957), 5.

Figures from the decennial census provide a picture of the entire decade, but the situation was actually far worse than the statistics reveal. Although estimates vary, the decline was actually much sharper between 1929 and 1933 than for the decade as a whole.

The urban areas were also affected by the agricultural problems. At first Omaha tried to take the depression lightly, but the years of drought and frozen credit struck one important activity after another. The city's livestock market slipped from second to third in the nation. The grain market was in shambles. The need to provide relief for an increasing number of persons in the industrial city drained county finances, which were relieved only by the inflow of federal funds. In the milk strike of 1933 the roads into Omaha were picketed by farmers who overturned milk trucks. Lincoln, too, was paralyzed. Many business firms failed, and unemployment became acute. Many buildings were vacant. The city's wholesale and retail trade, upon which it depended heavily, was inactive. The city was treated to the frightening spectacle of farmers marching on the state capitol to demand a moratorium on farm debts.

Everywhere the story was the same. As the authors of *Nebraska: A Guide to the Cornhusker State*, themselves victims of the depression, put it, "The condition of the farmers affected Nebraska merchants, lumber dealers, realtors, school teachers, laborers, and artisans. Housewives stocked their pantry shelves with the simplest essentials; construction lagged; school administrators curtailed their programs as tax receipts went down; day laborers, formerly sure of a place on Nebraska farms and in Nebraska industries, began the long trek of the unemployed."[7]

POLITICAL REPERCUSSIONS

Except in 1922, when Bryan was elected governor, Nebraskans followed their usual habit of voting Republican throughout the 1920s. In the congressional elections, however, the Democrats managed, with one exception, to elect candidates consistently from three of the six districts. These three were John H. Morehead, first district; Edgar Howard, third district; and Ashton C. Shallenberger, fifth district. The only exception occurred in 1928, when Fred G. Johnson defeated Shallenberger, and this loss was offset in the total statistics by the election of Democrat J. N. Norton from the normally Republican fourth district in 1926. The three perennially successful Democratic congressmen were all strong campaigners and had large personal followings. Morehead and Shallenberger had served the state as governor and Edgar Howard, the poker-playing, Quaker-garbed editor from Columbus, was easily the most colorful figure in Nebraska politics.

But the success of Morehead, Shallenberger, and Howard was based on more than a personal following. They represented three of the state's major farming areas, and their repeated reelection resulted, in part at least, from dissatisfaction on the part of the farmers with the efforts of Republican administrations and Republican Congresses to deal with the farm problem. Conversely, the urban areas seemed satisfied with Republican rule. Omaha, which before and after this period stood out as a Democratic stronghold, generally voted Republican. Lincoln, always a Republican stronghold, also voted Republican, but its pluralities in the congressional races were not sufficient to counterbalance the heavy Democratic vote in the rural counties of the first district. The fourth district, made up of the central South Platte section, was always a close battleground. The sixth district, including the Sand Hills, was always safely Republican, repeatedly returning Robert G. Simmons to Congress as it had his predecessor, Moses P. Kinkaid.

Further reflecting farm dissatisfaction was the Progressive vote in the presidential election of 1924. Though Robert M. La Follette did not split the Republican Party badly enough to result in a Democratic victory, as Theodore Roosevelt had done in 1912, he did poll 106,701 votes, or 23 percent of the total. The combined vote for La Follette and John W. Davis, the Democratic candidate, exceeded that of the victorious Calvin Coolidge by 25,405 and equaled 53 percent of the poll. Senator Norris, who had been a thorn in the flesh of the Republican regulars since his fight against Speaker Cannon in 1910, openly supported La Follette against Coolidge, which accounts in some measure for La Follette's success in the state. An indication that politics in Nebraska have always been complicated and that Nebraska voters have never slavishly followed party lines was Norris's reelection to the Senate as a Republican. Norris got 15,236 more votes than both of his opponents in the primaries (Fred G. Johnson and Charles H. Sloan) combined and won handily over John J. Thomas, who had the Progressive as well as the Democratic nomination. Norris took a leading role in the farm fight against the Coolidge administration and in 1928 supported Alfred E. Smith for the presidency, although even his support was not sufficient to carry the day for Smith in Nebraska, where the religious issue and prohibition entered significantly into the campaign, and Herbert Hoover won a landslide victory of 345,745 to 197,959.

Norris was rewarded in 1930 by a desperate effort to beat him in the primary through a trick designed to take advantage of the legal prohibition against any identification of candidates on the ballot other than name. At the last minute, Norris's enemies filed another George W. Norris, a grocery clerk at Broken Bow. The filing reached the secretary of state two days after the deadline had expired, but because it had been postmarked at Broken Bow within the prescribed time, Secretary Frank Marsh accepted it. Norris's friends, led by Attorney General C. A. Sorensen, immediately brought action, and an opinion by Chief Justice Charles A. Goss that the filing was invalid kept "Grocer Norris" off the ballot. But even though this skullduggery aroused national indignation and brought a Senate investigation, Norris faced a desperate fight for reelection. It was clear that the Republican National Committee wanted Norris defeated at any cost; he had been even more critical of Hoover than he had been of Coolidge. Large sums of money, some in excess of the amount allowed by the Nebraska primary law, were poured into the campaign to elect State Treasurer W. M. Stebbins, whom the organization had selected to oppose Norris. Former governor McKelvie, now a member of President Hoover's Federal Farm Board, took an active part in the campaign. Norris, however, rolled up an easy victory, 108,471 to 74,486.

In the general election, Norris faced former senator Gilbert M. Hitchcock. Norris proved to be the best vote-getter in the race, overwhelming Hitchcock 247,118 to 172,795, even though Hitchcock received substantial support from many Republican leaders. Democrat Charles W. Bryan defeated Arthur J. Weaver for the governorship, and Democrats won the fourth district (where Norton defeated Charles H. Sloan), in addition to their usual three congressional elections. It was evident that Norris not only had a greater hold on the rank-and-file Republicans than did the party leaders but that he was able to get a good many Democratic votes as well.

A vote for Norris was, of course, a vote against the Hoover administration, but it is difficult to determine just what part the protest vote played in his election and what part his great personal following played. The same is true in the case of Bryan, Morehead, Howard, and Shallenberger. Norton's defeat of Sloan in the fourth district may, perhaps, be classed as a protest against Hoover's farm policies. Generally, however, 1930 was a Republican year in Nebraska. Republicans elected all state officers except governor, and though the Democrats picked up some strength in the legislature, the Republicans retained a majority of both houses. But as the depression deepened, it became apparent that the Republicans, as the party in power nationally, were going to be held responsible for the economic distress ravaging the state and the nation.

Senator Norris came out early in support of Franklin D. Roosevelt for president, and as the campaign wore on, many independent and progressive Republicans in the state joined him in support of the New York governor. Roosevelt rolled up a greater vote than any candidate for president in the state's history and overwhelmed Hoover, 359,082 to 201,177. Bryan's victory over Dwight Griswold was much less impressive, but he and all Democratic candidates for state offices easily won election. Roosevelt had carried every county except Keya Paha and Lancaster; the Democrats for the first time since 1916 had elected their entire state ticket. The Democrats won the most complete control of the legislature they had ever enjoyed, electing all but two senators (both from Lancaster County) and all but seventeen representatives. As a result of the census of 1930, Nebraska had lost one representative in Congress, but the five elected were all Democrats—even Robert G. Simmons went down in defeat, beaten in the new fifth district by Terry Carpenter. The Socialists also were on the ballot in Nebraska and polled a substantial vote for a minor third party: Norman Thomas got 9,876 for president, and John M. Paul got 6,733 votes for governor. Glenn Griffith, Socialist candidate for railway commissioner, polled 15,222 votes.

The Democrats had rolled up the most substantial protest vote in the history of the state. In the state, as in the nation, they were completely in power and assumed virtually sole responsibility for dealing with the economic distress that had the nation in paralysis.

Relief, Recovery, and War

Nebraska had responded to Franklin D. Roosevelt's dramatic campaign, calling for government action to bring about recovery and reform with the largest majority it had ever given a presidential candidate. And on that snowy March 4, 1933, as Nebraskans sat with their ears to their radios to hear the new president tell them, "Only a foolish optimist can deny the dark realities of the moment," they knew whereof he spoke. Their banks were closed, their farms were going on the block for the benefit of mortgage holders, their city streets rumbled with the footfalls of the unemployed, their businesses were at a virtual standstill. As they listened to the inaugural address, many Nebraskans could hear echoes of the old Populist tradition, of William Jennings Bryan, of Theodore Roosevelt, and of Woodrow Wilson. Many others, too young to remember the old days, could sense that the reforms Senator Norris had been fighting for were now being advocated by the president.

In Lincoln, the state legislature, like the Congress, was preponderantly Democratic. The new legislature had been wrestling with the problem of depression for almost two months and had yet to inspire much confidence among the people. Although that body and succeeding legislatures did take significant steps designed to improve both state government and the condition of the people, it was clear that the great crisis of the early 1930s, in which financial distress was aggravated by prolonged drought, was beyond the power of the state government to solve. Nebraskans looked to Washington for the solution to their basic problems.

And a solution came from Washington. To be sure, it was not all that many people hoped. It brought anguished cries from certain segments of the population; it even disappointed some of its advocates. But it was a solution, a conscious effort to pull the nation out of the morass into which it had fallen since the end of World War I.

THE NEW DEAL IN AGRICULTURE

In agriculture, as in other segments of the economy, the immediate need was relief—not the soup kitchen variety but relief from the oppressive burden of debt which threatened to wipe away the individual's equity in the land. Auctioneers and sheriffs, cooperating voluntarily or otherwise with grim-faced farmers who attended foreclosure sales to ensure that bids were made only by the proper persons restored a few farms to their foreclosed owners, but this was no solution to the farm credit problem and everyone knew it.

Since before the war the federal government had been making efforts to alleviate the age-old problem of agricultural credit, a problem complicated by the farmers' need for both long-term and short-term credit in addition to some means of protection against the vicissitudes of nature and the price system. By 1933 reasonable credit facilities existed, but their administration was so encumbered by the operation of a complicated bureaucracy that many farmers were unwilling or unable to make full use of them.

On March 27, President Roosevelt, by executive order, consolidated all agricultural credit agencies under the Farm Credit Administration. Nebraska, Wyoming, South Dakota, and Iowa constituted the Eighth Farm Credit District with headquarters in Omaha. From May 1, 1933, to January 1, 1940, the institutions under the supervision of the Farm Credit Administration advanced $185 million to Nebraska farmers, the largest portion of which was loaned by the Federal Land Bank of Omaha.

Until 1935 most of the Federal Land Bank loans were used to pay off old debts; after 1935 a considerably greater portion went to purchase farms. By the end of 1939, the fourteen production credit associations operating in the state had made 18,719 loans amounting to $33.4 million. Another type of debt relief was provided by the Farm Security Administration (FSA), which extended supervised credit to certain destitute farm families, helping them to get back on their feet. By 1940 the FSA had aided 15,004 Nebraska farm families with rehabilitation loans amounting to $12.7 million, and FSA resettlement "homesteads" were established in the vicinity of North Platte and Scottsbluff.

The crushing burden of debt was the result rather than the cause of agricultural depression. As they had since the days of the Populists, most

Women filled the ranks of labor left vacant by men called to the service of their country. Here women perform dangerous yet vital duty in bomb construction at the Grand Island Ordnance Plant during World War II. Courtesy, NSHS, C817:3-1.

farmers believed the cause was low farm prices. There were many explanations for low farm prices, but most observers agreed that the farmers' principal difficulty was that they had no control over their production or their marketing. In 1929, after almost a decade of struggle against an unfriendly administration, farm congressmen had secured the creation of the Federal Farm Board to stabilize farm marketing through the use of government purchases. This effort failed largely because price stabilization served to increase production and thus aggravate the total situation. The Farm Board itself, of which former governor Samuel R. McKelvie was the grain member, concluded that effective price stabilization could not be accomplished without control of production.

The Agricultural Adjustment Act (AAA), passed on May 12, 1933, was designed to improve farm prices by controlling production. Its goal was to establish and maintain a purchasing power for agricultural commodities equivalent to that of the period from 1909 to 1914 through a system of crop reduction contracts under which the secretary of agriculture could pay farmers benefits for reducing production. The system was not compulsory, but the benefit payments were considered sufficient inducement to ensure compliance. The cost was to be borne by a processing tax on commodities covered by the act, and the program was to be administered through state and local farm committees organized by the secretary of agriculture.

Little could be done regarding crops for 1933, but emergency livestock reductions were carried out in the fall of the year. Approximately 470,000 Nebraska cattle were purchased by the government, either for shipment outside the state or for slaughter at a total of slightly more than $6 million. This was only about $10 to $12 per head, and resentment grew as farmers saw their herds disappear at a fraction of their value, but they also realized that they could not have maintained the herds under existing drought conditions. Similarly, approximately 438,000 pigs and about 36,000 farrowing sows were purchased and slaughtered.

Wheat growers who agreed to participate in the 1934 and 1935 crop reduction programs were given benefits in 1933. Approximately thirty-five thousand wheat growers participated. The corn-hog program included crop adjustment, hog contracts, and corn loans. The corn loans gave farmers an opportunity to obtain loans of forty-five cents per bushel on corn properly stored on their farms. Under this program a total of 53 million bushels of corn were sealed, and loans amounting to $23 million were advanced to farmers of the state. Participating farmers received cash for their corn at a rate ranging from 30 to 50 percent above the market price at the time the loans were made, and they benefited further because prices ranged from two to three times the initial market price when they sold their corn. In all, approximately forty-one thousand farmers, or about one-third of those in the state, took out corn loans.

The AAA, declared unconstitutional in 1936 because of its processing tax features, was promptly replaced by a soil conservation act which provided for direct subsidies to farmers who conformed to soil conservation and crop control standards established by the federal government. The program was administered through soil conservation districts organized under state law. In 1938 a new Agricultural Adjustment Act reintroduced adjustment of crop production by direct allotment of acreage. The law also provided for parity payments and standardized the conditions under which commodity loans would be offered. Another feature of the 1938 act was crop insurance for wheat.

Participation in the soil conservation program and the new AAA was substantial. Initially 98,583 farms, or 73.6 percent, participated in the soil conservation program in 1936 and received benefits totaling nearly $14 million. Likewise, participation in the new AAA program was widespread. By 1939, 81.2 percent of all cropland was covered and in 1940, 88.3 percent. By the end of 1940, 23.3 million bushels of corn were under seal, including 14.4 million bushels of 1938 and 1939 corn resealed. Relatively little wheat was resealed, and the total of 17 million bushels of wheat under loan on farms and in warehouses in 1940 included only 374,552 bushels of 1939 farm storage wheat resealed. Loans were made available on rye in 1939, and 44,000 bushels of this crop were sealed on the farms, of which 9,129 were resealed in 1940 along with 59,105 bushels of the new crop. In 1940, when loans were made available on barley, 335,280 bushels of that crop were sealed.

The commodity loans had marked price-stabilization features. If, for example, the price of corn had dropped thirty cents in 1940, as competent authority indicates it would have without the impetus of the loan rate of sixty-one cents per bushel, the loss to Nebraska farmers would have been about $30 million. Similarly, a decline of forty cents in the 1940 wheat price would have lowered the income of Nebraska's wheat farmers by about $14 million.

Altogether, Nebraska farmers received nearly $200 million during the years from 1933 to 1941 in government payments of one kind or another. Although this represented only about 9 percent of farmers' income during these years, the significance of this assistance in the economic life of the depression-racked state can hardly be ignored or underestimated in light of the significant decline in farm incomes throughout the 1930s.

At no time during the 1930s did farm income, either in dollars or purchasing power, attain the level achieved during the middle and late 1920s. Part of the reason may be that although prices increased greatly

Table 13. Farm Marketings and Government Payments, 1933–1941

Year	Cash Receipts from Crops and Livestock Amount (x 1,000)	Percent	Government Payments Amount (x 1,000)	Percent	Total Farm Income (x 1,000)	Percent Change from 1909–14
1909–14 (Ave.)	$ 340.1	100.0	—	—	$ 340.1	
1933	193.4	99.5	$ 1.0	0.5	194.4	−42.8
1934	227.2	90.6	23.5	9.4	250.7	−26.3
1935	209.4	86.4	33.1	13.6	242.5	−28.7
1936	281.0	94.2	17.3	5.8	298.3	−14.1
1937	250.8	93.5	17.5	6.5	268.3	−21.1
1938	200.5	86.8	15.4	13.2	215.9	−36.5
1939	221.5	88.7	28.1	11.3	249.6	−26.6
1940	224.3	82.9	46.3	17.1	270.6	−20.4
1941	290.0	94.8	15.9	5.2	305.9	−10.1
1933–41(Ave.)	$ 233.1	91.4	$ 22.0	8.6	$ 255.1	−25.0

Source: Nebraska Department of Agriculture and Inspection, *Nebraska Agricultural Statistics: Historical Record, 1866–1954* (Chicago: State-Federal Division of Agricultural Statistics, 1957), 127, 134, 138.

from the 1932 level, they stayed under the level of the 1920s, as well as under that for the years 1909–14, which was used to establish "parity" for the farm programs. More of the reason may be found in production. The decade was generally dry, but in 1934 and 1936 the state experienced the most severe drought ever, and low yields along with crop reduction programs decreased total production.

Despite these hardships, however, the condition of the farmers was so much better than it had been at the beginning of the depression that the slight recovery in the middle and late 1930s seemed almost like prosperity. Moreover, government guarantees removed the specter of foreclosure. Expanded programs in electric power, conservation, and irrigation added to the chances for the good life on the farm and were building the basis for what seemed like permanent farm prosperity.

Table 14. Per Acre Crop Yields, 1926–1941

Year	(inches)	Corn (bu.)	Wheat (bu.)	Oats (bu.)	Sorghum (bu.)	Hay (tons)
1926–30 (Ave.)	23.2	23.9	16.8	27.2	n.a	1.04
1931	19.3	17.0	16.6	21.5	14.0	.80
1932	20.5	25.0	12.3	29.5	13.5	1.02
1933	20.2	22.5	12.1	10.5	13.0	.87
1934	14.3	3.2	7.8	7.4	5.7	.58
1935	22.6	13.2	12.6	28.5	8.0	1.07
1936	14.4	3.5	14.2	11.5	7.4	.67
1937	17.7	10.5	13.2	21.0	9.9	.74
1938	22.2	15.0	11.8	29.5	14.5	.93
1939	16.3	12.0	11.1	14.7	10.1	.76
1940	17.4	17.0	13.1	24.0	11.0	.72
1941	24.5	23.5	15.4	29.5	17.0	.98

Mean rainfall for the state is 22.8 inches.
Source: Nebraska Department of Agriculture and Inspection, *Nebraska Agricultural Statistics: Historical Record, 1866–1954* (Chicago: State-Federal Division of Agricultural Statistics, 1957).

IN THE CITIES AND TOWNS

Nebraskans, and Americans generally, were wholly unprepared to meet the heavy demands for relief they faced in the early 1930s. Over the years the state had developed a group of institutions to care for the less fortunate, and in 1921 a Veterans Relief Fund had been established; but relief for the needy generally had been left to the counties. Some counties expanded their relief programs to meet the new situation, but it soon became clear that the problem was beyond the capabilities of county government, and in 1933 both the state and federal governments were forced to take cognizance of the destitute. The state legislature that year adopted an old-age pension act, to be administered by the counties, and authorized the counties to levy up to one mill for the relief of unemployed and indigent persons.

The federal government entered the field through the Federal Emergency Relief Administration, the Civilian Conservation Corps, and the

Civil Works Administration. These agencies were supplemented or replaced by other agencies, but the federal government continued to bear the greater part of the relief burden, and as late as January 1935, the Federal Emergency Relief Administration was contributing 87 percent of all public assistance. Under the impetus of the Social Security Act of 1935, the legislature, in a special session, enacted a series of measures providing for old-age assistance, aid to dependent and crippled children, and assistance to the blind.

The impact on state government of this effort to meet the needs of the indigent was second only to that resulting from the assumption of responsibility for providing highways to meet the needs of the automobile. Before 1936 public assistance was not an item in the state's regular expenditures; by 1938 it ranked second only to highways in amount of money expended, and in the biennium 1937–39 the budget for assistance accounted for nearly one-fourth of the state's total appropriations.

Relief payments reported by federal and state agencies indicate that as many as 100,322 individuals received approximately $30 million in relief payments during the fiscal year 1938–39 alone, but these figures fall short of describing the total impact of relief programs on the state. Nor do they provide an accurate picture of the number of persons actually affected by relief payments of one kind or another. The Legislative Council estimated in November 1938 that the ultimate number of recipients would almost certainly reach or exceed 250,000, more than 18 percent of the inhabitants of the state. Moreover, official figures in no way tell the story of the social benefits derived from the relief program, and particularly its work relief aspects. A great variety of projects were carried forward, from resodding a courthouse lawn to constructing public buildings, improving highways and other facilities, and inventorying archives and indexing newspaper files. The skills and self-respect of many professional and subprofessional people were kept alive by giving them an opportunity to earn a living along lines related to the fields in which they were trained. The figures do reveal, however, that before the onset of World War II, the state did not appreciably reduce the number of persons receiving relief or the expenditures for relief.

DEPRESSION POLITICS

In the 1930s the Democrats enjoyed greater and more sustained success politically than in any other period in Nebraska's history, and for the most part their control of state politics during this period was more complete than any the Republicans had had during their periods of supremacy since 1890. Though the Republicans cut into their majorities and picked up a few more seats in the legislature, the Democrats in 1934 generally repeated their landslide performance of 1932. Edward R. Burke, the Omaha congressman who had defeated Charles W. Bryan in a bitter primary fight, went to the Senate in an easy victory over Robert G. Simmons. For governor, Roy L. Cochran, former state engineer, who had received less than a third of the vote in the Democratic primary in besting a field of eight opponents (including Terry Carpenter and Eugene D. O'Sullivan), defeated Dwight Griswold, Gordon publisher and former member of the state legislature, by a much less substantial margin, 284,095 to 266,707. The Democrats won all state offices except that of commissioner of public lands and buildings and a large majority in both houses of the legislature. They also won all congressional races except in the third district, where the venerable Edgar Howard was soundly defeated by Norfolk radio man Karl Stefan, who was to remain in Congress until his death in 1951 and develop into as substantial, if not quite so picturesque, a figure in the Nebraska congressional delegation as his erstwhile opponent.

In 1936, though Roosevelt got only slightly more than 56 percent of the vote as compared with a little over 62 percent in 1932, the Democrats generally repeated their performance: Leo N. Swanson, commissioner of public lands, and Congressman Karl Stefan were the only Republicans elected, and Cochran, seeking reelection, defeated Griswold by a considerably larger margin than he had in 1934. There were signs, however, that the Democratic Party in the state was in serious trouble and that Democratic successes were based to at least some degree on the votes of Norris Republicans who supported the basic principles of the New Deal. Those signs showed up in the senatorial election. Senator Norris, who had supported Democratic presidential candidates since 1928, was one of Roosevelt's major bulwarks in the Senate and probably could not have gotten the Republican nomination if he had wanted it. In his autobiography he makes it clear that he did not want it and that he would not even have accepted a Democratic nomination, although he probably could have had it. He appeared to be ready to retire from politics at the expiration of his fourth term in 1937. He would be seventy-six.

By 1937 the *Omaha World-Herald* had drifted away from the New Deal, and the *Lincoln Star* became the state's leading Democratic newspaper. The *Star*'s editor, James E. Lawrence, began to circulate petitions to nominate Senator Norris as an Independent. This drive was successful, and Norris accepted the nomination. Meanwhile, Terry Carpenter, easily the state's most flamboyant politician, who had been elected to Congress in 1932 and had campaigned unsuccessfully for the Democratic nomination for governor in 1934, won the nomination for senator in the Democratic primary. The state convention, however, refused to recognize the action of the Democratic primary and instead endorsed Norris for the post. From the beginning, President Roosevelt had made it clear that he favored Norris's reelection, and during the campaign he visited the state to persuade Nebraskans that they owed a duty to the nation to return Norris to the Senate. Aided by this support, Norris was reelected and Carpenter ran a poor third, although his vote and that of Republican candidate Robert G. Simmons together totaled 72,967 more than that given Senator Norris.

By 1938, the pendulum had begun to swing toward the Republicans. Cochran won a third term as governor, defeating Republican Charles J. Warner, who had bested Griswold in the primary, and Charles W. Bryan, who was running by petition. Cochran was able to carry the secretary of state and treasurer with him, but Republicans William E. Johnson, Ray C. Johnson, Walter R. Johnson, and Duane T. Swanson were elected lieutenant governor, auditor, attorney general, and railway commissioner, respectively. Indeed, it seemed that anyone whose name ended in a Scandinavian suffix could get elected to office in Nebraska irrespective of the ticket, for the two Democratic victors on the state ticket were Harry R. Swanson and Walter H. Jensen. In the congressional races Republicans George Heinke, Karl Stefan, and Carl T. Curtis won in the first, third, and fourth districts; Democrats Charles F. McLaughlin and Harry B. Coffee won reelection in the second and fifth districts.

By 1940, the political pendulum had swung almost completely to the Republican side. Wendell Willkie took the state's electoral votes away from Roosevelt; Hugh A. Butler, Omaha grain dealer, defeated Governor Cochran for the Senate; and Dwight Griswold finally claimed the executive office by defeating Terry Carpenter. Griswold took the entire state ticket in with him. The only Democrat elected was Harry B. Coffee, who was returned to Congress from the fifth district.

THE UNICAMERAL LEGISLATURE

While wrestling with the problems of drought and depression, Nebraskans adopted a major innovation in state government—the unicameral legislature. The unicameral idea was not new, either in Nebraska or the nation. Most of the colonial assemblies originated as one-house bodies, although they gradually shifted over to the two-house system, and when state constitutions were formed, only Pennsylvania and Georgia adopted the one-house legislature. Even in these cases a Board of Censors acted as a virtual second house. When Vermont set itself up as an independent republic in 1777 it had a one-house legislature, but in 1836 the unicameral idea gave way there to the by then traditional two-house system. Interest in the unicameral idea slept until early in the twentieth century, when an increasing number of progressives became concerned with legislative reform. Over the years state legislatures had been subject to a great deal of criticism. Progressives especially condemned their inefficient methods and their frequent subservience to special interests. They were particularly critical of the conference committee between the two houses, which often resulted in reform legislation either dying or being emasculated. As Senator Norris put it: "It has been the stock argument that in a two house legislature one branch serves as a check upon the other in the ultimate molding of good and wholesome legislation. As a matter of practice, it has developed frequently that, through the Conference Committee, the politicians have the checks, and the special interests the balances."[1]

Nebraska's two-house legislature appears to have been no better or worse than most other state legislative bodies. The Conference Committee played an important role in legislation. For example, from 1921 to 1933, 10.95 percent of all measures enacted by the legislature passed through the Conference Committee, and in one instance involving a bill permitting municipally owned electric light plants to build lines beyond their corporate limits, the Conference Committee was able for six years to frustrate legislation which, as is evidenced by a heavy majority in a special election on the question, the people generally approved.

As early as 1915 a joint committee of the legislature, in a strongly worded statement which declared that "one body can more directly represent the public will of a democratic people than two or more," recommended the submission of a single-chamber amendment to the people and called for a constitutional convention to prepare the proposal for that purpose.[2] The legislature, possibly because it was interested in broader constitutional reform, refused to accept the recommendation of its joint committee. The proponents of unicameralism brought the issue up again without success in 1917. They came close to succeeding in the constitutional convention of 1919–20, when they were beaten only by the tie-breaking vote of the president. In 1923, after failing again in the legislature, they circulated an initiative petition but were unable to obtain enough signatures to put the proposition on the ballot. They tried the legislative route again in 1925 and in 1933 without success.

All this activity kept the idea before the people. In 1934, Senator Norris took an active interest in the proposal. He attended a conference on the issue in Lincoln on February 22 and urged the submission of an amendment to the constitution providing for a unicameral legislature. Before adjourning, the conference decided to try the initiative route again. The amendment, as finally initiated, provided for the election of a one-house legislature, to consist of not less than thirty or more than fifty members, for two-year terms, on a nonpartisan basis. There was some concern that the nonpartisan feature of the proposal might cause its defeat, but Norris insisted that it was basic to the whole idea, and his will prevailed.

The nonpartisan feature brought opposition from the leaders of both political parties. Some farm groups opposed the amendment on the grounds that the proposed legislature's membership was too restricted and farmers would not be adequately represented. Others opposed it as a dangerous experiment with the tried and true American legislative formula. Most of the press, led by the *Omaha World-Herald*, opposed the amendment. The only daily papers supporting it were the *Lincoln Star* and the *Hastings Tribune*.

At first it seemed that the effort might meet the same fate that had befallen it in 1923, but by June 5, a month before the deadline, seventy-five thousand persons had signed the initiative petition, exceeding the fifty-seven thousand signatures required to place it on the ballot. Thereafter, the unicameral movement rapidly gained ground. Senator Norris visited every section of the state in its behalf. He was assisted by many civic leaders, academic people, and others who volunteered their services in the cause.

As the campaign wore on, it appeared that Norris's leadership would be decisive. His large following in Nebraska, proud of his national reputation in the field of government reform, seemed willing to accept the unicameral idea if he favored it. Moreover, the proponents of the amendment pointed to the savings in expense that would result from a one-house legislature. This, perhaps more than other arguments, struck a responsive chord with Nebraskans during the depths of the depression, many of whom found the idea of a more efficient and economical government appealing, especially if it meant a reduction in taxes. And the argument was underscored by the fact that the legislature of 1933, which included many inexperienced members swept into office in the Roosevelt landslide, had not provided many examples of bicameral efficiency. Finally, the unicameral amendment was helped by the presence of two other amendments on the ballot, one repealing the state prohibition law and the other legalizing parimutuel betting at the race tracks. People who favored the latter two amendments apparently tended to vote for all three even though some of them may not have had any great interest in the science of government.

The amendment provided for the one-house legislature to be convened in 1937. The legislature of 1935, therefore, had the task of redistricting the state and establishing the number of members in the new body. The amendment limited membership to not less than thirty or more than fifty, but a further limitation was a provision that the combined salaries of all members should be $37,500 per year. The number of districts, therefore, would determine the salary of each member. Finally, the legislature agreed upon forty-three districts as nearly equal in population as was feasible.

Table 15. Vote on 1934 Amendments

Amendment	For		Against		Total
Repeal of prohibition	328,074	(60.1%)	218,107	(39.9%)	546,181
Unicameral legislature	286,068	(59.7%)	193,152	(40.3%)	479,220
Parimutuel betting	251,111	(57.3%)	187,455	(42.7%)	438,566

The amendment prohibited splitting counties to form legislative districts. Douglas County was given seven members and Lancaster three; Gage and Scotts Bluff were single-county districts; all the rest were composed of two or more counties, with District 39 in the Sand Hills consisting of ten counties.

Senator Norris, who had demonstrated his hold on the people of Nebraska by being reelected in 1936 as an Independent, was in Lincoln to address the first session of the unicameral legislature on January 5, 1937. Later in the month he witnessed the inauguration of the first president under what is generally known as the Norris amendment to the U.S. Constitution abolishing lame-duck sessions of Congress.[3]

The first unicameral legislature contained twenty-two Democrats and twenty-one Republicans. They had been elected on nonpartisan tickets, however, and to demonstrate their nonpartisan characteristics they chose Republican Charles J. Warner as Speaker. Later legislatures, dominated by Republicans, exhibited similar nonpartisanship in the selection of their leaders. Democrat Walter Raecke was chosen Speaker in 1947, and Democrat John Callan was selected to head the powerful Budget Committee in 1941, 1947, and 1949. The first session also took a long step toward eliminating one of the most criticized evils of the old system by providing for a public hearing on every bill while it was in committee. Votes were still taken, however, in executive session to which reporters were invited under a "gentleman's agreement" that they would disclose neither the content of the discussion nor the vote of any member. The first session also created a Legislative Council to replace the old legislative reference service. At first the Legislative Council consisted of sixteen members, but in 1949 the legislature provided that it should consist of all members of the legislature, thus creating a vehicle through which the legislature could function as a committee of the whole in the interim between sessions. The council was provided with a professional staff headed by a political scientist as director of research. In 1961, the office of fiscal analyst was created within the Legislative Council.

Adoption of the unicameral system did not cut off debate on its merits. Political leaders who had opposed the nonpartisan aspect of the new arrangement during the campaign for the amendment continued to press their opposition to this feature. They argued that the lack of partisanship in the legislature created both a power and a leadership vacuum in the legislature and made it difficult, if not impossible, for the governor to achieve effective liaison with the legislative branch of government. They received little encouragement from either the governors or the legislators, and the people to date have shown little interest in returning to a partisan system. Commenting on the unicameral system in 1957, A. C. Breckenridge suggested that "one reason for this may be that for the majority of the people of the state, and for a majority of the legislators past and present (possibly for some future ones too), the differences between Democrats and Republicans on most state questions are difficult to ascertain. Indeed, the bases for party distinctions may be difficult for most of them much of the time."[4]

Concern that the legislature was too small, an argument bolstered by pressure from the urban centers for redistricting to recognize the shift in population from the farms to the cities, was finally addressed when the 1961 session submitted a compromise amendment to the voters which provided that in redistricting the state, lines other than county lines could be followed, and though primary emphasis should be given to population, a certain amount of weight must be given to area. The voters approved the amendment in 1962, as well as one that provided four-year terms of office for legislators, half of the membership being elected each two years. Under this authority, the 1963 session redistricted the state to provide for forty-nine legislators, to be elected from one-member districts, with those from the odd-numbered districts to be elected for four years in 1964 and those from the even-numbered districts to be elected for two years.

In July 1964, a three-judge federal court panel held invalid the area amendment to the state constitution but agreed to permit legislators to be elected in 1964 under the reapportionment law of 1963, which had been enacted pursuant to the provisions of the amendment. Federal judges Harvey M. Johnsen, Robert Van Pelt, and Richard E. Robinson also held that though the legislature elected in 1964 would have de facto status in 1965, it would have to create a constitutionally valid legislative apportionment.

The legislature's first attempt to meet the court's demand was struck down by the same three judges on the grounds that the 48.4 percent disparity in the populations of the smallest and the largest districts provided in the apportionment was too great. At the same time, the judges warned the senators either to produce an acceptable law or run at large in 1966. A substitute measure, passed just before adjournment, reduced the disparity to 19.65 percent, but there was no assurance that this would be satisfactory, and the legislature adjourned with its members facing the gloomy prospect that they might have to run at large in 1966, which would have wiped out the four-year terms to which half of them had been elected in 1964. In February 1966, however, the three judges who had overthrown the two previous efforts at reapportionment expressed satisfaction with the new arrangement, and the cloud of uncertainty that had hung over the legislature for two years was lifted. The new apportionment breached seven county lines, and Hall County was sliced into three districts. Douglas County was given twelve of the forty-nine districts and Lancaster County six. At the other end of the scale, District 44 in the southwest corner of the state included six counties.

The apportionment crisis tended to deflect the debate on the merits of the unicameral legislature, and the successful weathering of that crisis seemed to have further entrenched the idea of unicameralism in Nebraska. Roger V. Shumate, director of research for the Legislative Council from its establishment until his death in 1954, observed in 1952: "The unicameral legislature is now beginning to enjoy the support of the very force which once constituted its greatest enemy—that is tradition."[5]

WORLD WAR II

During the 1930s, Nebraskans, like most Americans, were preoccupied with the problem of recovery from the depression and generally oblivious to events transpiring elsewhere in the world. Their reaction to the growing menace of European dictatorships seems to have been the hope that America could remain free from Europe's troubles. The debate was heated, though not as bitter as that preceding America's entry into World War I, and isolationist sentiment, at least as expressed in the state's newspapers, was strong. Although its importance is difficult to assess, the fear of foreign entanglement was a factor in the Republican victory of 1940. Opposition to a third term for the president was also strong. In addition, in light of improving economic conditions, there had been a general defection from the New Deal in much of the state. The debate over foreign policy continued, although the Japanese attack on Pearl Harbor precluded the continuation of opposition. Likewise, there was none of the home-front hysteria that had marred the state's history during World War I.

At home, the war years were characterized by unprecedented prosperity, both on the farms and in the towns, as heavy yields and high prices strengthened the state's agricultural economy. This prosperity continued and increased after the war, so that by 1954 the state had seen almost a decade and a half of the most prosperous years in its history.

The federalization of the armed services accomplished during World War I was continued and extended during World War II with the result that there was virtually no participation by state units as such, although Nebraska's National Guard, the 134th Infantry Regiment, was called to active duty in December 1940 and, under the command of General Butler B. Miltonberger of North Platte, fought with great distinction in France and Germany, playing a vital role in the breakthrough at St. Lo, one of the turning points in the war. Most of the 120,000 Nebraska men and women who served in the armed forces, however, were scattered throughout the army, navy, marines, and air forces. A total of 3,839 Nebraskans lost their lives in the service.

Primarily an agricultural state, Nebraska did not attract the great war industries, although many of the state's small enterprises subcontracted a wide variety of equipment, and heavy bombers were assembled in Bellevue. Ordnance plants were located at Mead, Grand Island, and Sidney, and the navy located one of its large ammunition depots at Hastings. The army air forces found that the broad prairies and sunny skies of

Nebraska provided excellent training facilities, and large air bases were located at Alliance, Ainsworth, Bruning, Fairmont, Grand Island, Harvard, Kearney, Lincoln, McCook, Scottsbluff, and Scribner. At Atlanta, near Holdrege, and also at Scottsbluff and at Fort Robinson there were prisoner-of-war camps. Historic Fort Robinson was pressed into service as a training center for the dogs of the K-9 corps. After the war, Offutt Field, near Omaha, became headquarters for the Strategic Air Command.

Nebraska's primary contribution during World War II, as in World War I, was the production of food, and in this the prisoner-of-war camps proved an unforeseen blessing. Because of a shortage of farm labor, POW labor was used by many area farmers and in other areas as well, including work on irrigation ditches for the Central Nebraska Public Power District. The experience of POW Bill Oberdieck reflects the wide variety of jobs filled by the POWs:

While at the main camp at Atlanta he worked for a lumber yard in Holdrege. In Grand Island he picked potatoes, and at Alma he worked for the Cudahy Chicken Processing Plant. His in-camp jobs included that of mess sergeant.

Later Oberdieck was transferred to the Weeping Water branch camp. While there he worked at the Robinson Seed Company in Waterloo and in the corn fields cutting weeds and stalks. He picked tomatoes for the canning factory in Nebraska City and worked for a time in the Kimmel Apple Orchards there as well.[6]

Through his many experiences Oberdieck developed a love for his new environment, and after the war he returned with his wife to Nebraska City and worked again for Kimmel Orchards, which he bought in 1964 upon Kimmel's retirement.

CHAPTER 26

Legacies of the Depression

After several attempts to discover and exploit potential resources under the ground, Nebraskans ultimately realized that the search for coal, salt, and other minerals was fruitless, that the state's real natural resource was under their feet, the soil itself. If there was enough water, the generally fertile soil would support a thriving agriculture. For a while, they comforted themselves with the theory that rainfall followed the plow and that agriculture would essentially provide its own solution to the problem of moisture. They also busied themselves with efforts to assist nature in increasing the moisture supply. Much of the early interest in tree planting was based on the theory that trees would improve moisture conditions. In the 1890s, there was some interest in rain making through concussion and other artificial means. Finally, however, Nebraskans came to realize that the only satisfactory solution to the problem of moisture was to use and conserve properly the relatively limited amount available. A little later they began to realize that their soil, too, needed to be conserved if it were to continue to support the state's principal economic activity. Thus in the twentieth century, soil conservation and irrigation have been integral parts of Nebraska's agricultural economy. Likewise, electric power has come to be looked upon as a natural resource and has been developed as a public enterprise.

CONSERVATION

The first conscious effort by Nebraskans to improve their environment was centered around tree planting. The absence of trees west of the Missouri had led many early observers to conclude that the area would not support agriculture. Even after this assumption was proved false, the lack of trees was keenly felt by pioneers who had grown up in the wooded states of the East. With typical western optimism, Nebraska's pioneer agriculturists were sure that this shortcoming of nature had a human solution. When early efforts to grow fruit proved successful in southeastern Nebraska, Robert W. Furnas, J. Sterling Morton, and others began to promote the growing of fruit trees not only as an important economic activity but as a means to the good life. Morton told the State Horticultural Society in 1871:

There is beauty in a well ordered orchard which is a "joy forever." It is a blessing to him who plants it, and it perpetuates his name and memory, keeping it fresh as the fruit it bears long after he has ceased to live. There is comfort in a good orchard, in that it makes the new home more like the "old home in the East," and with its thrifty growth and large luscious fruits, sows contentment in the mind of a family as the clouds scatter the rain. Orchards are missionaries of culture and refinement. They make the people among whom they grow a better and more thoughtful people. If every farmer in Nebraska will plant out and cultivate an orchard and a flower garden, together with a few forest trees, this will become mentally and morally the best agricultural State, the grandest community of producers in the American Union. Children reared among trees and flowers growing up with them will be better in mind and in heart, than children reared among hogs and cattle. The occupations and surroundings of boys and girls make them, to a great extent, either bad and coarse, or good and gentle.

If I had the power I would compel every man in the State who had a home of his own, to plant out and cultivate fruit trees.[1]

As a means of encouraging Nebraskans to plant trees, the State Board of Agriculture in 1872 adopted a resolution introduced by Morton designating April 10 as Arbor Day and providing a prize for the person who on that day planted the greatest number of trees. The Arbor Day idea spread rapidly. In 1874 Governor Furnas issued a proclamation calling upon Nebraskans to celebrate Arbor Day. In 1885 the legislature designated Morton's birthday, April 22, as Arbor Day and made it a legal holiday. Further efforts to encourage tree planting may be found in the constitution of 1875, which provided that improvements resulting from tree planting should not be included in assessments for tax purposes, in state legislation requiring towns and villages to plant trees along their

The construction of the Gerald Gentleman Nuclear Power Plant near Sutherland in June 1977. Courtesy, NSHS Jim Denney Collection, T7:5-9.

streets, and in the efforts of Senator Phineas W. Hitchcock that resulted in the Timber Culture Act of 1873. Lawrence and Uriah Bruner successfully grew trees in the Sand Hills, and Charles E. Bessey fought for the planting and establishment of a national forest in the Sand Hills, an effort that came to fruition under the administration of Theodore Roosevelt, a great conservationist himself. In the same tradition are the millions of trees set out each year on farms of the state through the Clark-McNary program and the windbreaks planted across the plains as part of the New Deal shelter-belt program in the 1930s.

During the early years Nebraskans exhibited little interest in conserving their soil. Although here and there a voice was raised to admonish them that the process of "mining the soil" would lead to undesirable results, most Nebraska farmers proceeded on the apparent assumption that the fertility of their soil was inexhaustible. The problem in the 1870s and 1880s was expansion, not conservation. The drought and depression of the 1890s caused considerable rethinking of the agricultural question, and agricultural leaders, both practical and academic, began to urge diversification and systematic crop rotation. The soil-building qualities of alfalfa particularly were stressed.

The problem of soil fertility was kept constantly before the farmers of the state during the early years of the twentieth century, and though many were slow to appreciate its importance, by 1930 systems of crop rotation best suited to the various sections were well recognized and were being practiced by a substantial number of farmers. Providing added impetus was the obvious economic need for diversifying crops to remove the hazards of one-crop agriculture and to try to find a combination of crops and livestock that would ensure a profit under conditions of high costs of production and static or declining prices. Much of the pioneering work was carried on under the direction of George E. Condra, director of the Conservation and Survey Division of the University of Nebraska, successor to the Conservation Commission, established by Governor Sheldon in 1908 and made permanent by act of the legislature in 1913.

Widespread soil conservation work began in earnest when the federal government took a direct hand in conservation during the 1930s. The Federal Soil Conservation Service, in cooperation with the College of

Agriculture and the Conservation and Survey Division, began a program of erosion control in 1934 with demonstration projects in Boone and Nance Counties. By 1936 there were projects in Douglas and Otoe Counties as well, and demonstration work in erosion control was being carried forward by sixteen Civilian Conservation Corps camps scattered throughout the central and eastern portions of the state.

Under the impetus of the Federal Soil Conservation Act, which replaced the Agricultural Adjustment Act, the legislature in 1937 provided for the establishment of soil conservation districts and created a State Soil Conservation Committee to represent the state in the organization and administration of the districts. By 1940 eight soil conservation districts had been organized; by 1944 more than one-half of the farms of the state were in soil conservation districts; and by 1950 100 percent of the acreage of all the farms and ranches in the state was included in eighty-seven soil conservation districts. Heavy rains in the late 1940s, which frequently sent small streams over their banks, resulted in considerable interest in the eastern part of the state in the development of an integrated conservation, flood, and erosion control program within the various watersheds, and in 1953 the legislature passed an act authorizing the establishment of watershed districts.

From the beginning, the soil conservation movement faced an uphill struggle. Everyone believes in conservation in principle, but conservation practices are expensive and frequently require deferring immediate returns in favor of long-term gains. Many individual farmers have been unable or unwilling to make that deferment. In any event, successful widespread conservation has been accomplished only through the expenditure of vast sums of federal money, both in technical assistance and direct payments to farmers.

IRRIGATION

Though there had been sporadic interest in irrigation since territorial days, and the army at Fort Sidney in the 1870s had successfully diverted water from Lodgepole Creek to irrigate a line of trees, there was little general interest in irrigation in Nebraska until 1890. A few private ditches had been constructed in the 1880s, but the Twelfth Census reports a total of only 11,744 irrigated acres in Nebraska in 1889, with Cheyenne, Lincoln, Scotts Bluff, and Sioux Counties leading in that order. In 1889, the legislature authorized the acquisition of water rights by appropriation, but initially only a few applications were filed. As M. A. Daugherty of Ogallala told the third annual convention of the Nebraska State Irrigation Association in 1895, "Through these early years to speak of irrigation as the solution for crop raising was to invite condemnation upon oneself."[2]

The drought years of the early 1890s caused a marked change in the attitude of many farmers in western Nebraska. Those who had scoffed at irrigation as a solution to the agricultural problems of the arid West were now quick to join the ranks of irrigators. A state irrigation convention was held in 1891, and Robert W. Furnas, whose name had been associated with almost every agricultural advance since territorial times, was elected its first president. The Nebraska State Irrigation Association, which grew out of the convention, met annually and campaigned tirelessly in the interest of irrigation. Its first major victory was achieved in 1895, when the legislature created the State Board of Irrigation to supervise applications for water rights under the law of 1889 and to provide for the organization of irrigation districts. The functions of the State Board of Irrigation were transferred to the new Department of Public Works in 1919 but remained basically the same.

As a result of drought conditions and active promotion of irrigation as a solution to the problem of dry-land farming, the number of irrigated acres in the state increased from 11,744 in 1889 to 148,538 in 1899. The leading counties, in order of acreage, were Scotts Bluff, Lincoln, Cheyenne, Dawson, Keith, and Deuel. Most of the irrigation works built in the 1890s were constructed by private companies, occasionally representing outside capital but more frequently associations of farmers. Most of the state's irrigation was carried on in the Platte Valley, but a small project was opened in the North Loup Valley in 1895, there was some activity in the Republican Valley, and Holt County had 2,218 irrigated acres. The cost of construction per mile of ditch was high compared with other sections having a similar topography, largely because canals of great length were required to bring the water out of the valleys onto the fields. In any event, it was becoming increasingly clear that extensive irrigation works were beyond the capacity of private capital.

The federal government entered the field with the Reclamation Act of 1902, creating a reclamation fund from the proceeds of public land sales in sixteen western states. The fund was to be used in the construction and maintenance of irrigation works; the costs were to be repaid by settlers on irrigated land. This system was supplemented in 1911 by the Warren Act, authorizing the sale of surplus water from federal projects to land already irrigated but in need of additional water.

Through the North Platte Project, constructed under the act of 1902, approximately 150,000 acres of land were reclaimed in Morrill and Scotts Bluff Counties. Water is stored in the Pathfinder Reservoir, completed in 1910, about forty miles southwest of Casper, Wyoming. From the Pathfinder Reservoir, the water is withdrawn through the channel of the North Platte for a distance of about two hundred miles, then is diverted into two canals, one on each side of the river, and conducted to crops needing water. A regulatory reservoir at Guernsey, Wyoming, was completed in 1928, with a net capacity of 61,000 acre-feet. Lake Alice and Lake Minatare, supplementary off-stream regulatory reservoirs, have a combined capacity of 72,000 acre-feet. Further regulatory storage is provided by the Sutherland Reservoir, constructed in the 1930s by the Platte Valley Public Power and Irrigation District with funds supplied by the Public Works Administration. Other major projects constructed with federal funds during the 1930s were the Central Nebraska Public Power and Irrigation District (Tri-County) and the public power and irrigation projects on the Loup River. These projects, involving the expenditure of millions of dollars, not only added to the agricultural resources of the state but added significantly to the income of drought- and depression-stricken Nebraskans during the decade.

Initially, virtually all irrigation was from streams, but beginning in the 1920s, pump irrigation from wells began to be used increasingly, particularly in the lower Platte Valley. During the 1890s an amazing variety of homemade windmills pumped water in the Platte Valley, some of it for irrigation.[3] In 1919 there were only 546 acres under pump irrigation; by 1929 the acreage thus irrigated had increased to 23,452 and by 1939 to 80,673. Since that time it has increased steadily. The state's vast groundwater resources provide excellent supplies for pump irrigation and furnish much of the surface supply of water.

Table 16. Irrigated Acres, 1890–1950

Year	Acres Irrigated	
1890	11,744	< 0.1%
1900	148,538	0.5
1910	255,950	0.7
1920	442,690	1.0
1930	532,617	1.2
1940	610,379	1.8
1950	1,066,250	2.2
1960	2,557,900	5.3
1970	3,998,000	8.3
1980	7,200,000	15.1
1990	8,000,000	17.0

Source: Annual Reports of Nebraska Department of Agriculture and Inspection, *Nebraska Agricultural Statistics*; *Nebraska Agricultural Statistics: Historical Record, 1866–1954*; and *Nebraska Blue Book*, 1992–93.

Less than 2 percent of the state's farmland was under irrigation in 1940, and only eleven counties had more than 10,000 acres each in irrigation. Five of these were in the northwest: Scotts Bluff, Morrill, Sioux, Dawes, and Garden; three in the southwest: Lincoln, Keith, and Hitchcock; and three in central Nebraska: Hall, Buffalo, and Dawson. Together they accounted for 516,696 acres of irrigated land, nearly 85 percent of the total irrigated area in the state. Nearly 40 percent of the state's irrigated land was in Scotts Bluff County, and except for that county, the total irrigated area in the above-mentioned counties was only a little more than 5 percent of their total area. Even in Scotts Bluff, the state's leading irrigation county, a little less than 43 percent of its farmland was irrigated in 1939. Despite these relatively insignificant percentages, however, the impact of irrigation on the economy of the counties where it was practiced and on the state as a whole has been highly significant.

Scotts Bluff County had a population of only 1,188 in 1890 and only 2,552 in 1900. By 1930, however, it had become the fourth most populous county in the state, and in 1940 it ranked third and was first in density of rural farm population. By 1940 the city of Scottsbluff, which in 1900 had been only a little huddle of tar-paper shacks, ranked sixth in the state. In the value of crops produced, the county ran well ahead of every other county in the state, and the margin greatly increased during the dry years. The county's agricultural economy was based to a large degree on specialized cash crops such as sugar beets, potatoes, beans, and canning crops grown under irrigation. In each of these it ranked first in the state and produced from about one-half to three-fourths of the state's entire production. Irrigation farmers also grew alfalfa, corn, barley, and oats for livestock feed, and the county ranked first in the number of sheep on feed. Other aspects of the economy reflected the high efficiency of the county's agriculture. In 1940 the county ranked third in manufacturing and third in retail sales. In freight shipments Scottsbluff was second only to Omaha.

Scotts Bluff County's relative prosperity was shared by the other irrigation counties, where dependable supplies of moisture combined with fertile soil to produce large yields even in dry years. Estimates indicated that irrigation could be expected to increase production as follows: alfalfa, 65 percent; barley, 116 percent; corn, 126 percent; oats, 96 percent; potatoes, 162 percent; and wheat, 131 percent. Irrigation made the sugar beet industry into an important agricultural enterprise that by the 1990s would be producing a crop valued in excess of $50 million annually. As early as the 1930s Nebraska was exceeded only by Colorado in the production of sugar beets. Dawson County, in the central Platte Valley, developed into the nation's leading alfalfa producer, and dehydration processes, developed by Nebraskans, greatly increased the crop's potential uses.

Irrigation thus made the Platte Valley from Grand Island west a veritable garden and greatly increased production elsewhere in the central and western portions of the state. Nevertheless, interest in irrigation fluctuated considerably, even after its value had been demonstrated. Irrigation farming is expensive, and after a couple of wet years people's inclination to depend solely on rainfall grows very strong. Then, too, irrigation, involving the use of water from streams flowing not only through many counties but across state lines, has been the subject of much legislation and litigation.

The state has been involved in controversy and litigation with Colorado and Wyoming over the use of water from the Platte River, and within the state the question of diverting water from one valley to another has on occasion so rocked the legislature that all other issues tended to revolve around it. Moreover, as irrigation developed, it became increasingly more apparent that neither the surface nor groundwater resources of the state were inexhaustible. The North Platte Valley at times faced the prospect of serious water shortages, and farming by irrigation required continuous study and planning to achieve the proper combination of land and water use.

If those who once thought the land unfit for farming were to drive through the valley of the Platte, the Loup, or the Republican today or stand on top of Scotts Bluff and look eastward down the North Platte Valley, they could not help but come to the conclusion that irrigation has supplied at least part of the answer to the problems involved in the occupation of the plains by an agricultural population.

PUBLIC POWER

Coincident with the large-scale irrigation projects of the late 1930s and early 1940s, Nebraska developed a statewide public power system. The system is complicated, and its operation, as well as the motives behind its creation cause much confusion at home and abroad. Although Nebraskans in general do not share the view, in some quarters Nebraska's public power system is looked upon with horror as a monstrous example of socialism. Bitterly fought over and opposed on ideological grounds, the system was brought about, not as the result of any particular political movement, but primarily as the result of an effort to harness the rivers of the state for their maximum beneficial use.

Before 1930 the public had little appreciation of the hydroelectric potential of Nebraska's rivers. The total installed power of all hydroelectric plants in the Platte River Basin in Nebraska was only 10,446 horsepower, and surveys by federal, state, and private engineers were not optimistic over the possibility of installing much more. In 1925 Senator Norris and others tried unsuccessfully to promote federal financing of irrigation and hydroelectric projects in central Nebraska through the Bureau of Reclamation. To be sure, there were a few men, including Phil Hockenberger,

Keith Neville, R. O. Canaday, C. W. McConaughy, and George Kingsley, who shared Senator Norris's concern, but there was little public interest.

The depression of the early 1930s and an amendment of the Reconstruction Finance Corporation Act in July 1932, permitting the Corporation to provide loans to public groups for irrigation and hydroelectric projects, stimulated considerable interest in the state in the development of such projects, not only for their inherent benefits but also for the employment their construction would provide. Groups organized in Columbus, North Platte, and Hastings raised over $200,000 to promote such activity.

Before anything could be done, however, the legislature had to authorize the organization of public corporations to undertake the work. Lawyers for the three groups drew up a bill, and the legislature in 1933, over heavy opposition from the private utilities, passed the necessary legislation. The act as passed and signed by Governor Bryan authorized the formation of public power and irrigation districts as political subdivisions with authority to borrow money backed by revenue bonds. The districts could be formed upon approval by the Department of Roads and Irrigation of petitions bearing signatures of 15 percent of the qualified electors of the area concerned.

The Columbus group was the first to comply with the legislative requirements, organizing on June 3, 1933, the Loup River Public Power District, with headquarters at Columbus. Charles B. Fricke was named president; Phil Hockenberger, vice-president; C. C. Sheldon, treasurer; and Harold Kramer, secretary and general manager. Retaining Arthur F. Mullen, Democratic national committeeman from Nebraska, who had been Roosevelt's floor leader at the Chicago convention of 1932, as its Washington attorney, the district submitted its application for funds to the Reconstruction Finance Corporation. The request was transferred to the newly created Public Works Administration, and by November 15, 1933, the Loup River plan was approved. Construction was started in October 1934, and by March 1937 the project started producing power. The cost of construction had been about $14 million.

Meanwhile, the North Platte Group was under way, formally organized in June 1933 as the Platte Valley Public Power and Irrigation District. It, too, retained Mullen as its Washington attorney. Its plans were approved on November 3, a few days before those of the Loup River district, but construction began several months earlier, in August 1934, and was completed in December 1936, at a cost of $11 million. Whereas the Loup River project produced only power, this district, known also as the Sutherland project, provided both power and irrigation; the Sutherland Reservoir has a capacity of about 175,000 acre-feet. The district embraces Keith, Lincoln, Dawson, Buffalo, and Hall Counties.

The Tri-County Project, organized on November 1, 1933, as the Central Nebraska Public Power and Irrigation District, embracing Adams, Gosper, Phelps, and Kearney Counties, did not fare so well. Its plan, denounced by Mullen as an engineering monstrosity, did not meet Public Works Administration approval and had to be resubmitted. Though Mullen fought the Tri-County project to the last, Senator Norris advocated it before both Secretary Harold Ickes and the president, and finally on September 28, 1935, a revised project was approved. Though the first contracts were awarded on December 14, 1935, construction did not get under way until the spring of 1938. It did not begin furnishing power until January 1941 and was not considered officially completed until December 31, 1943. Its principal feature is Kingsley Dam, near Ogallala, an earthen dam that forms Lake C. W. McConaughy. Built at a cost of $38 million, it irrigates land in four counties and can provide 233 million kilowatt-hours of power annually.

By the late 1930s, with the Loup River and Platte Valley projects completed and Tri-County building, it became clear that the hydros were going to have trouble marketing their power in sufficient quantities to pay their costs of operation and service their debt to the federal government. To provide outlets and to secure extra generating plants to increase their capacity to produce power, the hydros tried to buy the privately owned electric utilities serving Nebraska. When this failed, largely because of difficulties encountered in financing, the Consumers Public Power District was organized in 1939 to make the purchases. Consumers was organized as a separate legal entity, having no connection with the hydros other than agreements to purchase and market their power. The first private utility acquired was in Columbus, and headquarters of the district were established there. Initially, the members of its board of directors were all members of the Loup River board. In 1943, however, the legislature divided the entire state, except five eastern counties still served by a private utility, into seven districts for the purpose of electing a seven-member board to govern Consumers. Altogether, Consumers purchased fourteen private utility properties at a total price of slightly more than $40.7 million financed by revenue bonds. A great deal of public controversy surrounded the acquisition of the private utilities by Consumers and the sale of its bonds. At the center of the controversy was Guy C. Meyers, a New York broker, who handled all of Consumers' negotiations with the private utilities and the marketing of its bonds and who collected nearly $900,000 in commissions and expenses from the district over a five-year period.

Meanwhile, to provide a degree of stability in their operations, to prevent ruinous competition among themselves, and to make possible a refinancing of their obligations to the federal government, the three hydros in 1940 entered into a joint operating agreement under the name of the Nebraska Public Power System. They agreed to pool their production and revenues, thus securing the unification which Senator Norris had tried unsuccessfully to achieve through a "Little TVA" for Nebraska. In 1949, Tri-County, wishing to concentrate on irrigation in its own area, withdrew from the Nebraska Public Power System. It maintained a close relationship with the system, however, selling it the entire output of its hydros and the Canaday Steam Plant.

Electric power for the farms of the state was provided by rural public power districts, also organized under the act of 1933. President Roosevelt had created the Rural Electrification Administration by executive order in 1936 and had provided it with $100 million of work relief funds. Legislation sponsored by Senator Norris made it permanent and provided federal loans to rural electrification districts. In 1964 there were thirty-four rural public power districts in Nebraska. In addition, three electric cooperatives in South Dakota, two in Wyoming, and one in Colorado served areas of Nebraska bordering on those states. The twenty-seven rural systems east of North Platte purchased their power from the Nebraska Public Power System, and twenty-one of them belonged to the Nebraska Electric Generation and Transmission Cooperative, which constructed a 230,000-volt line from the Bureau of Reclamation power site at Fort Randall to a point near Columbus where it connected with the Nebraska

Public Power System. Except for the Southwest Public Power District, the rural systems west of North Platte purchased their power from the Bureau of Reclamation through the Tri-State Generation and Transmission Cooperative, which has headquarters in Denver. The Southwest Public Power District, a cooperative that became a public power district, produced part of its power and purchased the rest from the Nebraska Public Power System. Change had come quickly. In 1929 only 5.8 percent of Nebraska's farms enjoyed the benefits of electric power. By the mid-1960s the rural systems were supplying power to virtually all of the farms and ranches in the state.

Today Nebraska is the only state in the Union in which electric power facilities are either publicly owned and controlled or owned and controlled by member-only cooperatives. There are no private power companies. There are many rural power districts within the state, but the major districts are Loup River Public Power, Central Nebraska Public Power and Irrigation, Nebraska Public Power, and Omaha Public Power. The Omaha Public Power District, established in 1945 and consolidated with Eastern Nebraska Public Power District in 1965, sells half of all the electricity used in Nebraska. The most recent district is the Nebraska Public Power District, which was formed in 1970 as a merger of the old Consumers Public Power District, Platte Valley Public Power and Irrigation, and the Nebraska Public Power System.

CHAPTER 27

Postwar Prosperity

The war years ushered in a period of prosperity unprecedented in Nebraska's history, and as the state approached its centennial in 1967, its
citizens could reflect that the last quarter of a century had been almost
completely free of the drought-and-depression pattern that had characterized so much of the state's earlier history.

In the middle 1950s there was a mild recession; oldsters still harkened
back to the grim years of the 1930s; and much of the state's political
discussion seemed to reflect the desperation of the 1890s rather than the
promise of the 1960s. Yet by 1965 a generation of Nebraskans had been
born and reared to maturity without having experienced the trials that
had beset every previous generation in the history of the state.

An important reason for the state's prolonged prosperity was good
rainfall. In 1941, the ten-year drought that had shriveled crops and
blighted hopes was broken, and with the exception of three years (1943,
1955, and 1956) annual precipitation through 1965 was at or near the
normal mean of 22.84 inches and in some years was considerably above
the mean.

Crop production reflected the favorable moisture conditions. Although yields varied considerably from year to year, crops generally were
good, and some production records were attained. The average yield of
corn in the years 1959–63 was 53.6 bushels per acre and of wheat, 23.2
bushels per acre, compared to a corn yield of 25.7 bushels during the
1920s and 14.9 during the 1930s. Wheat had yielded 15.3 bushels during
the 1920s and 13.2 during the 1930s. The increases in yields were not
solely the result of rainfall but were largely caused by spectacularly improved methods, seed, and fertilizer. Corn and wheat remained the state's
leading crops, but in the 1950s and 1960s soybeans and sorghum, which
had been relatively unimportant before World War II, were increasingly
planted.

Ceremonies opening the fifty-two-mile stretch of Interstate 80 between Lincoln and Omaha on August 11, 1961. Governor Frank Morrison cut the ribbon amid hundreds of cheering visitors who lined the highway near Greenwood. © 1996 by the Journal-Star Printing Co. Used by permission.

Likewise, the production of livestock, particularly cattle, increased markedly. Near the end of the war there were more than four million cattle on Nebraska farms. The numbers declined in the immediate post-war years, but in the 1950s there were again more than four million cattle, and in the 1960s the number went above five million. Hog production recovered markedly during the war from the sharp decline of the 1930s but remained below what it had been in the 1920s and early 1930s. Sheep production, which was higher during the war than it had been before, declined to a position somewhat under that of the 1930s. Poultry production went into a steady decline after the war and in 1964 was less than half the volume of 1945. There was, of course, a steady and continued decline in horses and mules as mechanized power replaced horsepower, and "Old Dobbin" virtually disappeared, as did oats, from Nebraska farms.

Prices, although uneven, soared to unprecedented heights, and, combined with increased production, brought Nebraska farm income to record highs. Until 1945 total farm income had not returned to the record $700 million attained during World War I. Two years later, in 1947, it exceeded $1 billion and in subsequent years either exceeded or so closely approached that level that it came to be viewed as the new standard. By the mid-1960s, farm income began to edge up again toward $1.5 billion, and at the end of the decade it reached the $2 billion mark. It has continued to climb steadily, assisted to some extent by double-digit inflation in the 1970s and by 10 to 15 percent government subsidies in the 1980s, to exceed $10 billion annually by the 1990s.

During the war years, Nebraska's farmers were beset with many difficulties. Farm labor was siphoned off to war industry and to the armed forces. Many farmers, entering the war years with worn-out and inadequate machinery, found it difficult to obtain repairs and almost impossible to secure replacements. Nevertheless, they produced record amounts of food for the war effort; and, after the war, when labor became more plentiful and new and improved farm machinery became available, their position greatly improved.

Nebraska's mid-century agricultural prosperity was not encumbered by the speculation that shackled the apparent prosperity during and immediately after World War I. The number of mortgaged farms decreased from 54,246 in 1940 to 29,509 in 1950, or from 44.8 to 27.5 percent. The ratio of debt to value on the mortgaged farms decreased from 54.7 to 23.1 percent. Taken as a percentage of total farm value, mortgage debt decreased from 27.2 percent in 1940 to 5.9 percent in 1950. Farms have continued to decrease in number and increase in size. There were 133,616 farms in 1935, 102,000 in 1955, and 82,000 in 1965; the average size during the thirty-year period increased from 348.9 to 587 acres. This change both reflected and was a cause of the continued loss of farm population, which between 1940 and 1960 decreased by almost 38 percent.

Although the state's total population increased only slightly during the 1940s and 1950s, the decline in farm population, brought about in part by the farmers' ability to farm larger acreages, was more than

Table 17. Nebraska Manufactures, 1939–1967

Year	No. of Establishments	No. of Employees	Wages	Value Added by Manufacture
1939	1,161	26,739	$34,898,295	$69,087,373
1947	1,341	47,014	119,923,000	260,658,000
1958	1,536	59,000	265,000,000	536,000,000
1963	1,611	64,882	348,034,000	757,000,000
1967	1,608	77,600	479,500,000	926,342,000

Source: U.S. Bureau of the Census, *Sixteenth Census of the United States. Manufacturers: 1939* (Washington DC: Government Printing Office, 1942): 44–45; and Nebraska Department of Economic Development, *Nebraska Statistical Handbook, 1970*: 163, 155.

offset by the increase in urban population. Between 1940 and 1960, total urban population increased by almost 50 percent. Omaha's population increased by 30.3 percent, Lincoln's by 56.7 percent. The smaller cities scored gains, too, and the number of cities in addition to Omaha and Lincoln with ten thousand or more persons increased from eight to nine.

Manufacturing, though still relatively unimportant in the state's economy, increased considerably, particularly in the urban areas. Omaha remained the dominant manufacturing center. Of the 1,536 establishments reported in 1958, approximately 31 percent, or 490, were located in Douglas County; Lancaster County reported a total of 155. Most of the establishments were small: 1,124 had fewer than twenty employees, and only 114 had more than one hundred employees, including five, all in Omaha, with a thousand or more employees. As in the past, food and kindred products were the most important, accounting for more than half of the total manufactures of the state. Other important industries were printing and publishing, machinery, electrical equipment, chemicals, fabricated metal products, transportation equipment, stone and clay products, furniture and fixtures, and lumber products.

Wages and salaries increased markedly after the war, 106.36 percent between 1950 and 1962. The annual rate of growth for these years in all areas was 6.22 percent, ranging from 2.40 percent in farming to 20.82 in wholesale and retail trade.

Table 18. Retail Sales, 1939–1967

Year	Sales
1939	$ 397,196,000
1948	1,317,813,000
1958	1,730,000,000
1963	2,096,000,000
1967	2,555,498,000

Source: Nebraska Department of Economic Development, *Nebraska Statistical Handbook, 1970,* 169.

In response to high wages and farm prosperity, business flourished as never before. Retail sales, a pervasive indicator of general business health, spiraled upward. At the same time, the number of retail establishments steadily declined, from 19,330 in 1939 to 16,907 in 1967, as small businesses and family enterprises faced increasingly heavy competition from large operators.

As on the farms, signs of prosperity were everywhere in the towns and cities. Shabby, run-down buildings were repaired and remodeled or replaced with new structures. The characters as well as the faces of many cities were altered as bright new shopping centers were built for the convenience of a population that was increasingly dependent on the automobile.

THE POLITICS OF PROSPERITY

Since admission to the Union, Nebraska normally has been a Republican state. Its Republicanism, however, has been tempered by a considerable degree of independent voting, and in times of economic stress or uncertainty, Nebraskans have exhibited a tendency to abandon the Republican Party. In the 1890s the Democrats, through the magic personality of William Jennings Bryan and an uneasy alliance with the Populists, established themselves as a significant force in each contest, and they won elections frequently enough, particularly outside of state offices, to make Nebraska a close battleground in most years. When the Populists drifted back into the Republican Party and new voters, unimpressed by the issues of the Civil War, made their appearance, the Republicans, under the impetus of national leadership furnished by Theodore Roosevelt, came under the control of the progressive element of the party. Hence, during the early years of the twentieth century, the dominant spirit in Nebraska politics, Democratic and Republican, was progressive, certainly less conservative than before, but liberal only insofar as it advocated an expanded role for government in social and economic affairs. By the close of World War I, however, Bryan's influence had largely disappeared from the Democratic Party, and the Republicans were generally under the control of the conservative wing of the party in Nebraska as in the nation.

The old populist-progressive spirit was still strong in Nebraska, however, and it centered around Senator George W. Norris. As the rift between Senator Norris and the Republican administrations in Washington widened, that influence tended to gravitate toward the Democratic Party, culminating in the landslide for Franklin D. Roosevelt of 1932. The Democrats, however, were unable to maintain their alliance with the progressive Republicans and, hence, their domination of state politics. The Democratic dilemma came sharply into focus in 1936. Terry Carpenter won the senatorial nomination in the Democratic primary, but the state convention, under prodding from Roosevelt, endorsed the independent candidacy of Senator Norris, and Roosevelt came into the state to urge Norris's reelection.

The Norris-Roosevelt victory in 1936 was the last one achieved by the coalition between progressive Republicans and liberal Democrats. Norris, running again as an independent in 1942, was defeated by Kenneth S. Wherry, a Pawnee City merchant, former legislator, and former chairman of the Republican State Central Committee. This campaign ended Senator Norris's long and distinguished legislative career. Norris was closely identified with the New Deal, a liability in Nebraska politics by 1942. Moreover, he did not have the official blessing of the Democratic Party in the state as he had in 1936, although he was strongly supported by the *Lincoln Star*. His failure to get official support from the Democratic Party, however, was not a major factor in the outcome. Terry Carpenter had secured approximately 17 percent of the total vote without it in 1936, and Foster May got only a little more than 21 percent of the vote with it in 1942. Senator Norris was eighty-one years old, and his advanced age was highlighted by the opposition, but age has not always been a bar to success in Nebraska politics. The major reason for his defeat, it would appear, was simply resurgent Republicanism, spearheaded by an extremely energetic and effective campaigner. By 1942 Norris had lost the active support of many Republicans on whom he had counted in the past.

During the 1940s, the Republicans completely dominated politics in Nebraska. The Democrats tasted victory in a major contest only in 1948, when Eugene D. O'Sullivan unseated Howard Buffett in the second congressional district. Dwight Griswold, who gave the state a calm, careful wartime administration, served three terms as governor, to be succeeded for three terms by Val Peterson of Elgin. Peterson's administrations stirred up considerably more controversy than did Griswold's, and in 1950, seeking his third term, he had a comparatively difficult time defeating Walter R. Raecke, former Speaker of the legislature. Hugh Butler easily won reelection to the Senate in 1946 and 1952, as did Kenneth S. Wherry in 1948.

Most of the major contests occurred in the Republican primaries. In 1948, a group led by Raymond A. McConnell Jr., editor of the *Lincoln Journal*, took advantage of a provision in the election laws which permitted candidates' names to be placed on the ballot in the presidential primary without their consent, to provide voters with a wide choice of candidates; of the seven Republican candidates, including Thomas E. Dewey and Robert A. Taft, Harold Stassen received the largest vote. By 1952 the legislature had changed the election laws so that a candidate could not be entered in the presidential primaries without the individual's personal consent. In this contest supporters of Senator Taft and General Dwight D. Eisenhower conducted vigorous write-in campaigns; Taft received the largest number of votes and Eisenhower ran second. Stassen, whose name was on the ballot, was third. But although the presidential primaries attracted wide attention, they did not bind the delegates to the national conventions.

In the nominating primaries the most heated contests occurred in connection with unsuccessful efforts by Republican governors to unseat Senator Butler: Dwight Griswold in 1946 and Val Peterson in 1952. Indeed, for a governor to move directly to the United States Senate appeared almost impossible. Governor R. L. Cochran won the Democratic nomination in 1940 but was defeated by Butler. Governor Robert B. Crosby ran unsuccessfully for the Republican senatorial nomination in 1954 but was defeated by Carl T. Curtis, congressman from the first district. The Republicans continued their hold on Nebraska's politics by electing their candidates to all state and national offices in the general election of 1954. Victor Anderson was elected governor; Carl T. Curtis, United States senator for the full term; Roman Hruska, senator for the remainder of the late Hugh Butler's term; and Hazel Abel to fill the final two months of Senator Griswold's term. The deaths of Senators Griswold and Butler in 1954 had complicated the senatorial situation. Eve Bowring and Sam Reynolds, appointed to fill the vacancies, did not seek election.

The 1956 presidential year saw the Republicans sweep Nebraska again, although there were some signs that their hold on the electorate was beginning to weaken. President Eisenhower's margin over Adlai Stevenson was down almost one-fourth from 1952, and in the third congressional district, Robert D. Harrison had great difficulty defeating Lawrence Brock. The trend away from the Republicans continued, and in 1958 the Democrats elected a governor for the first time in two decades when Ralph Brooks, superintendent of schools at McCook, who was making his first try for a statewide public office, defeated Governor Victor Anderson, who was seeking his third term. The Democrats also elected two congressmen, Brock eking out a victory over Harrison and Donald F. McGinley defeating A. L. Miller, who was seeking his ninth term as representative from the fourth district. Although stunned by these reverses, the Republicans were by no means routed. Senator Roman Hruska was reelected as were Congressmen Phil Weaver and Glenn Cunningham; the Republicans also elected all state officers except the treasurer.

After giving the state a colorful, controversial term, Governor Brooks died on September 9, 1960. He had received the Democratic nomination for United States senator. Indeed, his death came on the last day he could have withdrawn from the race and only four hours after he had announced that he would not withdraw. The Democratic State Central Committee named Governor Brooks's administrative assistant, Robert B. Conrad, to make the race against Senator Carl T. Curtis, who was seeking his second term. The veteran Minden lawmaker easily won reelection in a Republican landslide that brought defeat to Congressmen Brock and McGinley and victory to all Republican candidates except John R. Cooper of Humboldt, who was defeated in the race for governor by Frank B. Morrison, a McCook and Lincoln lawyer who had made five unsuccessful races for major offices.

In 1962, Governor Morrison again demonstrated his personal vote-getting abilities when he defeated Fred A. Seaton, Hastings publisher and former secretary of the interior, while Republicans won all other state and national offices. In 1964, Morrison won a third term by defeating Lieutenant Governor Dwight W. Burney, one of the most consistently successful campaigners in the history of the Republican Party. This time, however, Morrison was not bucking as strong a Republican tide as he had in his two earlier victories. The Democrats won the state's electoral votes for the first time since 1936; Philip C. Sorensen was elected lieutenant governor over Charles Thone, and in the first district, Clair Callan unseated Ralph Beerman.

POSTWAR PROBLEMS

For Nebraska, like other states, the postwar era brought increased demands from its citizens for services, particularly in the areas of transportation and education. The state's highway system came out of the war in critical condition, wholly unsuited to meet the growing needs of automobile transportation, and educational systems everywhere were inadequate to meet the demands of the increasing number of children of the Baby Boom.

Both maintenance and construction of highways had lagged during the war, resulting in an accumulated deficiency that was aggravated by the existence of many lightly built bituminous roads that could not withstand heavy traffic and by the excessive maintenance required on a considerable portion of relatively new pavement. Some areas, particularly in the Sand Hills, had no hard-surfaced roads, and many rural sections were even without adequate gravel roads. Adding to the overall burden, many miles of streets in the cities and towns were in serious need of repair. There was simply not enough money to do all that was needed, and the basic problem was allocating funds available.

The problem of how to allocate funds was not new. There had long been a conflict between those who insisted that local, rural "farm-to-market" roads should have first priority and those who insisted that the state trunk system should be favored. The conflict centered around the allocation of motor vehicle revenues (gasoline taxes and registration fees), the largest single source of highway funds. The legislature revised the allocation of gasoline tax revenue during each session from 1939 to 1943. In 1947, the cent of gasoline tax going to the assistance fund was allocated to the counties to gravel mail routes. In 1949 the legislature tried to increase the amount of money available for highways by increasing the gasoline tax and motor vehicle registration fees, but these measures were repealed by popular vote, through the referendum, in the election of 1950.

Passage of the Federal Aid Highway Act of 1956, which provided federal aid to the states at a 90 to 10 ratio for the construction of the interstate highway system, added an entirely new dimension to highway financing and construction. Nebraska's principal segment of the interstate was to be an east-west road connecting Omaha with Denver and Cheyenne. From the beginning there was concern and controversy over the precise location of the highway. As finally approved, it ran southwest from Omaha to just north of Lincoln and then headed west to Grand Island; from Grand Island it followed the north bank of the Platte River to Brady Island, where it crossed to the south bank and headed west past North Platte, Ogallala, and Sidney to the Wyoming state line near Pine Bluffs. Controversy over the route was accompanied by controversy over the rate of construction on various segments, particularly between urban and rural interests.

The first contract under the act of 1956 was let in June 1957. By 1965, over 25 percent, or 127 miles, of Nebraska's interstate highway had been built, and it was expected that by 1972, the scheduled completion date, all of Nebraska's 478 miles would have been completed.

Even with massive federal aid, Nebraska's highway problem remained complicated because the relatively small population of the state was required to provide a proportionately very extensive highway system.

Another serious problem facing Nebraska, as well as the country, was the provision of adequate school facilities. Although state, and particularly federal, aid increased markedly, the primary source of school support remained the local property tax. Considerable variation existed from district to district in the support given the public schools, and increasingly school people came to favor equalizing school support through a broader program of state aid. A constitutional amendment providing for state aid was defeated in 1946 by a margin of more than two to one. To strengthen the public school system by reducing the number of districts, the legislature passed an act in 1949 providing for the permissive reorganization of school districts. By 1965 the number of school districts had been reduced from 7,200 to 2,332.

The postwar years brought an increased interest, both public and private, in the diversification of the state's primarily agricultural economy and the conservation of its resources. The state benefited somewhat from the national trend toward decentralization of industry and from the inventiveness and ingenuity of its citizens. Out-of-state manufacturers established branch plants, notably in Omaha and Lincoln; and numerous small homegrown industries developed in various parts of the state. Oil and gas fields in southwestern Nebraska, notably in the Sidney area, added greatly to the economy of the region and the state.

DEVELOPMENTS IN CONSERVATION AND IRRIGATION

There was a growing realization that conservation of the state's water resources was essential to its prosperity. After 1940, the use of irrigation grew steadily. The number of acres under irrigation doubled from 873,960 in 1945 to 1.7 million in 1955 and nearly doubled again by 1965 with 2.9 million. The most spectacular increases occurred in the Tri-County area and in the central Platte Valley. Most of the land in the Tri-County area is irrigated from reservoirs, but elsewhere in the central Platte Valley most of the water comes from wells. Indeed, the vast increase in pump irrigation was the major factor in the increase in the state's irrigated acreage. Acreage under pump irrigation increased from 80,673 in 1939 to 2.1 million in 1965. That is, wells accounted for approximately 13 percent of the total irrigated acreage in 1939 and for approximately 72 percent by 1965.

By the state's centennial in 1967, Nebraskans were benefiting from federal projects built under a comprehensive plan for Missouri River

Basin development commonly known as the Pick-Sloan plan. This plan, which grew out of the Flood Control Act of 1944, envisioned multiple-purpose projects to provide for irrigation, flood control, power, navigation, conservation, and recreation throughout the basin. Major projects completed include Lewis and Clark Lake on the Missouri River, Merritt Reservoir on the Snake River, and a series of reservoirs on the Republican River and its tributaries: Harlan County and Enders Reservoirs, Harry Strunk, Swanson, and Hugh Butler Lakes. In the Lincoln area significant flood control and recreational facilities were provided by a system of twelve reservoirs in the Salt Creek Watershed. Omaha and many smaller communities also benefited greatly from flood control projects.

CHAPTER 28

Into the Second Century: New Realities

As Nebraskans demanded more and more from their government in the postwar era, government grew bigger and costlier. The phenomenon was not unique to Nebraska, however. Citizens throughout the nation had come to expect more from national and state governments and would have to pay more for additional services through increased taxation. In Nebraska, where the chief source of revenue had long been the property tax, those upon whom this burden fell began to protest that the tax system was unfair.

In part the taxation issue was made more compelling because more and more Nebraskans were living in cities, leaving fewer farmers on larger tracts of land to bear an increasingly disproportionate share of the tax burden for the rising cost of government. The number of farms in Nebraska had peaked at around 134,000 in 1935 and had steadily declined to 112,000 by the end of World War II, to 93,000 by 1960, and to just under 82,000 by the state's centennial. Conversely the average size of farms in the state had gone from approximately 350 acres to nearly 600 acres in that same period. Likewise, the population shift from rural to urban areas increased after World War II. This growth was apparent not only in Omaha and Lincoln but in other cities such as Norfolk, Fremont, and Grand Island. In addition, suburban growth detracted from the rural areas, as evidenced by dramatic population increases in Lancaster County around Lincoln, Dakota County south of Sioux City, Iowa, Sarpy County south and west of Omaha, and the western part of Douglas County to the west of Omaha.

As the population trend from rural to urban and suburban continued, the controversy became more heated between those who favored and those who intransigently opposed broadening the tax base to reduce reliance on the property tax. Politicians of both parties tried to avoid the issue. A notable exception was Dwight Burney, who called for a broad-ened tax base in his unsuccessful attempt to unseat Governor Morrison in 1964.

Increasingly, the legislature, struggling to find funds to meet the mounting costs of state government, became involved with the tax issue, and bills providing for a state income or sales tax received mounting support. Finally, in 1965, the legislature enacted an income tax law. Imme-diately, however, referendum proceedings put the measure on the ballot in the 1966 general election, and it was defeated by a margin in excess of two to one. The voters had made their antipathy to the income tax clear. To compound the revenue problems of the state, the voters in the same election narrowly approved by 51 percent another referendum prohibiting the state from levying a property tax. The combination of the two actions deprived the state of its major means of generating income at a time of mounting fiscal obligations and demands.

REPUBLICANS REFORM STATE GOVERNMENT

After six years of Democratic leadership in the governor's office, the voters, in the 1966 election, gave the nod to the Republicans, who made a virtual clean sweep. The only Democrat to win in the partisan contests was James F. Munnally of Omaha, who was elected to fill one of the five seats on the State Railway Commission. For governor Nebraskans elected Norbert T. Tiemann, a forty-two-year-old banker from Wausa and a newcomer to the political scene, over former lieutenant governor Philip Sorensen. Three-term governor Frank Morrison, banking on his popu-larity, had decided to make a bid for the U.S. Senate seat held by Carl T. Curtis, only to be "blasted into political retirement."[1] In the race for congressional seats, Republican Robert V. Denney defeated Democratic incumbent Clair A. Callan in the first district, and Republican incum-bents Glenn Cunningham and David Martin were returned to Congress from the second and third districts.

TAX REFORMS OF 1968

Tiemann had referred to the tax problem numerous times in the cam-paign, insisting that the heavy reliance on the property tax for state

In response to news of the U.S. invasion of Cambodia, some two thousand University of Nebraska students staged a sit-in at the Military and Naval Science Building on May 5, 1970. © 1996 by the Journal-Star Printing Co. Used by permission.

revenues was inequitable in light of current demographic trends and that a broadened tax base was absolutely essential if the state were to continue to serve its citizens adequately. It should have come as no surprise to the public when just hours after his election was assured, he responded to the tax crisis by introducing a combined sales-income tax in the legislative session scheduled to begin on January 3. Tiemann was wasting no time in asserting both leadership and courage. In setting the tone for his administration, he added, "There's a time for dreaming and a time for doing. Well the time for dreaming is over. From here on its going to be a matter of doing . . . of getting Nebraska on the move."[2]

Though he was inexperienced in politics, Tiemann's business experience and leadership abilities served him well in working out compromises with Scottsbluff senator Terry Carpenter, who introduced a bill calling for personal and corporate taxes, and Alliance senator George Gerdes, who introduced a sales tax bill. Governor Tiemann was also successful in urging the legislature to create a balanced tax program incorporating both a sales tax and an income tax that spread the burden of financing state government more equitably among the urban and rural people of the state. Again in 1968 the citizens used the referendum to challenge the taxation plan, but this time they mustered only a 35.6 percent negative vote; ironically the margin of support for the combined sales-income tax in 1968 was close to the margin by which the income tax had been defeated in 1966.

For Tiemann, the taxation controversy was symptomatic of larger issues and challenges facing the state. He believed that the state's leaders must examine current issues realistically and look to the future because the state's future well-being depended on its ability to deal with new realities. The approaching centennial observance provided the opportunity to look at the state's accomplishments as well as its liabilities as it faced the future. In his inaugural address to the centennial legislature, Tiemann pointed to the state's assets and potential for future growth. He noted the state's central geographic position which, he said, was "suitable for the location of transportation industries and for the development of other industries with nationwide distribution systems." He pointed to "a balanced and stable agricultural industry," which, he declared, had "the resources and technical capability to become the leader and the model for our country and the world." He also reminded Nebraskans that they had a strong and "proven educational system and a major university," which could "train our young people and provide scientific assistance to our industries." But, he warned, "Our population has declined in comparative terms. Our state highway system is inadequate. Our natural and human resources have not been fully appreciated or employed. We have a student explosion in our colleges and university and have not increased the size of our faculties sufficiently to give adequate instruction to these young people. We have made virtually no provision for the scientific research facility necessary to attract and support modern industry. And we have been neither imaginative nor aggressive in the operation of state government."[3]

Tiemann was not alone in his desire to streamline state government and make it more efficient. Many in and out of government recognized that times had changed since the major overhaul of the state's constitution in 1919 and called for a constitutional convention to address the problems facing state government. Milford senator Stanley Matzke was the chief sponsor of a bill calling for such a convention, but it failed to gain sufficient support. The *Lincoln Journal*, which supported a constitutional convention as an appropriate tribute to the state's centennial, responded to this reluctance with thinly veiled disgust when it said, "The resistance to holding a constitutional convention to give the state a constitution in time with the times is hard to understand. . . . The last constitutional convention was held in 1919. Life in the state has changed greatly and the state is entering its second century and should not be saddled with a 'horse and buggy' constitution."[4]

Tiemann provided the leadership necessary for the legislature to deal with many of the issues that might have been addressed by a constitutional convention. In addition to the immediate taxation crisis, he led the reform charge to eliminate several outdated tax measures that had become increasingly cumbersome and difficult to administer, particularly a $3.50 per person head tax, a $2.00 per person medical aid to the aged tax, a tax on intangible property such as stocks, bonds, and cash on hand, and a property tax on household goods.

Tiemann also provided leadership in other areas needing reform, some of which addressed the future economic well-being of the state. Particularly important was the creation of a state department of economic development and a state personnel office. The legislature also passed the state's first minimum wage law and fair housing act.

It was an aggressive agenda, but Tiemann could afford to be more aggressive than former governors, in part because he was the first to serve a four-year term and thus had more time to bring his goals to fruition independent of the concern for reelection. Four years earlier, in 1962, the legislature had prepared and the voters approved by a slim margin of 50.4 percent to 49.6 percent a constitutional amendment to lengthen the terms of governor and lieutenant governor to four years. In the 1964 election the voters approved an additional amendment limiting the terms of governors and lieutenant governors to two terms.

Tiemann was the first beneficiary of the new system, and, during his four-year term, the legislature prepared thirty-three constitutional amendments, of which twenty-three found favor with the voters. Some of these also addressed the effectiveness and efficiency of government. Voters approved the creation of a Board of Pardons and a redistricting and expansion of the University Board of Regents. They also approved an amendment providing for long-term loans to college students and lowering the voting age to twenty. And though fraught with controversy, the legislature took the necessary steps to make the Municipal University of Omaha part of the University of Nebraska, thus paving the way for a larger University of Nebraska system.

REFORMING HIGHWAY FINANCING: BONDED INDEBTEDNESS

Of the concerns Tiemann laid before the centennial legislature, the improvement of the state's highway system had the greatest financial implications. In 1967 the report of a study commissioned by the legislature two years earlier put the price tag for completing Nebraska's portion of the interstate highway system and developing additional roads to meet the state's needs through 1985 at $3.2 billion. Few could argue against the need to improve the state's road system or the completion of the interstate highway. The larger issue was the funding of such projects because the state's constitution forbade public indebtedness in excess of $100,000. Many argued, as did the *Omaha World Herald,* that the traditional pay-as-you-go plan for road financing had served the state well. The opponents argued that if the state did not have the money in hand, it could not afford the expenditure. Besides, they argued, if highways were built with borrowed money, the time would surely come when the roads were worn out but the debt remained.

Tiemann, along with Senator Jerome Warner, who succeeded Senator Jules Burbach as chair of the special legislative study committee in 1967, and other supporters of public bond issues for highway construction, including the *Lincoln Evening Journal,* argued that "credit financing could be, in the long run, an economical method of supplemental financing of highway construction" because "inflation could justify the interest cost of borrowing money." They pointed out that "$50 borrowed today could buy more than $50 plus $5 interest repaid at a later date."[5] Further, they argued, the state's roads would always be inadequate if it improved them only when money was available. Other states had obviously discovered the wisdom of bond issues, they argued, because Nebraska was one of only two states that did not allow public indebtedness for highway construction. Tiemann pointed out that the Federal Aid to Highway Act allowed states that issued bonds to speed up construction of toll-free highway systems to apply for federal funds to repay the bonds. It made no sense to Roads Department officials or to Tiemann for Nebraska to fail to benefit from these federal resources.

It was a hard-fought battle, but in the 1968 general election 53.9 percent of the voters approved Amendment 14 allowing the state to issue bonds for highway construction. As a result, Nebraska became the first state to complete its portion of the interstate highway system. Two years later, the voters would again agree to a constitutional change by approving an amendment allowing for revenue bonds for the construction of college and university facilities. Public financing through bond issues would become another new reality for the state in its second century.

RECRUITING INDUSTRY

Underlying all other issues for Tiemann was the health of the economy, and, as he had emphasized in his inaugural address, he continued to believe the state's future depended on its ability to develop a broader industrial base. Again, and perhaps more clearly, he emphasized this theme in March in a televised message kicking off the state's centennial celebration. In addition to the optimism of the moment, he sounded a note of warning. If Nebraskans failed to address issues necessary to encourage industrial expansion within the state, he said, then Nebraska was at risk of becoming "a mere conduit between the states on either coast."[6]

Tiemann's concern for expanding and attracting industries to Nebraska was well founded. In 1967 the state had 1,672 manufacturing establishments, approximately the same as in 1900. Expanding opportunities in this area, however, proved difficult. Tiemann's most important accomplishment and contribution to that end was, perhaps, the creation of the State Department of Economic Development.

Even following the creation of a state agency to foster industrial and business expansion, however, the goal proved elusive, and over the next thirty years Nebraskans would realize that agriculture and agriculture-related industries would remain its best economic prospects. For the time being, however, Nebraskans could share in the optimism for a bright future and an expanding economy.

Perhaps it was the spirit of celebration that caused many to miss other realities that threatened to dampen the enthusiasm. By March 1967, the war in Vietnam was being brought home to Nebraskans even as it was becoming an urgent issue for the nation as a whole. So, too, rumblings from minority groups within Nebraska threatened to mar the optimism.

THE WAR IN VIETNAM

The conflict in Vietnam slipped up on Nebraskans as it did the rest of the nation. Most thought of it as President Lyndon Johnson's war, but its roots went back to World War II. The war had, of course, escalated under Johnson, particularly after August 1964, when U.S. Navy ships had been fired on in the Gulf of Tonkin and the Senate had responded with the Tonkin Gulf Resolution, granting the president broad authority to retaliate as he deemed necessary. The commitment of military personnel to offensive combat and bombing raids was soon apparent by the increasing reports in hometown newspapers of those killed in action.

Before 1967 the state's newspapers had witnessed occasional letters to the editor calling on the United States to "Get Out of Vietnam," but the debate was clearly one-sided in favor of U.S. policy. A representative editorial in the *Lincoln Evening Journal* on November 9, 1966, criticized students at Harvard University for openly confronting and shouting down Secretary of Defense Robert McNamara as he attempted to explain the government's strategy in Vietnam. The paper condemned the students for their disrespectful behavior and expressed relief that Nebraska students were more tolerant.

There were, however, occasional cracks in the facade of respect and tolerance. One such incident occurred at Wayne State College in March 1967, when two assistant professors were asked to resign for their role in instigating an antiwar sit-in. But with the exception of an occasional sit-in or teach-in on the campuses across the state, there was little disruptive behavior on the part of antiwar protesters until May 1970, when students at the University of Nebraska in Lincoln took over the Military and Naval Science Building, which housed the ROTC program. The incident had been motivated by the killing of four students at Kent State University in Ohio by troops in the National Guard. The Nebraska students were enraged by the incident and sought to express their disgust for the war, the military, and the administration. Governor Tiemann wanted to call out the Nebraska National Guard, but to do so might have risked a repeat of the Kent State debacle. The situation was defused when university chancellor Joseph Soshnik prevailed, and university administrators and faculty sought a peaceful resolution by authorizing a university-sanctioned strike and an open forum at which students could express their frustrations with the war.

The late 1960s also provided the backdrop for a growing militancy among blacks in the United States, particularly in the urban areas. Between 1965 and 1968 urban rioting, which first broke out in the Watts section of Los Angeles during the summer of 1965, erupted in major cities across America. And, though mild by comparison to the level of violence and destruction experienced by many cities, Nebraska's largest city, Omaha, where most black Nebraskans lived, experienced its share of racial tension and rioting beginning in the summer of 1966. Omaha could also claim, although for some time it was reticent to do so, the man who by the mid-1960s had become the symbol of "Black Power." Malcolm X had been born Malcolm Little in Omaha in 1925.

At the root of black frustrations were the war in Vietnam, which relied on a disproportionate number of black soldiers, and the reality that the barriers to greater equality and social well-being, held out by President Johnson's Great Society, were being lowered too slowly, if at all. Most black Americans were not experiencing economic and social improvement or greater access to the political system. Although black Americans fought and died for American freedom, the dawning reality, particularly among the youth, was that America was owned, controlled, and governed by whites, and they were fighting a "white man's war" in Southeast Asia.

Racial strife in urban America was exacerbated by long periods of high heat and humidity, which seemed to characterize the long, hot summers of the mid-1960s. In July 1966 on Omaha's Near North Side, the area where most of the city's black citizens resided, temperatures had exceeded 100 degrees for several days and on July 4 reached 103. The Near North Side neighborhood spread out along North 24th Street, the district's main business artery, and police had been cruising the area for several nights in an effort to break up the crowds, particularly at the intersection of North 24th and Lake Streets, the hub of the district's business area. There had been several incidents of rock throwing, both at patrol cars and store windows, and minor vandalism, but the situation escalated on July 4, when the area turned into a mob scene resulting in increased vandalism, smashed store windows, and looting of businesses. Fortunately, there were no fatalities, but a fifteen-year-old black was shot in the leg by an off-duty policeman during a break-in. In response to Mayor A. V. Sorensen's request for assistance, Lieutenant Governor Philip Sorensen, acting for Governor Morrison, who was attending the National Governors Conference, dispatched two companies of the National Guard to Omaha shortly after midnight. The Guard restored some measure of calm, but not before some seventy-eight arrests had been made.

Until the July 4 incident, Mayor Sorensen had steadfastly insisted that the unrest on the Near North Side was caused by groups of young rowdies with little respect for the law. Now, however, he acknowledged that racial issues were involved and needed to be resolved. Julius Williams, who had been sent to observe the conflict in Omaha by the National Association for the Advancement of Colored People, agreed that Sorensen had essentially been correct in his assessment but that he was partly responsible for the situation becoming a racial issue.

[The incident] was not a racial one when it began, but the "press" and mayor Sorensen blew it into something by the way they handled it.

The whole problem . . . stemmed from the fact white policemen were sent to quell a small noisy Negro disturbance in a Negro neighborhood. If Negro policemen would have been sent the whole incident might have been different.[7]

Acknowledging that the problems stemmed partly from unemployment, Governor Morrison offered to help and ordered that an employment office be established in the Near North Side neighborhood to assist people in finding jobs. There were still many unresolved issues, however, and a second wave of rioting erupted three weeks later, on August 1.

Community leaders claimed that tension between area residents and the police had been mounting for a week, triggered by an incident on July 25, when a nineteen-year-old black man had been fatally shot by a night watchman following a burglary. Rioting broke out on August 1 when police attempted to arrest a man for drunkenness at a parking lot at 24th and Lake. In the commotion that followed, a crowd gathered, and when police attempted to disperse the group, it turned into an angry mob that started throwing rocks and bottles at police and store windows. Three buildings were fire-bombed. It took 170 police equipped with riot gear and assault weapons to gain control of the situation. Again there were no fatalities, but numerous people were injured, including one of the rioters, an eighteen-year-old black.

In response to this second wave of violence, Mayor Sorensen, who had been criticized for not involving the leaders of the black community before calling for the National Guard to restore order in July, now tried to enlist the support of community leaders in identifying the causes of the unrest, but there was little meeting of minds. Community leaders criticized the actions of the police, and Mayor Sorensen vigorously defended both law enforcement policies and officials. Governor Morrison, concerned with the series of events, appointed Edward Danner of Omaha, the only black senator in the legislature, to be his liaison to the Omaha black community.

Although little had been resolved, the situation appeared relatively calm for the next year and a half, but beginning in the spring of 1968 and extending into the summer, several more incidents of vandalism and looting occurred. The period of calm was interrupted when presidential candidate George Wallace of Alabama brought his campaign to Omaha on March 3. A crowd had gathered to protest Wallace's appearance at the City Auditorium on March 4, but when a sixteen-year-old black was shot and killed at a vandalized pawn shop in the black neighborhood, a riot broke out.

Twenty-five persons, including concerned whites as well as blacks, called on Mayor Sorensen to take immediate action to avoid future troubles. The mayor appointed a "community committee," made up of Jack Clayter, executive director of the Omaha Urban League; city planner Michael Adams; Rev. Rodney Wead, director of the United Methodist Community Center; Rev. John McCaslin of St. Cecelia Cathedral; and a young barber and activist for black rights, Ernest Chambers, who had walked out on the mayor's meeting convinced that he was incapable of dealing with the issue. Chambers, however, was committed to resolving the conflict, as well as helping the black community, and he proved to be a valuable member of the community team that helped restore calm to the Near North Side. On March 5, he helped quell a disturbance at Horace Mann Junior High School, where students were protesting, breaking windows, and refusing to attend classes. Chambers addressed the students, pointing out the television cameras, and saying: "You are putting on a show for the crackers. They are going to make it look like you are a bunch of thugs. Don't let them make a show out of you. You know they think we're monkeys and we're ignorant. You guys aren't doing anything to help yourselves."[8]

By the end of the week, tensions had eased, but state and local officials decided to move the final games of the state basketball tournament, scheduled to begin in Omaha that weekend, to Lincoln's Pershing Auditorium to lessen the risk of renewed violence. The problems were far from over, however. Tension mounted, tempers flared, and rioting broke out several more times over the next two years until the last major disturbance in 1969 when three nights of fire-bombing and vandalism began on June 24 and again disrupted the Near North Side neighborhood. The disturbance began when a white police officer, who had responded to a break-in call at a public housing project on North 21st Street, shot and killed Vivian Strong, a black teenage girl. In the aftermath of the shooting, five businesses were destroyed by fire and ten others vandalized and looted.[9]

By 1969 both city and state leaders were awakening to the reality that the problems in Omaha could not be addressed simply as law and order issues but that poverty, discrimination, and racism in general were at the root of the disturbances. The legislature took some important first steps that year when it created an equal opportunities commission and adopted a civil rights code that made certain discriminatory housing and hiring practices illegal.

The racial disturbances in Omaha, as well as the youth protest against the war in Vietnam, served to illustrate to Nebraskans that their state was diverse, both in opinion and culture. It was a new reality that would manifest itself several more times as Nebraska moved into its second century when its Native-American inhabitants became more vocal and new immigrants arrived from Asia and Latin America.

The 1970s: Holding the Line

The voting behavior of Nebraskans has long been of interest to political analysts because it does not always follow the voting pattern exhibited by either Democrats or Republicans on a national scale. For this reason it has been categorized by some as more independent than traditional. Historically, party identity and loyalty has often played a secondary role in determining the support Nebraskans have given political candidates. Correspondingly, the Republican or Democratic labels have not necessarily connoted the degree of conservatism or liberalism which at any point might describe the same parties on a national level. The 1970 election, particularly the gubernatorial race, illustrated once again the independent character of Nebraska politics.

Although the 1966 election had been a clean sweep for the Republicans, it was clear as the 1970 election approached that many Nebraskans were nervous about another four years with Tiemann at the helm. Few could argue that the state had suffered from the programs or changes instituted under Tiemann's leadership, but many felt they had come too quickly and at either excessive costs or long-term future commitments. And though it was clear that the Republicans would not deny him the party's nomination for reelection, the strength of that support at the polls was not nearly so certain.

Tiemann's challenger was Lincoln businessman J. James Exon, who had been Frank Morrison's campaign manager in his three successful runs for governor in 1960, 1962, and 1964. A longtime Democrat who had learned Democratic Party politics from his grandfather, who had been active in the Democratic Party organization in South Dakota, and his father, who had been the Nebraska state Democratic Party chairman during the early years of Franklin Roosevelt's presidency, Jim Exon was a shrewd and tireless campaigner. He was also a fiscal conservative, which appealed to voters concerned about the high costs of the programs introduced during

Tiemann's governorship. His campaign staff popularized the slogan "Tax for Tiemann," referring to the sales tax, which Tiemann had promoted as part of his broadened tax base.

Perhaps the incident that helped Exon more than anything else was an offhand comment made by Tiemann when NBC's *Meet the Press* program interviewed a group of midwestern governors in August 1970. Tiemann was asked if the farmers in Nebraska were happy with the Nixon administration's economic policies, and he responded, "I suppose, to make a pragmatic statement, I have never seen any farmers happy anytime, whether it is in prosperity or not prosperity."[1] The Exon election committee immediately launched a campaign of stickers carrying the slogan "I'm a Happy Farmer for Exon." The timing could not have been more opportune; the State Fair had just opened in Lincoln and thousands of farmers could be seen sporting the round paper badges.

Many "happy farmers," as well as other Republicans, crossed over to vote for Exon on election day, giving him 53.8 percent of the vote. It was not a victory for the Democrats as much as for Exon, who was the only Democrat to win in any state or national contest in the election. The Republicans, clearly holding the balance of power, won in every other contest. The *Lincoln Evening Journal* analyzed it as an obvious repudiation of Tiemann. With a measure of sarcasm, a *Journal* editorial proclaimed that Tiemann lost the election because he had led courageously in difficult times and had tried to "move Nebraska off dead center."[2] Even though not fully appreciated by the voters of the state, the governor had accomplished much needed change and pointed the state in the proper direction for meeting future challenges. As the same editorial expressed it:

Probably it was too much to expect that any governor could preside over such profound change as the last four years have wrought in Nebraska and still be returned to office.

Although Gov. Norbert Tiemann has now been soundly repudiated by the voters of the state, the far reaching programs initiated during his term—a new state tax system, a pattern of state support for local governments, ambitious highway and expressway building plans, institutional reorganization—are not likely to be abandoned.[3]

374

Outgoing Republican governor Norbert Tiemann (left) congratulates incoming Democratic governor J. James Exon (right) on his November 1970 victory. © 1996 by the Journal-Star Printing Co. Used by permission.

Exon's challenge would now be to make good on his promises to maintain essential services while curbing the state's appetite for funds. It was no surprise to political observers when he announced in his inaugural address that his budget would be austere but adequate. "No essential services of the state will be sacrificed," he said, "nor will the foundations for the future be surrendered to expedite the present."[4] At the same time, he declared, there would be no increase in the sales and income taxes. In addition to holding taxes at 1970 levels, he proposed the elimination of the sales tax on food and a halt to the sale of Nebraska's school lands, action that would decrease state government revenues.

In part, Exon sought to enhance state services by exploiting available federal funds. If the state paid its required portion, for example, Nebraska cities would qualify for federal matching funds to develop secondary sewage treatment facilities. Federal money was also available for water and air pollution control if the states were willing to pay their share. For Exon, it made sense not only environmentally but economically.

Exon also felt the state could save money by eliminating areas in which state and federal services were duplicated. Nebraska's programs in meat and dairy inspection, for example, could be eliminated because federal inspection programs already existed. Federal help could also be used in correcting abuses, as well as enhancing funding, in the state's welfare programs. In other areas, he declared, Nebraskans would have to curb their economic appetites and "do more with what we have."[5] In education, for example, state aid to local school districts would have to remain at the current level. Likewise, he said, agricultural, as well as industrial development could be furthered by strengthening the already existing vocational education schools. And in the area of road building, Exon took a slap at the previous administration by declaring that he would "shun additional bonded debt unless there is no reasonable alternative."[6]

The Democrat Exon had set a far different tone for his administration than the Republican Tiemann, yet his message eased the anxieties of many Nebraskans, both Republicans and Democrats, who were nervous about the growth of the state budget. "It is not that Nebraskans are necessarily opposed to progress," the *Lincoln Evening Journal* had declared with some sarcasm in the aftermath of the election, "they just don't want to pay for it."[7]

The cautious tone that Governor Exon had set in his inaugural address was a reflection of the concerns of many that, regardless of the progress being enjoyed, Nebraska was spending beyond the means of its citizens to pay. By the latter half of the 1960s, government expenditures in Nebraska were far outpacing either inflation or the personal per capita income of Nebraskans. By the end of the decade the economic productivity of the nation was beginning to slow, but for Nebraska, agricultural prices during most of the 1960s were down significantly from the 1950s. The state's most important crop, corn, which had brought as much as $2.12 per bushel in 1947 and held at approximately $1.50 per bushel through the mid-1950s, was bringing only $1.10 to $1.15 through most of the 1960s.

Given the state of the nation's economy, which by the election of 1970 was beginning to exhibit signs of a worsening future replete with rising unemployment and runaway prices, maintaining, as Exon was fond of saying, "Nebraska: The Good Life" by "holding the line on spending" made not only good political rhetoric but a good deal of sense to many Nebraskans. Exon repeated the popular theme each year in his budget message to the legislature. Likewise, for four years he insisted that the legislature hold the line on taxes as well, maintaining the state sales and income taxes at 1970 levels: 2.5 percent for the state sales tax and 13 percent for the state income tax. It was the only way Nebraskans could continue to enjoy "The Good Life."

While Democrats made major gains nationally in the 1974 elections, voters in Nebraska stood firmly behind Republican contenders in congressional and state posts yet remained happy with the conservative Democrat Exon, supporting his reelection bid in 1974 for another four-year term by giving him over 60 percent of the vote against Republican Richard D. Marvel, veteran state senator and political science professor from Nebraska Wesleyan University, and state senator Ernest Chambers, who had been elected to represent Omaha's Near North Side (District 11) in 1970 and who had launched an independent campaign for the governor's office. Chambers, known for his articulate and polished wit, commented about his third-place finish: "This proves that politically I am no Muhammad Ali . . . sometimes the people, at large, voting blindly in their uninformed ignorance, will be led out of the wilderness and into the swamp."[8]

Table 19. Nebraska Personal Income and
Government Expenditures, 1960–1970

Year	Consumer Price Index (1967 = 100)	% Increase	Personal Income of Nebraskans (per capita)	% Increase	Nebraska Government Expenditures	% Increase
1960	88.7		$2,116		$176,582,000	
1965	94.5	5.8	2,640	24.8	237,538,000	34.5
1970	116.3	21.8	3,759	42.4	452,301,000	90.4

Source: Department of Economic Development, *Nebraska Statistical Handbook*, 1972.

Republicans Charles Thone and John Y. McCollister easily won reelection to third terms in the first and second districts. In the third congressional district, Republicans nominated Mrs. Haven (Virginia) Smith to replace retiring congressman David Martin. It was a close race; Smith won by less than a thousand votes over Democratic state senator Wayne Ziebarth, who appealed the loss in U.S. District Court, but Smith's victory was sustained. Although women had served in the Nebraska legislature since 1925, when Mabel Gillespie of Gretna, Clara Humphrey of Mullen, and Sara Muir of Lincoln were elected, it was the first time Nebraskans sent a woman to Congress. Smith's victory held a certain irony in light of the 1973 legislature's repeal of Nebraska's previous ratification of the Equal Rights Amendment to the U.S. Constitution.

Holding the line on spending, however, proved an almost insurmountable task. In spite of Exon's plea for fiscal restraint, state government spending for 1971 increased by a record 18.6 percent over the previous year. In 1972 and 1973, he was more successful; and the legislature held increases to slightly over 7 percent annually, but by 1974 spending increases were again at double-digit levels and by 1975 they were setting new records.

By 1975 Exon and the legislature were at odds over the necessity of a tax increase. Exon insisted that his legislative program could be enacted without increasing taxes, but the legislature was not convinced that a tax increase could be avoided. To resolve the issue, Exon called the legislature into special session. Exon's foes wanted to adjourn, convinced that his

Table 20. Nebraska Personal Income and
Government Expenditures, 1970–1975

Year	Consumer Price Index (1967 = 100)	% Increase	Personal Income of Nebraskans (per capita)	% Increase	Nebraska Government Expenditures	% Increase
1969	109.8		$3,573		$ 395,904,000	
1970	116.3	6.5	3,788	6.0	452,301,000	14.2
1971	121.3	5.0	3,974	4.9	536,430,000	18.6
1972	125.3	4.0	4,442	11.8	575,479,000	7.3
1973	133.1	7.8	5,187	16.8	616,116,000	7.1
1974	147.7	14.6	5,278	1.8	698,260,000	13.3
1975	161.2	13.5	6,040	14.4	866,032,000	24.0
1976	170.5	9.3	6,209	2.8	983,070,000	13.1
1977	181.5	11.0	6,748	8.7	1,042,162,000	6.0
1978	195.4	13.9	7,581	12.3	1,144,827,000	9.9

Source: Department of Economic Development, *Nebraska Statistical Handbook*, 1972, 1976–77, 1982–83.

legislative program would run the state into the red, and Exon could be blamed; the majority, however, insisted on raising the state income tax to assure a balanced budget. In the end, Exon placed the blame on the legislature for the $40 million tax hike, which placed the income tax rate at the record levels of the Tiemann administration.

The unemployment picture in the state was not as bleak as that of the nation. By the mid-1970s, national unemployment figures reached nearly 10 percent, the highest level since the Great Depression. For Nebraska, unemployment fluctuated between 2.5 and 3.0 percent through the 1960s and slightly higher than that from 1970 to 1974, when it reached 4.3 percent. Unemployment figures for the state reached a decade high of 6.1 percent in 1975 and declined to 5.0 percent the following year, before falling back to 3 percent by the end of the decade.

In other areas, however, the problems of the nation were reflected in Nebraska as well. Annual economic growth for the nation by the mid-1970s was down 25 percent from 1950 levels and inflation was being measured in double-digit numbers. For Nebraska, ironically, the early

1970s were relatively good years for agricultural prices. Total crop values exceeded $1 billion for the first time in 1971 and $2 billion in 1973. By the end of the decade, total crop values in Nebraska were reported at $3.5 billion.

Yet this seemingly rosy picture was offset by rapid inflation, particularly devastating because oil prices had been climbing since the end of the 1960s. Inflation in oil prices reached crisis proportions in October 1973 when the Organization of Petroleum Exporting Countries (OPEC), made up largely of Arab producers, imposed an embargo on oil shipments to Israel's allies, including the United States, in retaliation for their support of Israel after the Yom Kippur War. The embargo caused oil prices almost to double overnight and brought Americans face to face with the reality that they were too dependent upon oil, particularly foreign oil. Even when the embargo was lifted in March 1974, prices continued to rise, causing the nation to look seriously to conservation measures to reduce dependency.

Congress created the Department of Energy in 1977 to deal with the energy crisis and implement conservation measures to lessen the nation's dependence on oil. Governor Exon addressed the legislature in February 1977 to declare a sixty-day energy emergency, asking businesses and public institutions to reduce their consumption of energy and imposing a six-point voluntary program for the public to conserve energy: (1) setting thermostats between 55 and 58 degrees at night and between 65 and 68 degrees during the day; (2) cutting back on electric power usage by refraining from nonessential use to help reduce fuel consumption at electric generating facilities; (3) temporarily converting from fuel oil to coal by industries where possible; (4) reducing the temperature in all buildings and schools to 45 degrees when unoccupied over weekends and holidays; (5) recommending the cooperation of jobbers and suppliers of fuel in allocating fuel to customers; and (6) creating a legislative subcommittee to work with the State Energy Office and the governor to develop conservation proposals.

The energy crisis and rising oil prices pushed the price of gasoline and fertilizer almost out of reach for farmers, who turned to the banks to borrow at higher and higher rates of interest to maintain their operations. They soon found themselves faced with the same crises they had experienced nearly one hundred years earlier with spiraling debt and mortgage foreclosures. The high costs and risks of farming soon took their toll, resulting in a significant decrease in the number of family farms. The number of farms decreased 12.3 percent from seventy-three thousand in 1970 to sixty-five thousand by 1979.

The farm crisis of the 1970s had a major impact on the state's economic health. In spite of efforts to expand the state's manufacturing base inaugurated by the Tiemann administration from 1967 to 1970 and encouraged by the Exon administration, which increased the emphasis on technical training programs, there was little increase in manufacturing through the 1970s. The percentage of the state's labor force rose less than 2 percent from 10.9 percent in 1965 to 12.6 percent by the end of the 1970s. In spite of an increasing shift of population from rural to urban areas by the mid-1970s, and the fact that the greatest percentage of manufacturing employment was in eastern Nebraska, with 40 percent concentrated in Douglas County alone, more than one-third of Nebraska's manufacturing remained connected to the production of agricultural products or farm machinery. By the 1970s Nebraska's economic well-being clearly was still heavily dependent on agriculture.

Some Nebraskans identified easily with the popularization of Exon's image for the state, "Nebraska: The Good Life," but others were not so certain. Just as young Hispanics, Asians, and Native Americans across the nation were learning the lessons of the black experience of the 1960s and expressing their identity as they sought to claim their own niche in society in the early 1970s, so too Mexican Americans and Indians were becoming more visible in Nebraska. Asians, too, would become a visible group within the state in another decade.

To its credit, the Nebraska legislature facilitated advocacy efforts among Indians in the state by creating the Nebraska Commission on Indian Affairs in 1971. The commission was made up of fourteen representatives of Nebraska Indians, distributed tribally and geographically, to review issues of Indian rights and to monitor legislation and provide coordination for activities among the various tribes and state and federal agencies. The legislature also converted the Governor's Commission on the Status of Women, which had been created in 1965, to a state agency in 1971 and changed its name to the Nebraska Commission on the Status of Women in 1975. The following year the legislature created a similar commission to deal with Mexican-American issues. The Nebraska Commission on Mexican-Americans was charged specifically with concern for "education, employment, health, housing and welfare."

Indian issues became a central focus in the 1970s because of incidents either in northwestern Nebraska or across the border in South Dakota. Awareness of the concerns of Native Americans and racial conflict became prominent issues beginning in February 1972, when the body of Raymond Yellow Thunder, a fifty-one-year-old Oglala was found in a pickup truck in a used car lot in Gordon. Two men were arrested, charged and convicted for his murder. In the investigation, issues of racism quickly surfaced. Yellow Thunder had been beaten, stripped, and forced to dance at the American Legion Hall. When the evidence from the investigation became public, the American Indian Movement (AIM) led a protest claiming that the treatment of Yellow Thunder, which ultimately led to a cerebral hemorrhage and death, was symbolic of white attitudes toward Indians throughout Nebraska. In a later confrontation with authorities, Indian rights activists associated with AIM staged a protest in which they took over the museum at Fort Robinson for a brief period.

Less than a year after the Yellow Thunder case, in February 1973, some two hundred AIM supporters raided the trading post at Wounded Knee, South Dakota, also on the Lakota reservation, seizing weapons and ammunition and barricading themselves in a church in defiance of law enforcement officers. The protesters demanded that the government investigate the Bureau of Indian Affairs, as well as the hundreds of broken treaties between various tribes and the United States. The stalemate lasted for seventy days until Indian representatives agreed to surrender after receiving a letter from a counsel to President Richard Nixon offering to have White House representatives participate in the investigation and talks to consider Indian grievances. AIM leaders Dennis Banks and Russell Means were arrested and charged with conspiracy, but the charges were dismissed in September 1974 by U.S. District Court judge Fred Nichol in St. Paul, Minnesota, who cited government misconduct and criticized the actions of the FBI, saying, "I was ashamed the government was not represented better. . . . I didn't realize the F.B.I. was stooping so low." Over the course of the next year and a half, 125 of the nonleadership defendants were tried by U.S. District Court judge Warren Urbom in Lincoln. The trials, which lasted into 1976 before being moved to Council Bluffs, Iowa, served to heighten the awareness of Nebraskans to Native American issues.

The treatment of Indians by whites became an issue again when Jo Ann Yellow Bird, an Oglala, filed a lawsuit against Gordon police, claiming that their rough treatment of her in 1976 had led to the death of her unborn child. The Yellow Bird trial attracted national attention because of the underlying racism which emerged from the case and the fact that an Indian had taken the offensive, charging white police officers with a violation of civil rights. Yellow Bird won a $300,000 settlement in a U.S. District Court in 1979.

During the next decade Native Americans became more active in pursuing legal channels to assert their rights and demand redress for past injustices. Lengthy litigation over the Omaha claims to Black Bird Bend and the attempts of the Northern Ponca to regain tribal lands on the Niobrara represented a new reality in Indian-white relations: the battleground had moved from the prairie to the courtroom.

REPUBLICANS LOSE A SENATE SEAT

When Republican senator Roman Hruska announced in 1975 that he was retiring after twenty-two years in the Senate and would not seek reelection in 1976, second district Republican congressman John Y. McCollister declared his intention to seek the GOP nomination for Hruska's Senate seat. There was speculation that Governor Exon would seek the position, but when he decided not to do so, Democrats were concerned about finding a candidate who could run a strong race against McCollister. Former Democratic state chairman Hess Dyas, who had run a strong campaign for the first district congressional seat against Charles Thone in 1974, announced his intention to run for the Senate, but party leaders, disappointed by Exon's decision, were not united in believing that Dyas could defeat McCollister, who was almost certain to carry Douglas County. In a surprise move, Omaha's Republican mayor, Edward Zorinsky, announced he was switching his party affiliation to Democratic and at the same time announced he would seek the Democratic nomination for the Senate race.

Zorinsky's victory over McCollister was the first successful Democratic senatorial race since the New Deal. It was little wonder that political analysts found Nebraska politics interesting. As the *Lincoln Star* was quick to observe, however, "Although historic in terms of political party fortunes, the Zorinsky Senate win did not work any tumultuous change in Nebraska's conservative political philosophy."⁹ Perhaps of greater interest was Democrat John Cavanaugh's successful bid for McCollister's second district congressional seat, which put a Democrat in the seat for the first time since 1948. In the presidential race, as in most other in-state contests, Nebraskans voted Republican, giving the state's electoral votes to the Ford-Dole ticket with 57.6 percent of the popular vote and supporting Carter and Mondale with only 37.4 percent of the vote.

Political surprises did not end with the 1976 elections. When Republican senator Carl T. Curtis, who had held his seat since 1955, announced his plans to retire at the conclusion of his term in 1979, Governor Exon, concluding his second term as governor, announced that he would seek the seat. Exon's four years as a fiscally conservative governor made him a strong contender, and his victory was not unexpected. He won by a margin of over two to one over Republican Don Shasteen, who had been Senator Curtis's administrative aide but a relative unknown to Nebraskans. Yet, as the *Lincoln Star* expressed it, Exon's win "shattered more than a century of political tradition." For the first time in its 111-year history, both Senate seats were held by Democrats. Republicans regained the governorship, however, by electing first district congressman Charles Thone and hung on to the first and third district congressional seats, reelecting Virginia Smith in the third and Doug Bereuter over Hess Dyas for the seat vacated by Thone. John Cavanaugh, however, won an easy reelection over Omaha Republican business executive Hal Daub, maintaining that seat for the Democrats. Two years later, Cavanaugh gave up the seat, and Hal Daub won it over Douglas County commissioner Richard Fellman. When Doug Bereuter and Virginia Smith were reelected, Nebraska's House delegation was completely in Republican hands, while its Senate delegation belonged to the Democrats.

CHAPTER 30

The Politics of Recession: The 1980s and Beyond

As Nebraskans approached the end of the 1970s, the question for many was, "The Good Life: Where and for Whom?" The nation was again on the verge of recession, the second in less than a decade. Nebraska was also experiencing record inflation with costs of food, housing, and fuel increasing by double digits. The United States was still too dependent on foreign oil. The price of regular unleaded gasoline prices at the pump in Nebraska increased from approximately $.70 a gallon in January 1979 to $.85 in May to $1.15 by the end of the year. In 1980 it exceeded $1.30 per gallon across the state. Grocery bills increased by an average of 10 percent each year between 1978 and 1980.[1]

THE REPUBLICANS BACK IN POWER

After eight years of a Democratic governor, now senator, whose "hold the line" rhetoric and "Nebraska: The Good Life" optimism had become so popular with the voters, the new Republican administration of Charles Thone could hardly launch new spending programs or initiate or increase taxes. Thone had little choice but to ride out the recession and try to limit increases in government spending. Thone's inaugural address mimicked much of his predecessor's. "We must live within our means," he declared, and that "will require the adoption of a state budget and appropriations which require no tax increases."[2]

GOVERNOR THONE AND THE POLITICS OF TAXES

Exon had successfully placed the responsibility for the only tax hike during his administration on Republicans in the legislature, and Thone, as the first Republican governor in eight years, did not want to be linked to higher taxes. Nor were any governors, Republican or Democrat, for the foreseeable future willing to stake their political fortunes on increased taxation. To the contrary, Thone set out to maintain a 7 percent lid on increases in government spending and, at the same time, lower taxes. In December he recommended to the State Board of Equalization that the tax rate for 1980 be lowered from 18 percent to 17 percent of federal liability and, as a symbolic gesture of his commitment to reducing the tax burden on Nebraskans, supported a suspension of the withholding tax for the month of December to provide what he called "not a tax reduction, but an early refund."[3]

THE WORSENING FARM ECONOMY

The efforts of the governor and the legislature could not offset the worsening economy of the early 1980s, however. By 1981 inflation was eating up the small salary gains made by Nebraskans, resulting in declining sales across the state. Manufacturing establishments responded with layoffs. Sperry New Holland in Grand Island announced a layoff of 178 workers, Valmont Industries laid off 75 and reduced some 300 workers to thirty-two hours per week, and the Morton House plant in Nebraska City ceased operations, leaving 175 persons out of work.[4] The Union Pacific Railroad, citing the depressed farm economy, reduced its labor force by 652 persons over the course of the year. Unemployment climbed to over 6 percent to the levels of mid-1970s and many people who had jobs demanded higher wages to offset the crippling effects of inflation. By 1981 teachers, police officers, firefighters, and government employees across the state had joined or were considering joining unions to improve their bargaining positions.

In spite of higher than average crop yields, farmers across the state were also losing ground to the twin effects of declining crop prices and inflation. From May to November 1981 corn prices dropped 27.6 percent from $3.19 to $2.31 per bushel; from January to November soybeans declined 25.1 percent from $7.50 to 5.62 per bushel, and milo decreased 31.6 percent from $5.29 to $3.62 per hundredweight. In addition, several elevators declared bankruptcy, leaving hundreds of farmers holding

Gubernatorial candidates Kay Orr and Helen Boosalis shake hands outside the capitol after the May primaries in 1986, which virtually guaranteed that Nebraska's next governor would be a woman. © 1996 by the Journal-Star Printing Co. Used by permission.

worthless receipts for their grain. For livestock producers the story was no better; higher cattle prices in the spring simply resulted in diminished demand for beef on the part of consumers.[5]

CHOOSING BETWEEN TAXES AND BUDGET CUTS

In October Governor Thone called the legislature into special session to cut the budget further because of a predicted shortfall in state revenues caused by declining sales. Citing a $200 million decline in livestock values and a $1 billion drop in the value of farm commodities, "stifling interest rates," and reports of increased unemployment, Thone told the legislature it had two choices: raise taxes or cut spending. Reiterating his opposition to the first, he asked the legislature to cut the budget by $25 million.[6] The legislature did its job, but not all were convinced that the real problem had been addressed. In December the *Lincoln Journal* quoted state senator Jerome Warner as saying, "Nebraska had not been in such a precarious financial position since the Depression years of the 1930's" and he had "never seen a budget mess like the one that will face the state's lawmakers in January."

Fortunately for Nebraskans, the economy began to recover in 1982. Inflation settled back to just over 6 percent, the first time in several years that it was measured in single rather than double digits. The following year it was reported at 3.2 percent. For the first three years of Thone's term in office, however, it had averaged over 13 percent a year. Thone and the legislature had held the line on spending, managing to keep the annual increases in government expenditures slightly below those of inflation and achieving the budget cuts he had asked for in 1982. Thone had kept the increase at 5.6 percent that year.[7]

DEMOCRATS RECAPTURE THE GOVERNOR'S OFFICE

As the 1982 election approached, political observers were confident that Thone would easily win reelection. The Democratic contender was a thirty-eight-year-old Lincoln pharmacist turned restaurant owner, Robert Kerrey. He was personable and energetic, but he was also divorced. Worse, he spoke with enthusiasm about getting Nebraska moving again. He favored spending more money for education and for soil and water conservation. He talked about making hard decisions "for the benefit of the next generation."[8] He talked about running state government like a business, making sound decisions but willing to take risks. And he risked the ire of Nebraskans by criticizing the Reagan administration's farm policies. "I think agriculture has been abandoned by the Reagan administration. This administration's farm bill is a budget bill designed to reduce the budget, not help the farmer. I don't think we have spoken as strongly for agriculture as we should have."[9]

Kerrey did not fit the image of a Nebraska governor; he was a stark contrast to Thone, as became clear in debates between Kerrey and Thone at the State Fair in September. Thone at first bristled at the inference that he was a colorless conservative but conceded that he didn't mind the label. "After all," he said, "that's what Nebraska is all about."[10] It appeared to be a safe statement; on September 10, the *Lincoln Star* carried an article headlined "Few Voters Swayed by Debate," and two days later it reported that a poll conducted by the *Lincoln Journal-Star* indicated that seven weeks before the election Thone was leading Kerrey 46 to 38 percent.[11] The following day *Lincoln Star* columnist Don Walton commented on the vagaries of Nebraska politics:

This "safe" Republican state is represented in the U.S. Senate by two Democrats. Although we are all used to that fact by now, it nevertheless is amazing, representing nothing short of a political revolution from the days of Carl Curtis and Roman Hruska. . . . And the governorship in this "Republican state" hasn't been "safe" for Republicans for more than two decades. In fact, it has been almost a Democratic preserve since 1958. Since then a Republican governor has been the exception, not the rule.[12]

Walton's comments proved prophetic when Kerrey squeaked out a narrow victory over Thone in the November election, winning with 50.7 percent of the popular vote. The governorship had been turned over once again to the Democrats. Yet the Republicans maintained a strong grip on the rest of state government, even electing for the first time a Republican woman, Kay Orr, over Democrat Orval Keyes for a statewide office. As state treasurer, Orr often sparred publicly with Kerrey, which helped lead to her successful race for governor four years later.

Kerrey proved to be more fiscally conservative than his opponents had feared or than some of his supporters had hoped. Government employees, tired of years of austerity and salary increases that failed to keep pace with inflation, had rallied around Kerrey only to be disappointed by his agenda to streamline government operations. Given his business background and campaign promises, it should have come as little surprise when he announced his plans to study the functions of state government and reduce or eliminate positions of low priority. In so doing, he asserted, "we will pay only for those necessary facets of government which we can afford under realistic tax rates."[13]

GOVERNOR KERREY AND THE POLITICS OF
ECONOMIC DEVELOPMENT

In his inaugural address Kerrey reiterated his campaign promises to emphasize economic development. In March he returned to the legislature to address the issue specifically. Citing a Massachusetts Institute of Technology study which reported that businesses with fewer than twenty employees had generated 66 percent of all new jobs in the nation in the 1970s, he urged the legislators to focus on programs to attract new small businesses as well as issues important to maintaining the viability of existing small businesses within the state.[14] Asserting that "the quality of life in a state can be either an incentive or disincentive to prospective business," he urged the legislature to explore new financing mechanisms for housing, industry, and agriculture, as well as the availability and quality of the state's educational facilities.

To Kerrey, effective and efficient integration and use of technology was the key to small business success, and the colleges and universities of the state should be encouraged to develop programs to provide the latest technical skills. He also created a Communications Industry Development Task Force to study both the development of communications technology through the support of science and engineering and issues of regulation.

Kerrey laid out the most aggressive economic development plan since the Tiemann administration. In his first budget message to the legislature he announced increased funding for the Department of Economic Development, including money for a Food Research Center to assist in advancing Nebraska's food processing industries and the creation of the Small Business Revitalization Program to promote the development of private sector jobs. In addition, he established four business financing offices within the state to assist small business ventures. He also appointed the Nebraska State Job Training Council to hold hearings to determine the job training needs across the state, and he announced that the Nebraska Department of Labor would train some fourteen hundred youths through the 1983 Summer Youth Employment program.

During the campaign Kerrey had repeatedly criticized the Reagan farm policies and Thone for failing to represent the interests of Nebraska farmers during his term as congressman and more recently as governor. Upon taking office, Kerrey created the Agricultural Recovery Program Task Force to work with the Farmers Home Administration, Nebraska bankers, and representatives from agriculture-related industries in the state to develop a new method of providing financial support for the state's farmers and ranchers. The result was the Nebraska Investment Finance Authority (NIFA), a consolidation of three existing boards, to issue bonds for housing, agriculture, and development.

Kerrey also emphasized energy conservation. He announced that the Nebraska Energy Office would have $3.8 million to inject into the construction industry through weatherization programs that encouraged insulation, energy-efficient windows, and new energy systems for government, schools, hospitals, and elderly and low-income housing.

A DIFFERENT KIND OF GOVERNOR

After twelve years of "holding the line" and a mentality of austerity, Kerrey's energetic and enthusiastic leadership was psychologically uplifting. Kerrey captured the imagination of Nebraskans, in part by his exuberance and charisma and in part by his association with Hollywood actress Debra Winger, who arrived on location in Lincoln in 1985 as a major player in the film, *Terms of Endearment*. Kerrey and Winger were soon being observed lunching at K's Restaurant, the site of some of the filming, and at jazz concerts at the Zoo Bar and other nightspots in Lincoln. Far from being scandalized, Nebraskans seemed amused by the youthful Kerrey and Winger. The public even seemed amused when Winger, while driving the governor's vehicle, was stopped by a patrolman for speeding and operating a motor vehicle with an expired driver's license. In response to the incident, Weird Wally, a Lincoln used car dealer, started a fund to buy Debra her own car so she wouldn't have to drive the governor's vehicle, which was provided by the taxpayers. Winger gave the car back and donated the proceeds to charity.

THE COLLAPSE OF FINANCIAL INSTITUTIONS

In spite of the public's general affirmation of Kerrey's activities, his administration was marred by some serious concerns. The failure of the Commonwealth Savings Company in Lincoln in November 1983 touched off an investigation that exposed the weaknesses of such state institutions as well as the inadequacy of the Nebraska Depository Institution Guarantee Corporation (NDIGC), which had been created by the legislature to protect depositors in state-chartered banking institutions. Some sixty-seven hundred depositors, who had assumed that NDIGC provided protection similar to that provided federal banks through the Federal Deposit Insurance Corporation, lost $67 million and found themselves at the mercy of an unsympathetic legislature.

The investigation that followed the Commonwealth collapse led to criminal charges against Commonwealth's president, S. E. Copple, and several others associated with the institution. State banking director Paul Amen resigned during the controversy, and Attorney General Paul Douglas was impeached by the legislature for his personal business dealings with Commonwealth and his conduct during the investigation. Convicted of perjury, Douglas was later acquitted in a trial before the Nebraska Supreme Court. The beleaguered Douglas was subsequently indicted by a Lancaster County grand jury for perjury and obstruction of government, found guilty of the perjury charges, and resigned his post as attorney general. In 1985 the legislature approved an $8.5 million settlement for depositors of the failed Commonwealth, an amount that fell far short of covering the actual losses incurred by depositors. By 1989 depositors had recovered slightly over half of their losses, and in 1995 surviving depositors were still seeking redress through litigation.

The Commonwealth collapse was just the beginning. Six more banks were closed by the state the following year in Blair, David City, Verdigre, Kilgore, Cody, and Uehling, and the State Security Savings Company of Lincoln closed and filed for reorganization. In 1985 thirteen more Nebraska banks failed, followed by nine more the following year. Most of the failures were directly tied to farm loans and the struggling farm economy. Analysts reported that 25 percent of the loans made by each of the banks were related to agriculture. In spite of a record harvest in 1985, low commodity prices left farmers with little ability to repay their loans.

The slumping farm economy was reflected throughout Nebraska. As farmland values continued to decline, the economy of small towns across the state became depressed. Many forecast that the state was headed into another recession, though it was hardly out of the last one. Economic forecasters estimated that the state would face a $41 million deficit by the end of the year. Because of the depressed economy, Kerrey called the legislature into special session in October 1985 to cut the budget by more than $17 million and pass a one-year retroactive increase in the state sales tax. Also in October he announced that he would not seek reelection, "lacking the desire," he said, "to be governor for another four years."[15]

THE YEAR OF THE WOMAN: ORR AND BOOSALIS

Kerrey's unexpected decision not to seek reelection was welcomed by Republicans and State Treasurer Kay Orr. Orr's disagreements with Kerrey over fiscal policy had been publicly aired several times during his first three years in office. Orr had helped manage Charles Thone's successful race for the governor's office in 1978 and had subsequently served as his chief of staff. Her fiscal stance and outspokenness placed her in a prime position for the Republican nomination, which she received in May 1986. And in a surprising turn of events, Helen Boosalis, who had served three terms on Lincoln's City Council and been elected to two terms as mayor beginning in 1975, emerged from the May primaries as the Democratic nominee.

Nebraska, assured of a female governor, was soon making national news. It was the first time in the nation's history that two women faced each other in a gubernatorial race. Indeed, it seemed to be the "Year of the Woman" in politics as 130 women across the nation were engaged in national or statewide races, nine of them for governor. Nebraska would add another political first to its list when Orr emerged victorious as the first Republican woman governor in the nation.

Both women had waged an aggressive campaign, but Orr successfully capitalized on her fiscal conservatism and strong statements opposing any tax increase. President Ronald Reagan came to Nebraska to campaign personally for Orr, but whether influenced by the president's visit or simply frightened by Kerrey's aggressive leadership or concerned about Nebraska's sluggish economy and prospects of future financial hardship, Nebraskans gave the office back to the Republicans by a margin of over thirty thousand votes. Orr won in seventy-nine of Nebraska's ninety-three

393

counties, including Douglas County, which had long been a safe haven for the Democratic Party in the state.

THE REPUBLICANS AGAIN

The 1986 election represented a solid victory for Republicans. Orr won the governor's race with nearly 53 percent of the vote. Doug Bereuter won a fifth congressional term from the first district against Lincoln attorney Steve Burns with 65 percent of the vote; Hal Daub won a fourth congressional term from the second district against Omaha City councilman Walt Calinger with 59 percent of the vote; and Virginia Smith claimed 70 percent of the vote in the third congressional district in her race for a seventh term, defeating Kearney attorney Scott Sidwell. State offices remained solidly in Republican hands as well with Secretary of State Allen Beerman and Auditor Ray Johnson winning reelection and Frank Marsh and Robert Spire winning their races for state treasurer and attorney general. And the following March, when Democratic senator Ed Zorinsky died of a heart attack at the age of fifty-eight, Governor Orr appointed Republican businessman David Karnes to fill his unexpired term.

Orr had broken the Democrats' solid hold on Nebraska Senate seats, but it was a short-lived victory. In the 1988 election, Bob Kerrey reentered the political arena to challenge Karnes's bid for election, and Nebraskans responded enthusiastically, giving him a winning margin of over one hundred thousand votes.

GOVERNOR ORR AND THE POLITICS OF TAX REVISION

Taxation issues had been at the forefront of every administration since the major revisions during the late 1960s, and Orr was forced to address them. Based on federal tax liabilities, the Nebraska income tax revenues were placed in jeopardy by the Tax Reform Act passed by Congress in 1986. Estimates by the Nebraska Department of Revenue indicated that the state stood to lose as much as $24 million in 1987–88 and $36 million in 1988–89. Nebraska had no choice but to increase the individual's percentage of federal liability above the current 19 percent or change its tax system. Orr opted for the latter and presented a plan in which individuals would pay an average of 3.47 percent of their adjusted gross income. In an effort to improve the state's ability to attract new industry and to address the concerns of several corporations demanding tax relief, Orr's tax plan altered the formula by which corporations calculated their tax liability. By eliminating corporate property and payroll as factors in the computation, the plan reduced the tax liability of in-state corporations by $21 million spread over a five-year period.

Orr insisted that her plan did not raise taxes and that it allowed the state to collect no additional tax dollars. In effect, however, it did increase the tax burden on lower and middle incomes, while lessening it on higher incomes. And though she insisted that the program would raise only the necessary dollars for the budget, it was anything but "revenue neutral"; the state actually collected $18 million in surplus revenue over the course of the following year.[16] Orr also supported revisions in the Homestead exemption which were predicted to create savings in excess of $5 million, but the bill as amended and finally passed by the legislature was projected to save only about $400,000 per year. In addition to altering Nebraska's tax system, Orr attempted to cut budget expenditures by streamlining some facets of state government and eliminating others, but though the governor and the legislature may have shared the same goals of reducing the budget, they did not always agree on the methods. Orr advocated phasing out state funding for the advocacy agencies, the Commission on the Status of Women, the Native American Commission, and the Mexican-American Commission, by reducing their funding by one-third over each of the successive two years, while exploring sources of alternative funding. The legislature, however, disagreed and restored funding to all three agencies at the close of the session. Funding for those agencies had been eliminated in 1985 and partially restored in 1986. The governor did succeed in abolishing the Liquor Control Commission, transferring its enforcement functions to the State Patrol and its tax functions to the Department of Revenue.

TAX INCENTIVES FOR INDUSTRY

Kay Orr placed economic development issues at the forefront of her administration. She insisted that the legislature needed to improve the competitive ability of the state to attract new industries, as well as to encourage present industries to expand. For Orr, the key incentive was tax relief. The administration's bill, LB775, consumed most of the legislature's 1987 session. As finally passed, it provided a 5 percent tax credit on salaries paid to new employees and a 10 percent credit on investments in expansion for companies that created thirty new jobs and invested $3 million. In addition, the law allowed a property tax exemption on mainframe computers and aircraft, provided the company created one hundred new jobs and invested more than $10 million in expansion. In either case, the credits could be carried forward for fifteen years. In a companion measure passed by the legislature, small businesses, as well as farm and ranch operations, were allowed $1,000 tax credits for each new employee and for each $100,000 invested in expansion.

Orr and legislative proponents of tax incentives for business growth insisted that "this would send a message to Nebraska Corporations that the state wants to keep them and tell companies outside Nebraska that the state wants them to locate here." These concerns were well founded. In 1967, Governor Tiemann decried that the 1,672 manufacturing establishments in Nebraska were about the same number that the state boasted at the beginning of the century. By 1970 the number had slipped to 1,634. By 1975 the census of manufacturers indicated some growth, showing 1,719 manufacturing establishments in Nebraska. At the beginning of Orr's term as governor, the number had increased to 1,806, but the total number of employees was only 87,438 compared to 77,000 in 1967.[17] Manufacturing was not offsetting the flight from the farms to any significant degree.

Some followed Orr's lead, convinced that tax incentives were the way to attract industry, but others were not so convinced. Some felt the legislature was being "blackmailed" by large corporations such as ConAgra, which suggested that it might leave Nebraska to locate in a state with more favorable corporate taxation. Others felt that over the long run the costs would become far greater than any benefits the state would realize.[18] The debate over the impact of this measure continues today and emerges each time the state loses another bid for a major outside corporation. In the recent past those losses have included IBM, Mercedes-Benz, and Micron Technologies.

In 1990 the legislature passed a bill requiring the state Department of Revenue to report annually the employment and investment statistics related to LB775. The March 1991 report revealed that from the passage of the law in 1987 through December 1990, a total of seventy-nine companies had been approved for investment and new job credits of $123.6 million for the creation of 13,138 new jobs and slightly more than $1.5 billion in plant investments.[19] Through December 1991, the number of companies had increased to one hundred that had been approved for investment and new job credits of $208.4 million for the creation of 18,366 new jobs and $2.4 billion in plant investments.[20]

THE BRAIN DRAIN?

"A lot of good people came out of Nebraska; and the better they were the faster they came!" So commented a network television late-night talk show host, who had been born and raised in Nebraska, to another network television late-night talk show host when asked about the co-incidence that both were from Nebraska. It was in the 1970s, and some, maybe many, Nebraskans found the remark less than amusing. For some, particularly in state government and educational institutions, it hit a raw nerve. Nebraska governors from Tiemann through Orr were plagued with the fact that many Nebraskans were growing up and being educated in the state, only to leave for better opportunities elsewhere. The phenomenon came to be known as the "Brain Drain."

Tiemann had addressed the issue in the late 1960s, when he urged Nebraskans to adopt an aggressive economic development program to attract industry and provide the kinds of jobs for which young Nebraskans were being trained in the state's colleges and universities. Governors since have placed greater or lesser importance on the phenomenon and the degree of its reality. In a study conducted by the Federal Reserve Bank of Kansas City between 1985 and 1990, it was estimated that Nebraska lost more than thirteen thousand highly trained professionals during the period, the equivalent of the loss of over $1.23 billion in personal income.

THE 1990 ELECTIONS

Although the 1990 gubernatorial election would continue the same pattern of changing parties, it had an exciting beginning, particularly for

Democrats, because voters had to wait forty-eight days for a recount of the May primary vote to find out who they had nominated to challenge incumbent Kay Orr. The Republicans offered a degree of excitement during the primaries as top-ranking Republican officials and the president came to Nebraska to campaign for the reelection of their Republican woman governor, but on the Democratic side, voters had difficulty deciding between Omaha attorney Ben Nelson and former Kerrey campaign manager and aide Bill Hoppner. On successive days after the primary it appeared that first one had won, then the other. A statewide recount ultimately determined Nelson the winner by forty-two votes.

For Nelson the primary was just the beginning. The general election in November was one of the closest in Nebraska history, and Nelson waited three days for Orr to concede. In the final count, Nelson won by only 4,030 votes. With 0.9 percent of the votes going to write-in candidates, Nelson received 49.9 percent of the vote and Orr received 49.2; it was one of the closest gubernatorial elections in the state's history. Issues centered around taxation, government expenditures, economic development, farm policies, and school financing, all of which divided Nebraskans as they approached the last decade of the millennium.

TOWARD A NEW MILLENNIUM

Nearly a quarter-century since their centennial celebration, Nebraskans continue to struggle with many of the same issues. Their society is still heavily dependent on agriculture yet is seeking a broader economic diversity through the expansion of industry. The out-migration of Nebraskans remains a concern; the fairness of the tax system is still being debated; urban residents clamor for sales and income tax relief and farmers demand property tax relief.

Political fortunes rise and fall on the answers; since the centennial voters have systematically rotated the governor's office between Republicans and Democrats, seemingly dissatisfied with the most recent party in power. Indeed, since 1978, there has been little inclination to grant a second chance to any governor, whether Democrat or Republican. Such are the vagaries of the Nebraska political landscape.

As Nebraskans look to the new century, there is much in their past to celebrate. Both creative and pragmatic solutions have resolved the challenges of the past and will likely do so in the future. The land and the pioneer spirit of its people remain Nebraska's most valuable resources for meeting the challenges of the twenty-first century.

APPENDIX I. OFFICIALS OF THE TERRITORY OF NEBRASKA, 1854–1867

GOVERNORS

Francis Burt	October 16, 1854, to October 18, 1854 (Died)
Thomas B. Cuming	October 18, 1854, to February 20, 1855
Mark W. Izard	February 20, 1855, to October 25, 1857 (Resigned)
Thomas B. Cuming	October 25, 1857, to January 12, 1858
William A. Richardson	January 12, 1858, to December 5, 1858 (Resigned)
J. Sterling Morton	December 5, 1858, to May 2, 1859
Samuel W. Black	May 2, 1859, to February 24, 1861 (Resigned)
J. Sterling Morton	February 24, 1861, to May 6, 1861
Alvin Saunders	May 15, 1861, to March 27, 1867

SECRETARIES

Thomas B. Cuming	August 13, 1854, to March 12, 1858
John B. Motley	March 23, 1858, to July 12, 1858
J. Sterling Morton	July 12, 1858, to May 6, 1861
Algernon S. Paddock	May 6, 1861, to February 21, 1867

APPENDIX II: GOVERNORS OF THE STATE OF NEBRASKA

David Butler (R)	1867–71
William H. James (R), Acting	1871–73
Robert W. Furnas (R)	1873–75
Silas Garber (R)	1875–79
Albinus Nance (R)	1879–83
James W. Dawes (R)	1883–87
John M. Thayer (R)	1887–91
James E. Boyd (D)	1891
John M. Thayer (R)	1891–92
James E. Boyd (D)	1892–93
Lorenzo Crounse (R)	1893–95
Silas A. Holcomb (Fusion)	1895–99
William A. Poynter (Fusion)	1899–1901
Charles H. Dietrich (R)	1901
Ezra P. Savage (R)	1901–3
John H. Mickey (R)	1903–7
George L. Sheldon (R)	1907–9
Ashton C. Shallenberger(D)	1909–11
Chester H. Aldrich (R)	1911–13
John H. Morehead (D)	1913–17
Keith Neville (D)	1917–19
Samuel R. McKelvie (R)	1919–23
Charles W. Bryan (D)	1923–25

Adam McMullen (R)	1925–29
Arthur J. Weaver (R)	1929–31
Charles W. Bryan (D)	1931–35
Robert Leroy Cochran (D)	1935–41
Dwight Griswold (R)	1941–47
Val Peterson (R)	1947–53
Robert B. Crosby (R)	1953–55
Victor E. Anderson (R)	1955–59
Ralph G. Brooks (D)	1959–60
Dwight W. Burney (R)	1960–61
Frank B. Morrison (D)	1961–67
Norbert T. Tiemann (R)	1967–71
J. James Exon (D)	1971–79
Charles Thone (R)	1979–83
J. Robert Kerrey (D)	1983–87
Kay A. Orr (R)	1987–91
E. Benjamin Nelson (D)	1991–

APPENDIX III, RAINFALL IN NEBRASKA, BY DIVISION, 1865–1993

	Division					Division		
Year	*East*	*Central*	*West*	*State*	*Year*	*East*	*Central*	*West*	*State*
1865	29.8				1901	24.4	25.5	19.2	23.0
1866	27.1				1902	38.1	28.7	21.7	29.5
1867	28.5				1903	36.9	26.5	16.6	26.7
1868	39.6				1904	28.1	25.1	17.5	23.5
1869	43.9				1905	36.1	32.4	26.0	31.5
1870	26.3				1906	30.5	26.6	21.0	26.0
1871	31.9				1907	26.3	18.3	15.8	20.1
1872	31.9				1908	35.1	23.8	20.6	26.5
1873	31.8				1909	32.9	21.7	19.3	24.6
1874	33.0				1910	21.2	16.9	11.9	16.7
1875	36.7				1911	25.5	23.0	15.0	21.2
1876	32.6	15.7	11.4	19.9	1912	24.4	18.7	21.2	21.5
1877	36.5	21.8	15.5	24.6	1913	27.0	21.3	17.3	21.9
1878	29.4	23.5	20.5	24.4	1914	27.0	20.6	14.6	20.7
1879	28.8	24.6	20.7	24.7	1915	41.0	36.4	29.4	35.6
1880	25.9	21.5	13.1	20.2	1916	22.6	18.8	15.1	18.8
1881	33.0	31.6	23.3	29.3	1917	24.5	20.5	16.6	20.5
1882	28.7	23.6	16.7	23.0	1918	24.9	21.6	20.6	22.4
1883	37.3	29.3	24.6	30.4	1919	32.6	24.5	18.2	25.1
1884	29.5	21.4	20.6	23.8	1920	28.5	24.9	20.0	24.5
1885	28.7	28.1	19.9	25.6	1921	24.6	21.0	15.9	20.5
1886	27.8	27.1	14.5	23.1	1922	24.2	18.7	17.6	20.2
1887	23.3	22.0	20.0	21.8	1923	30.7	28.7	25.2	28.2
1888	27.8	22.9	16.5	22.4	1924	26.6	19.9	16.3	20.9
1889	26.4	22.5	18.0	22.3	1925	25.4	19.0	18.0	20.8
1890	21.7	16.1	13.6	17.2	1926	26.0	19.4	17.1	20.8
1891	36.8	29.8	25.3	30.6	1927	26.8	22.6	21.7	23.7
1892	26.8	23.6	22.6	24.3	1928	26.4	21.4	20.6	22.8
1893	22.3	16.6	9.9	16.3	1929	27.3	22.1	18.9	22.7
1894	17.2	12.3	11.2	13.5	1930	26.7	27.8	23.3	25.9
1895	22.4	20.1	14.6	19.0	1931	27.1	17.9	12.9	19.3
1896	35.6	25.3	16.6	25.9	1932	26.3	20.0	15.3	20.5
1897	28.6	24.4	18.0	23.7	1933	21.6	20.5	18.6	20.2
1898	24.9	19.8	17.1	20.6	1934	17.1	13.7	12.1	14.3
1899	25.9	18.7	14.1	19.6	1935	26.7	22.2	19.0	22.6
1900	33.0	22.4	16.4	23.9					

Appendix 3 / Rainfall in Nebraska

	Division						Division			
Year	East	Central	West	State		Year	East	Central	West	State
1936	16.1	14.4	12.8	14.4		1966	21.7	18.5	16.1	19.4
1937	21.3	18.3	13.4	17.7		1967	27.6	21.2	19.1	23.3
1938	27.0	20.5	19.2	22.2		1968	29.1	21.1	16.9	23.6
1939	18.9	16.7	13.3	16.3		1969	28.5	22.8	15.6	24.0
1940	22.6	15.8	13.6	17.4		1970	25.9	17.7	14.8	20.4
1941	28.7	24.0	20.7	24.5		1971	26.9	24.1	18.4	24.4
1942	26.8	25.5	23.3	25.2		1972	30.7	22.0	17.2	24.7
1943	21.4	16.8	13.4	17.2		1973	38.6	28.3	20.5	31.2
1944	35.1	26.6	20.4	27.4		1974	19.2	15.4	11.2	16.3
1945	29.2	20.4	18.6	22.7		1975	25.9	18.1	14.1	20.6
1946	27.6	27.1	19.0	24.6		1976	19.6	17.8	13.3	17.9
1947	27.9	22.6	19.6	23.4		1977	35.5	29.7	18.8	30.3
1948	27.6	19.9	16.6	21.6		1978	28.5	20.4	18.3	23.2
1949	30.5	25.3	19.8	25.4		1979	30.9	25.5	18.2	26.6
1950	28.0	23.5	16.1	22.7		1980	21.8	16.9	13.1	18.3
1951	38.8	29.5	22.4	30.5		1981	27.2	26.1	17.0	25.4
1952	28.8	16.9	14.4	20.3		1982	36.3	25.9	21.2	29.2
1953	22.7	21.5	16.9	20.4		1983	31.5	24.3	19.0	26.3
1954	26.1	17.6	14.4	19.6		1984	36.0	25.3	15.4	28.1
1955	18.8	16.4	17.7	17.4		1985	27.8	23.4	14.7	27.9
1956	19.4	15.1	12.0	16.3		1986	36.6	23.1	20.1	27.8
1957	32.0	27.0	20.6	28.1		1987	32.3	26.2	18.1	27.5
1958	28.6	22.4	18.3	24.2		1988	19.7	21.6	17.0	20.3
1959	33.3	21.5	15.8	25.2		1989	23.4	15.2	12.0	17.1
1960	31.0	22.5	13.8	24.6		1990	26.5	21.1	16.7	22.5
1961	29.3	21.8	17.2	24.0		1991	27.7	21.8	16.7	23.4
1962	28.6	27.4	19.0	26.8		1992	34.3	24.0	17.1	25.8
1963	25.0	20.2	17.0	21.6		1993	41.2	32.1	21.8	32.1
1964	28.1	18.6	11.4	21.3						
1965	35.7	29.6	21.7	30.9		Mean	27.7	22.3	17.9	22.8

Source: Data for 1865 to 1875 are estimates from the Nebraska State Board of Agriculture. See State of Nebraska, *Transactions of the State Board of Agriculture: From September 1876 to September 1879* (Lincoln: Journal Company, State Printers, 1880), 107. Data for 1876 to 1954 are from the U.S. Weather Bureau and compiled by the Nebraska Department of Agriculture and Inspection. See Nebraska Department of Agriculture and Inspection, *Nebraska Agricultural Statistics: Historical Record, 1866–1954* (Chicago: State-Federal Division of Agricultural Statistics, 1957), 173. Data for 1955 to 1991 are compiled from weather data recorded in the *Nebraska Blue Book, 1992–93.* Data for 1993–94 are compiled from the annual reports of the Nebraska Department of Agriculture, *Nebraska Agricultural Statistics.*

Table 1. Nebraska Farm and Crop Values, 1860–1994

Year	No. of farms	Average size of farms (acres)	Average value of farms	Average value per acre	% Change in acre values (annual average)	Value of all crops (x 1,000)	% Change value of all crops (annual average)
1860	3,000	226.3	$ 1,293	$ 5.82			
1867				3,798			
1870	12,301	172.8	2,520	10.68	8.4%	4,196	14.5
1875						9,843	26.9
1880	63,387	156.9	2,322	10.65	0.0	29,457	39.9
1885						52,460	15.6
1890	113,608	190.1	4,505	18.63	7.5	89,589	14.2
1895						42,752	(−10.5)
1900	121,525	246.1	6,155	19.31	0.4	97,504	25.6
1905						139,298	8.6
1910	129,678	297.8	16,038	49.95	15.9	176,613	5.4
1915						187,291	1.2
1920	124,417	339.4	33,771	87.91	7.6	314,139	13.5
1925	128,000	329.0	19,760	60.00	(−6.3)	284,513	(−1.9)
1930	129,000	345.4	19,274	56.00	(−1.3)	236,399	(−3.4)
1935	134,000	348.9	11,696	32.00	(−8.6)	157,354	(−6.7)
1940	121,000	391.1	9,399	24.00	(−5.0)	146,027	(−1.4)
1945	112,000	427.3	15,205	36.00	10.0	545,579	54.7
1950	107,000	442.9	25,517	58.00	12.2	718,289	6.3
1955	102,000	474.0				492,582	(−6.3)
1960	93,000	518.0	46,392	89.00	5.3	712,502	8.9
1965	82,000	588.0				698,492	(−0.4)
1970	73,000	659.0	101,465	154.00	7.3	886,756	5.4
1975	67,000	715.0	201,611	282.00	16.6	2,424,371	34.7
1980	65,000	734.0	469,985	635.00	25.0	3,554,507	9.3
1985	60,000	787.0	381,850	485.00	(−4.7)	3,488,928	(−1.8)
1990	57,000	826.0	454,473	550.00	2.7	3,599,297	(−3.2)
1994	52,923	839.0	516,335	635.00	3.1		

Table 2. Nebraska Crop Values: All Crops, 1867–1993

Year	Value (x 1,000)	Percent Change	Year	Value (x 1,000)	Percent Change
1866			1901	$103,139	5.8
1867	$3,798		1902	123,781	20.0
1868	4,018	5.8	1903	105,097	−15.1
1869	3,533	−12.7	1904	135,652	29.1
1870	4,196	18.8	1905	139,298	2.7
1871	4,460	6.3	1906	132,939	−4.6
1872	5,489	22.8	1907	141,535	6.5
1873	10,437	90.5	1908	174,476	23.3
1874	11,044	5.8	1909	195,663	12.1
1875	9,843	−10.9	1910	176,613	−9.7
1876	15,857	61.1	1911	187,291	6.1
1877	21,142	33.3	1912	197,518	5.5
1878	20,329	−3.8	1913	177,127	−10.3
1879	29,382	44.5	1914	241,563	36.4
1880	29,457	0.3	1915	268,541	11.2
1881	44,345	50.5	1916	423,120	57.6
1882	50,708	14.3	1917	478,466	13.1
1883	53,300	5.1	1918	402,179	−15.9
1884	45,535	−14.6	1919	507,427	26.2
1885	52,460	15.2	1920	314,139	−38.1
1886	44,967	−16.2	1921	198,329	−36.9
1887	60,056	33.6	1922	238,888	20.5
1888	69,432	15.6	1923	309,107	29.4
1889	59,393	−14.5	1924	339,118	9.7
1890	89,589	50.8	1925	284,513	−16.1
1891	103,233	15.2	1926	241,797	−15.0
1892	87,093	−15.6	1927	399,285	65.1
1893	67,876	−22.1	1928	312,967	−21.6
1894	46,167	−32.0	1929	315,773	0.9
1895	42,752	−7.4	1930	236,399	−25.1
1896	57,842	35.3	1931	122,308	−48.3
1897	74,104	28.1	1932	121,781	−0.4
1898	71,590	−3.4	1933	163,106	33.9
1899	80,363	12.3	1934	77,358	−52.6
1900	97,504	21.3	1935	157,354	103.4

Table 2 *continued*

Year	Value (x 1,000)	Percent Change	Year	Value (x 1,000)	Percent Change
1936	$136,837	−13.0	1966	$938,679	34.4
1937	140,063	2.4	1967	792,163	−15.6
1938	129,848	−7.3	1968	774,759	−2.2
1939	118,143	−9.0	1969	938,707	21.2
1940	146,027	23.6	1970	886,756	−5.5
1941	233,528	60.0	1971	1,000,615	12.8
1942	379,384	62.5	1972	1,487,554	48.7
1943	474,926	25.2	1973	2,492,900	67.6
1944	459,574	−3.2	1974	2,305,288	−7.5
1945	545,579	18.7	1975	2,424,371	5.2
1946	695,112	27.4	1976	2,209,187	−8.9
1947	725,356	4.4	1977	2,375,869	7.5
1948	693,035	−4.5	1978	2,779,383	17.0
1949	545,846	−21.2	1979	3,419,327	23.0
1950	718,289	31.6	1980	3,554,507	4.0
1951	627,332	−12.7	1981	3,742,028	5.3[1]
1952	831,806	32.6	1982	3,662,195	−2.1
1953	661,273	−20.5	1983	2,922,175	−20.2
1954	641,144	−3.0	1984	3,483,519	19.2
1955	492,582	−23.2	1985	3,488,928	0.2
1956	456,365	−7.4	1986	2,538,138	−27.3
1957	647,110	41.8	1987	2,867,238	13.0
1958	747,755	15.6	1988	3,640,080	27.0
1959	659,147	−11.8	1989	3,394,956	−6.7
1960	712,502	8.1	1990	3,599,297	6.0
1961	675,839	−5.1	1991	3,894,943	11.4
1962	725,043	7.2	1992	3,712,702	−4.7
1963	714,624	−1.4	1993	3,377,626	−9.0
1964	651,824	−8.8			
1965	698,492	7.2			

Table 3. Total Acres Harvested: All Nebraska Crops, 1866–1993

Year	Acres (x 1,000)	3 yr. Average (x 1,000)	5 yr. Average (x 1,000)	Year	Acres (x 1,000)	3 yr. Average (x 1,000)	5 yr. Average (x 1,000)
1866	162			1900	12,884	12,775	12,693
1867	223	229		1901	12,760	12,883	12,830
1868	303	272	307	1902	13,005	12,862	12,874
1869	389	383	456	1903	12,822	12,908	12,954
1870	456	483	504	1904	12,898	13,002	13,057
1871	603	610	669	1905	13,285	13,152	13,162
1872	770	833	849	1906	13,274	13,364	13,362
1873	1,126	1,062	1,120	1907	13,533	13,483	13,543
1874	1,290	1,409	1,422	1908	13,642	13,720	13,749
1875	1,811	1,739	1,759	1909	13,982	13,979	13,997
1876	2,117	2,126	2,165	1910	14,314	14,271	14,204
1877	2,449	2,575	2,648	1911	14,516	14,476	14,438
1878	3,158	3,103	3,112	1912	17,630	14,632	14,639[2]
1879	3,703	3,663	3,565	1913	17,876	17,864	14,870[3]
1880	4,129	4,073	4,020	1914	18,085	18,244	18,227[4]
1881	4,387	4,414	4,490	1915	18,770	18,544	18,222
1882	4,725	4,873	5,027	1916	18,776	18,383	18,217
1883	5,507	5,539	5,587	1917	17,604	18,474	18,450
1884	6,386	6,275	6,186	1918	19,043	18,718	18,735
1885	6,931	6,900	6,896	1919	19,506	19,278	18,838
1886	7,382	7,528	7,543	1920	19,285	19,340	18,928
1887	8,272	8,132	8,136	1921	19,230	19,357	19,319
1888	8,742	8,789	8,667	1922	19,556	19,587	19,505
1889	9,354	9,228	9,357	1923	19,976	19,750	19,683
1890	9,587	9,929	9,869	1924	19,717	19,877	19,944
1891	10,828	10,416	10,403	1925	19,937	20,062	20,238
1892	10,832	11,025	10,815	1926	20,533	20,500	20,425
1893	11,414	11,220	11,277	1927	21,029	20,824	20,794
1894	11,413	11,575	11,459	1928	20,909	21,116	21,227
1895	11,899	11,683	11,742	1929	21,560	21,525	21,463
1896	11,736	11,961	11,886	1930	22,105	21,793	21,583
1897	12,247	12,039	12,139	1931	21,713	21,816	21,662
1898	12,134	12,354	12,336	1932	21,630	21,555	20,193
1899	12,680	12,566	12,541	1933	21,323	19,050	19,757

Table 3 *continued*

Year	Acres (x 1,000)	3 yr. Average (x 1,000)	5 yr. Average (x 1,000)	Year	Acres (x 1,000)	3 yr. Average (x 1,000)	5 yr. Average (x 1,000)
1934	14,196	18,481	19,059	1964	16,403	16,318	16,297
1935	19,923	17,447	18,413	1965	15,447	15,860	16,275
1936	18,223	18,851	18,165	1966	15,730	15,955	15,999
1937	18,398	18,903	18,844	1967	16,688	16,048	15,841
1938	20,087	18,692	18,326	1968	15,725	16,010	15,889
1939	17,591	18,336	18,373	1969	15,616	15,675	15,997
1940	17,331	17,794	18,544	1970	15,684	15,857	15,742
1941	18,459	18,348	18,601	1971	16,271	15,790	16,057
1942	19,253	19,362	19,057	1972	15,415	16,328	16,443
1943	20,373	19,831	19,643	1973	17,298	16,754	16,840
1944	19,868	20,167	19,884	1974	17,548	17,505	17,138
1945	20,260	19,931	19,970	1975	17,669	17,658	17,712
1946	19,665	19,870	19,826	1976	17,758	17,904	17,723
1947	19,686	19,668	19,824	1977	18,285	17,799	17,855
1948	19,653	19,731	19,719	1978	17,353	17,950	18,112
1949	19,854	19,748	19,574	1979	18,213	18,172	18,380
1950	19,737	19,632	19,756	1980	18,951	18,755	18,515
1951	19,304	19,637	19,668	1981	19,100	19,003	18,069
1952	19,869	19,583	19,566	1982	18,959	17,727	18,143
1953	19,575	19,597	19,366	1983	15,122	17,555	18,071
1954	19,346	19,219	18,987	1984	18,584	17,432	17,757
1955	18,736	18,497	18,449	1985	18,589	18,235	17,151
1956	17,410	18,104	18,646	1986	17,533	17,350	17,480
1957	18,165	18,054	18,256	1987	15,927	16,742	17,253
1958	18,588	18,378	18,241	1988	16,765	16,714	17,144
1959	18,381	18,543	18,144	1989	17,450	17,420	17,310
1960	18,660	17,989	17,871	1990	18,044	17,953	17,791
1961	16,926	17,463	17,575	1991	18,366	18,247	18,021
1962	16,802	16,944	17,179	1992	18,330	18,204	
1963	17,105	16,770	16,537	1993	17,917		

Table 4. Nebraska Corn Production and Price: 1866–1993

Year	Rainfall (inches)	Acres (x 1,000)	Yield Bu.	Price Per Bu.	Value (x 1,000)	Percent of Total Crop Value	Percent of Total Crop Acres
1866	29.8	72	29.5				44.4
1867	27.1	90	33.0	$.53	$1,813	47.7	40.4
1868	39.6	115	28.0	.51	1,642	40.9	38.0
1869	43.9	125	38.5	.29	1,395	39.5	32.1
1870	26.3	155	33.5	.32	1,661	39.6	34.0
1871	31.9	225	38.0	.22	1,881	42.2	37.3
1872	31.9	295	37.0	.16	1,746	31.9	38.3
1873	31.8	370	22.0	.26	2,116	20.3	32.9
1874	33.0	380	15.0	.66	3,462	34.1	29.5
1875	36.4	625	31.0	.17	3,294	33.5	34.5
1876	10.9	780	32.0	.25	6,240	39.4	36.8
1877	24.6	1,130	34.0	.18	6,916	32.7	46.1
1878	24.4	1,340	41.0	.16	8,790	43.2	42.4
1879	24.7	1,631	40.1	.21	13,735	46.7	44.0
1880	20.2	1,970	31.0	.25	15,268	51.2	47.7
1881	29.3	2,150	29.5	.39	24,736	55.8	49.0
1882	23.0	2,460	38.0	.33	30,848	60.8	52.1
1883	30.4	2,990	37.5	.24	26,910	50.5	54.3
1884	23.8	3,500	41.0	.18	25,830	56.7	54.8
1885	25.6	3,910	40.0	.19	29,716	56.6	56.4
1886	23.1	4,380	31.0	.20	27,156	60.4	59.3
1887	21.8	4,740	27.5	.30	39,105	65.1	57.3
1888	22.4	5,120	38.0	.22	42,803	61.6	58.6
1889	22.3	5,480	39.4	.17	36,705	61.8	58.6
1890	17.2	5,525	20.0	.48	53,040	59.2	57.6
1891	30.6	6,150	37.5	.26	59,962	58.1	56.8
1892	24.3	5,975	32.0	.28	53,536	61.5	55.2
1893	16.3	6,400	26.5	.27	45,792	67.5	56.1
1894	13.5	6,825	7.0	.50	23,888	51.7	59.8
1895	19.0	7,300	16.5	.18	21,681	50.7	61.3
1896	25.9	7,425	37.5	.13	36,197	62.6	63.3
1897	23.7	7,500	30.0	.17	38,250	51.6	61.2
1898	20.6	7,000	21.0	.22	32,340	45.2	57.7
1899	19.6	7,380	28.8	.23	48,885	60.8	58.2
1900	23.9	7,350	26.0	.31	59,241	60.8	57.0

Table 4 *continued*

Year	Rainfall (inches)	Acres (x 1,000)	Yield Bu.	Price Per Bu.	Value (x 1,000)	Percent of Total	
						Crop Value	Crop Acres
1901	23.0	7,175	14.0	.54	54,243	52.6	56.3
1902	29.5	7,350	32.5	.30	71,662	57.9	56.5
1903	26.7	7,075	27.5	.28	54,477	51.8	55.2
1904	23.5	7,275	33.0	.33	79,225	58.4	56.4
1905	31.5	7,200	34.0	.32	78,336	56.2	54.2
1906	26.0	7,075	34.0	.29	69,760	52.5	53.3
1907	20.1	7,075	24.0	.41	69,618	49.2	52.3
1908	26.5	7,150	27.0	.51	98,456	56.4[2]	52.4
1909	24.6	7,327	24.8	.50	90,855	46.4	52.4
1910	16.7	7,425	26.0	.44	84,941	48.1	51.9
1911	21.2	7,350	21.5	.62	97,976	52.3	50.6
1912	21.5	7,500	27.0	.49	99,225	50.2	42.5[2]
1913	21.9	7,650	15.0	.64	73,440	41.5	48.8
1914	20.7	7,350	24.5	.61	109,846	45.5	40.6
1915	35.6	7,350	31.0	.58	132,153	49.2	39.2
1916	18.8	7,600	27.0	1.15	235,980	54.6	40.5
1917	20.5	8,350	27.0	1.37	308,866	64.6	47.4
1918	22.4	7,000	18.0	1.45	182,700	45.4	36.8
1919	25.1	7,080	24.0	1.32	224,294	44.2	36.3
1920	24.5	7,660	33.2	.38	96,639	30.8	39.7
1921	20.5	7,520	27.0	.37	75,125	37.9	39.1
1922	20.2	7,440	24.0	.62	110,707	46.3	38.0
1923	28.2	8,500	32.0	.67	182,240	59.0	42.6
1924	20.9	8,718	21.5	.97	181,814	53.6	44.2
1925	20.8	9,200	25.0	.63	144,900	50.9	46.1
1926	20.8	9,290	15.0	.73	101,726	42.1	45.2
1927	23.7	9,160	32.1	.74	217,587	54.5	43.6
1928	22.8	9,250	22.0	.77	156,695	50.1	44.2
1929	22.7	9,516	25.2	.67	160,668	50.9	44.1
1930	25.9	9,564	25.0	.46	109,986	46.5	43.3
1931	19.3	10,042	17.0	.30	51,214	41.9	46.2
1932	20.5	10,644	25.0	.27	71,847	59.0	49.2
1933	20.2	10,431	22.5	.41	96,226	59.0	48.9
1934	14.3	6,676	3.2	.87	18,586	24.0	47.0
1935	22.6	8,078	13.2	.61	65,044	41.3	40.5

Table 4 *continued*

Year	Rainfall (inches)	Acres (x 1,000)	Yield Bu.	Price Per Bu.	Value (x 1,000)	Percent of Total	
						Crop Value	Crop Acres
1936	14.4	7,674	3.5	1.16	31,156	22.8	42.1
1937	17.7	7,904	10.5	.51	42,326	30.2	43.0
1938	22.2	7,430	15.0	.47	52,382	40.3	37.0
1939	16.3	6,538	12.0	.56	43,935	37.2	37.2
1940	17.4	6,211	17.0	.58	61,240	41.9	35.8
1941	24.5	6,708	23.5	.67	105,617	45.2	36.3
1942	25.2	7,245	31.5	.82	187,139	49.3	37.6
1943	17.2	8,332	26.0	1.03	223,470	47.0	40.9
1944	27.4	8,749	33.0	.97	280,055	60.9	44.0
1945	22.7	8,587	28.5	1.13	273,324	50.1	42.4
1946	24.6	7,103	29.0	1.51	341,912	49.2	36.1
1947	23.4	7,340	19.5	2.12	303,436	41.8	37.3
1948	21.6	7,160	35.0	1.29	323,274	46.6	35.1
1949	25.4	7,518	31.0	1.21	282,000	51.7	37.8
1950	22.7	6,917	36.0	1.45	367,067	51.1	34.1
1951	30.5	7,080	27.5	1.55	301,785	48.1	36.7
1952	20.3	6,938	38.0	1.49	392,830	47.2	34.9
1953	20.4	7,146	29.0	1.47	304,634	46.1	43.5
1954	19.6	6,860	29.0	1.46	290,452	45.3	42.2
1955	17.4	5,958	20.0	1.45	155,765	31.6	31.8
1956	16.3	5,312	22.0	1.36	158,935	34.8	30.5
1957	28.1	4,940	46.0	1.09	247,692	38.3	27.2
1958	24.2	5,582	52.5	1.11	325,291	43.5	30.0
1959	25.2	6,558	48.5	1.02	336,891	51.1	35.7
1960	24.6	6,538	51.0	.96	320,100	44.9	35.0
1961	24.0	5,296	52.0	1.10	302,931	44.7	31.3
1962	26.8	5,031	60.5	1.10	334,814	46.2	29.9
1963	21.6	5,081	56.0	1.08	307,299	43.0	29.7
1964	21.3	4,166	53.0	1.15	253,918	39.0	25.4
1965	30.9	3,565	70.0	1.17	291,974	41.8	23.1
1966	19.4	4,100	80.0	1.19	390,320	41.6	26.1
1967	23.3	4,510	74.0	1.05	350,427	44.2	27.0
1968	23.6	4,239	74.0	1.09	341,918	44.1	27.0
1969	24.0	4,620	93.0	1.09	468,329	49.9	29.6
1970	20.4	4,805	75.0	1.25	450,469	50.8	30.6

Table 4 *continued*

Year	Rainfall (inches)	Acres (x 1,000)	Yield Bu.	Price Per Bu.	Value (x 1,000)	Percent of Total	
						Crop Value	Crop Acres
1971	24.4	5,300	85.0	1.11	500,055	50.0	32.6
1972	24.7	5,135	104.0	1.53	817,081	54.9	33.3
1973	31.2	5,900	94.0	2.41	1,336,586	53.6	34.3
1974	16.3	5,700	68.0	2.92	1,131,792	49.1	32.5
1975	20.6	5,920	85.0	2.48	1,247,936	51.5	33.5
1976	17.9	6,100	85.0	2.06	1,068,110	48.3	34.4
1977	30.3	6,550	99.0	1.97	1,277,447	53.8	35.8
1978	23.2	6,750	113.0	2.22	1,643,133	59.1	38.9
1979	26.6	7,150	115.0	2.42	1,989,845	58.2	39.3
1980	18.3	7,100	85.0	3.04	1,834,640	51.6	37.5
1981	25.4	6,880	115.0	2.51	1,985,912	53.1	36.0
1982	29.2	6,800	110.0	2.85	2,195,469	59.9	35.9
1983	26.3	4,860	97.0	3.12	1,467,800	50.2	32.1
1984	28.1	6,950	116.0	2.56	2,063,872	59.2	37.4
1985	27.9	7,450	128.0	2.22	2,269,568	65.1	40.1
1986	27.8	7,000	128.0	1.52	1,361,920	53.7	39.9
1987	27.5	6,200	131.0	1.96	1,591,912	55.5	38.9
1988	20.3	6,600	124.0	2.48	2,029,632	55.8	39.4
1989	17.1	7,000	121.0	2.30	1,948,100	57.4	40.1
1990	22.5	7,300	128.0	2.28	2,130,432	59.2	40.5
1991	23.4	7,800	127.0	2.34	2,318,004	59.5	42.5
1992	25.8	7,900	135.0	2.10	2,228,985	60.0	43.1
1993	32.1	7,550	104.0	2.51	1,970,852	58.3	42.1

Table 5. Nebraska Wheat Production and Price, 1866–1993

Year	Rainfall (inches)	Acres (x 1,000)	Yield Bu.	Price Per Bu.	Value (x 1,000)	Percent of Total Crop Value	Crop Acres
1866	29.8	43	14.0				26.5
1867	27.1	83	10.5	.95	828	21.8	37.2
1868	39.6	123	12.0	.71	1,048	26.1	40.6
1869	43.9	160	14.0	.40	896	25.4	41.1
1870	26.3	170	11.5	.57	1,114	26.5	37.3
1871	31.9	225	8.0	.81	1,458	32.7	37.3
1872	31.9	285	12.0	.69	2,360	43.1	37.0
1873	31.8	515	15.5	.69	5,508	52.2	45.7
1874	33.0	640	11.5	.54	3,974	36.0	49.6
1875	36.4	790	9.5	.56	4,203	42.7	43.6
1876	10.9	890	11.0	.72	7,049	44.5	42.0
1877	24.6	850	16.0	.81	11,016	52.1	34.7
1878	24.4	1,250	13.0	.49	7,962	39.2	39.6
1879	24.7	1,470	9.4	.84	11,607	39.5	39.7
1880	20.2	1,520	8.5	.73	9,432	32.0	36.8
1881	29.3	1,550	7.0	.97	10,524	23.7	35.3
1882	23.0	1,450	13.0	.67	12,630	24.9	30.7
1883	30.4	1,550	17.5	.70	18,988	35.6	28.1
1884	23.8	1,700	16.5	.42	11,781	25.9	26.6
1885	25.6	1,650	13.5	.57	12,697	24.2	23.8
1886	23.1	1,450	11.0	.47	7,496	16.7	19.6
1887	21.8	1,700	10.0	.53	9,010	15.0	20.6
1888	22.4	1,600	10.0	.83	13,280	19.1	18.3
1889	22.3	1,675	13.2	.52	11,497	19.4	17.9
1890	17.2	1,775	12.0	.76	16,188	18.1	18.5
1891	30.6	2,150	15.0	.73	23,542	22.8	19.9
1892	24.3	2,225	13.5	.50	15,019	17.2	20.5
1893	16.3	2,425	8.5	.40	8,245	12.1	21.2
1894	13.5	2,125	7.0	.49	7,289	15.8	18.6
1895	19.0	2,075	12.0	.40	9,960	23.3	17.4
1896	25.9	1,650	14.0	.58	13,398	23.2	14.1
1897	23.7	2,200	14.5	.69	22,011	29.7	18.0
1898	20.6	2,475	16.5	.47	19,194	26.8	20.4
1899	19.6	2,539	9.8	.49	12,192	15.2	20.0
1900	23.9	2,750	13.7	.53	20,034	20.5	21.3

Table 5 *continued*

Year	Rainfall (inches)	Acres (x 1,000)	Yield Bu.	Price Per Bu.	Value (x 1,000)	Percent of Total Crop Value	Crop Acres
1901	23.0	2,875	17.2	.54	26,674	25.9	22.5
1902	29.5	3,000	19.4	.49	28,550	23.1	23.1
1903	26.7	2,750	16.5	.54	24,462	23.3	21.4
1904	23.5	2,350	14.8	.87	30,259	22.3	18.2
1905	31.5	2,425	19.5	.66	31,262	22.4	18.3
1906	26.0	2,500	21.8	.57	31,133	23.4	18.8
1907	20.1	2,600	17.4	.79	35,733	25.2	19.2
1908	26.5	2,625	17.1	.84	37,605	21.6[2]	19.2
1909	24.6	2,663	17.9	.90	42,925	21.9	19.0
1910	16.7	2,855	15.8	.82	37,039	21.0	19.9
1911	21.2	3,265	12.3	.85	34,015	18.2	22.5
1912	21.5	3,335	15.8	.76	40,166	20.3	18.9[2]
1913	21.9	3,410	17.6	.73	43,764	24.7	19.1
1914	20.7	3,650	17.6	.94	60,230	24.9	20.2
1915	35.6	3,800	18.3	.91	63,404	23.6	20.2
1916	18.8	3,600	18.5	1.44	96,156	22.3	19.2
1917	20.5	975	12.5	2.00	24,376	5.1	5.5
1918	22.4	3,826	11.3	2.01	86,828	21.6	20.1
1919	25.1	4,427	13.2	2.07	120,689	23.8	22.7
1920	24.5	3,593	16.8	1.59	96,163	30.6	18.6
1921	20.5	3,967	15.1	.96	57,421	29.0	20.6
1922	20.2	4,177	13.8	.92	53,151	22.2	21.4
1923	28.2	3,252	9.9	.85	27,343	8.8	16.3
1924	20.9	3,033	18.4	1.19	66,266	19.5	15.4
1925	20.8	2,711	12.1	1.42	46,424	16.3	13.6
1926	20.8	3,146	13.1	1.18	48,722	20.1	15.3
1927	23.7	3,733	19.3	1.16	83,738	21.0	17.8
1928	22.8	3,757	18.0	.94	63,399	20.3	18.0
1929	22.7	3,700	15.0	.90	54,849	17.4	17.2
1930	25.9	3,974	18.8	.59	44,160	18.7	18.0
1931	19.3	3,420	16.6	.34	19,361	15.8	15.8
1932	20.5	2,265	12.3	.36	10,022	8.3	10.5
1933	20.2	2,388	12.1	.72	20,746	12.7	11.2
1934	14.3	2,251	7.8	.84	14,736	19.0	15.9
1935	22.6	3,045	12.6	.85	32,735	20.8	15.3

Table 5 *continued*

Year	Rainfall (inches)	Acres (x 1,000)	Yield Bu.	Price Per Bu.	Value (x 1,000)	Percent of Total	
						Crop Value	Crop Acres
1936	14.4	3,325	14.2	1.05	49,645	36.3	18.2
1937	17.7	3,567	13.2	.98	46,090	32.9	19.4
1938	22.2	4,691	11.8	.54	30,008	23.1	23.4
1939	16.3	3,186	11.1	.67	23,612	20.0	18.1
1940	17.4	2,643	13.1	.68	23,613	16.2	15.3
1941	24.5	2,354	15.4	.98	35,432	15.2	12.8
1942	25.2	2,947	23.7	1.13	78,996	20.8	15.3
1943	17.2	2,948	20.8	1.35	82,679	17.4	14.5
1944	27.4	2,675	12.6	1.40	47,248	10.3	13.5
1945	22.7	3,596	22.9	1.47	121,042	22.2	17.7
1946	24.6	3,954	22.9	1.89	171,370	24.7	20.1
1947	23.4	4,434	20.9	2.23	206,802	28.5	22.5
1948	21.6	4,674	20.4	1.98	172,411	24.9	23.8
1949	25.4	4,165	14.0	1.91	111,123	20.4	21.0
1950	22.7	4,051	21.8	2.04	180,458	25.1	20.5
1951	30.5	4,005	14.5	2.16	125,370	20.0	20.7
1952	20.3	4,390	22.4	2.09	205,561	24.7	22.1
1953	20.4	3,856	22.3	2.08	178,848	27.0	19.7
1954	19.6	3,107	19.3	2.16	129,784	20.2	16.1
1955	17.4	3,141	24.9	2.00	156,508	31.8	16.8
1956	16.3	3,324	19.5	1.99	128,741	28.2	19.1
1957	28.1	2,920	27.0	1.92	151,171	23.4	16.1
1958	24.2	3,442	33.0	1.74	197,238	26.4	18.5
1959	25.2	3,092	22.0	1.76	119,722	18.2	16.8
1960	24.6	3,011	28.5	1.73	148,263	20.8	16.1
1961	24.0	3,209	24.5	1.77	139,157	20.6	19.0
1962	26.8	2,760	19.5	1.94	104,411	14.4	16.4
1963	21.6	2,953	21.5	1.83	116,187	16.3	17.3
1964	21.3	2,953	25.0	1.33	98,187	15.1	18.0
1965	30.9	2,727	20.0	1.33	72,538	10.4	17.7
1966	19.4	2,891	35.0	1.63	164,932	17.6	18.4
1967	23.3	3,325	26.5	1.32	116,308	14.7	19.9
1968	23.6	3,159	32.0	1.17	118,273	15.3	20.1
1969	24.0	2,780	31.5	1.17	102,457	10.9	17.8
1970	20.4	2,558	38.0	1.22	118,589	13.4	16.3

Table 5 *continued*

Year	Rainfall (inches)	Acres (x 1,000)	Yield Bu.	Price Per Bu.	Value (x 1,000)	Percent of Total	
						Crop Value	Crop Acres
1971	24.4	2,434	42.0	1.24	126,763	12.7	15.0
1972	24.7	2,509	37.0	1.74	161,529	10.9	16.3
1973	31.2	2,680	35.0	3.80	356,440	14.3	15.5
1974	16.3	2,900	34.0	3.81	375,666	16.3	16.5
1975	20.6	3,070	32.0	3.39	333,034	13.7	17.4
1976	17.9	2,950	32.0	2.38	224,672	10.2	16.6
1977	30.3	2,950	35.0	2.22	229,215	9.6	16.1
1978	23.2	2,550	32.0	2.79	227,664	8.2	14.7
1979	26.6	2,550	34.0	3.64	315,588	9.2	14.0
1980	18.3	2,850	38.0	3.72	402,876	11.3	15.0
1981	25.4	2,900	36.0	3.65	381,060	10.2	15.2
1982	29.2	2,900	35.0	3.45	350,175	9.6	15.3
1983	26.3	2,300	43.0	3.39	335,300	11.5	15.2
1984	28.1	2,250	36.0	3.28	265,680	7.6	12.1
1985	27.9	2,300	39.0	2.79	264,615	7.6	12.4
1986	27.8	2,000	38.0	2.23	169,480	6.7	11.4
1987	27.5	1,950	44.0	2.45	210,210	7.3	12.2
1988	20.3	2,000	36.0	3.66	263,520	7.2	11.9
1989	17.1	2,050	27.0	3.75	207,563	6.1	11.7
1990	22.5	2,250	38.0	2.53	455,138	12.6	12.5
1991	23.4	2,100	32.0	3.01	450,783	11.6	11.4
1992	25.8	1,850	30.0	3.15	175,380	4.7	10.1
1993	32.1	2,100	35.0	3.04	223,440	6.6	11.7

Table 6. Nebraska Livestock, Market Values, 1867–1994

Year	Cattle Number (x 1,000)	Cattle Value per Head	Hogs Number (x 1,000)	Hogs Value per Head	Sheep Number (x 1,000)	Sheep Value per Head
1867	115	$20.10	250	$6.00	29	$2.70
1868	122	19.90	270	4.60	85	2.30
1869	136	23.00	300	4.70	40	2.00
1870	157	26.00	340	6.60	36	2.05
1871	202	29.10	360	7.80	36	2.00
1872	247	24.20	395	5.20	36	2.25
1873	296	23.30	475	4.90	39	2.50
1874	349	22.40	580	4.10	42	2.00
1875	375	21.30	500	3.65	50	2.30
1876	431	19.20	510	6.60	75	2.45
1877	517	20.10	720	6.60	105	2.55
1878	657	21.50	925	5.60	126	2.70
1879	787	20.00	1,025	3.05	168	2.30
1880	1,000	22.20	1,300	5.20	244	2.75
1881	1,055	22.20	1,226	5.10	325	2.75
1882	1,420	23.60	1,389	6.90	425	2.60
1883	1,830	26.40	2,275	8.00	580	2.45
1884	2,200	27.20	2,600	7.30	530	2.20
1885	2,400	26.60	2,090	6.20	475	2.10
1886	2,385	25.50	1,791	5.10	369	2.15
1887	2,200	24.60	2,028	5.50	277	1.90
1888	1,800	22.00	2,095	5.70	222	2.00
1889	1,750	19.80	2,238	7.10	204	1.85
1890	2,208	17.60	2,920	5.60	204	2.10
1891	2,251	17.00	2,765	4.25	204	2.35
1892	2,211	17.00	2,190	5.20	184	2.55
1893	2,010	16.70	2,167	6.00	193	2.65
1894	1,900	17.30	2,385	8.00	212	2.30
1895	1,800	14.40	1,792	4.90	201	1.85
1896	1,750	18.90	2,040	5.00	250	2.15
1897	1,900	20.70	2,710	4.75	325	2.45
1898	2,175	27.60	3,180	5.40	350	2.85
1899	2,400	28.90	3,160	5.30	385	3.15
1900	2,808	31.20	2,969	6.00	380	3.40
1901	2,953	27.20	2,680	7.20	415	3.40

Table 6 *continued*

Year	Cattle		Hogs		Sheep	
	Number (x 1,000)	*Value per Head*	*Number (x 1,000)*	*Value per Head*	*Number (x 1,000)*	*Value per Head*
1902	3,074	22.10	2,600	8.40	350	3.00
1903	3,230	21.00	2,640	8.70	330	2.75
1904	3,557	18.80	3,622	6.40	355	2.80
1905	3,596	18.50	3,765	6.50	375	3.00
1906	3,527	19.70	3,745	6.60	370	3.70
1907	3,460	20.60	4,020	8.70	350	4.10
1908	3,290	20.70	4,135	6.20	350	3.75
1909	3,228	22.00	3,290	7.20	325	3.50
1910	2,972	24.50	2,960	11.00	319	4.40
1911	2,753	25.60	3,435	10.90	395	4.05
1912	2,561	27.80	3,805	8.80	301	3.60
1913	2,561	36.00	3,230	11.40	300	4.40
1914	2,764	42.60	2,975	11.80	270	4.50
1915	3,040	44.90	3,440	10.90	174	4.80
1916	3,253	44.00	3,690	9.40	200	5.40
1917	3,578	48.20	3,670	14.00	240	7.50
1918	3,758	54.00	4,110	24.40	300	11.00
1919	3,382	55.90	4,005	26.50	232	11.90
1920	3,154	47.40	3,436	23.00	241	11.60
1921	2,953	35.30	3,558	14.80	195	6.50
1922	3,026	29.60	4,100	11.00	180	5.40
1923	3,224	33.40	5,633	13.20	170	8.20
1924	3,386	32.10	5,983	11.00	175	8.10
1925	3,314	31.40	5,200	14.50	180	10.80
1926	3,191	35.80	4,405	17.60	190	11.30
1927	2,819	37.00	4,660	19.50	209	9.80
1928	2,766	49.40	5,340	15.50	215	10.10
1929	2,931	59.00	5,305	15.00	230	10.60
1930	3,060	55.00	5,010	15.60	258	8.90
1931	3,242	39.00	4,820	13.40	270	4.70
1932	3,330	24.00	5,334	6.00	275	3.00
1933	3,610	18.80	4,534	4.30	280	2.80
1934	3,980	17.50	5,010	4.30	295	3.70
1935	3,232	18.00	2,034	6.10	274	4.10
1936	3,491	34.30	2,238	14.70	288	6.60

Table 6 *continued*

	Cattle		Hogs		Sheep	
Year	Number (x 1,000)	Value per Head	Number (x 1,000)	Value per Head	Number (x 1,000)	Value per Head
1937	3,037	30.90	1,567	13.90	271	5.40
1938	2,780	32.00	1,507	12.30	274	5.90
1939	2,810	38.60	1,869	13.50	310	6.10
1940	2,904	41.20	2,385	8.70	370	6.20
1941	3,009	43.10	1,813	9.70	377	6.70
1942	3,285	53.80	2,375	19.30	434	9.10
1943	3,765	70.30	3,491	27.80	395	10.10
1944	3,957	65.30	4,329	21.90	348	9.20
1945	4,176	61.80	2,597	26.90	278	8.60
1946	4,026	72.00	3,168	28.60	222	10.10
1947	3,922	91.40	2,503	42.70	178	12.80
1948	3,797	120.00	2,403	55.10	169	14.30
1949	3,856	135.00	2,403	45.70	179	15.00
1950	3,843	124.00	2,499	32.00	168	16.60
1951	4,105	167.00	2,999	39.00	185	24.60
1952	4,575	184.00	3,239	30.70	239	26.90
1953	4,992	120.00	2,397	30.00	220	14.70
1954	4,752	90.00	2,061	45.90	233	11.70
1955	5,065	93.00	2,423	17.50	261	14.60
1956	4,759	82.00	1,841	28.70	242	12.60
1957	4,531	88.00	2,044	34.60	273	13.60
1958	4,630	128.00	2,579	35.50	308	18.40
1959	4,886	167.00	2,502	19.20	357	20.80
1960	5,072	131.00	2,452	29.20	375	15.30
1961	5,134	136.00	2,648	28.70	375	15.20
1962	5,434	145.00	2,727	28.70	320	13.40
1963	5,773	155.00	2,809	24.40	320	15.40
1964	6,048	132.00	2,696	25.40	301	13.60
1965	6,077	116.00	2,561	48.30	283	15.60
1966	6,259	138.00	2,766	35.30	283	19.50
1967	6,377	151.00	3,043	28.70	269	19.50
1968	6,394	149.00	3,226	30.40	241	19.40
1969	6,330	159.00	2,839	40.20	393	21.70
1970	6,330	185.00	3,691	23.50	377	24.50
1971	6,457	185.00	3,320	29.50	370	21.50

Table 6 *continued*

Year	Cattle		Hogs		Sheep	
	Number (x 1,000)	*Value per Head*	*Number (x 1,000)*	*Value per Head*	*Number (x 1,000)*	*Value per Head*
1972	6,780	215.00	3,300	43.50	366	23.50
1973	6,865	255.00	3,455	62.00	370	26.00
1974	7,410	355.00	3,050	44.00	320	32.50
1975	6,900	150.00	2,700	85.50	280	29.50
1976	6,550	190.00	3,100	47.50	210	34.50
1977	6,450	205.00	3,150	67.00	190	37.00
1978	6,500	240.00	3,650	88.50	237	49.00
1979	6,450	410.00	4,150	60.50	175	65.00
1980	6,400	495.00	3,900	79.00	210	39.50
1981	6,850	455.00	4,100	74.50	250	65.50
1982	7,250	405.00	3,600	94.00	225	54.50
1983	7,200	380.00	4,000	64.00	205	53.00
1984	6,900	400.00	3,700	80.50	195	50.00
1985	6,100	410.00	3,900	74.00	165	52.00
1986	5,800	395.00	3,950	95.00	160	60.00
1987	5,500	410.00	4,050	78.00	173	76.00
1988	5,700	510.00	4,150	70.50	180	83.00
1989	5,500	585.00	4,200	83.00	169	80.00
1990	5,800	595.00	4,300	88.00	177	72.50
1991	6,000	685.00	4,500	69.00	165	67.00
1992	5,800	635.00	4,600	71.00	144	51.00
1993	5,900	670.00	4,300	75.00	136	63.00
1994	6,100	685.00			92	70.00

Source: Tables in Appendix 4 compiled from Nebraska Department of Agriculture and Inspection, *Nebraska Agricultural Statistics: Historical Record, 1866–1954* (Chicago: State-Federal Division of Agricultural Statistics, 1957), and from the annual volumes of *Nebraska Agricultural Statistics* since 1957.

Notes for Appendix 4
1. Beginning in 1981, All Crop Value is based on ten major crops: corn, wheat, oats, barley, sorghum, soybeans, rye, sugar beets, dry beans, and hay.
2. Acres of Harvested Wild Hay were included for the first time in 1912, accounting for the 21.5 percent increase.
3. Acres of Harvested Wild Hay included in three-year average beginning in 1913.
4. Acres of Harvested Wild Hay included in five-year average beginning in 1914.

APPENDIX V. NEBRASKA FARM MARKETINGS
AND GOVERNMENT PAYMENTS, 1909–1992
(MILLION DOLLARS)

Year	Cash Receipts from Crops and Livestock	Government Payments		Total Farm Income
		Amount	Percent	
1909–14 (Ave.)	$ 340.1	—	—	$ 340.1
1915–16 (Ave.)	392.5	—	—	392.5
1917–19 (Ave.)	711.8	—	—	711.8
1920	680.6	—	—	680.6
1921	374.8	—	—	374.8
1922	383.2	—	—	383.2
1923	399.6	—	—	399.6
1924	421.1	—	—	421.1
1925	444.9	—	—	444.9
1926	434.2	—	—	434.2
1927	418.4	—	—	418.4
1928	484.6	—	—	484.6
1929	489.1	—	—	489.1
1930	408.4	—	—	408.4
1931	279.1	—	—	279.1
1932	166.7	—	—	166.7
1933	193.4	$ 1.0	0.5%	194.4
1934	227.2	23.5	9.4	250.7
1935	209.4	33.1	13.6	242.5
1936	281.0	17.3	5.8	298.3
1937	250.8	17.5	6.5	268.3
1938	200.5	15.4	13.2	215.9
1939	221.5	28.1	11.3	249.6
1940	224.3	46.3	17.1	270.6
1941	290.0	15.9	5.2	305.9
1942	468.9	36.4	7.2	505.3
1943	653.6	37.1	5.4	690.7
1944	634.5	21.6	3.3	656.1
1945	734.6	18.7	2.5	753.3
1946	841.1	23.6	2.3	864.7

Year	Cash Receipts from Crops and Livestock	Government Payments		Total Farm Income
		Amount	Percent	
1947	1,072.6	13.5	1.2	1,086.1
1948	1,030.2	8.5	0.8	1,038.7
1949	955.0	6.8	0.7	961.8
1950	1,009.6	8.8	0.9	1,018.4
1951	1,188.9	9.1	0.8	1,198.0
1952	1,173.6	10.0	0.8	1,183.6
1953	1,120.3	7.9	0.7	1,128.2
1954	1,060.8	8.6	0.8	1,069.4
1955	1,017.7	7.7	0.8	1,025.4
1956	914.7	42.7	4.5	957.4
1957	902.3	54.8	5.7	957.1
1958	1,217.2	36.9	2.9	1,254.1
1959	1,233.0	19.9	1.6	1,252.9
1960	1,187.9	22.1	1.8	1,210.0
1961	1,213.4	88.6	6.8	1,302.0
1962	1,253.2	101.4	7.5	1,354.6
1963	1,315.6	106.9	7.5	1,422.5
1964	1,273.5	164.9	11.5	1,438.4
1965	1,343.2	184.7	12.1	1,527.9
1966	1,681.8	175.4	9.4	1,857.2
1967	1,743.7	134.5	7.2	1,878.2
1968	1,731.7	185.3	9.7	1,917.0
1969	1,961.0	200.6	9.3	2,161.6
1970	2,124.4	203.0	8.7	2,327.4
1971	2,285.8	171.0	7.0	2,456.8
1972	2,821.4	233.3	7.6	3,054.7
1973	3,943.3	151.8	3.7	4,095.1
1974	4,107.4	21.0	0.5	4,128.4
1975	3,860.1	71.7	1.8	3,931.8
1976	3,841.0	36.6	0.9	3,877.6
1977	3,975.0	92.9	2.3	4,067.9
1978	3,084.1	268.6	5.4	4,948.2

Appendix 5 / Farm Marketings and Government Payments

Year	Cash Receipts from Crops and Livestock	Government Payments		Total Farm Income
		Amount	Percent	
1979	4,266.6	132.7	2.1	6,433.7
1980	6,830.1	82.9	1.2	6,913.0
1981	6,622.5	101.0	1.5	6,723.5
1982	7,024.2	277.5	3.8	7,301.7
1983	6,451.3	786.8	10.9	7,238.1
1984	6,836.9	533.0	7.2	7,369.9
1985	7,388.6	518.4	6.6	7,907.0
1986	6,761.1	858.4	11.3	7,619.5
1987	7,139.1	1,274.8	15.2	8,413.9
1988	7,802.0	1,091.5	12.3	8,893.5
1989	8,725.8	542.3	5.9	9,268.1
1990	8,715.0	624.6	6.6	9,339.6
1991	9,044.5	490.7	5.1	9,535.2
1992	8,782.7	478.7	5.2	9,261.4

Source: Nebraska Department of Agriculture and Inspection, *Nebraska Agricultural Statistics: Historical Record, 1866–1954* (Chicago: State-Federal Division of Agricultural Statistics, 1957), 127, 134,138; *Nebraska Blue Book* (1993–94), 459–60.

NOTES

1. THE LAND

1. Rueben Gold Thwaites, ed., *Early Western Travels* (Cleveland: Arthur H. Clark, 1905), vol. 14, *Accounts of an Expedition from Pittsburgh to the Rocky Mountains, Performed in the Years 1819, 1820 under the Command of Stephen H. Long*, ed. Edwin James, 20.
2. Elliott Coues, *The Expeditions of Zebulon Montgomery Pike* (New York: Francis P. Harper, 1895), 2:525.
3. Walter Prescott Webb, *The Great Plains* (Boston: Ginn and Company, 1931), 8–9.
4. John Bradbury, *Travels in the Interior of America in the Years 1809, 1810 and 1811* (1819; rpt. Lincoln: University of Nebraska Press, 1986), 266–67.
5. Bayard Taylor, *Colorado: A Summer Trip* (New York, 1867), 20–49, quoted in Ralph C. Morris, "The Notion of a Great American Desert East of the Rockies," *Mississippi Valley Historical Review* 13 (December 1926): 198.
6. Others, of course, have added to and redefined Professor Aughey's lists.

2. THE FIRST PEOPLE

1. See Kingley M. Bray, "Teton Sioux Population History, 1655–1881," *Nebraska History* 75 (summer 1994): 165–88.

3. SPAIN AND FRANCE ON THE PLAINS

1. "Coronado to the King, October 2, 1541," quoted in G. P. Winship, "The Coronado Expedition, 1540–1542," *Fourteenth Annual Report of the Bureau of American Ethnology*, 583.
2. "Coronado to the King," 582.
3. Baron Marc de Villiers, *La découverte du Missouri et l'histoire du Fort d'Orléans, 1673–1728* (Paris, 1925).
4. The exact location of Fort Charles is unknown, but recent research suggests that it was probably near present-day Homer, Nebraska, and very likely on or near modern Blyburg Lake at the southern edge of Dakota County. See W. Raymond Wood, "Fort Charles or Mr. Mackey's Trading House," *Nebraska History* 76 (spring 1995): 2–7; and Gayle F. Carlson, "The Search for Fort Charles," *Nebraska History* 76 (spring 1995): 8–9.

4. THE LOUISIANA PURCHASE

1. York has been the subject of numerous novelists, poets, and historians through the years who have created in him a legendary hero. Some have suggested that his size and strength and the darkness of his skin, as well as his entertainment abilities, so fascinated Indians who had never seen a black person that he succeeded in establishing a foundation for friendship with the tribes where the expedition's diplomatic efforts had failed. Such conclusions are based on conjecture, for there is little evidence to support them in the Lewis and Clark journals. Clark mentions York numerous times in his journal, usually in the context of sharing in the normal duties and routines of the expedition. See Gary E. Moulton, ed., *The Journals of the Lewis and Clark Expedition* (Lincoln: University of Nebraska Press, 1986), 2:525.

2. Clark, "Journal Entry, May 14, 1804," in Moulton, *Journals of the Lewis and Clark Expedition*, 2:227.

3. Clark, "Journal Entry, July 15, 1804," in Moulton, *Journals of the Lewis and Clark Expedition*, 2:381.

4. Clark, "Journal Entry, August 3, 1804," in Moulton, *Journals of the Lewis and Clark Expedition*, 2:440.

5. Clark, "Journal Entry, August 3, 1804," 441.

6. Clark, "Journal Entry, August 19, 1804," in Moulton, *Journals of the Lewis and Clark Expedition*, 2:493.

7. In the 1920s an interesting controversy over the exact location of these villages developed between Kansas and Nebraska. The Kansas State Historical Society erected a monument to Pike in Republic County, Kansas, on the presumed site of the village. Later, archaeological research by A. T. Hill demonstrated conclusively that the villages were located in Webster County, Nebraska. See *Nebraska History* 10 (July–September 1927): 157–261.

8. Lisa was accompanied by Henry M. Brackenridge, well-known author and traveler; accompanying Hunt was John Bradbury, naturalist and traveler. Each kept a journal that contains information regarding the two expeditions and the Missouri Valley. They were published as volumes 5 and 6 of Reuben Gold Thwaites, ed., *Early Western Travels* (Cleveland: Arthur H. Clark Company, 1904).

9. *American State Papers, Military Affairs* (Washington DC: Gales and Seaton, 1860), 2:33.

10. Fitzpatrick and Clyman were but two of the men sent by Ashley after the Arickara War to explore the mountain region south of the Missouri. The party, as H. C. Dale suggests, "was the most significant group of continental

explorers ever brought together." Their wanderings during the next ten to fifteen years covered the entire West. The group included, in addition to Henry, Fitzpatrick and Clyman, Edward Rose, Louis Vasquez, Jim Bridger, David E. Jackson, Hugh Glass, Seth Grant, and Jedediah Smith. See H. C. Dale, ed., *The Ashley-Smith Explorations and the Discovery of a Central Route to the Pacific* (Cleveland: Arthur H. Clark Company, 1918), 86–87.

11. Edgar Bruce Wesley, "Life at Fort Atkinson," *Nebraska History* 30 (December 1949): 352–53.

12. "Letters Concerning the Presbyterian Mission in the Pawnee Country, near Bellevue, Neb., 1831–1849," *Collections of the Kansas State Historical Society* 14 (1915–18): 608.

5. THE GREAT PLATTE RIVER ROAD

1. "Jedediah Smith, David E. Jackson, and W. L. Sublette, St. Louis, to J. H. Eaton, Secretary of War, 29 October 1833," in *The Documentary Background of the Days of the First Wagon Train on the Road to Oregon*, ed. Archer B. Hulbert (Missoula: University of Montana, 1930), 20–21.

2. Bernard DeVoto assessed Young's place in American history, commenting, "Nothing in American history . . . is like Winter Quarters" and that few leaders can compare with Brigham Young—"a great leader, a great diplomat, a great administrator, and at need a great liar and a great scoundrel . . . one of the finders and one of the makers of the West." See Bernard DeVoto, *The Year of Decision: 1846* (Boston: Little, Brown, 1943), 435, 439.

3. Because Brigham Young's brother Lorenzo insisted on taking his wife, Harriett, and her two young sons by a previous marriage, Brigham Young and Heber Kimball also selected wives to take along. The record also indicates that they took along ninety-three horses, fifty-two mules, sixty-six oxen, nineteen cows, seventeen dogs, and a few coops of chickens.

4. Douglas C. McMurtrie, ed., *The General Epistle of the Latter Day Saints Dated: Winter Quarters, Nebraska, December 23, 1847 . . .* (Chicago: Black Cat Press, 1935).

5. William A. Linn, *The Story of the Mormons* (New York: Macmillan, 1902), 422–23, quoted in Jay Monaghan, "Handcarts on the Overland Trail," *Nebraska History* 30 (March 1949): 3–18.

6. "Diary of the Overland Trail, 1849, and Letters 1849–50 of Captain David DeWolf," *Transactions of the Illinois Historical Society* 32 (1925): 186.

7. One of the best-recorded cholera deaths was that of George Winslow of Massachusetts, whose grave is in Jefferson County, near Fairbury. See George W.

Hansen, "A Tragedy of the Oregon Trail," Nebraska State Historical Society *Collections* 17 (1913): 110–26.

8. Franklin Langworthy, *Scenery of the Plains, Mountains, and Mines*, ed. Paul C Phillips (Princeton: Princeton University Press, 1932), 37–38.

9. John Wood, *Journal* . . . (Columbus: Nevins and Meyers, 1871), 31.

10. Kanesville, so named for its founder, Thomas Kane, would later be renamed Council Bluffs.

11. Merrill J. Mattes, "The Council Bluffs Road: A New Perspective on the Northern Branch of the Great Platte River Road," *Nebraska History* 65 (summer 1984): 190.

12. Merrill J. Mattes, *The Great Platte River Road* (Lincoln: Nebraska State Historical Society, 1969), 82.

13. John D. Unruh, *The Plains Across: The Overland Emigrants and the Trans-Mississippi West, 1840–60* (Urbana: University of Illinois Press, 1979), 124, 516.

6. THE KANSAS-NEBRASKA ACT

1. Senate Reports, 33d Cong., 1st sess., No. 15, 4.

7. THE NEBRASKA TERRITORY

1. *Nebraska Palladium*, July 15, 1854.

2. President Pierce earlier had offered the job to William O. Butler of Kentucky, who had declined.

3. Residents of Bellevue maintained that he intended to locate the territorial capital there permanently. Armistead Burt, the governor's son, who accompanied him to Bellevue, later recalled: "The governor's intention was to convene the first legislature at Bellevue; I think the Rev. Mr. Hamilton had offered the mission house for the purpose. As to locating the capital I remember hearing him say he intended to choose a place that would, he hoped, be permanently the capital of the state. He intended to make Nebraska his home." See J. Sterling Morton and Albert Watkins, *Illustrated History of Nebraska*, 3 vols. (Lincoln: Jacob North and Co. and Western Publishing and Engraving Co., 1905–13), 1:163n.

4. *Nebraska Palladium*, January 3, 1855.

5. Morton and Watkins, *Illustrated History*, 1:194.

6. Addison E. Sheldon, *Nebraska: The Land and the People* (Chicago: Lewis Publishing Company, 1931), 1:277.

8. TERRITORIAL GROWTH AND DEVELOPMENT

1. The exact number was 2,420,062.88 acres.
2. Morton and Watkins, *Illustrated History*, 1:231.
3. The Omaha land office, though nominally established in 1854, was not opened until 1856. In 1857, additional land offices were established at Brownville, Nebraska City, and Dakota City.
4. *Brownville Advertiser*, May 2, 1872.
5. James C. Olson, *J. Sterling Morton* (Lincoln: University of Nebraska Press, 1942), 52–53.
6. Olson, *J. Sterling Morton*, 52–53.
7. Everett Dick, *Sod House Frontier* (New York: Appleton-Century, 1937), 90.
8. *Nebraska City News*, September 25, 1858.
9. Compiled from U.S. Department of the Interior, Bureau of the Census, *Agriculture of the United States in 1860* (Washington DC: Government Printing Office, 1864), 172–75; and Nebraska Department of Agriculture and Inspection, *Nebraska Agricultural Statistics: Historical Record, 1866–1954* (Chicago: State-Federal Division of Agricultural Statistics, 1957). See agricultural statistics in the Appendix for comparative data.
10. Nebraska Legislature, 6th Session, *Report of the Honorable Robert W. Furnas, President of the State Board of Agriculture* (Omaha City, 1860), 3–4.
11. *Omaha Herald*, October 27, 1865.
12. U.S. Department of the Interior, Bureau of the Census, *Manufactures of the United States in 1860* (Washington DC: Government Printing Office, 1865), 665.
13. Governor David Butler, "Second Inaugural Message, January 8, 1869," in *Messages and Proclamations of the Governors, 1854–1941*, 4 vols. (Lincoln: Works Progress Administration, 1941–42), 1:284.
14. U.S. Department of the Interior, Bureau of the Census, *The Population of the United States in 1860* (Washington DC: Government Printing Office, 1864), 554–55, 592; U.S. Department of the Interior, Bureau of the Census, *The Statistics of the Population of the United States in 1860* (Washington DC: Government Printing Office, 1866), 507; U.S. Department of the Interior, Bureau of the Census, *The Statistics of the Population of the United States in 1870* (Washington DC: Government Printing Office, 1872), 394–95, 618.
15. George W. Barnes, "Pioneer Preacher—An Autobiography," *Nebraska History* 27 (April–June 1946): 79–80.
16. U.S. Department of the Interior, Bureau of the Census, *Statistics of the United States in 1860*, 499.

9. HIGHWAY TO THE WEST

1. *Western Guide* (Rulo, Nebraska), August 13 and September 17, 1858, quoted in Donald F. Danker, "The Influence of Transportation upon Nebraska Territory," *Nebraska History* 47 (June 1966): 190.
2. William E. Lass, *A History of Steamboating on the Upper Missouri River* (Lincoln: University of Nebraska Press, 1976), 108.
3. Jerome E. Petsche, *The Steamboat Bertrand: History, Excavation, and Architecture* (Washington DC: National Park Service, 1974), 1.
4. Petsche, *Steamboat Bertrand*, 77.
5. Petsche, *Steamboat Bertrand*, 45.
6. Petsche, *Steamboat Bertrand*, 48–49.
7. Brown had been appointed a major general in the Minnesota State militia.
8. Noel M. Loomis, *Wells Fargo* (New York: Bramhall House, 1968), 126–27.
9. Samuel Bowles, *Across the Continent* (Springfield MA 1865), 20–22.
10. Bowles, *Across the Continent*, 20.
11. *Nebraska Advertiser*, August 30,1860.
12. Howard P. Chudacoff, "Where Rolls the Dark Missouri Down," *Nebraska History* 52 (spring 1971): 5.
13. Charles W. Martin, ed., "Omaha in 1868–1869: Selections from the Letters of Joseph Barker," *Nebraska History* 59 (winter 1978): 510.

10. SECURING THE LAND

1. *U.S. Senate Documents*, 32d Cong., 2d sess., "Report of the Commissioner of Indian Affairs, November 25, 1852," 1:299.
2. This encounter, initially referred to as the Battle of Blue Water, later came to be known as the Battle of Ash Hollow. See R. Eli Paul, ed., "Battle of Ash Hollow: The 1909–1910 Recollections of General N. A. M. Dudley," *Nebraska History* 62 (fall 1981): 373.
3. A letter dated January 23, 1901, to the Nebraska Historical Society from retired general N. A. M. Dudley indicates that the number killed at Ash Hollow was more than one hundred and that a significant number were captured. He claims personally to have taken in fifteen of the prisoners. See Paul, ed., "Battle of Ash Hollow," 373–99.
4. Gouverneur K. Warren, *Explorations in the Dacota Country in the Year 1855* (Washington DC: A. O. P. Nicholson, Senate Printing, 1856), 21, quoted in Vincent J. Flanagan, "Gouverneur Kemble Warren: Explorer of the Nebraska Territory," *Nebraska History* 51 (summer 1970): 176.

5. Draft of letter by G. K. Warren, January 29, 1858, in Gouverneur Kemble Warren Papers, New York State Library, Albany, 8:13, quoted in Flanagan, "Gouverneur Kemble Warren," 193.

6. "Report to the President by the Indian Peace Commission, January 7, 1868," *Annual Report of the Commissioner of Indian Affairs* (1868), 29, in House Executive Documents, 40th Cong., 3d sess., 1:492.

7. Robert W. Mardock, "The Plains Frontier and the Indian Peace Policy, 1865–1880," *Nebraska History* 49 (summer 1968): 194.

II. THE POLITICS OF STATEHOOD

1. *Nebraska Palladium*, February 7, 1855.

2. Ruth K. Nuermberger, ed., "Letters from Pioneer Nebraska by Edward Randolph Harden," *Nebraska History* 27 (January–March 1946): 27.

3. *Nebraska Advertiser*, November 17, 1859.

4. Olson, *J. Sterling Morton*, 85–94. Also see Morton and Watkins, *Illustrated History*, 1:469–72.

5. Governor Alvin Saunders, "Opening Message to the Eleventh Session of the Legislative Assembly, January 9, 1866," in *Messages and Proclamations of the Governors, 1854–1941*, 1:199–200.

6. Olson, *J. Sterling Morton*, 142.

7. *Congressional Globe*, 39th Cong., 2d sess., 1866–67, pt. 1, 360.

12. ESTABLISHING THE STATE GOVERNMENT

1. *Senate Journal of the Legislative Assembly of Nebraska*, June 4, 1867, 110.

2. "Report of the Commission to Locate the Seat of Government of Nebraska," *House Journal of the Legislative Assembly of Nebraska*, 6th sess., January 7, 1869, Appendix A, 347.

3. *Omaha Republican*, July 17, 1867.

4. *Omaha Republican*, June 7, 1867.

5. *Senate Journal of the Legislative Assembly of Nebraska*, 6th sess., 92; and *House Journal of the Legislative Assembly of Nebraska*, 6th sess., 98.

13. YEARS OF SETTLEMENT

1. *House Journal of the Territorial Legislature of Nebraska*, 9th sess., January 7, 1864, 13.

2. *U.S. Statutes at Large*, 12:392.

3. *U.S. Statutes at Large*, 12:392.

4. The United States government reacquired the Freeman homestead in 1936 and established it as Homestead National Monument of America.

5. *Report of the Commissioner of the General Land Office* (1883), 3.

6. *Report of the Commissioner of the General Land Office* (1885), 51.

7. The Union Pacific's land grant, of course, extended all the way across the state, and much of it lay in the subhumid region of the central and western area, whereas virtually all of the Burlington's land lay in the more humid section.

8. Theodore C. Wentzlaff, ed., "The Russian Germans Come to the United States," *Nebraska History* 49 (winter 1968): 382.

9. According to Union Pacific Museum curator Don Snoddy, as of October 1994 the Union Pacific still retained 1,335 acres from the original land grant.

10. Samuel Aughey, *Sketches of the Physical Geography and Geology of Nebraska* (Omaha: Daily Republican Book and Job Office, 1880), 44–45.

14. THE 1870S: GROWING PAINS

1. Sheldon, *Nebraska*, 1:579.

2. U.S. Department of the Interior, Bureau of the Census, *Population of the United States at the Tenth Census: 1880* (Washington DC: Government Printing Office, 1883), 492–95.

3. Sheldon, *Nebraska*, 1:494.

4. Sheldon, *Nebraska*, 1: 494.

5. Addison E. Sheldon., ed., *Official Report of the Debates and Proceedings in the Nebraska Constitutional Convention, 1871* (Lincoln: Nebraska State Historical Society, 1907).

6. See Sheldon, ed., *Official Report of the Debates and Proceedings in the Nebraska Constitutional Convention, 1871*, 405, 407, 422.

15. THE RANGE CATTLE INDUSTRY

1. Edward Everett Dale, *The Range Cattle Industry* (Norman: University of Oklahoma Press, 1930), 21.

2. Norbert Mahnken, "Ogallala—Nebraska's Cowboy Capital," *Nebraska History* 27 (April–June 1947): 85.

3. James S. Brisbin, *The Beef Bonanza; or, How to Get Rich on the Plains* (Philadelphia: J. B. Lippincott, 1881).

4. Harry E. Chrisman, *Ladder of Rivers: The Story of I. P. (Print) Olive* (Denver: Sage Books, 1962). The incident was also reported in S. D. Butcher, *Pioneer History of Custer County* (Broken Bow NE, 1901), 43–62.

5. Bartlett Richards Jr. with Ruth Van Ackerman, *Bartlett Richards: Nebraska Sandhills Cattleman* (Lincoln: Nebraska State Historical Society, 1980), 143–55, 175.

6. *Alliance Times*, May 10, 1904.

16. THE 1880S: PROGRESS AND PROSPERITY

1. See yearly rainfall figures in Appendix.

2. There has been a widespread belief that the census returns for 1890 were heavily padded in certain Nebraska cities. Though apparently there was some padding, it does not appear to have been as heavy as generally believed. See Edgar Z. Palmer, "The Correctness of the 1890 Census of Population for Nebraska Cities," *Nebraska History* 32 (December 1951): 259–67.

3. Boyd County was organized in 1891 from land added to the state in an adjustment of the South Dakota boundary; Thurston County was added in 1892 in an area occupied by the Omaha Indian Reservation.

4. Sheldon, *Nebraska*, 1:661–62.

5. See agricultural acreage statistics in Appendix.

6. See oat production statistics in Appendix.

7. From statements about J. Sterling Morton by Governor Robert Furnas when announcing Morton's death on April 27, 1902, in *Proceedings of the Nebraska State Historical Society* 15 (1907): 147–53.

8. "Report of the President," *Journal of the Proceedings of the State Board of Agriculture, September 4, 1873–January 26, 1876* (Lincoln: Journal Company, State Printers, 1876), 40–47.

9. See wheat production statistics in Appendix.

10. *Conservative*, January 19, 1899.

11. Virginia V. Ott, *Sterling's Carrie: Mrs. J. Sterling Morton* (Lincoln: Media Publishing, 1989), 191.

12. *Western Resources*, February 1887, p. 36.

13. The legislature had memorialized Congress in 1871 to relocate the nation's capital to Nebraska. See Sheldon, *Nebraska*, 1:460.

14. C. M. Harger, "New Era in the Middle West," *New Harpers Magazine* 97 (July 1898): 276–77.

15. H. J. Fletcher, "Western Real Estate Booms, and After," *Atlantic Monthly* 81 (May 1898): 689–704.

16. See Addison E. Sheldon, "A Hero of the Nebraska Frontier," *Nebraska History and Record of Pioneer Days* 1 (February 1918): 5.

17. THE 1880S: WHOSE PROSPERITY?

1. James J. Blake, "The Brownville, Fort Kearney and Pacific Railroad," *Nebraska History* 29 (September 1948): 238–72.
2. George W. Berge, *The Free Pass Bribery System* (Lincoln: Independent Publishing Company, 1905), 9.
3. Nebraska State Farmers' Alliance, "Declaration of Principles, 1887," in Sheldon, *Nebraska*, 1:672.

18. THE POPULIST REVOLT

1. *Omaha Bee*, January 15, 1890.
2. "Declaration of Principles and Popular Call for a People's Independent State Convention," in Sheldon, *Nebraska*, 1:673.
3. Sheldon, *Nebraska*, 1:682.
4. Sheldon, *Nebraska*, 1:682.
5. *Nebraska State Journal*, Lincoln, July 29,1890.
6. *Nebraska State Journal*, Lincoln, July 30, 1890.
7. Sheldon, *Nebraska*, 1:684.
8. Sheldon, *Nebraska*, 1:688–89.
9. Written by Arthur L. Kellog and published in the *Farmers' Alliance*, October 4, 1890. For the lyrics to this and other populist songs, see also John D. Hicks, *The Populist Revolt* (Lincoln: University of Nebraska Press, 1961), 167–70.
10. *Farmers' Alliance*, September 27, 1890. See Hicks, *Populist Revolt*, 168.
11. Jane Taylor Nelsen, ed., *A Prairie Populist: The Memoirs of Luna Keillie* (Iowa City: University of Iowa Press, 1992), 159.
12. The phrase "hogs in the parlor" was in an editorial in the *Lincoln Daily State Journal* of September 14, 1890, written by the newspaper's editor C. H. Gere. See Sheldon, *Nebraska*, 1:690.
13. Sheldon, *Nebraska*, 1:745.

19. THE FADING FRONTIER

1. U.S. Department of the Interior, Bureau of the Census, *Compendium of the Eleventh Census: 1890*, vol. 1: *Population* (Washington DC: Government Printing Office, 1892), xlviii.

2. Frederick Jackson Turner, "The Significance of the Frontier in American History," in *The Turner Thesis*, ed. George Rogers Taylor (1949; rpt. Lexington MA: D. C. Heath, 1972), 3.

3. Willa Cather, "Nebraska: The End of the First Cycle," in *Roundup: A Nebraska Reader*, ed. Virginia Faulkner (Lincoln: University of Nebraska Press, 1957), 7.

4. Whitmore was a prolific writer and speaker on Nebraska agriculture. See William Gunn Whitmore Manuscript Collection, MS3742, Nebraska State Historical Society.

20. EMERGING AWARENESS: CULTURAL EXPRESSIONS

1. Sheldon, *Nebraska*, 1:864.

2. Willa Cather, "Nebraska: The End of the First Cycle," 4.

3. See John E. Carter, *Solomon D. Butcher: Photographing the American Dream* (Lincoln: University of Nebraska Press, 1985).

4. See Edward Everett Dale, "The Frontier Literary Society," *Nebraska History* 31 (September 1950): 167–82.

21. NEBRASKA POLITICS AND PROGRESSIVISM

1. Charles H. Morrill, *The Morrills and Reminiscences* (Chicago: University Publishing Co., 1918), 70–71.

2. *Omaha Weekly Bee*, August 10, 1898.

3. *Nebraska State Journal*, February 26, 1902.

4. *Schuyler Free Lance*, May 20, 1904.

5. Frederick Jackson Turner, *The Frontier in American History* (New York: Henry Holt, 1920), 281.

6. *Nebraska State Journal*, June 17, 1906.

22. NEBRASKA AND WORLD WAR I

1. The vote in the Republican primary of 1918 for United States senator was as follows: George W. Norris, 23,715; Charles H. Sloan, 17,070; Ross L. Hammond, 16,948; William Madgett, 4,301; and Dave Mercer, 4,089.

2. *Laws of Nebraska*, 35th sess., 1917, 489.

3. Governor Keith Neville, "Opening Message to the Extra Session of the Legislature, March 26, 1918," in *Messages and Proclamations of the Governors of Nebraska, 1854–1941*, 3:288.

4. Douglas R. Hartman, *Nebraska's Milita: The History of the Army and Air National Guard, 1854–1991* (Virginia Beach VA: Donning Company, 1994), 93.

5. Nebraska Department of Agriculture and Inspection, *Nebraska Agricultural Statistics: Historical Record, 1866–1954*, 8. For data from 1954 to the present, see the annual reports of the same title.

6. Nebraska Department of Agriculture and Inspection, *Nebraska Agricultural Statistics: Historical Record, 1866–1954*, 14–15.

7. To be sure, some prices were guaranteed by the government, although prices on the open market generally stayed above government-guaranteed minimums.

8. U.S. Department of Commerce, Bureau of the Census, *Fourteenth Census of the United States: 1920* (Washington DC: Government Printing Office, 1922).

23. THE 1920S: ADAPTING TO CHANGE

1. Michael L. Lawson, "Omaha, a City in Ferment: Summer of 1919," *Nebraska History* 58 (fall 1977): 415.

2. *Lincoln Star*, July 1, 2, 1924, quoted in Michael W. Schuyler, "The Ku Klux Klan in Nebraska," *Nebraska History* 66 (fall 1985): 235.

3. Governor Samuel R. McKelvie, "First Inaugural Message, January 9, 1919," *Messages and Proclamations of the Governors of Nebraska, 1854–1941*, 3:352.

4. *Messages and Proclamations of the Governors of Nebraska, 1854–1941*, 3:353.

5. According to Nebraska Roads Department figures, the Nebraska highway system in 1995 consisted of approximately ten thousand miles of roads. Approximately ninety thousand miles of additional roadways are designated within the various systems of counties, cities, and towns.

6. *Twenty-Third Biennial Report of the Department of Roads and Irrigation* (1939–40), vi–vii.

24. THE GREAT DEPRESSION

1. Cather, "Nebraska: The End of the First Cycle," 7.

2. See agricultural tables in Appendix.

3. H. C. Filley, *Effects of Inflation and Deflation upon Nebraska Agriculture, 1914 to 1932* (Lincoln: University of Nebraska, Agricultural Experiment Station, 1934), 115.

4. U.S. Bureau of the Census, *Statistical Abstract of the United States: 1930* (Washington DC: Government Printing Office, 1933), 758–59.

5. U.S. Bureau of the Census, *Statistical Abstract of the United States, 1930*, 758–59, 1940, 4.
6. Nebraska Department of Economic Development, *Nebraska Statistical Handbook*, 1970.
7. Works Progress Administration, *Nebraska: A Guide to the Cornhusker State* (1939; rpt. Lincoln: University of Nebraska Press, 1979), 67.

25. RELIEF, RECOVERY, AND WAR

1. George W. Norris, *Fighting Liberal* (New York: Macmillan, 1945), 351–52.
2. Report of the Joint Committee of the Senate and House of Representatives, Nebraska Legislative Reference Bureau, Bulletin No. 4 (Lincoln, 1914).
3. Amendment 20, adopted in January 1933, after the experience of the long "lame-duck" presidency of Herbert Hoover between the election of Franklin Roosevelt on November 20, 1932, and his inauguration on March 4, 1933, set the date of future presidential inaugurations on January 20.
4. A. C. Breckenridge, *One House for Two* (Washington DC: Public Affairs Press, 1957), 46.
5. Roger V. Shumate, "The Nebraska Unicameral Legislature," *Western Political Quarterly* 5 (September 1952): 512.
6. Glenn Thompson, *Prisoners on the Plains: The German POWs at Camp Atlanta* (Holdrege NE: Phelps County Historical Society, 1993), 78, 82–83.

26. LEGACIES OF THE DEPRESSION

1. J. Sterling Morton, "Address to the Horticultural Society," Brownville, October 5, 1871, *Transactions of the Nebraska State Horticultural Society* (1871), 17–22.
2. *Nebraska Irrigation Annual* (Lincoln, 1896), 28–29.
3. See Walter Prescott Webb, "The Story of Some Prairie Inventions," *Nebraska History* 34 (December 1953): 229–44.

28. INTO THE SECOND CENTURY: NEW REALITIES

1. *Lincoln Evening Journal*, November 9, 1966.
2. *Lincoln Evening Journal*, November 9, 1966.
3. "Inaugural Address of Governor Norbert T. Tiemann, January 5, 1967," *Legislative Journal of the State of Nebraska*, 77th sess., 1:71.
4. *Lincoln Evening Journal*, January 25, 1967.
5. *Lincoln Evening Journal*, November 1, 1968.

6. *Lincoln Evening Journal*, March 1, 1967.

7. *Lincoln Evening Journal*, July 5, 1966.

8. Quoted in *Omaha World Herald*, March 5, 1968.

9. *Omaha World Herald*, June 25, 1969.

29. THE 1970S: HOLDING THE LINE

1. Duane Hutchinson, *Exon: Biography of a Governor* (Lincoln: Foundation Books, 1973), 208–9. There is some disagreement about exactly what Tiemann said. The *Omaha World Herald* of August 10, 1970, quoted him as saying, "I have never seen farmers happy in prosperity or not prosperity," and the *Lincoln Evening Journal* of the same date gave the words as "Farmers never seem happy about anything."

2. *Lincoln Evening Journal*, November 4, 1970.

3. *Lincoln Evening Journal*, November 4, 1970.

4. J. James Exon, "Inaugural Message," *Nebraska Legislative Journal*, 82d Legislature, 1st sess. (January 5, 1971-May 26, 1971), 66.

5. Exon, "Inaugural Message," 67.

6. Exon, "Inaugural Message," 68.

7. *Lincoln Evening Journal*, November 4, 1970.

8. "1974 Year in Review," Archives and Library, *Lincoln Journal Star*.

9. *Lincoln Star*, November 3, 1976.

30. THE POLITICS OF RECESSION: THE 1980S AND BEYOND

1. Economic data compiled from the *Nebraska Statistical Handbook*, published biennially by the State Department of Economic Development from 1970 to 1990.

2. Charles Thone, "Inauguration Address," January 4, 1979, *Legislative Journal of the State of Nebraska*, 86th Legislature, 1st sess., 1:91.

3. Charles Thone, "State of the State Address, January 10, 1980," *Legislative Journal of the State of Nebraska*, 86th Legislature, 2d sess., 161.

4. *Lincoln Evening Journal*, December 26, 1981.

5. *Lincoln Star*, January 2, 1982.

6. Charles Thone, "Address to the Legislature, October 30, 1981," *Legislative Journal of the State of Nebraska*, 87th Legislature, 1st special sess., 17.

7. Compiled from Department of Economic Development, *Nebraska Statistical Handbook*, 1972, 1976–77, 1982–83, 1990–91.

8. *Lincoln Journal Star*, September 10, 1982

9. *Lincoln Star*, September 10, 1982

10. "Star Picks Top Stories from 1982," *Lincoln Star*, January 1, 1983.

11. *Lincoln Journal-Star*, September 12, 1982.

12. *Lincoln Star*, September 13, 1982.

13. Governor Robert Kerrey, "Inaugural Address, January 6, 1983," *Legislative Journal of the State of Nebraska*, 88th Legislature, 1st sess., 82.

14. Governor Robert Kerrey, "Economic Development Policies for a More Productive Nebraska," March 24, 1983, *Legislative Journal of the State of Nebraska*, 88th Legislature, 1st sess., 1144.

15. *Lincoln Journal*, December 6, 1985.

16. *Lincoln Journal*, December 23, 1988.

17. Department of Economic Statistics, *Nebraska Statistical Handbook*, 1970, 1990–92.

18. *Unicameral Update* 10 (June 2, 1987): 4.

19. Nebraska Department of Revenue, *Annual Report to the Nebraska Legislature on the Employment and Investment Growth Act (LB775) and the Employment Expansion and Investment Incentive Act (LB270)*, March 15, 1991.

20. Nebraska Department of Revenue, *Annual Report to the Nebraska Legislature on the Employment and Investment Growth Act (LB775) and the Employment Expansion and Investment Incentive Act (LB270)*, March 13, 1992.

SUGGESTIONS FOR FURTHER READING

There is a wealth of material relating to the state's past. This bibliography is not intended to be exhaustive, but it does make an effort to call attention to works that should be generally useful and available. For a more extensive bibliography, the reader should refer to Michael L. Tate, *Nebraska History: An Annotated Bibliography* (1995).

GENERAL SUGGESTIONS

There are several older works, which are generally available in the academic and larger libraries of the state, that are of particular value. Originally published in 1882, Alfred T. Andreas, *History of the State of Nebraska* (rpt. 1995) is a mine of information regarding the local history of communities that had been established by 1882. Also of considerable usefulness for its treatment of the political history of the territorial period is J. Sterling Morton and Albert Watkins, *Illustrated History of Nebraska* (3 vols., 1905–13). In 1931 Addison E. Sheldon published *Nebraska: The Land and the People* (3 vols.), which is particularly good on the settlement and Populist periods.

A somewhat dated yet indispensable guide to ethnic studies and resources relevant to Nebraska is *Broken Hoops and Plains People: A Catalogue of Ethnic Resources in the Humanities, Nebraska and Thereabouts* (1976) published by the Nebraska Curriculum Development Center. Also dated but useful for its interpretive approach to Nebraska history is Dorothy Weyer Creigh, *Nebraska: A Bicentennial History* (1977).

Readers will find valuable Frederick C. Luebke, *Nebraska: An Illustrated History* (1995), as well as two collections of descriptive pieces about Nebraska issues and personalities: Dorothy Weyer Creigh, *Nebraska, Where Dreams Grow* (1981) and Donald R. Hickey, *Nebraska Moments: Glimpses of Nebraska's Past* (1992). Frederick C. Luebke, "Time, Place and Culture in Nebraska," *Nebraska History* 69 (winter, 1988), 150–68, is particularly useful and thought-provoking.

Nebraska History, the quarterly journal of the Nebraska State Historical Society, publishes valuable and interesting articles on all aspects of the state's history. *Nebraskaland*, the publication of the Nebraska Game and Parks Commission, is a valuable source of articles on a wide range of topics, both current and historical.

CHAPTER I: THE LAND

Basic to an understanding of the history of the plains is Walter Prescott Webb, *The Great Plains* (1931; rpt., 1981). Also essential are James C. Malin, *The Grassland of North America* (1947; rev. ed., 1967) and Everett Dick, *Conquering the Great American Desert* (1975). A useful guide to the work of James C. Malin is Thomas H. LeDuc, "An Ecological Interpretation of Grasslands History," *Nebraska History* 31 (September 1950): 226–33. Also useful is Brian W. Blouet and Merlin P. Lawson, *Images of the Plains: The Role of Human Adaptation in Settlement* (1975). Useful for its summary and interpretation of human adaptation to changes in the land is Paul A. Johnsgard, *The Platte: Channels in Time* (1984), as well as John W. Bennett, "Human Adaptation to the North American Great Plains," in *The Struggle for the Land: Indigenous Insights and Industrial Empire in the Semi-Arid West*, ed.Paul A. Olson (1990). A convenient summary of early attitudes regarding the plains will be found in Ralph C. Morris, "The Notion of a Great American Desert East of the Rockies," *Mississippi Valley Historical Review* 13 (September 1926): 190–200; Terry Alford, "The West as a Desert in American Thought Prior to Long's 1819–1820 Expedition," *Journal of the West* 8 (October 1969): 515–25; and Roger Nichols, "The Army and Early Perceptions of the Plains," *Nebraska History* 56 (spring 1975): 121–35.

Carl F. Kraenzel, *The Great Plains in Transition* (1955), vividly portrays the problems of the plains and suggests solutions; Robert G. Athearn, *High Country Empire* (1965), discusses the history of the plains and mountains with particular emphasis on the influence of environment; Brian W. Blouet and Frederick C. Luebke, *The Great Plains: Environment and Culture* (1979), is a compilation of essays dealing with the impact of the plains on political and institutional change. Also useful is John Francis McDermott, *The Frontier Re-examined* (1967), and Arrell Morgan Gibson, *The West in the Life of the Nation* (1976).

Older works on Nebraska geography, including George E. Condra, *Geography, Agriculture, Industries of Nebraska* (1946), will still be found useful, but readers will also want to consult Bradley H. Baltensperger, *Nebraska: A Geography* (1985). John Wesley Powell, *Report on the Lands of the Arid Region of the United States* (1879; rpt. 1983), is an important pioneer study, and Wallace Stegner, *Beyond the Hundredth Meridian* (1954; rpt. 1982), is an interesting discussion of the work of John Wesley Powell.

Although not for the general reader, J. E. Weaver, *North American Prairie* (1954), which summarizes the life work of the noted plant ecologist, contains much of significance, as does his *Native Vegetation of Nebraska* (1965) and *Prairie Plants and Their Environment* (1968). Of more contemporary interest and particularly valuable for its treatment of the ecology of the Sand Hills is Paul A. Johnsgard, *This Fragile Land: A Natural History of the Nebraska Sandhills* (1995).

The destruction of the buffalo is described dramatically in Mari Sandoz, *The Buffalo Hunters* (1954; rpt. 1978), but David A. Dary, *The Buffalo Book: The Full Saga of the American Animal* (1974), should also be consulted.

CHAPTER 2: THE FIRST PEOPLE

In recent years historians as well as anthropologists and archaeologists have been active in the interpretation of the prehistory of the plains. Valuable reports on archaeological work in Nebraska will be found in the publications of the Nebraska State Historical Society, but the general reader will find particularly valuable the spring 1994 volume of *Nebraska History*, entitled *The Cellars of Time: Paleontology and Archaeology in Nebraska*. The January–February 1984 issue of *Nebraskaland*, entitled *First Voices*, is also of interest.

Several recent general guides to Native Americans will also be found useful. Among these are David Hurst Thomas, Richard White, Peter Nabokov, and Philip J. Deloria, *The Native Americans: An Illustrated History* (1993); Philip Kopper, *The Smithsonian Book of North American Indians Before the Coming of the Europeans* (1986); Herman J. Viola and Carolyn Margolis, *Seeds of Change: Five Hundred Years Since Columbus* (1991); and William T. Hagan, *American Indians* (1993). On Plains Indians in general, see Karl H. Schlesier, ed., *Plains Indians, A.D. 500–1500* (1994); Preston Holder, *The Hoe and the Horse on the Plains* (1970); and Bernard Mishkin, *Rank and Warfare Among the Plains Indians* (1992).

Readers will want to look at the chapter titled "First People" in Paul Johnsgard, *The Platte: Channels in Time* (1984) for a general treatment of the prehistoric Indians in Nebraska. Several notable works have been produced on specific tribes. On the Pawnees, see George E. Hyde, *Pawnee Indians* (1988); Gene Weltfish, *The Lost Universe: Pawnee Life and Culture* (1977); Martha Royce Blaine, *Pawnee Passages* (1990); and James R. Murie, *Ceremonies of the Pawnee* (1989). The Pawnee Scouts are treated in George Bird Grinnell, *Two Great Scouts and Their Pawnee Battalion* (1928; rpt. 1973), and Donald F. Danker, "The North Brothers and the Pawnee Scouts," *Nebraska History* 42 (September 1961): 161–80.

Berlin B. Chapman, *The Otoes and Missourias* (1965), is a detailed study of the Otoes and Missourias with particular emphasis on their lands. Also of value is R. David Edmunds, *The Otoe-Missouria People* (1976).

For information on the Omahas see the recently reissued two-volume work by Alice Fletcher and Francis La Flesche, *The Omaha Tribe* (1911; rpt. 1992); John M. O'Shea and John Ludwickson, *Archaeology and Ethnohistory of the Omaha Indians: The Big Village Site* (1992); and Donald Ross, "The Omaha People," *Indian Historian* 3 (1970): 19–21.

For the Poncas, see Thomas Henry Tibbles, *Buckskin and Blanket Days* (1969), originally published in 1905, and Joseph H. Cash and Gerald W. Wolff, *The Ponca People* (1975).

For the Teton Sioux or Lakota, see Amos Bad Heart Bull and Helen H. Blish, *A Photographic History of the Oglala Sioux* (1967), which includes artwork depicting Oglala life; Royal B. Hasrick, *The Sioux: Life and Customs of a Warrior Society* (1964); George E. Hyde, *Spotted Tail's Folk: A History of the Brule Sioux* (1961); and Kingley M. Bray, "Teton Sioux Population History, 1655–1881," *Nebraska History* 75 (summer 1994): 165–88.

CHAPTER 3: SPAIN AND FRANCE ON THE PLAINS

Bernard De Voto, *The Course of Empire* (1952; rpt. 1983), covers in sweeping style the exploration of North America through the time of Lewis and Clark. Particularly valuable as a reference on events on the central plains in this era is Louise Barry, *The Beginnings of the West: Annals of the Kansas Gateway to the American West, 1540–1854* (1972). For a general account of both French and Spanish struggles for control of the North American West, see Russell McKee, *The Last West: A History of the Great Plains* (1974), and Arrell Morgan Gibson, *The West in the Life of the Nation* (1976). The best account of French and Spanish activity in the Missouri Valley will be found in the Introduction to Abraham P. Nasatir, ed., *Before Lewis and Clark* (2 vols., 1952; rpt. 1990).

Accounts of Spanish activity on the plains in general is found in Ralph H. Vigil, "Spanish Exporation and the Great Plains in the Age of Discovery: Myth and Reality," *Great Plains Quarterly* 10 (winter 1990): 3–17; and James A. Hanson, "Spain on the Plains," *Nebraska History* 74 (spring 1993): 2–21.

Documents relating to the Coronado expedition will be found in George P. Winship, *The Coronado Expedition, 1540–1542* (1896; rpt. 1964), but the best and most recent work on the career of Coronado with a careful discussion of the route of his exploration is Herbert E. Bolton, *Coronado, Knight of Pueblos and Plains* (1990).

For Spanish activity subsequent to Coronado, and particularly the Villasur expedition, see A. B. Thomas, *After Coronado: Spanish Exploration Northeast of New Mexico, 1696–1727* (1935), and William Brandon, "The Quivira Trail," in *Quivira: Europeans in the Region of the Santa Fe Trail, 1540–1820* (1990). For information on research on Fort Charles, see W. Raymond Wood, "Fort Charles or Mr. Mackey's Trading House," *Nebraska History* 76 (spring 1995): 2–7; and Gayle F. Carlson, "The Search for Fort Charles," *Nebraska History* 76 (spring 1995): 8–9.

For information on the Bourgmont expedition, see Frank Norall, *Bourgmont, Explorer of the Missouri, 1698–1725* (1988). Also useful for its insights into intertribal conflict is John C. Ewers, "Intertribal Warfare as a Precursor of Indian-White Warfare on the Northern Great Plains," *Western Historical Quarterly* 6 (October 1975): 66–88.

CHAPTER 4: THE LOUISIANA PURCHASE

The best source for the Lewis and Clark expedition is the journals themselves, easily available in Gary Moulton. See Gary Moulton, ed., *The Journals of the Lewis and Clark Expedition* (11 vols., 1985–97). Also useful is an excellent analysis of the Lewis and Clark expedition in James P. Ronda, *Lewis and Clark Among the Indians* (1984), as well as the analysis by John Logan Allen, *Passage Through the Garden: Lewis and Clark and the Image of the American Northwest* (1975). See also Ernest S. Osgood, ed., *The Field Notes of William Clark* (1964); Raymond D. Burroughs, ed., *The Natural History of the Lewis and Clark Expedition* (1961); and Donald Jackson, ed., *Letters of the Lewis and Clark Expedition, with Related Documents, 1783–1854* (1978).

The best source of information for the expeditions of Pike and Long is also the journals. For the Pike expedition, see Elliott Coues, ed., *The Expeditions of Zebulon Montgomery Pike . . .* (3 vols., 1895; rpt. 1972). Also useful are W. Eugene Hollon, *The Lost Pathfinder: Zebulon Montgomery Pike* (1949), and Donald Jackson, "Zebulon Pike and Nebraska," *Nebraska History* 47 (December 1966): 355–69. For the expeditions of Stephen Long, see Edwin James, *Account of an Expedition from Pittsburgh to the Rocky Mountains . . .* (1823; rpt. 1972). Readers will also find useful Richard G. Wood, *Stephen Harriman Long, 1784–1864: Army Engineer, Explorer, Inventor* (1966), and Roger Nichols's *Stephen Long and American Frontier Exploration* (1980). For works on the Frémont expedition see John C. Frémont, *Report of the Exploring Expedition to the Rocky Mountains . . .* (1845); Donald Jackson and Mary Lee Spence, eds., *The Expedition of John C. Frémont* (3 vols., 1970–84); and Allan Nevins, *Frémont: Pathmarker of the West* (1992).

The classic work on the fur trade is Hiram M. Chittenden, *The American Fur Trade of the Far West* (3 vols., 1902), also available in a more recent two-volume reprint with forewords by James P. Ronda (vol. 1, 1986) and William R. Swagerty (vol. 2, 1986). See also Donald McKay Frost, *General Ashley, the Overland Trail and the South Pass* (1960); Dale L. Morgan, *The West of William Ashley* (1964); James P. Ronda, *Astoria and Empire* (1990); and David J. Wishart, *The Fur Trade of the American West, 1807–1840: A Geographical Synthesis* (1992). Several articles in *Nebraska History* will also be found useful, including Charles E. Hanson Jr. and Veronica Sue Walters, "The Early Fur Trade in Northeastern Nebraska," 57 (fall 1976): 291–314; Richard E. Jensen, "Bellevue: The First Twenty Years,

1822–1842," 56 (fall 1975): 339–74; Charles E. Hanson Jr., "Reconstruction of the Bordeaux Trading Post," 53 (summer 1972): 137–65. For the career of Manuel Lisa, see Richard E. Oglesby, *Manuel Lisa and the Opening of the Missouri Fur Trade* (1963), and Walter B. Douglas, *Manuel Lisa, with Hitherto Unpublished Material*, annotated and edited by Abraham P. Nasatir (1964).

For a general treatment of the Yellowstone Expedition and Fort Atkinson, see Edgar Bruce Wesley, *Guarding the Frontier* (1935; rpt. 1970). See also Roger L. Nichols, *The Missouri Expedition, 1818–1820: The Journal of Surgeon John Gale* (1969). Over the years, *Nebraska History* has contained valuable articles on Fort Atkinson. More recent ones include Roger L. Nichols, "Scurvy at Cantonment Missouri, 1819–1820," 49 (winter 1968): 333–47; Roger L Nichols, "Soldiers as Farmers: Army Agriculture in the Missouri Valley, 1818–1827," 52 (fall 1971): 239–54; Virgil Ney, "Prairie Generals and Colonels at Cantonment Missouri and Fort Atkinson," 56 (spring 1975): 51–76; and Stewart Miller Jr., "To Plow, to Sow, to Reap, to Mow: The U.S. Army Agricultural Program," 63 (summer 1982): 194–215. Readers will also find useful Roger L. Nichols, *General Henry Atkinson: A Western Military Career* (1965), and Virgil Ney's article, "Daily Life at Fort Atkinson on the Missouri, 1820–1827," *Military Review* 57 (1977): 36–48, 50–66, as well as his larger work, *Fort on the Prairie: Fort Atkinson on the Council Bluff, 1819–1827* (1978).

No satisfactory general account of missionary activity in the region exists, but there are interesting works on particular missions and missionaries. Father DeSmet's life is exhaustively treated in H. M. Chittenden and Alfred T. Richardson, *Life, Letters, and Travels of Father Pierre Jean DeSmet, S.J.* (4 vols., 1905; rpt. 1969); and E. Laveille, *The Life of Father DeSmet* (1981). Particularly interesting and valuable are two new works on Father DeSmet: John J. Killoren, *"Come Blackrobe," DeSmet and the Indian Tragedy* (1994), and Robert C. Carriker, *Father Peter John DeSmet, Jesuit in the West* (1995). Nebraska State Historical Society, *Transactions and Reports*, contain some documentary material relating to the work of missionaries in Nebraska, including Samuel Allis, "Forty Years Among the Indians and on the Eastern Borders of Nebraska," 2 (1887): 133–66, and Moses Merrill, "Extracts from the Diary of Rev. Moses Merrill, a Missionary to the Otoe Indians from 1832 to 1840," 4 (1892): 160–91.

Also see John Dunbar, "Missionary Life Among the Pawnee," *Collections of the Nebraska Historical Society*, 16 (1911): 268–87, as well as numerous articles in *Nebraska History* including Phillips G. Davies, "David Jones and Gwen Davies, "Missionaries in Nebraska Territory, 1853–1860," 60 (spring 1979): 77–91; Norma Kidd Green, "The Presbyterian Mission to the Omaha Indian Tribe," 48 (autumn 1967): 267–88; Gail DeBuse Potter, "A Note on the Samuel Allis Family: Missionaries to the Pawnee, 1834–46," 67 (spring 1986): 1–7; and Richard E. Jensen, "The Pawnee Mission, 1834–1846," *Nebraska History* 75 (winter 1994): 301–10.

CHAPTER 5: THE GREAT PLATTE RIVER ROAD

The best accounts of the overland migration to the Pacific are found in two works by Merrill J Mattes—*The Great Platte River Road* (1969) and *Platte River Road Narratives* (1988)—and John D. Unruh Jr., *The Plains Across* (1979). For a discussion of the Council Bluffs Road north of the Platte River, see Merrill J. Mattes, "The Council Bluffs Road: A New Perspective on the Northern Branch of the Great Platte River Road," *Nebraska History* 65 (summer 1984): 179–94.

The Mormons have been the subject of a voluminous literature, much of it controversial. For their experiences in Nebraska, consult Leroy R. Hafen and Ann W. Hafen, *Handcarts to Zion: the Story of a Unique Western Migration, 1856–1860* (1992); Wallace Stegner, *The Gathering of Zion: The Story of the Mormon Trail* (1992); and recent articles in *Nebraska History*, including A. R. Mortensen, "Mormons, Nebraska and the Way West," 46 (December 1965): 259–72; Michael W. Homer, "After Winter Quarters and Council Bluffs: The Mormons in Nebraska Territory, 1854–1867," 65 (winter 1984): 467–83; and Richard Jensen, "By Handcart to Utah: The Account of C. C. A. Christensen," 66 (winter 1985): 333–48. See also Stanley B. Kimball, "Mormon Trail Network in Nebraska, 1846–1868: A New Look," *Brigham Young University Studies* 24 (1984): 3–18.

There are several works of interest dealing with women and their role in the western migration, including John Mack Farragher, *Women and Men on the Overland Trail* (1979); Julie Roy Jeffrey, *Frontier Women: The Trans-Mississippi West, 1840–1880* (1979); Glenda Riley, *Women and Indians on the Frontier, 1825–1915* (1984); and Lillian Schlissel, *Women's Diaries of the Westward Journey* (1982).

On Fort Kearny see Albert Watkins, "History of Fort Kearny," Nebraska State Historical Society, *Collections* 16 (1911): 227–67; Lillian M. Willman, "The History of Fort Kearny," Nebraska State Historical Society, *Publications* 21 (1930): 211–68; Lyle E. Mantor, "Fort Kearny and the Westward Movement," *Nebraska History* 29 (September 1948): 175–207; and Milton E. Holtz, "Old Fort Kearny, 1846–1848: Symbol of a Changing Frontier," *Montana* 22 (1972): 44–55. The definitive study of Fort Laramie is LeRoy Hafen and Francis M. Young, *Fort Laramie and the Pageant of the West* (1938; rpt. 1984).

Landmarks and facilities along the trail have been of considerable interest to historians. For those in Nebraska see particularly Merrill J. Mattes, *Scotts Bluff* (1958), and the same author's articles in *Nebraska History*: "Robidoux's Trading Post at 'Scott's Bluffs,' and the California Gold Rush," 30 (June 1949): 95–138; "Fort Mitchell, Scotts Bluff, Nebraska Territory," 33 (March 1952): 1–34; "Chimney Rock on the Oregon Trail," 36 (March 1955): 1–26. See also in *Nebraska History* Earl R. Harris, "Courthouse and Jail Rocks: Landmarks on the Oregon Trail," 43 (March 1962): 29–52; T. L. Green, "A Forgotten Fur Trading Post in Scotts Bluff County," 15 (January 1934): 38–46, and "Scotts Bluffs, Fort John," 19 (July 1938): 175–190; and David Walker Lupton, "Fort Bernard on the Oregon Trail," 60 (June 1949): 21–35.

There are countless journals and reminiscences of the overland trail, but readers will find a useful compilation of narratives in Merrill J. Mattes, *Platte River Road Narratives* (1988). In addition, readers will want to consult Dale L. Morgan, ed., *Overland in 1846: Diaries and Letters of the California-Oregon Trail* (2 vols., 1993). For the Mormon Trail, consult Mary Ann Hafen, *Recollections of a Handcart Pioneer of 1860: A Woman's Life on the Mormon Frontier* (1983). For the gold rush readers will find useful Georgia Willis and Ruth Louis Gaines, *Gold Rush: The Journals, Drawings, and Other Pictures of J. Goldsborough Bruff* (1944). One of the best-recorded cholera deaths is detailed in George W. Hansen, "A Tragedy of the Oregon Trail," Nebraska State Historical Society *Collections* 17 (1913): 110–26.

The Kansas-Nebraska Act has been the subject of much controversy among American historians. A dated but useful introduction to that debate, at least up to the 1950s, can be found in Roy F. Nichols, "The Kansas-Nebraska Act: A Century of Historiography," *Mississippi Valley Historical Review* 43 (September 1956): 187–212. For general treatments of the failure of statesmanship in the 1850s, of which the Kansas-Nebraska Act was a part, see Roy F. Nichols, *The Disruption of American Democracy* (1948; rpt. 1962); Michael F. Holt, *The Political Crisis of the 1850s* (1973); David M. Potter, *The Impending Crisis, 1848–1861* (1976); and James A. Rawley, *Bleeding Kansas and the Coming of the Civil War* (1969).

Of special importance are the works of James C. Malin, particularly *The Nebraska Question* (1953); "Thomas Jefferson Sutherland, Nebraska Boomer," *Nebraska History* 34 (September 1953): 181–214; "The Nebraska Question: A Ten Year Record, 1844–1854," *Nebraska History* 35 (March 1954): 1–16; "The Motives of Stephen A. Douglas in the Organization of Nebraska Territory: A Letter Dated December 17, 1853," *Kansas Historical Quarterly* 19 (November 1951): 321–53; and "Aspects of the Nebraska Question, 1852–1854," *Kansas Historical Quarterly* 21 (May 1953): 385–91.

Many of the foregoing are concerned, in part at least, with an analysis of the motives of Stephen A. Douglas. Throwing additional light on the subject are the biographies of Douglas, of which the best is George Fort Milton, *The Eve of Conflict: Stephen A. Douglas and the Needless War* (1934; rpt. 1963). Also interesting is a more recent treatment in Robert Walter Johannsen, *Stephen A. Douglas* (1973).

Documents relating to the provisional government of Nebraska Territory are published in William E. Connelley, ed., *The Provisional Government of Nebraska Territory . . .* (1899). Hadley D. Johnson, "How the Kansas-Nebraska Line Was Established," Nebraska State Historical Society, *Transactions and Reports* 2 (1887): 80–92, is a discussion of the division of the territory by a participant. Of interest also will be the two general histories of the Republican and Democratic Parties as they relate to Nebraska history. See William E. Gienapp, *The Origins of the Republican Party, 1852–1856* (1987), and James F. Pedersen and Kenneth D. Wald, *Shall the People Rule? A History of the Democratic Party in Nebraska Politics, 1854–1972* (1967).

CHAPTER 7: THE NEBRASKA TERRITORY

The best and most detailed account of the establishment of territorial government will be found in J. Sterling Morton and Albert Watkins, *Illustrated History of Nebraska*, 1:194–255. A briefer treatment is provided by Addison Sheldon, *Nebraska: The Land and the People*, 1:238–63. These studies concentrate on the political history of the territory. See also James C. Olson, *J. Sterling Morton* (1942); David H. Price, "Sectionalism in Nebraska: When Kansas Considered Annexing Southern Nebraska, 1856–1860," *Nebraska History* 53 (winter 1972): 447–62; and James B. Potts, "The Nebraska Capital Controversy, 1854–1859," *Great Plains Quarterly* 8 (1988): 172–82.

CHAPTER 8: TERRITORIAL GROWTH AND DEVELOPMENT

Norman A. Graebner, "Nebraska's Missouri River Frontier, 1854–1860," *Nebraska History* 42 (December 1961): 213–36, is an excellent brief discussion of the urban aspects of Nebraska's territorial development. Donald F. Danker has authored important articles on territorial town building in *Nebraska History*: "C. W. Giddings and the Founding of Table Rock," 34 (March 1953): 33–54; "Columbus, a Territorial Town in the Platte Valley," 34 (December 1953): 275–88; "The Nebraska Winter Quarters Company and Florence," 37 (March 1956): 27–50. For early Omaha see Walker D. Wyman, "Omaha: Frontier Depot and Prodigy of Council Bluffs," *Nebraska History* 27 (July–September 1936): 143–55; Wallace Brown, "George L. Miller and the Boosting of Omaha," *Nebraska History* 50 (fall 1969): 277–91. For Brownville see Marion Marsh Brown, "The Brownville Story: Portrait of a Phoenix, 1854–1974," *Nebraska History* 55 (spring 1974): 1–141. For Bellevue see J. Q. Goss, "Bellevue, Its Past and Present," Nebraska State Historical Society, *Proceedings and Collections* 7 (1898): 36–47, and William J. Shallcross, *Romance of a Village* (1954).

Everett Dick, *The Sod House Frontier* (1937; rpt. 1954), is particularly valuable for the territorial period. Also important are Morton and

Watkins and Sheldon, cited above; volume 2 of the former contains much information on territorial banking, territorial products, the press, and various church groups. In addition, readers will find valuable Paul Schach, "German-Language Newspapers in Nebraska, 1860–1890," *Nebraska History* 65 (spring 1984): 84–107; Michael W. Homer, "The Territorial Judiciary: An Overview of the Nebraska Experience, 1854–1867." *Nebraska History* 63 (fall 1986): 349–80; and Gordon J. Blake, "Government and Banking in Territorial Nebraska," *Nebraska History* 51 (winter 1970): 425–35.

The standard land history of Nebraska is Sheldon, *Land Systems and Land Policies in Nebraska* (1936), of which pages 25–79 are useful for the territorial period. See also Orville H. Zabel, "To Reclaim the Wilderness: The Immigrant's Image of Territorial Nebraska," *Nebraska History* 46 (December 1965): 315–25; C. Howard Richardson, "The Nebraska Prairies: Dilemma to Early Territorial Farmers," *Nebraska History* 50 (winter 1969): 359–72; and Betty Stevens, *Bright Lights and Blue Ribbons: 125 Years of the Nebraska State Fair* (1994). A brief summary of the educational history of the territory will be found in Helen Siampos, "Early Education in Nebraska," *Nebraska History* 29 (June 1948): 113–33.

Personal documents of importance are Donald F. Danker, ed., *Mollie: The Journal of Mollie Dorsey Sanford in Nebraska and Colorado Territories, 1857–1866* (1959, rpt. 1976); Ruth K. Nuermberger, "Letters from Pioneer Nebraska by Edward R. Harden," *Nebraska History* 27 (January–March 1946): 18–47; George W. Barnes, "Pioneer Preacher," *Nebraska History* 27 (April–June 1946): 71–91. In addition, the publications of the Nebraska State Historical Society contain many reminiscences of territorial pioneers which are useful for social and economic as well as political history.

CHAPTER 9: HIGHWAY TO THE WEST

For a summary of the history of transportation in the West, see Oscar O. Winther, *The Transportation Frontier: Trans-Mississippi West, 1865–1890* (1964). For steamboating on the Missouri River, see William E. Lass, *A History of Steamboating on the Upper Missouri* (1977). For information about the steamboat *Bertrand*, see Jerome E. Petsche, *The Steamboat Bertrand: History, Excavation, and Architecture* (1974).

For a history of overland freighting, see William E. Lass, *From the Missouri to the Great Salt Lake: An Account of Overland Freighting* (1972). Raymond W. Settle and Mary Lund Settle, *War Drums and Wagon Wheels: The Story of Russell, Majors and Waddel* (1966), is an excellent study of the firm of Russell, Majors and Waddell. Alexander Majors, *Seventy Years on the Frontier* (1893; rpt. 1989), is a valuable reminiscence. For the stagecoach and Pony Express, see LeRoy R. Hafen, *The Overland Mail* (1969). Also useful are Frank A. Root and William E. Connelley, *The Overland Stage to California* (1901; rpt. 1950); Settle and Settle, *Saddles and Spurs: The Pony Express Saga* (1972); Noel M. Loomis, *Wells Fargo* (1968); Merrill J. Mattes and Paul C. Henderson, "The Pony Express: Across Nebraska from St. Joseph to Fort Laramie," *Nebraska History* 41 (June 1960): 83–122; and Norbert R. Mahnken, "The Sidney–Black Hills Trail," *Nebraska History* 30 (September 1949): 203–25. Musetta Gilman, *Pump on the Prairie* (1975), is an excellent history of the Gilman Brothers' road ranch.

Nebraska History is a source for several good articles which focus on Omaha as a freighting and outfitting post: Merrill J. Mattes, "The Council Bluffs Road: A New Perspective on the Northern Branch of the Great Platte River Road," 65 (spring 1984): 179–94; Howard P. Chudacoff, "Where Rolls the Dark Missouri Down," 52 (spring 1971): 1–30; Carol Gendler, "Territorial Omaha as a Staging and Freighting Center," 49 (summer 1968): 103–20; and Charles W. Martin, ed., "Omaha in 1868–1869: Selections from the Letters of Joseph Barker," 59 (winter 1978): 501–25.

Maury Klein has prepared a definitive history of the Union Pacific in two volumes: *Union Pacific: The Birth of a Railroad, 1862–1893* (1986) and *Union Pacific: The Rebirth, 1894–1969* (1989). Also consult Wallace D. Farnham, "The Pacific Railroad Act of 1862," *Nebraska History* 43 (September 1962): 141–68.

For an account of the building of the transcontinental railroad, see Wesley S. Griswold, *A Work of Giants* (1962), and Grenville M. Dodge's own account, *How We Built the Union Pacific Railway* (1910; rpt. 1965) Also useful are Robert G. Althearn, *Union Pacific Country* (1971), and

Thomas Buecker, "The Post of North Platte Station, 1867–1878," *Nebraska History* 63 (fall 1982): 381–98. More popular treatments are Barry Combs, *Westward to Promontory: Building the Union Pacific Across the Plains and Mountains, A Pictorial Documentary* (1969), and John Hoyt Williams, *A Great and Shiny Road: The Epic Story of the Transcontinental Railroad* (1988). A popular biography of the man who built the Union Pacific is Jacob R. Perkins, *Trails, Rails, and War: The Life of General G. M. Dodge* (1929)

CHAPTER 10: SECURING THE LAND

Indian problems constituted an important aspect of the Civil War in the West. For a general survey, see Robert Huhn Jones, *The Civil War in the Northwest: Nebraska, Wisconsin, Iowa, Minnesota, and the Dakotas* (1960). Nebraska's military participation in the Civil War is treated specifically in the first chapter of Douglas R. Hartman, *Nebraska's Militia* (1994), as well as in Earl G. Curtis, "John Milton Thayer," *Nebraska History* 28 (October–December 1947): 225–38; Benjamin F. Cooling, "The First Nebraska Infantry Regiment and the Battle of Fort Donelson," *Nebraska History* 45 (June 1964): 131–45; Robert C. Farb, "The Military Career of Robert W. Furnas," *Nebraska History* 32 (March 1951): 18–41; and James E. Potter, "A Nebraska Cavalryman in Dixie: The Letters of Martin Stowell," *Nebraska History* 74 (spring 1993): 21–31.

Indian difficulties and the role of the army in Nebraska during the Civil War are covered in Jennings C. Haggerty, "Indian Raids Along the Platte and Little Blue Rivers, 1864–1865," *Nebraska History* 28 (July–September, October–December 1947): 176–86, 239–60; Dee Brown, *The Galvanized Yankees* (1986); Larry D. Duke, "Nebraska Territory," *Journal of the West* 16 (April 1977): 72–84; R. Eli Paul, ed., "A Galvanized Yankee Along the Niobrara River," *Nebraska History* 70 (summer 1989): 146–57; Merrill J. Mattes, "Old Fort Mitchell, Nebraska, Revisited," *Overland Journal* 7 (1989): 2–11; and Eugene F. Ware, *The Indian War of 1864* (1911; rpt. 1960). Ware also discusses the establishment of Fort McPherson, which is treated definitively in Louis A. Holmes, *Fort McPherson, Nebraska, Fort Cottonwood, N.T.* (1963).

Suggestions for Further Reading

There is a voluminous literature on the subjugation of the plains Indians and the establishment of the reservation system in the West. Ralph K. Andrist, *The Long Death: The Last Days of the Plains Indians* (1993), is a popular general account. The Cheyennes are treated in George B. Grinnell, *The Fighting Cheyennes* (1915; rpt. 1956), and Mari Sandoz, *Cheyenne Autumn* (1953; rpt. 1992). Three volumes by George E. Hyde deal with the Lakota: *Red Cloud's Folk* (1937), *A Sioux Chronicle* (1956), and *Spotted Tail's Folk* (1961); see also James C. Olson, *Red Cloud and the Sioux Problem* (1965; rpt. 1975), and Mari Sandoz, *Crazy Horse* (1942; rpt. 1961). Particularly valuable is David J. Wishart, *An Unspeakable Sadness: The Dispossession of the Nebraska Indians* (1994). Also useful are Martha Royce Blaine, *Pawnee Passage, 1870–1875* (1990); James T. King, "A Better Way: General George Crook and the Ponca Indians," *Nebraska History* 50 (fall 1969): 239–56; Robert W. Mardock, "The Plains Frontier and the Indian Peace Policy, 1865–1880," *Nebraska History* 49 (summer 1968): 187–201; Roy W. Meyer, "The Establishment of the Santee Reservation, 1866–1869," *Nebraska History* 45 (March 1964): 49–97; and the Society of Friends Delegation Report, "Quaker Report on Indian Agencies in Nebraska, 1869," *Nebraska History* 54 (summer 1973): 151–219.

Military studies of particular interest to Nebraskans are Robert G. Athearn, *William Tecumseh Sherman and the Settlement of the West* (1956); James T. King, *War Eagle: A Life of General Eugene A. Carr* (1963); Merrill J. Mattes, *Indians, Infants and Infantry: Andrew and Elizabeth Burt on the Frontier* (1988); Dee Brown, *Fort Phil Kearny: An American Saga* (1962); Vincent J. Flanagan, "Gouvernor Kemble Warren, Explorer of the Nebraska Territory," *Nebraska History* 51 (summer 1970): 171–98; R. Eli Paul, "Battle of Ash Hollow: The 1909–1910 Recollections of General N. A. M. Dudley," *Nebraska History* 62 (fall 1981): 373–99; and Richard Guentzel, "The Department of the Platte and Western Settlement, 1866–1877," *Nebraska History* 56 (fall 1975): 389–417. For an account of the Republic River expedition, see two articles by James T. King: "The Republic River Expedition," *Nebraska History* 41 (September 1960): 165–200, and "The Battle of Summit Springs," *Nebraska History* 41 (December 1960): 281–98. The best of numerous accounts of the ghost-dance troubles and the Battle of Wounded Knee is Robert M. Utley, *The Last Days of the Sioux Nation* (1963).

CHAPTER 11: THE POLITICS OF STATEHOOD

Morton and Watkins, *Illustrated History of Nebraska* (3 vols., 1905–13), remains the best and most detailed source on the political history of Nebraska during the period of admission to the Union and establishment of the state government. For details of legislation involved in the statehood struggle, readers may want to consult Albert Watkins, "How Nebraska Was Brought into the Union," Nebraska State Historical Society, *Publications* 18 (1917): 375–434. Also useful for its chronology of key legislation is Douglas Bakken, "Chronology of Nebraska Statehood," *Nebraska History* 48 (spring 1967): 81–89. *Nebraska History* has included numerous articles over the years about the statehood struggle. Particularly useful are Wallace Brown, "George L. Miller and the Struggle over Nebraska Statehood," 41 (December 1960): 299–318, and Dennis Thavenet, "The Territorial Governorship: Nebraska Territory as Example." 51 (winter 1970): 387–409, as well as his "Governor William A. Richardson: Champion of Popular Sovereignty in Territorial Nebraska," 53 (winter 1972): 463–76; and two articles by James B. Potts, "Nebraska Statehood and Reconstruction," 69 (summer 1988): 73–83, and "North of 'Bleeding Kansas': The 1850s Political Crisis in Nebraska Territory," 73 (fall 1992): 110–18.

CHAPTER 12: ESTABLISHING THE STATE GOVERNMENT

Morton and Watkins, *Illustrated History of Nebraska* (3 vols., 1905–13), and Sheldon, *Nebraska: The Land and the People* (1931), are also valuable sources here. In addition, readers may want to consult the older yet still useful history of Lincoln, Andrew J. Sawyer, ed., *Lincoln and Lancaster County* (1916), which discusses the founding and early development of the capital city in great detail and reproduces the report of the Capital Commissioners on the location of the capital. A more recent history of Lincoln is Neale Copple, *Tower on the Plains* (1959). See also Louise Pound, "The Legend of the Lincoln Salt Basin," *Western Folklore* 10 (April 1951): 109–16.

For the location and disposition of the state lands, see Addison Sheldon, *Land Systems and Land Policies in Nebraska* (1936), particularly pages

219–85; Agnes Horton, "Nebraska's Agricultural College Land Grant," *Nebraska History* 30 (March 1949), 19–49; and "The History of Nebraska's Saline Land Grant," *Nebraska History* 40 (June 1959): 89–104.

CHAPTER 13: YEARS OF SETTLEMENT

The standard work on Nebraska's land history for this time period is Addison E. Sheldon, *Land Systems and Land Policies in Nebraska* (1936). For a briefer statement, see Fred A. Shannon, *The Farmer's Last Frontier* (1945). Howard W. Ottoson, ed., *Land Use Policy and Problems in the United States* (1963), consists of the papers presented at the Homestead Centennial Symposium at the University of Nebraska in 1962; of particular value for the settlement period is Paul W. Gates, "The Homestead Act Free Land Policy in Operation, 1862–1935." For a general survey, see Roy M. Robbins, *Our Landed Heritage* (1942; rpt. 1976). Also useful are Everett Dick, *The Lure of Land: A Social History of the Public Lands from the Articles of Confederation to the New Deal* (1970), and William H. Beezley, "Homesteading in Nebraska, 1862–1872," *Nebraska History* 53 (spring 1972): 59–75.

Essential to an understanding of the settlement of Nebraska is Richard C. Overton, *Burlington West: A Colonization History of the Burlington Railroad* (1941); also of importance is his *Burlington Route* (1965). James C. Olson, *J. Sterling Morton* (1942), discusses railroad promotional activity. See also articles in *Nebraska History*, including James J. Blake, "The Brownville, Fort Kearney and Pacific Railroad," 29 (September 1948): 238–72; Thomas M. Davis, "Building the Burlington Through Nebraska —A Summary View," 30 (December 1949): 317–47; "Lines West!—The Story of George W. Holdrege," 31 (March 1950): 25, 47; (June 1950): 107–25; (September 1950): 204–25; C. Clyde Jones, "A Survey of the Agricultural Development Program of the Chicago, Quincy and Burlington Railroad," 30 (September 1949): 226–56; Ray H. Mattison, "Burlington Tax Controversy in Nebraska Over the Federal Land Grants," 28 (April–June 1947): 110–31; Richard C. Overton, "Why Did the C. B. & Q. Build to Denver?" 40 (September 1959): 177–206; John D. Unruh Jr., "The Burlington and Missouri River Railroad Brings the Mennonites to Nebraska, 1873–1878," 45 (June 1964): 177–206; and Theodore C.

Wentzlaff, ed., "The Russian Germans Come to the United States," 49 (winter 1968): 379–400.

CHAPTER 14: THE 1870S

A useful general guide to ethnic settlement in Nebraska beginning in the 1870s is Wayne Wheeler, *An Almanac of Nebraska* (1975). Also useful for its overview of settlement patterns is David J. Wishart, "Settling the Great Plains, 1850–1930," in *North America: The Historical Geography of a Changing Continent*, ed. R. D. Mitchell and P. A. Groves (1987), 255–78.

For Swedish immigration to Nebraska, see James I. Dowie, *Prairie Grass Dividing* (1959), as well as his articles, "Sven Gustaf Larson, Pioneer Pastor to the Swedes of Nebraska," *Nebraska History* 40 (September 1959): 207–22, and "Unge Man, Ga Westerhut," *Nebraska History* 54 (spring 1973): 47–63. Also interesting are Louise Pound, "Olaf Bergstrom: Swedish Pioneer," *Nebraska History* 31 (March 1950): 64–74; Joseph Alexis, "Swedes in Nebraska," Nebraska State Historical Society, *Proceedings and Collections* 19 (1919): 78–85; and Paul A. Olson, "Scandinavians: The Search for Zion," in *Broken Hoops and Plains People* (1976), 237–90.

For Czech immigration see Rose Rosicky, comp., *A History of Czechs (Bohemians) in Nebraska* (1929; rpt. 1976); Bruce M. Garven, "Czech-American Freethinkers on the Great Plains, 1871–1914," in *Ethnicity on the Great Plains*, ed. Frederick C. Luebke (1980); Joseph G. Svoboda, "Czechs: The Love of Liberty," in *Broken Hoops and Plains People* (1976), 153–91, and "Czech-Americans: The Love of Liberty," *Nebraska History* 74 (fall–winter 1993): 109–19; and Sarka B. Hrbkova, "Bohemians in Nebraska," Nebraska State Historical Society, *Publications* 19 (1919): 140–58.

For English immigration to Nebraska see Richard Wake, "English Settlement in Palmyra," *Collections of the Nebraska Historical Society* 16 (1911): 224–26, and Oscar O. Winther, "The English in Nebraska, 1857–1880," *Nebraska History* 48 (autumn 1967): 209–23. For German-Russian immigration see Hattie Plum Williams, *The Czar's Germans* (1975); Richard Sallet, *Russian-German Settlements in the United States* (1974); James Ruben Griess, *The German-Russians: Those Who Came to Sutton* (1968);

Roger L. Welch, "Germans from Russia: A Place to Call Home," in *Broken Hoops and Plains People* (1976), 193–235; and Theodoere C. Wenzlaff, ed., "The Russian-Germans Come to the United States," *Nebraska History* 49 (winter 1968): 379–99. For Jewish settlement in Nebraska, readers will find of interest Betty Levitov, "Jews: The Exodus People," in *Broken Hoops and Plains People* (1976), 291–335; and F. A. Long and J. O. Trine, "Jewish Homesteaders in Madison Township," *Memories of the Jewish Midwest* 3 (1987): 24–26. For discussion of the black homesteading experience see Lillian Anthony-Welch, "Black People: The Nation-Building Vision," in *Broken Hoops and Plains People* (1976), 99–151; Forrest M. Stith, *Sunrises and Sunsets for Freedom* (1973); and Beryl Decker, "The Lost Pioneers: Negro Homesteaders in Nebraska," *Negro Digest* 12 (May 1963): 63–66.

Everett Dick, *The Sod House Frontier* (1954; rpt. 1975), is an excellent survey of the social and economic history of homesteading. See also Martha Ferguson McKeown, *Them Was the Days* (1950; rpt. 1961), and the following articles in *Nebraska History*: Edward Everett Dale, "Wood and Water: Twin Problems of the Prairie Plains," 29 (June 1948): 87–106; Dick, "Free Homes for the Millions," 43 (December 1962): 211–28; Robert N. Manley, "In the Wake of the Grasshoppers: Public Relief in Nebraska, 1874–1875," 44 (December 1963): 255–76; Homer E. Socolofsky, "Why Settle in Nebraska—The Case of John Rogers Maltby," 44 (June 1963): 123–31; Walter Prescott Webb, "The Story of Some Prairie Inventions," 34 (December 1953): 229–44; Walker D. Wyman, ed., "Reminiscences of a Nebraska Pioneer of the '70's," 28 (July–September 1947): 187–95; and William H. Beezley, "Homesteading in Nebraska, 1862–1872," 53 (spring 1972): 59–75.

For a discussion of women homesteaders and the role of women in general on the frontier, see Glenda Riley, *The Female Frontier: A Comparative View of Women on the Prairie and the Plains* (1978); Anne Polk Diffendal, "Women in Nebraska History," *Nebraska Humanist* 9 (1986): 18–23; and Everett Dick, "Sunbonnets and Calico: The Homesteader's Consort," *Nebraska History* 47 (March 1966): 3–13.

For railroad colonization in Nebraska, see Robert G. Athearn, *Union Pacific Country* (1976), and Richard C. Overton, *Burlington West: A Colonization History of the Burlington Railroad* (1941). Still valuable are two older works in *Proceedings and Collections of the Nebraska State Historical*

Society 15 (1907): John R. Buchanan, "The Great Railroad Migration into Northern Nebraska," 25–34, and E. L. Lomax, "The Work of the Union Pacific in Nebraska," 181–88.

There is no published history of the Granger movement in Nebraska, but a relatively recent survey of the movement generally can be found in D. Sven Norden, *Rich Harvest: A History of the Grange, 1867–1900* (1974), as well as the older Solon J. Buck, *The Granger Movement* (1913; rpt. 1963).

CHAPTER 15: THE RANGE CATTLE INDUSTRY

General histories of the range cattle industry include Edward Everett Dale, *The Range Cattle Industry* (1930); Ernest S. Osgood, *The Day of the Cattleman* (1929; rpt. 1957); Louis Pelzer, *The Cattlemen's Frontier* (1926; rpt. 1969); and Mari Sandoz, *The Cattlemen* (1958; rpt. 1978). On the destruction of the bison, see Sandoz, *The Buffalo Hunters* (1954; rpt. 1978); Wayne Gard, *The Great Buffalo Hunt* (1968); and David A. Dary, *The Buffalo Book: The Full Saga of the American Animal* (1974).

Accounts of the long trail drive north from Texas are John Bratt, *Trails of Yesterday* (1921; rpt. 1980); James H. Cook, "Trailing Texas Long-Horn Cattle Through Nebraska," Nebraska State Historical Society, *Publications* 18 (1917) 260–68; and the following articles in *Nebraska History*: James H. Cook, "Early Days in Ogallala," 14 (April–June 1933): 86–99; "The Texas Trail," 16 (October–December 1935): 229–40; Marshall M. Davis, "Last Trail Herd of Texas Longhorns," 19 (October–December 1938): 374–76; Norbert R. Mahnken, "Early Nebraska Markets for Texas Cattle," 26 (January–March 1945): 3–25; "Ogallala—Nebraska's Cowboy Capital," 28 (April–June 1947): 85–109.

The development of the cattle industry in the Sand Hills is treated in William D. Aeschbacher, "Development of the Sandhill Lake Country," *Nebraska History* 27 (July–September 1946): 205–21; "Development of Cattle Raising in the Sandhills," 28 (January—March 1947): 41–64; and H. E. Wolf, "Taming the Sandhills," in *The Westerners: New York Posse Brand Book* (1959). For an account of the Print Olive affair, see Harry E. Chrisman, *The Ladder of River: The Story of I. P. (Print) Olive* (1962), and Richard Crabb, *Empire on the Platte* (1967). For a general discussion of herd law see Rodney O. Davis, "Before Barbed Wire: Herd Law Agitation in Kansas and Nebraska," *Journal of the West* 6 (January 1967): 41–52.

Accounts of individual cattlemen and women include A. B. Snyder and Nellie Snyder Yost, *Pinnacle Jake* (1951; rpt. 1963); Nellie Snyder Yost, *Boss Cowman: The Recollections of Ed Lemmon, 1857–1946* (1969); Barlett Richards Jr. with Ruth Van Ackeren, *Bartlett Richards: Nebraska Sandhills Cattleman* (1980); Harold J. Cook, *Tales of the 04 Ranch* (1968); Martha McKelvie, *Sandhills Essie* (1964); and the following articles in *Nebraska History*: Robert H. Burns, "The Newman Ranches: Pioneer Cattle Ranches of the West," 34 (March 1953): 22–32; James C. Dahlman, "Recollections of Cowboy Life in Western Nebraska," 10 (October–December 1927): 335–39; Asa B. Wood, "The Coad Brothers: Panhandle Cattle Kings," 19 (January–March 1938): 28–43; Harriett Persinger Searcy Murphy, " A. B. Persinger, Nebraska Panhandle Pioneer, " 54 (summer 1973): 251–306; and James E. Potter, ed., "The Ranch Letters of Emma Robertson, 1891–1892," 56 (summer 1975): 221–29.

CHAPTERS 16: AND 17: THE 1880S

For the development of Lincoln, see Andrew J. Sawyer, *Lincoln, the Capital City, and Lancaster County* (2 vols., 1916); Neale Copple, *Tower on the Plains* (1959); James L. McKee and Arthur Duershner, *Lincoln: A Photographic History* (1976); James L. McKee, *Lincoln, the Prairie Capital: An Illustrated History* (1984); and Everett N. Dick, "Problems of the Post-Frontier Prairie City as Portrayed by Lincoln, Nebraska, 1880–1890," *Nebraska History* 27 (April–June 1947): 132–43.

For Omaha see Alfred Sorenson, *The Story of Omaha* (1923; rpt. 1993); and two works by Lawrence H. Larsen, *The Gate City: A History of Omaha* (1982; rpt. 1997), and *Frontier Omaha and Its Relationship to Other Urban Centers* (1989). The development of urban and interurban transportation is treated in three articles by E. Bryant Phillips in *Nebraska History*: "Horsecar Days and Ways in Nebraska," 29 (March 1948): 16–32; "Interurban Projects in Nebraska," 30 (June 1949): 163–82; "Interurban Projects in and Around Omaha," 30 (September 1949): 257–85. See also, Charles Jenkins, "The Kearney Cotton Mill—A Bubble That Burst," *Nebraska History* 38 (September 1957): 207–20. More recent articles about the history of Omaha are Howard P. Chudacoff, "Where Rolls the Dark Missouri Down," *Nebraska History* 52 (spring 1971): 1–30, and Charles W. Martin, ed., "Omaha in 1868–1869: Selections from the Letters of Joseph Barker," *Nebraska History* 59 (winter 1978): 501–25.

For labor unrest see Donald L. McMurray, *The Great Burlington Strike of 1888* (1956), which has some significance for Nebraska. A specific treatment of labor unrest in Nebraska is Roland M. Gephart, "Politicians, Soldiers and Strikes: The Reorganization of the Nebraska Militia and the Omaha Strike of 1882," *Nebraska History* 46 (June 1965): 89–120.

For biographical material on J. Sterling Morton, see James C. Olson, *J. Sterling Morton* (1942; rpt. 1972). Also useful is Virginia V. Ott, *Sterling's Carrie: Mrs. J. Sterling Morton* (1989). Ora A. Clement and W. H. O'Gara, *In All Its Fury: A History of the Blizzard of January 12, 1888* (1947), is a detailed account of the most celebrated natural disaster in the history of the state. Also of interest for its insight into the early years of the women's suffrage movement in Nebraska is Ann L. Wilhite, "Sixty Five Years Till Victory: A History of Woman's Suffrage Movement in Nebraska," *Nebraska History* 49 (summer 1968): 149–63.

CHAPTER 18: THE POPULIST REVOLT

For a general overview of Populism, see Stanley B. Parsons, *The Populist Context* (1973), as well as his earlier, briefer work, "Who Were the Nebraska Populists?" *Nebraska History* 44 (June 1963): 83–100. See also Robert W. Cherny, *Populism, Progressivism, and the Transformation of Nebraska Politics, 1885–1915* (1981). Highly academic is Jeffrey Don Ostler, *Prairie Populism* (1993).

For specific perspectives in the historiography of Populism, refer to several older works, including the old standard yet generally sympathetic John D. Hicks, *The Populist Revolt* (1931; rpt. 1961). More critical of the Populists is Richard Hofstadter, *The Age of Reform: From Bryan to F.D.R.* (1955; rpt. 1960). Rejecting many of Hofstadter's interpretations are Norman Pollack, *The Populist Response to Industrial America: Midwestern Populist Thought* (1962); and Walter T. K. Nugent, *The Tolerant Populists* (1963). Other contributions to the historiography of Populism are David F. Trask, "A Note on the Politics of Populism," *Nebraska History* 46 (June

1965): 157–61, and Frederick C. Luebke, "Mainstreet and Countryside: Patterns opf Voting in Nebraska During the Populist Era," *Nebraska History* 50 (fall 1969): 257–75, which tests Trask's suggestions.

Studies that examine the conditions that produced Populism are John D. Barnhart, "Rainfall and the Populist Party in Nebraska," *American Political Science Review* 19 (1925): 527–40; Hallie Farmer, "The Economic Background of Frontier Populism," *Mississippi Valley Historical Review* 10 (March 1924): 406–27; "The Railroads and Frontier Populism," *Mississippi Valley Historical Review* 13 (December 1926): 387–97; and two contributions by David S. Trask, "Formation and Failure: The Populist Party in Seward County, 1890–1892," *Mississippi Valley Historical Review* 51 (fall 1970): 281–301, and "Nebraska Populism as a Response to Environmental and Political Problems," in *The Great Plains: Environment and Culture*, ed. Brian W. Blouet and Frederick C. Luebke (1979), 61–80.

Biographical sketches of important Nebraska Populists include the following in *Nebraska History*: Marie U. Harmer and James L. Sellers, "Charles H. Van Wyck—Soldier and Statesman," 12 (1929, printed 1931), 81–128, 190–246, 322–73; 13 (1932), 3–36; N. C. Abbott, "Silas A. Holcomb," 26 (October–December 1945), 187–200; 27 (January–March 1946): 3–17; Addison E. Sheldon, "William Vincent Allen," 19 (July–September 1938): 191–206; and "John Holbrook Powers," (October–December 1938): 331–39. For studies of Luna Kellie see Jane Taylor Nelson, ed., *A Prairie Populist: The Memoirs of Luna Kellie* (1992); Mary Jo Wagner, "Prairie Populists: Luna Kellie and Mary Elizabeth Leese," in *Northwest Women's Heritage*, ed. Karen Blair (1985), 200–210; and Douglas A. Bakken, ed., "Luna Kellie and the Farmers' Alliance," *Nebraska History* 50 (summer 1969): 185–205.

CHAPTER 19: THE FADING FRONTIER

Much has been written recently about Indian-white relations in the late nineteenth century. An excellent overview of the removal of Native Americans from Nebraska is David J. Wishart, *An Unspeakable Sadness: The Dispossession of the Nebraska Indians* (1994). For other works dealing with removal and assimilation, see Leonard A. Carlson, *Indians, Bureaucrats, and Land: The Dawes Act and the Decline of Indian Farming* (1981);

Clyde A. Milner II, "Off the White Road: Seven Nebraska Indian Societies in the 1870s: A Statistical Analysis of Assimilation, Population and Prosperity." *Western Historical Quarterly* 12 (1981): 37–52; Kay Graber, ed., *Sister to the Sioux: The Memoirs of Elaine Goodale Eastman* (1978); Ronald C. Naugle and Nancy Svoboda, "The Genoa Indian School," *Nebraskaland Magazine* 62 (January–February 1984): 98–99; and the following articles in *Nebraska History*: Wilma A. Darrio, "'They Get Milk Practically Every Day:' The Genoa Indian Industrial School, 1884–1934," 73 (spring 1992): 2–11; Richard E. Jensen, ed., "Commissioner Theodore Roosevelt Visits Indian Reservations, 1892," 62 (spring 1981): 85–106; Oliver Knight, "War or Peace: The Anxious Wait for Crazy Horse," 54 (winter 1973): 521–44; Sarah McAnulty, "Angel DeCora: American Indian Artist and Educator," 57 (summer 1976): 143–99; and Valerie Sherer Mathes, "Susan LaFlesche Picotte: Nebraska's Indian Physician, 1865–1915," 63 (winter 1982): 502–30. An excellent multigenerational study of the Lakota people is Joe Starita, *The Dull Knifes of Pine Ridge: A Lakota Odyssey* (1995). For the massacre at Wounded Knee, readers should consult Richard E. Jensen, R. Eli Paul, and John Carter, *Eyewitness at Wounded Knee* (1991).

Nebraska's role in the Spanish-American War is well covered in four articles by J. R. Johnson in *Nebraska History*: "Nebraska's 'Rough Riders' in the Spanish-American War," 29 (June 1948): 105–12; "The Saga of the First Nebraska in the Philippines," 30 (June 1949): 139–62; "The Second Nebraska's 'Battle' of Chickamauga," 32 (June 1951): 77–93; "Imperialism in Nebraska," 44 (September 1963): 141–66. More recent articles in *Nebraska History* that have contributed to this area are John R. Johnson, "Colonel John Miller Stotsenburg: Man of Valor," 50 (winter 1969): 339–57; Margaret Inglehart Reilly, "Andrew Wadsworth, a Nebraska Soldier in the Philippines, 1898–1899," 68 (winter 1987): 183–99; and Thomas D. Thiessen, "The Fighting First Nebraska: Nebraska's Imperial Adventure in the Philippines, 1898–1899," 70 (fall 1989): 210–72.

CHAPTER 20: EMERGING AWARENESS

For a discussion of the Trans-Missippi Exposition see Kenneth Gerald Alfers, "Triumph of the West: The Trans-Mississippi Exposition,"

Nebraska History 53 (fall 1972): 313–29, and Patrice K. Beam, "The Last Victorian Fair: The Trans-Mississippi International Exposition," *Journal of the West* 33 (January 1994): 10–23.

For population distribution at the turn of the century, George Evert Condra, *Geography in Nebraska* (1906) is particularly useful. Other studies of value are Esther S. Anderson, "The Significance of Some Population Changes in Nebraska Since 1880," *Journal of Geography* 21 (October 1922): 254–63; Gilbert C. Fite, "Flight from the Farms," *Nebraska History* 40 (September 1959): 159–76; and Howard P. Chudacoff, *Mobile Americans: Residential and Social Mobility of Omaha* (1972).

Perhaps the best brief interpretation of cultural factors in Nebraska life is Willa Cather's essay "Nebraska: The End of the First Cycle," in *Roundup: A Nebraska Reader*, ed. Virginia Faulkner (1957), which also contains many other pieces of value. There is also much of value in volume 2 of the previously cited Morton and Watkins, *Illustrated History of Nebraska*.

For the history of churches and religion at this time in Nebraska's history, see Orville H. Zabel, *God and Caesar in Nebraska: A Study of the Legal Relationship of Church and State* (1955). An interesting account of missionary work in western Nebraska is C. H. Frady, "First Years' Gospel Giving on the Frontier," *Nebraska History* 10 (October–December 1927): 269–325. George W. Barnes, "Pioneer Preacher," *Nebraska History* 27 (April–June 1946): 71–91, also contributes to an understanding of the early churches of Nebraska.

Numerous works recount the histories of individual religious denominations in Nebraska. The Catholics are treated in Henry W. Casper, *History of the Catholic Church in Nebraska* (3 vols., 1960–66). The Congregationalists are discussed in Motier A. Bullock, *Congregational Nebraska* (1905), and Annadora F. Gregory, "The Reverend Harmon Bross and Nebraska Congregationalists, 1873–1928," *Nebraska History* 54 (fall 1973): 445–74. For the history of Methodists, see David Marquette, *History of Methodism, First Half Century* (1904), as well as the more recent Don W. Holter, *Flames on the Plains: A History of United Methodism in Nebraska* (1983). For the various groups of Lutherans, see Knud C. Bodholdt, *Pioneer Days on the Prairie* (1980); Jena M. Matteson and Edith H. Matteson, *Blossoms on the Prairie: The History of Danish Lutherans in*

Nebraska (1988); Charles Frederick Sandahl, *The Nebraska Conference of the Augustana Synod* (1931); and Frederick C. Luebke, "German Immigrants and the Churches in Nebraska, 1910–1917," *Mid-America* 50 (April 1968): 116–30. For Presbyterians see Julius F. Schwarz, *History of the Presbyterian Church in Nebraska* (1924). For the Episcopal Church, see William Joseph Barnds, *The Episcopal Church in Nebraska* (1969). For Mennonites, see Anthony R. Epp, "Visions Shaping the Mennonites of the Plains," *Nebraska Humanist* 6 (fall 1983): 14–19, and Royden K. Loewen, "Ethnic Farmers and the 'Outside' World: Mennonites in Manitoba and Nebraska, 1874–1900," *Journal of the Canadian Historical Association* 1 (1990): 195–213.

A good brief account of education will be found in Helen Siampos, "Early Education in Nebraska," *Nebraska History* 29 (June 1948): 113–33. Howard W. Caldwell, *Education in Nebraska* (1902), is invaluable on the early history of education. See also Wayne E. Fuller, *The Old Country School: The Story of Rural Education in the Midwest* (1982); Mary Hurlbut Cordier, "Prairie Schoolwomen, Mid 1850s to 1920s in Iowa, Kansas, and Nebraska," *Great Plains Quarterly* 8 (spring 1988): 102–19; Richard E. Dudley, "Nebraska Public School Education, 1890–1910," *Nebraska History* 54 (spring 1973): 65–90; and Rosalie Trail Fuller, "A Nebraska High School Teacher in the 1890s: The Letters of Sadie B. Smith," *Nebraska History* 58 (winter 1977), 447–73.

Numerous works examine the history of colleges and universities in Nebraska around the turn of the century. For an excellent interpretive study of the University of Nebraska, see Robert E. Knoll, *Prairie University: A History of the University of Nebraska* (1995). For a history of agricultural education at the University of Nebraska, see Elvin F. Frolik and Ralston J. Graham, *The University of Nebraska–Lincoln College of Agriculture* (1987). Robert Coleman, *First Hundred Years of the University of Nebraska College of Medicine* (1980), deals with the early history of the University of Nebraska Medical Center. For a history of the University of Omaha, see Tommy R. Thompson, *A History of the University of Nebraska at Omaha, 1908–1983* (1983). For Dana College see Peter L. Peterson, *A Placed Called Dana* (1984). James Iverne Dowie, *Prairie Grass Dividing* (1959), is a history of Luther College. For Union College see David D. Rees and Everett Dick, *Union College: Fifty Years of Service* (1941). For Creighton University see M. P. Dowling, *Creighton University: Reminis-*

cences of the First Twenty-Five Years (1903). For Peru State College see Ernest Longfellow, *The Normal on the Hill: One Hundred Years of Peru State College* (1967). For Doane College see Donald J. Ziegler, *A College on a Hill: Life at Doane, 1872–1987* (1990). For Nebraska Wesleyan University see David H. Mickey, *Of Sunflowers, Coyotes and Plainsmen* (2 vols., 1992–93).

For a history of Chautauqua in Nebraska see James P. Eckman, "Missionaries of Culture: Chautauqua Literary and Scientific Circles in Nebraska, 1878–1900," *Nebraska History* 73 (spring 1992): 18–24. For the arts, the best general survey is that found in the Federal Writers' Project's *Nebraska: A Guide to the Cornhusker State* (1939). Clarissa Bucklin, *Nebraska Art and Artists* (1932), is a useful compilation. See also Norman A. Geske, *Art and Artists in Nebraska* (1983); Fred N. Wells, *The Nebraska Art Association: A History, 1888–1971* (1972); and Patricia Cox Crews and Ronald C. Naugle, *Nebraska Quilts and Quiltmakers* (1991). For music see Karen M. Dyer, "Musical Expression on the Great Plains: Nebraska, 1854–1904," *American Music* 3 (summer 1985): 143–51.

For a general discussion of literature see James C. Olson, "The Literary Tradition in Pioneer Nebraska," *Prairie Schooner* 24 (summer 1950): 161–67. For newspapers see Benjamin Pfeiffer, "The Role of Joseph E. Johnson and His Pioneer Newspapers in the Development of Territorial Nebraska," *Nebraska History* 40 (June 1959): 119–36.

On Willa Cather, see Mildred R. Bennett, *The World of Willa Cather* (1951, rev. ed. 1961); John March, *A Reader's Companion to the Fiction of Willa Cather* (1993); Sheryl L. Meyerling, *A Reader's Companion to the Short Stories of Willa Cather* (1994); Robert L. Gale, "Willa Cather and the Usable Past," *Nebraska History* 42 (September 1961): 181–90; Edith Lewis, *Willa Cather Living: A Personal Record* (1953; rpt. 1963); Bernice Slote, "Willa Cather and Her First Book," in Willa Cather, *April Twilights* (1903; rpt. 1962); and Slote, "Writer in Nebraska" and "The Kingdom of Art," in *The Kingdom of Art: Willa Cather's First Principles and Critical Theories, 1893–1896* (1966). Readers will also find valuable Brent L. Bohlke, ed., *Willa Cather in Person* (1986); Phyllis C. Robinson, *Willa: The Life of Willa Cather* (1983); James Woodress, *Willa Cather: A Literary Life* (1987); Marilyn Arnold, "The Other Side of Willa Cather," *Nebraska History* 68 (summer 1987): 74–82.

For autobiographical sketches by Mari Sandoz, see "Recollections," in *Hostiles and Friendlies: Selected Short Writings of Mari Sandoz* (1959); "Outpost in New York," *Prairie Schooner* 37 (summer 1963): 95–106; and *The Christmas of the Phonograph Records* (1966). Also see Carolyn Sandoz Pifer, *Making of an Author* (1984).

For John G. Neihardt, see his two-volume autobiography, *All Is But a Beginning* (1972) and *Patterns and Consequences* (1978). Readers will also want to consult Lucille F. Aly, *John G. Neihardt* (1976); Fred L. Lee, "John G. Neihardt: The Man and His Western Writings, the Bancroft Years, 1900–1921," *Trail Guide* 17 (September–December 1973): 1–35; and John T. Flanagan, "John G. Neihardt: Chronicler of the West," *Arizona History Quarterly* 21 (spring 1965): 7–20.

CHAPTER 21: NEBRASKA POLITICS AND PROGRESSIVISM

William Jennings Bryan has been the subject of much controversy among historians. For a brief and balanced view of Bryan, see Robert Cherny, *A Righteous Cause: The Life of William Jennings Bryan* (1985). The most extensive, thorough presentation of Bryan is a three-volume work by Paolo E. Coletta, *William Jennings Bryan: I, Political Evangelist, 1860–1908* (1964); *William Jennings Bryan: II, Progrssive Politician and Moral Statesman, 1909–1915* (1969); and *William Jennings Bryan: III, Political Puritan, 1915–1925* (1969). In the preparation of his work, Coletta also published numerous articles about Bryan in *Nebraska History*. See also David Stephens Trask, "A Natural Partnership: Nebraska's Populists and Democrats and the Development of Fusion," *Nebraska History* (fall 1975): 419–38.

For the career of George W. Norris, the definitive study is Richard Lowitt's three-volume work, *George W. Norris: The Making of a Progressive, 1861–1912* (1963), *George W. Norris: The Persistence of a Progressive, 1913–1933* (1971), and *George W. Norris: The Triumph of a Progressive, 1933–1944* (1978). Readers will also be interested in comparing these with Norris's autobiography, *Fighting Liberal* (1945; rpt. 1966).

Also of interest in this time period are Victor Rosewater, *Back Stage in 1912* (1932), a personal account of the Nebraskan who served as chairman of the Republican National Committee in that year; Donald F. Danker,

"The Election of 1912 in Nebraska," *Nebraska History* 37 (December 1956): 283–310, a useful summary of that election; and Fred Carey, *Mayor Jim: The Life of James Dahlman* (1930), an account of Omaha's colorful cowboy mayor.

CHAPTER 22: NEBRASKA AND WORLD WAR I

Relatively little has been written on Nebraska's military participation in World War I. Douglas R. Hartman, *Nebraska's Militia* (1994), is useful here. For General Pershing, see Frederick Palmer, *John J. Pershing, General of the Armies* (1948); Donald L. Smythe, "John J. Pershing at the University of Nebraska, 1891–1895," *Nebraska History* 43 (September 1962): 169–95; "The Early Years of John J. Pershing," *Missouri Historical Review* 48 (October 1963): 1–20.

For a discussion of the difficulties of the Non-Partisan League in Nebraska during World War I, see Robert N. Manley, "The Nebraska State Council of Defense and the Non-Partisan League," *Nebraska History* 43 (December 1962): 229–52; and Burton W. Folsom, "Immigrant Voters and the Nonpartisan League in Nebraska, 1917–1920," *Great Plains Quarterly* 1 (summer 1981): 159–68. Also see Frederick C. Luebke, "The German-American Alliance in Nebraska, 1910–1917," *Great Plains Quarterly* 49 (summer 1968): 165–85; and David George Wagaman, "The Industrial Workers of the World in Nebraska, 1914–1920," *Great Plains Quarterly* 56 (fall 1975): 295–337.

For the foreign language problem that grew out of the war, see Frederick C. Luebke, "Legal Restrictions on Foreign Languages in the Great Plains States, 1917–1923," in *Languages in Conflict: Linguistic Acculturation on the Great Plains*, ed. Paul Schach (1980). See also Luebke, ed., "Superpatriotism in World War I: The Experience of a Lutheran Pastor," *Concordia Historical Institute Quarterly* 41 (February 1968): 3–11; Robert N. Manley, "Language, Loyalty and Liberty: The Nebraska State Council of Defense and the Lutheran Church, 1917–1918," *Concordia Historical Institute Quarterly* 37 (April 1964): 1–17; Frederick Nohl, "The Lutheran Church–Missouri Synod Reacts to United States Anti-Germanism during World War I," *Concordia Historical Institute Quarterly* 35 (July 1962):

49–66; and Jack W. Rodgers, "The Foreign Language Issue in Nebraska, 1918–1923," *Nebraska History* 39 (March 1958): 1–22.

H. C. Filley, *Effects of Inflation and Deflation upon Nebraska Agriculture, 1914–1932* (1934), and Eleanor Hinman, *History of Farm Land Prices in Eleven Nebraska Counties* (1934) are older works but useful for illuminating some facets of agriculture during World War I.

CHAPTER 23: THE 1920S

Sheldon, *Nebraska: The Land and the People*, 1:961–1097, discusses in some detail the constitutional convention and the decade of the 1920s. For the early history of the automobile in Nebraska through the 1920s, see Michael Berger L., *The Devil Wagon in God's Country* (1979); Drake Hokanson, *The Lincoln Highway* (1988); Carol Ahlgren and David Anthone, "The Lincoln Highway in Nebraska: The Pioneer Trail of the Automotive Age," *Nebraska History* 73 (winter 1992): 173–79; Tommy R. Thompson, "The Devil Wagon Comes to Omaha: The First Decade of the Automobile, 1900–1910," *Nebraska History* 61 (summer 1980): 172–91; Clinton Lee Warne, "The Acceptance of the Automobile in Nebraska," *Nebraska History* 37 (September 1956): 221–35; and Warne, "Some Effects of the Introduction of the Automobile on Highways and Land Values in Nebraska," *Nebraska History* 38 (March 1957): 43–58.

Several recent articles in *Nebraska History* have dealt with the Omaha Race Riot of 1919: Carol Gendler, "The U.S. Army and the Omaha Race Riot of 1919," 72 (fall 1991): 135–43; Orville D. Menard, "Tom Dennison, the Omaha Bee, and the 1919 Omaha Race Riot," 68 (winter 1987): 152–65; Clayton D. Laurie, "The U.S. Army and the Omaha Race Riot of 1919," 72 (fall 1991): 135–43; and Michael A. Lawson, "Omaha, a City in Ferment: Summer of 1919," 58 (fall 1977): 395–417. Of related interest is Michael W. Schuyler, "The Ku Klux Klan in Nebraska, 1920–1930," 66 (fall 1985): 234–56.

Nebraska History also contains several other articles relevant to various aspects of Nebraska in the post–World War I era: Robert E. Bader, "The Curtailment of Railroad Service in Nebraska, 1920–1941," 36 (March 1955): 27–42; R. E. Dale, "Back to Normal," 38 (September 1957): 179–206; C. Clyde Jones, "Purebred Dairy Sire Development in Nebraska,"

42 (September 1961): 191–200; Maurice C. Latta, "The Economic Development of Custer County Through World War I and the New Era, 1914–1929," 33 (September 1952): 139–53; Floyd W. Rodine, "The County Agent and the Nebraska Farm Bureau," 36 (September 1955): 205–12; Kurt Wimer, "Senator Hitchcock and the League of Nations," 44 (September 1963): 189–204; and Larry G. Osnes, "Charles W. Bryan: 'His Brother's Keeper,'" 48 (spring 1967): 45–67.

The career of Governor McKelvie is treated in Bruce Nicoll and Ken R. Keller, *Sam McKelvie: Son of the Soil* (1954).

CHAPTERS 24 AND 25: THE GREAT DEPRESSION AND WORLD WAR II

Sheldon, *Nebraska: The Land and the People*, 1:961–1097, discusses the politics of the period in some detail. Gilbert C. Fite, *George N. Peek and the Fight for Farm Parity* (1954); John R. Crampton, *The National Farmers Union* (1965); and Theodore Saloutos, *The American Farmer and the New Deal* (1982), though dealing with the national situation, are of value for the understanding of the local problem. More specific to Nebraska and other plains states is Michael W. Schuyler, *The Dread of Plenty: Agricultural Relief Activities of the Federal Government in the Middle West, 1933–1939* (1989). For George Norris's efforts to assist Nebraska during the depression see Richard Lowitt, "George W. Norris and the New Deal in Nebraska, 1933–1936," *Nebraska History* 51 (April 1977): 396–405, as well as Lowitt's three-volume biography of Norris mentioned in the preceding chapter.

For the role of a specific New Deal program in Nebraska, see Elizabeth Anderson, "Depression Legacy: Post Office Art," *Nebraska History* 71 (spring 1990): 23–33; and Charles E. Humberger, "The Civilian Conservation Corps in Nebraska: Memoirs of Company 762," *Nebraska History* 75 (winter 1994): 292–300. Readers will also find useful Dennis N. Mihelich, "The Lincoln Urban League: the Travail of Depression and War," *Nebraska History* 70 (winter 1989): 303–16; and Lawrence H. Larsen, "Omaha and the Great Depression: Progress in the Face of the Adversity," *Journal of the West* 24 (October 1985): 27–34. For everyday life during the 1930s, Patricia A. Schneider, *A Bundle of Nebraska Memories* (1989), is an interesting and useful reminiscence.

Other useful but older articles in *Nebraska History* include Walter Johnson, "Politics in the Midwest," 32 (March 1951): 1–19; Maurice C. Latta, "The Economic Effects of Drouth and Depression upon Custer County, 1929–1942," 33 (December 1952): 221–36; John L. Shover, "The Farm Holiday Movement in Nebraska," 43 (March 1962): 53–78.

For the unicameral legislature, two older works still deserve attention: John P. Senning, *The One-House Legislature* (1937), and Adam C. Breckenridge, *One House for Two* (1957). Readers should also consult Breckenridge's more recent article, "Innovation in State Government: Origin and Development of the Nebraska Nonpartisan Unicameral Legislature," *Nebraska History* 59 (spring 1978): 31–46. George Norris's autobiography, *Fighting Liberal*, already mentioned, is also useful for an understanding of the struggle surrounding the adoption of the unicameral system. See also Robert F. Wesser, "George W. Norris: The Unicameral Legislature and the Progressive Ideal," *Nebraska History* 45 (December 1964): 309–21.

No comprehensive story of Nebraska's participation in World War II is available, but much of interest will be found in James A. Huston, *Biography of a Battalion* (1950), a detailed history of the Third Battalion, 134th Infantry Regiment, during World War II. Douglas R. Hartman, *Nebraska's Militia*, is of interest as well. *Nebraska History* contains many useful and interesting articles about different aspects of Nebraska's as well as Nebraskans' involvement in World War II, including, Todd L. Petersen, "Kearney, Nebraska, and the Kearney Army Air Field in World War II," 72 (fall 1991): 118–26; and George A. Larson, "Nebraska's World War II Bomber Plant: The Glenn L. Martin–Nebraska Company," 74 (spring 1993): 32–43. Articles in *Nebraska History* 76 (summer–fall 1995), a special issue devoted to Nebraskans in World War II, include Richard O. Joyce with Samuel Van Pelt, "You Bet I Was Scared": A Doolittle Raider Remembers," 54–65; Frederick T. Daly, "Nebraska-Related Names of United States Navy Ships," 66–74; Beverly Russell, "World War II Boomtown: Hastings and the Naval Ammunition Depot," 75–83; W. Raymond Wood, "Or Go Down in Flame: A Navigator's Death over Schweinfurt," 84–99; Douglas R. Hartman, "Lawrence W. Youngman: War Correspondent for the Omaha *World-Herald*," 100–105; Michele L. Fagan, "Overseas with the ANC: Experiences of Nebraska Nurses in World War II," 106–21; Alex Meyer, "Karl Timmermann: From Pebble Creek to the Rhine," 122–28; and Robert Hurst, "Nebraska Army Air Fields, A Pictorial Review," 129–43.

CHAPTER 26: LEGACIES OF THE DEPRESSION

There has been very little material of a comprehensive nature published in recent years in this area. The most current information can be found in *The Nebraska Blue Book*, published biannually by the Nebraska legislature, the reports of the Nebraska Department of Water Resources, the proceedings of the Nebraska Irrigation Association, and various reports issued by the State Department of Agriculture and Inspection and the State-Federal Division of Agricultural Statistics.

Robert E. Firth, *Public Power in Nebraska: A Report on State Ownership* (1962), is a good general survey of public power in the state to its date of publication. For irrigation, see Sam S. Kepfield, "El Dorado on the Platte: The Development of Agricultural Irrigation and Water Law in Nebraska, 1860–1895," *Nebraska History* 75 (fall 1994): 232–43. Gene E. Hamaker, *Irrigation Pioneers: A History of the Tri-County Project to 1935* (1964), is a careful study of both irrigation and power in Gosper, Phelps, and Kearney Counties.

Marquis Childs, *The Farmer Takes a Hand: The Electric Power Revolution in Rural America* (1952), is general but useful; more specific on rural electrification is H. S. Person, "The Rural Electrification Administration in Perspective," *Agricultural History* 24 (April 1950): 70–88. Supplementing Firth on municipal power is C. G. Wallace and Harold O. Johnson, "Municipally Owned Power Plants in Nebraska," *Nebraska History* 43 (September 1962): 197–202.

Olson, *J. Sterling Morton*, previously cited, is useful on the establishment and growth of Arbor Day, as is his more recent article, "Arbor Day—A Pioneer Expression of Concern for the Environment," *Nebraska History* 53 (spring 1972): 1–13. For accounts of the development of Nebraska's national forest, see Raymond J. Pool, "Fifty Years on the Nebraska National Forest," *Nebraska History* 34 (September 1953): 139–80; and Richard A. Overfield, "Trees for the Great Plains: Charles E. Bessey and Forestry," *Journal of Forest History* 23 (January 1979): 18–31.

CHAPTER 27: POSTWAR PROSPERITY

Much has been written on the problems of the Missouri River Basin. Of particular interest for this time period are *Missouri: Land and Water, Report of the Missouri Basin Survey Commission* (1953); Rufus Terral, *The Missouri Valley: Land of Drouth, Flood, and Promise* (1947); Henry C. Hart, *The Dark Missouri* (1957); Marian E. Ridgeway, *The Missouri Basin's Pick-Sloan Plan: A Case Study in Congressional Policy Determination* (1955); and Thomas H. Langevin, "Development of Multiple-Purpose Water Planning by the Federal Government in the Missouri Basin," *Nebraska History* 34 (March 1953): 1–21.

For a useful source for key Nebraska political figures in the post–World War II era, see James Reichly, "Nebraska Sons of the Pioneers," in *States in Crisis: Politics in Ten American States, 1950–1962* (1964); and Neal R. Peirce, "Nebraska: 'A Place to Come from or a Place to Die?,'" in *The Great Plains States of America: People, Politics and Power in Nine Great Plains States* (1973). See also Marvin E. Stromer, *The Making of a Political Leader: Kenneth S. Wherry and the United States Senate* (1969).

For a history of the construction of the interstate highway system in Nebraska, see James C. Creigh, "Constructing the Interstate Highway in Nebraska: Route and Funding Controversies," *Nebraska History* 72 (spring 1991): 44–53; and David M. Ambrose, "The Importance of Interstate Highways to Economic Development in Nebraska," in *Nebraska Policy Crisis*, ed. Russell L. Smith (1988).

CHAPTERS 28–30: THE 1960S TO THE PRESENT

For a discussion of Governor Tiemann and the controversies of his administration, see Frederick C. Luebke, "Tiemann, Taxes, and the Centennial Legislature, 1967," *Nebraska History* 71 (fall 1990): 107–20. The Yellow Thunder incident is addressed as background material in Roland Dewing,

Suggestions for Further Reading

Wounded Knee: The Meaning and Significance of the Second Incident (1985). For a biography of Robert Kerrey, see Ivy Harper, *Walzing Matilda: Life and Times of Nebraska Senator Robert Kerrey* (1992). For Kay Orr and Helen Boosalis and the gubernatorial campaign and election of 1986, see John Barette, *Prairie Politics* (1987).

INDEX